REASONING FROM RACE

REASONING FROM RACE

Feminism, Law, and the Civil Rights Revolution

SERENA MAYERI

HARVARD UNIVERSITY PRESS | Cambridge, Massachusetts | London, England   2011

Library of Congress Cataloging-in-Publication Data

Mayeri, Serena.
    Reasoning from race : feminism, law, and the civil rights revolution / Serena Mayeri.
        p. cm.
    Includes bibliographical references and index.
    ISBN 978-0-674-04759-4 (alk. paper)
1. Sex discrimination against women—Law and legislation—United States—History—
20th century. 2. Women's rights—United States—Philosophy. 3. Feminist jurisprudence—
United States. 4. Women's rights—United States—History—20th century. 5. Civil rights
movements—United States. 6. Women—Legal status, laws, etc.—United States—History—
20th century. 7. Constitutional law—United States—Methodology. 8. Feminist theory—
United States. I. Title.
    KF4758.M39 2011
    342.7308'78—dc22   2010048448

FOR MY PARENTS

Harriet and Ray Mayeri

CONTENTS

ABBREVIATIONS USED IN TEXT

Organizations

ACLU	American Civil Liberties Union
CCR	Center for Constitutional Rights
CEDAPW	Campaign to End Discrimination Against Pregnant Workers
CESA	Committee to End Sterilization Abuse
FEW	Federally employed women
LCCR	Leadership Conference on Civil Rights
LDF	NAACP Legal Defense and Educational Fund, Inc.
NAACP	National Association for the Advancement of Colored People
NBFO	National Black Feminist Organization
NEA	National Education Association
NOW	National Organization for Women
NOW LDEF	NOW Legal Defense and Education Fund
NUL	National Urban League
NWP	National Woman's Party
PCSW	President's Commission on the Status of Women
SPLC	Southern Poverty Law Center
WEAL	Women's Equity Action League
WLF	Washington Legal Foundation
WRP	ACLU Women's Rights Project

Government Agencies

DOJ	Department of Justice
EEOC	Equal Employment Opportunity Commission
HEW	Department of Health, Education, and Welfare

REASONING FROM RACE

In October 2008, LaDoris Cordell was hopeful. Polls showing that Americans would likely elect the first black president buoyed Cordell, a university administrator and former judge. Her optimism extended to the likely fate of Proposition 8, a ballot measure that would prohibit same-sex marriage in California. Though she was "well aware of the black community's discomfort with things gay," Cordell nevertheless believed that "the African American electorate will come through" and vote against the ban.[1]

Less than a week later, Cordell felt "angry" and "betrayed." Barack Obama had won, but so had Prop 8. Worse, many pundits attributed both victories to historically high African American turnout.[2] After a "long and tortured history of fighting against discrimination and exclusion," Cordell lamented, "black folks . . . vote[d] to oppress others in exactly the same way."[3] A mother of two who was once married to a man, Cordell described herself as an "African American lesbian who [has] been in a loving relationship for over two decades." She wrote, "I did not choose to be gay anymore than I chose to be black."[4] Cordell's rhetorical analogy between sexual orientation and race and between gay rights and civil rights echoed the legal arguments adopted by California's highest court less than six months earlier. In a stirring opinion legalizing same-sex marriage, the court had declared that "an individual's sexual orientation—like a person's race or gender—does not constitute a legitimate basis upon which to deny or withhold legal rights."[5]

Not everyone embraced the parallels that seemed so self-evident to Cordell. Opponents of same-sex marriage rejected the moral equivalence they implied. Some more sympathetic to gay rights worried about alienating African Americans whose religious beliefs or memories of Jim Crow made comparisons to antigay discrimination offensive or painful. Others feared that pithy slogans like "Gay Is the New Black" trivialized both racial oppression and homophobia while implying that gayness and blackness were mutually exclusive.[6]

Stanford law professor Richard Thompson Ford offered a different critique. Much opposition to same-sex marriage, he argued, stemmed not from "prejudice and bigotry" but from a desire to preserve "distinctive sex roles" within marriage. "Civil rights law," wrote Ford in an article published the week after the election, "reflects this ambivalence about sex difference." Judges scrutinized sex discrimination less carefully than race discrimination under the federal Constitution; employment laws allowed for sex-specific workplace grooming standards and other sex-based distinctions.[7] Ford's logic suggested that the same misgivings that had prevented courts and legislatures from embracing a full-blown analogy between race and sex might stand in the way of including gay Americans under the civil rights umbrella.

The unfinished business of sex equality is often expressed in such comparative terms by legal scholars, political pundits, and casual observers alike. The African American quest for civil rights has become so deeply ingrained in American consciousness that it is the yardstick against which all other reform movements are measured.[8] In the American legal system, analogical reasoning often justifies applying accepted principles to new circumstances; analogies to race have therefore held particular salience to those who demand changes in the law. "The African American struggle for social equality . . . has provided the deep structure, social resonance, and primary referent for legal equality," the feminist legal theorist Catharine MacKinnon observed in 1991.[9] By the twentieth century's end, the use of race as a template for other rights claims had become routine. In the words of legal scholar Janet Halley, "asking the advocates of gay, women's, or disabled peoples' rights to give up 'like race' similes would be like asking them to write their speeches and briefs without using the word *the*."[10]

Although such analogies now carry an aura of inevitability, it was not always so. Nineteenth-century women's rights movements famously compared marriage to slavery and women to freedmen in the hope of enfranchising women through the Reconstruction Amendments.[11] Race-sex analogies then lay largely, though not entirely, dormant for almost a century, until their resurrection in the early 1960s.[12]

Beginning in the 1960s, "second-wave" feminists conscripted legal strategies developed to combat race discrimination into the service of women's rights.[13] They compared discrimination against women to the injustices suffered by racial minority groups, asserting that sex inequality, like racial subordination, betrayed the American promise of egalitarian democracy. Feminists also promoted parallels between race and sex as legal categories. Litigators argued that sex, like race, should be a "suspect classification" under the Fourteenth Amendment's equal protection clause. Supporters of the Equal Rights Amendment (ERA) insisted that women, like African Americans, needed constitutional protection of their rights. Feminists sought to codify race-sex analogies in employment discrimination statutes, educational equity laws, and affirmative action policies by listing sex alongside race as a prohibited category of discrimination and as a basis for remedies.

By the early 1980s, feminists had secured significant legal and constitutional advances. But their success had limits. So did race-sex analogies, according to many feminist theorists. Such comparisons, they charged, epitomized white women's exploitation of African Americans' hard-won victories and ignored the complicated interactions between race and sex. Moreover, race-sex analogies obscured the experiences of women of color. The title of an influential anthology published in 1982 said it all: *All the Women Are White, All the Blacks Are Men, But Some of Us Are Brave.*[14]

The modern origins of the legal race-sex analogy could not have been further removed from the parasitic and marginalizing tendencies decried by this new generation of feminists. Two decades earlier, Pauli Murray, an African American attorney, scholar, and activist, engineered the rebirth of reasoning from race as the centerpiece of feminist legal strategy. Murray was determined to fight "Jane Crow"—laws and practices that segregated or discriminated against women—by emulating the battle against Jim Crow. For Murray, the race-sex analogy depicted the struggles for racial justice and sex equality as intertwined and rooted in century-old alliances between movements against slavery and for women's rights. Murray's analogy placed African American women's advancement at the center of an integrated campaign for what she called "human rights." Murray linked the battles against Jim and Jane Crow because she hoped to close the divide between the reawakening feminist movement and the black civil rights cause. In civil rights advocacy she found both an effective strategic model and a compelling source of moral legitimacy for the feminist legal battles of her time.

"Reasoning from race" eventually included a variety of strategies. Feminists tried to emulate the civil rights movement's organizational structure and tactics: most famously, the NAACP Legal Defense Fund's triumphant litigation campaign against state-sponsored racial segregation inspired feminists to seek judicial redress. Feminists also used analogies rhetorically, to unsettle habits of thought and practices that seemed natural and just, as racial difference and subordination once did. If advertisements had formerly included "No Negroes Need Apply," then perhaps "Men Only" labels on some jobs were equally problematic.[15] Legal analogies took this rhetorical parallel a step further, justifying similar legislative, administrative, or judicial responses to various forms of injustice. In legislatures, feminists sought the inclusion of sex alongside race and other categories in antidiscrimination laws. In court, they urged judges to examine legal classifications based on sex with the same skepticism applied to racial distinctions. In administrative agencies, they lobbied for the enforcement of laws and regulations against sex as well as race discrimination.

From its inception, reasoning from race provoked controversy. Some civil rights advocates charged that it belittled the African American freedom struggle and risked squandering the movement's hard-won moral and political capital. Some feminists worried that women too wedded to the civil rights example would be unable to develop an independent agenda. Women of color feared that comparing "women" to "blacks" or other "minorities" erased white women's complicity in racial oppression and downplayed the class differences so highly correlated with racial identity. Others simply believed that analogies between race and sex were descriptively inaccurate. Nevertheless, social movement activists and politicians, lawyers and judges, journalists and laypeople continued to use race as an all-purpose comparator.

This book is a history of reasoning from race as a legal strategy pursued by feminists during the 1960s and 1970s. To understand the history of feminist legal advocacy is to recognize reasoning from race as a fluid, historically variable practice rather than as a fixed or foregone conclusion. The social meaning and legal content of reasoning from race varied widely over time. Political and economic context mattered tremendously, as did the audience to whom feminists presented their demands.

And reasoning from race did not only involve simple parallels or assertions of equivalence. When advocates reasoned from race, they often engaged in more sophisticated uses of comparative analysis. Analogies illuminated differences as well as similarities between race and sex. As the legal scholar Paulette Caldwell has written, analogies can lead "to important insights, which in turn may assist in conceptualizing new approaches to challenging oppression based on either [race or sex]."[16] Reasoning from race allowed feminists to reimagine as well as to emulate ideas, strategies, legal precedents, and policies conceived as responses to racial injustice. As a legal strategy, reasoning from race could be unifying as well as divisive, binding together groups that might otherwise compete for recognition and resources in a shared quest to win or preserve legal rights and remedies.

Why study feminism and the law through the prism of reasoning from race? In the latter years of the civil rights era, reasoning from race transcended legal doctrines, categories, and forums. It cast a long shadow over debates about education and employment, citizenship and reproduction, sexuality and class, political economy and cultural mores. Race and sex had always been deeply intertwined in American culture; feminists' investment in the civil rights revolution married race and sex equality as a matter of law and policy. By the 1970s, it had become impossible to understand one without reference to the other.

The history of reasoning from race illuminates the rich but often troubled relationship between civil rights and feminism.[17] The connections between race and sex as categories of legislation and jurisprudence reflected and shaped interactions among social groups and social movements. The stories of women like Murray who attempted to bridge these movements expose moments of effective cooperation as well as conflict and competition. These stories also highlight the integral role played by African American women—as strategists, plaintiffs, theorists, and government officials—in shaping both equality law and the infrastructure of the civil rights–feminist coalition.

Finally, the civil rights paradigm continues to influence movements for legal change in ways both obvious and subtle. Advocates grapple with how to frame their claims in relation to the civil rights struggle, how to win the support of established civil rights constituencies, and how to build upon race equality law precedents.[18] Conservative movements, too, have sought to assume the civil rights mantle even as they resist and revise its core premises.[19]

Historians and sociologists, political scientists and legal scholars have acknowledged the centrality of race-sex analogies to feminist advocacy in the United States.[20] But we know remarkably little about how reasoning from race has evolved over time, especially after race-sex parallels were incorporated—often partially and problematically—into the law.[21] This book fills that gap by examining both the origins of modern race-sex analogies in the period before 1970 and their subsequent career as a building block of equality law in the 1970s.

Reasoning from race has often borne blame, explicitly or implicitly, for the shortcomings of 1970s sex equality law. Commentators routinely characterized feminists' legal agenda during this period as limited to "formal equality," an "equal treatment" or "sameness" model that required women's assimilation to a male norm. The resulting jurisprudence removed overt, sex-based classifications from the law but failed to grapple with enduring physical and cultural sex differences or with racial and economic stratification among women. Feminists, these critiques suggested, took from civil rights the principle of colorblindness and applied it to sex. In doing so, they embraced an impoverished version of equal rights that allowed for the continued subordination of women, especially those who were poor or of color.

Or did they? Recent historical work has persuasively debunked popular characterizations of second-wave feminism as a white, middle-class, myopic endeavor populated by disaffected housewives, disillusioned young refugees from the civil rights and antiwar movements, radicals seeking sexual freedom but oblivious to bread-and-butter economic concerns, and naïve liberals who placed too much faith in principles like neutrality and equal opportunity. Historians have uncovered instead tremendous diversity of background, thought, and activism, a multiplicity of movements within a movement obscured by an exclusive focus on mainstream, predominantly white organizations and advocacy.[22] A few of these studies have examined legal advocacy in particular areas, such as affirmative action and sexual harassment, often at the less visible but no less important grassroots level.[23] Historians have also begun to explore the pivotal contributions of Murray and other African American women to the revitalization of feminist advocacy in the 1960s and early 1970s.[24]

Tracing the career of reasoning from race across time helps to bridge the gap between these two disparate pictures. How did the rich, intersectional vision promoted by African American feminist advocates and their allies become the more limited version of legal equality, largely divorced from race and reproduction, that prevailed by the early 1980s? Answering this question will take us to schools and workplaces from the rural South to the urban North, to the pages of local newspapers and law reviews, and to intricate doctrinal debates in law offices, judges' chambers, and the halls of Congress. Looking beneath the surface of Supreme Court opinions reveals the arguments and strategies that did not prevail, the disappointments and missed opportunities—the "lost promise" of feminist advocacy.[25] It also helps to explain why these efforts have largely vanished from our historical memory.

The story of feminist legal advocacy is in part one of constraint and compromise. Feminists enjoyed their first substantial legal success just as a conservative resurgence and an economic downturn narrowed the possibilities for progressive reform. Movements against abortion, affirmative action, and other rights claims put feminists and civil rights advocates on the defensive. Reasoning from race became a less attractive strategy to the extent that Americans harbored second thoughts about the civil rights revolution and began to see economic opportunity as a zero-sum game.

But the 1970s also offered opportunities for creativity and coalition. Throughout the decade, feminists continued to promote much more expansive conceptions of equality than those that survived in published Supreme Court opinions. When the strategy of reasoning from race foundered, feminists reshaped the relationship between race and sex equality law. When formal equality principles fell short, they turned to more capacious theories, many of which implicated race as well as sex equality. When conservatives organized, feminists and civil rights advocates united against a common adversary. And when Ronald Reagan's election and the ERA's demise ended the civil rights era, feminist defeats proved not merely demoralizing but liberating.

This book uncovers the myriad ways that Americans reconfigured the relationship between racial injustice, sex inequality, and the law in the 1960s and 1970s.[26] During this period, reasoning from race usually—

though not always—concerned a particular racial group's historical struggle: even rhetoric that compared "women" to "minorities" frequently treated "minorities" as synonymous with "Negroes" or "blacks," and "civil rights" as the concern of African Americans.[27] The "feminism" of this book's title refers to the strands of activism that sought to remedy the injustice and inequality that advocates for women identified within American society and law. Feminist advocates lobbied, litigated, organized, demonstrated, and educated. They supported legislation, the repeal or judicial invalidation of discriminatory laws and policies, and the amendment of state and federal constitutions. The courts were a particularly crucial arena for feminists' reasoning from race, an homage to the civil rights movement's successful constitutional litigation strategy.

Feminist legal advocacy was only one component of the post–World War II women's movement: other feminist objectives were not primarily, or even nominally, legal in nature. Not only legal decision makers but also members of nongovernmental organizations, employees, professors, litigants, and homemakers all played important roles. Other historical actors included the politicians, journalists, attorneys, fellow activists, and members of the public to whom feminists presented their demands. Still, legal and constitutional reform played a starring role in the feminist constellation. The civil rights revolution shaped feminists' imagination— especially the imagination of those for whom racial justice and sex equality were inseparable.

Like Pauli Murray a half-century earlier, LaDoris Cordell placed her faith in the law as an instrument of social change. Despite her keen disappointment in the passage of Prop 8, Cordell remained optimistic about the future of same-sex marriage in California. "The courts," she predicted, "will reopen the doors of marriage to the gay community"— just as they had to mixed-race couples decades earlier.[28] Whether advocates embrace or reject civil rights as a model, they cannot escape the power of its legacy.

1

THE REBIRTH OF RACE-SEX ANALOGIES

"The similarities of the societal positions of women and Negroes are fundamental rather than superficial," wrote college student Florynce "Flo" Kennedy in 1946. "[A] dispassionate consideration of the economic, sociological, historical, psychological, political, and even physiological aspects reveals some rather startling parallels." Both groups were "generally dependent economically upon the dominant group"; they were "barred from many specialized fields," penalized more severely for "sex 'transgressions,'" considered "naturally inferior," and their "[i]ndividual distinctions [were] minimized." Kennedy condemned "segregation, discrimination, and limitation" and hoped that comparing "women" and "Negroes" would "hasten the formation of alliances" and "counteract the divide-and-rule technique" endemic to social domination.[1]

Kennedy's analysis, written for a Columbia sociology course, reflected and anticipated a flowering of social science scholarship in the 1940s and 1950s that analogized "women" to "Negroes." Gunnar Myrdal's landmark *An American Dilemma* (1944) contained a six-page appendix titled "A Parallel to the Negro Problem," in which he described how women, like African Americans, were branded intellectual inferiors, deemed ineducable, confined to certain societal roles, excluded from many fields of employment, denied citizenship rights, and mythologized as "content" in their subordinate positions.[2]

Myrdal's insight had many adherents, setting the stage for the analogical reasoning that became a powerful tool for feminist lawyers in subsequent decades. In 1945, anthropologist Ashley Montagu compared "antifeminism" with "race prejudice," urging his readers to "recall that almost every one of the arguments used by the racists to 'prove' the inferiority of one or another so-called 'race' was not so long ago used by the antifeminists to 'prove' the inferiority of the female."[3] Social psychologist Helen Mayer Hacker's 1951 article "Women as a Minority Group" argued that "women and Negroes" occupied a "caste-like status," and described the similar operation of race- and sex-based subordination.[4] In one of the pivotal texts of second-wave feminism, *The Second Sex,* the French social theorist Simone de Beauvoir identified "deep similarities between the situation of the woman and that of the Negro."[5]

These writers laid the groundwork for the rhetorical and constitutional arguments that revolutionized American law in the 1960s and 1970s. Prior to 1960, however, race-sex parallels were of limited use to feminists. In 1951, for example, Flo Kennedy became the second African American woman to receive a law degree from Columbia. But several years later, when Columbia Law Professor Herbert Wechsler questioned whether racially segregated schools should always be held to violate the Constitution's equal protection guarantee, he invoked sex segregation as an uncontroversial example of legitimate discrimination. "Does enforced separation of the sexes discriminate against females merely because it may be the females who resent it and it is imposed by judgments predominantly male?"[6] he asked rhetorically. To Wechsler—and likely to many Americans—the answer was almost surely no.

In the century before 1960, a few advocates for women argued that similarities between sex and race warranted comparable treatment.[7] But it was not until the early 1960s that reasoning from race became a centerpiece of feminist legal advocacy. As African Americans enjoyed greater success in the courts in the years after World War II, black civil rights became a more promising template for other reforms, including women's rights. Even then, many advocates for women remained skeptical of the race-sex analogy. Its acceptance required a concerted effort to overcome long-standing racial and ideological divisions, and achieving unity was not without costs.

*   *   *

Although the social science literature comparing race and sex was new in the mid-twentieth century, such comparisons had a long history in American political and legal discourse. Analogies between servitude and marriage had long legitimated both white dominion over blacks and male domination of women as natural, even divinely sanctioned.[8] Apologists for racial slavery in the seventeenth and eighteenth centuries drew upon common understandings of women's supposed inherent inferiority to justify a similar subordination for persons of African descent. In the nineteenth century, slaveholders defended the South's "peculiar institution" as an indispensable element of other social hierarchies, most prominently marriage.[9] In a sense, then, women's rights advocates of the nineteenth century answered proslavery theorists on their own terms when they invoked similarities between the legal status of married free women and slaves. These rhetorical parallels were useful in that they both attracted white Northern women to abolitionism and alerted them to their own subordination.[10] Sojourner Truth and others subtly challenged such comparisons and highlighted the particular plight of African American women by telling their own stories of suffering and strength.[11]

Analogical arguments resurfaced among advocates of racial and sexual equality after the Civil War. For a time in the 1860s, feminists and abolitionists united behind the American Equal Rights Association to promote universal suffrage for African American men and all women, and they made freedwomen a central symbol of their struggle. The Reconstruction Amendments proved an enticing template for the enfranchisement of women as well as black men. Republican politicians' reluctance to accept any analogy between black male suffrage and women's enfranchisement provoked bitter and lasting divisions between those who believed it was better to achieve black male enfranchisement, even if woman suffrage was not forthcoming, and those who thought abolitionists should oppose anything short of universal suffrage.[12] Beginning in the late 1860s, some white woman suffragists turned to racist and nativist arguments, compromising the link between white women's rights and the struggle for racial equality.[13] This betrayal signaled the end of an interracial abolitionist-feminist alliance.

Race-sex analogies survived in pockets, especially among African American advocates of woman suffrage. In a typical formulation, W. E. B.

Du Bois declared in 1917 that disenfranchisement for women was "as unjust as . . . the denial of the right to vote to American Negroes." Activists James Weldon Johnson and Mary Church Terrell drew parallels between proslavery and antifeminist ideologies.[14] These woman suffragists used analogical arguments to resist white women's racism and to convince African Americans that the movement's exclusionary tactics made woman suffrage a no less laudable goal.

Conflicts among advocates for women erupted after the Nineteenth Amendment gave women the vote, reshaping the stakes of debates over the relationship between race and sex inequality.[15] When suffragist Alice Paul proposed an Equal Rights Amendment (ERA) in 1923, she ignited a controversy between two opposing camps. One, which included Paul's National Woman's Party (NWP) and some professional women's groups, insisted that an ERA eliminating all legal distinctions between men and women was necessary to achieve women's equal status in American society.[16] The other faction, composed of labor-oriented advocates, had fought hard for protective legislation for working women, such as minimum wage and maximum hours laws and weight-lifting regulations.[17] Members of the NWP argued that special laws for women were insidious, "protecting" women not from dangerous working conditions so much as from meaningful advancement in traditionally male occupations. From 1923 until the late 1950s, the NWP's small but determined band of stalwarts pressed the ERA in Congress, without success. Allies of the protectionists were equally determined, often attaching riders and amendments to exempt protective laws from coverage.[18]

Race-sex parallels paid few dividends in the interwar period, and advocates for women invoked them only occasionally. In 1935, NWP member and lawyer Blanche Crozier read the Fourteenth Amendment to prohibit the exclusion of women from juries. Crozier contended that race and sex "are in every way comparable. . . . They are large, permanent, unchangeable, natural classes . . . susceptible to implications of innate inferiority." She also lamented the apparently "ineradicable tendency of legislatures and courts to draw distinctions upon sex lines."[19] Crozier had little ammunition with which to attack sex discrimination, however. The Fourteenth Amendment, the pillar of Reconstruction-era legal remedies for slavery, had been largely emptied of meaning by post-adoption court decisions.[20] Courts had construed protections against racial discrimination narrowly, and severe segregation and subjugation prevailed on the ground.

Even the civil rights advances of the 1940s and 1950s did not guarantee the appeal of race-sex analogies to feminists. Instead, the NWP appealed to Southerners' belief in white supremacy and their opposition to protective labor laws. The ERA's early congressional sponsors included Strom Thurmond of South Carolina, who championed the amendment as a means of elevating white women's rights over African-American claims for equality. During this period, Alice Paul and many of her colleagues distanced themselves from black civil rights, openly courting segregationist legislators in ill-fated attempts to push the ERA through Congress.[21]

The protectionist opponents of the ERA also were wary of staking women's claims on an analogy to race under the Fourteenth Amendment, but for different reasons. Those who defended sex-specific protective legislation usually supported the civil rights movement and believed the law should treat blacks and whites equally. At the same time, they had little interest in proclaiming the irrelevance of differences between men and women.[22] Moreover, their disappointment in the Fourteenth Amendment as a vehicle for racial justice made them reluctant to place their hopes in an ERA. New Haven lawyer Catherine Tilson wrote in 1946, "[M]any of the fundamental injustices to the negro [sic] have been held to be unaffected" by the Fourteenth Amendment. She feared that the ERA would suffer the same fate. The lack of a general societal endorsement of sex equality, Tilson worried, would result in "judicial emasculation" of the amendment. Like the Fourteenth Amendment, the ERA would not apply to the actions of private individuals and institutions. And while "the negro [sic] had much to gain, and nothing to lose, by the adoption of the 14th amendment," the ERA could cost working women important protections and subject all women to the military draft.[23]

Dorothy Kenyon of the American Civil Liberties Union was among the few feminists during this period who believed that litigation under the Fourteenth Amendment could bring about meaningful change in women's status.[24] Kenyon had championed workers, the poor, radicals, and African Americans as well as women since graduating from law school in 1917.[25] Like most who toiled for progressive causes in the decades between 1920 and 1970, Kenyon saw the ERA as a threat to protective labor laws. Unlike many of her liberal male colleagues, though, she saw promise for women's rights in *Brown v. Board of Education,* the 1954 school desegregation decision. Kenyon and ACLU attorney Rowland Watts hoped that a 1958 suit challenging women's exclusion from

Texas A&M University would "build up a 'sociological' record—insofar as time and our research facilities permit—comparable to that done in the racial segregation cases."[26]

Success seemed possible at first. In *Heaton v. Bristol,* the trial judge found that "as a matter of law separate but equal facilities are inherently unequal as applied to males and females."[27] The Texas Court of Civil Appeals reversed, however, and the U.S. Supreme Court declined to hear the women's petition.[28] The lesson was that judicial decisions requiring the admission of African Americans to all-white graduate and professional schools remained inapplicable to women applying to all-male institutions.[29]

Kenyon's crusade foundered again in the jury service case *Hoyt v. Florida,* decided by the Supreme Court in 1961. Gwendolyn Hoyt had been convicted by an all-male jury of murdering her husband. She protested that Florida's exemption of women from jury service violated the Constitution.[30] Kenyon's amicus brief for the ACLU noted, "It has long been the law that the express exclusion of Negroes from juries or jury lists, on the sole ground of race or color—whether by statute or administrative act—was an unreasonable classification and therefore a denial to Negro defendants of the equal protection of the laws." She posed the question in *Hoyt* in parallel terms: "Is the same thing true in the case of women? Or is the rationale back of their classification in a category different from men, on the sole ground of sex, reasonable?"[31] The Supreme Court rejected Kenyon's arguments, with Justice John Marshall Harlan declaring that "woman is still regarded as the center of home and family life."[32] Women's primary responsibility for family care and their secondary status as workers and economic actors were central to federal policy throughout the first two-thirds of the twentieth century.[33] In the four decades after the Nineteenth Amendment's adoption in 1920, race-sex analogies remained at the margins of American legal thought.

Anna Pauline "Pauli" Murray set out to change all that. No one did more than Murray to make race-sex analogies the legal currency of feminism. A North Carolinian descended from slaves and slave owners, Murray was a veteran of the civil rights struggle by the time she emerged as the architect of feminist legal strategy. Born in 1910, she spent her childhood in Durham with her aunt, Pauline Fitzgerald Dame, a schoolteacher. Determined to escape Southern segregation, Murray attended Hunter College in New York, graduating to bleak economic prospects in 1933. After a difficult search for work, she found employment in the Works Progress Administration (WPA). There, she developed an abiding awareness of the crossracial impact of poverty and began a long friendship with Eleanor Roosevelt. In 1938, Murray applied to the University of North Carolina's graduate program in sociology, hoping to study race relations in one of the South's most progressive academic departments. State officials, however, pledged to build a separate Negro graduate school rather than admit Murray to UNC. Instead, she moved to Washington in the early 1940s to attend Howard University's law school. She led sit-ins in the nation's capital and fought on behalf of a black sharecropper sentenced to death for allegedly murdering his white landlord. She also excelled academically.[34]

At Howard, Murray received excellent civil rights training, as well as lessons in the evils of sexism, which she labeled "Jane Crow." In 1944, her classmates reacted with "hoots of derisive laughter" when she argued that civil rights lawyers should challenge segregation head-on, rather than proceeding piecemeal by proving individual facilities unequal. Spottswood Robinson, then a young Howard law professor and civil rights attorney, accepted Murray's wager of ten dollars that *Plessy v. Ferguson* would be overruled within twenty-five years. Murray applied for the Rosenwald Fellowship at Harvard Law School, traditionally awarded to Howard's top graduate—which Murray was. Harvard sent a terse rejection based on her photograph and college transcript, which demonstrated that she was not "of the sex entitled to be admitted to Harvard Law School."[35]

To Murray, the letter from Harvard was a piercing reprise of her earlier correspondence with University of North Carolina officials, who had informed her that "members of your race are not admitted to the University." This blow was even more devastating, however. Harvard's rejection was "a source of mild amusement to many of my male colleagues who were ardent civil rights advocates," she wrote in her autobiography. "The harsh reality was that I was a minority within a minority."[36] Murray appealed to the Harvard Corporation, mixing ironic humor with incisive critique. "Very recent medical examination reveals me to be a functionally normal woman with perhaps a 'male slant' on things, which may account for my insistence upon getting into Harvard," she told the Corporation.

She asked that Harvard not "allow tradition to stand in the way of progress."[37]

The Corporation punted Murray's application to the law school faculty. Her next submission closed with what appeared to be a bit of pointed levity: "Gentlemen," she wrote, "I would gladly change my sex to meet your requirements but since the way to such change has not been revealed to me, I have no recourse but to appeal to you to change your minds on this subject. Are you to tell me that one is as difficult as the other?" Murray's remark about changing her sex was not just an off-hand attempt at humor. In the late 1930s and early 1940s, Murray struggled to resolve the disjuncture between her "masculine sense of self" and her biological sex. In notes prepared for one of many medical professionals Murray consulted during this period, she described her "inverted sex instinct," and her tendency to "fall in love with the female sex," as well as her desire to wear pants, "be one of the men," and "do things that fellows do." She tried in vain to find a doctor who would allow her to experiment with injections of male sex hormone, and apparently resigned herself to living her life as a woman.[38] Murray kept these struggles over sexual identity private, but they likely influenced her intuition that sex, like race, was a complicated social construction rather than a fixed biological category.

By the time Murray learned that her appeal for admission to Harvard had been denied, she had moved on to pursue a master's degree at the University of California at Berkeley. There, Murray authored an important law review article on race and labor, as well as a paper arguing that the separate-but-equal doctrine violated the right of Negro children "not to be set aside or marked with a badge of inferiority." She used psychological and sociological data to show that segregation did "violence to the personality of the individual affected." The paper found its way into the hands of Spottswood Robinson, who initially dismissed her arguments as unrealistic. But he revisited them in 1953, when he and other members of the NAACP legal team prepared the briefs for *Brown*. Meanwhile, Murray spent the 1950s writing an acclaimed book about her family, practicing at the New York City law firm of Paul, Weiss, Rikfind, Wharton & Garrison, and teaching law in Ghana.[39] While working on her doctorate at Yale Law School in the early 1960s, she served on the Civil and Political Rights Committee (CCPR) of the President's Commission on the Status of Women (PCSW).[40] There, Murray began to make her mark on the emerging feminist legal renaissance.

The PCSW convened in 1961 against the backdrop of a standoff between proponents of protective laws and ERA supporters. The CCPR asked Murray to research and report on alternative strategies for legal and constitutional change. The result was a pivotal and widely circulated memorandum that prominently featured analogies between race and sex inequality and proposed a litigation campaign for women's rights modeled on the NAACP's successful struggle against racial segregation. Like racial minorities, Murray wrote, women were "an easily identifiable group, to a large degree unrepresented in the formal decision-making processes." Their "legal history [was] one of slow progress against considerable resistance from the dominant (male) group." Women's inferior position, like that of blacks, was predicated upon supposedly inherent differences. Therefore, "legal distinctions based upon sex [were] particularly susceptible" to applications prolonging and reinforcing "women's inferior status."[41] Murray's memo drew upon social scientists' postwar explorations of the subordinate status of women and of African Americans. Myrdal and Hacker were early sources; later influences included Ashley Montagu, Simone de Beauvoir, and historian Eleanor Flexner.[42]

Murray's analogy went beyond rhetorical and descriptive comparisons of race and sex inequality. She suggested that a women's rights coalition craft "Brandeis briefs" and bring lawsuits under the equal protection clause of the Fourteenth Amendment. The original Brandeis briefs, written in the early twentieth century to defend protective labor laws, had marshaled evidence about women's particular physiological and social needs. Murray maintained, instead, that social, economic, and technological transformations in women's lives rendered obsolete older legal doctrines that emphasized women's physical weakness and underwrote their political inferiority. Murray also emphasized the importance of building institutions comparable to those that had sustained civil rights advocacy.

The Fourteenth Amendment litigation strategy allowed Murray to straddle the line that divided ERA advocates and opponents. Murray believed that insufficient support among women's groups for a new amendment precluded its imminent success but did not bar a constructive campaign for judicial reinterpretation of existing constitutional provisions.[43] In contrast to the ERA's complete prohibition on any classification by sex, equal protection stood for a flexible, case-by-case approach. Equal protection, Murray argued, could eliminate pernicious discriminations against women, such as exclusion from jury service or from traditionally male occupations, without disrupting protections important to labor advocates.

Women had enjoyed little success in bringing challenges under the equal protection clause. Courts consistently upheld laws that distinguished between men and women. Judges asked only whether a challenged law was "reasonable" or if it had a "rational basis," which gave government free rein to classify on the basis of sex.[44] Under Murray's proposed standard of "heightened reasonableness," the law could treat women differently from men under much more limited circumstances. Murray left the door open to some protective labor laws "designed to protect the maternal and family functions through compensatory measures" or to address women's "special health needs." The law should also be permitted to help women overcome their "traditionally disadvantaged position in society," she contended. But Murray distinguished between "policies which are genuinely protective of the family and maternal functions and those which are unjustly discriminatory against women as individuals."[45] Murray's standard would not allow sex-based legal classifications that "imply inferiority or enforce an inferior status by singling women out as a class for restrictive treatment."[46]

The analogy to race, Murray believed, could help expose policies that excluded women from economic and political life as pernicious and discriminatory. Although Murray did not argue for the identical treatment of race and sex—or of men and women—some skeptics argued that this was the inevitable result of her proposal. Among others, Harvard Law School Dean Erwin Griswold rejected Murray's efforts "to equate racial discriminations with discriminations based on sex."[47] Griswold, a prominent supporter of civil rights for African Americans, wrote Murray a cordial note praising her "excellent memorandum" but refusing to endorse her conclusions. "[I]t has always seemed to me that there are differences in sex, and these differences may, in appropriate cases, be the basis of classification,"[48] he wrote. Others embraced Murray's approach as a welcome alternative to the ERA. The ACLU's Kenyon sent her endorsement, as did Harvard Law Professor Paul Freund, a protégé of Louis Brandeis who both championed black civil rights and opposed the ERA.[49] And even skeptics acknowledged that the Supreme Court's apparent willingness to recognize new rights boded well for women.[50] Murray hoped that feminists of various stripes could unite around the Fourteenth Amendment approach.[51] She recommended that the CCPR endorse "the underlying principle of the Equal Rights Amendment . . . without taking any position on that Amendment or referring to it by name." She wrote, "If we could build up the Fourteenth Amendment in this way without sacrificing the principle of the ER Amendment, we may escape from our dilemma."[52]

The Fourteenth Amendment strategy also linked women's rights advocacy to the existing civil rights agenda, the objective closest to Murray's heart. Murray's memo called explicitly for stronger ties between women's organizations and civil rights groups such as the NAACP and the ACLU, as well as the Department of Justice.[53] Litigation appealed to Murray because thus far "court action on the 14th amendment" had been "more effective than legislative efforts in the struggle for Negro rights."[54] Moreover, using the Fourteenth Amendment could unite civil rights and feminism under one constitutional banner, mitigating conflicts that had long pained Murray. For Murray, this unification was at least as important as closing the divide between protectionists and ERA supporters.

Murray won over much of the anti-ERA women's rights contingent with her new approach. But she struggled to convince ERA partisans that her strategy would not undermine their quest for women's legal equality. In public statements, leaders of the NWP described the Fourteenth Amendment path as "wishful thinking"—utterly hopeless and counterproductive.[55] Privately, some were suspicious of Murray's motives and her civil rights connections. Murray's "preoccupation," Miriam Holden wrote to Anita Pollitzer, "is with the Negro problem, and her primary purpose seems largely to be an attempt to hitch that wagon to our Equal Rights Amendment star." Such a linkage, Holden worried, would "spell disaster for our hopes," for "[t]he Southern states are sure to look with disfavor on any Constitutional legislation that is linked with the Negro problem." Holden accused the NAACP of conspiring to "infiltrate" the women's movement so that they could "make use of it as a springboard for their own propaganda." She advised feminists to "at all costs, avoid comparisons of our position with the position of the American Negro."[56]

Murray made it her mission to bridge these divides between white feminists and African American rights activists. Invoking history, Murray argued to supporters of black civil rights that a failure to assuage women's concerns would be racially divisive, reenacting the Reconstruction-era demise of the equal rights alliance.[57] In such a scenario,

Murray emphasized, black women would be left without effective redress. To audiences of white women, Murray spoke of past alliances as precedents for a renewed joint effort. In effect, she retrospectively credited white women with racial progressivism. She often noted a precipitous drop in lynching after the adoption of woman suffrage and pointed out that the states that still barred women from jury service were the very ones "which have given most stubborn resistance to desegregation."[58]

Murray's optimism buoyed the prospects for coalition. "Many white women today," she wrote, "are earnestly seeking to make common cause with Negro women and are holding out their hands . . . Negro women must be courageous enough to grasp the hand whenever it is held out."[59] But in 1963, the year of the landmark March on Washington for civil rights, some National Woman's Party members marched to the segregationist beat. For them, equal rights for women would only be undermined by an association with black civil rights. The prohibition of sex discrimination in employment, part of Title VII of the Civil Rights Act of 1964, finally began to disentangle the ERA and its proponents from racial segregationists.

In February 1964, with the NWP's encouragement, segregationist Democratic Rep. Howard W. Smith of Virginia proposed adding sex to the list of prohibited categories of discrimination in the civil rights bill's employment section. The ensuing debate framed the inclusion of sex in Title VII as a favor to white women that might well undermine the primary purpose of the bill—to protect African Americans from racial discrimination. When Smith introduced the sex amendment, Rep. Emanuel Celler, Democrat of New York, and a primary sponsor of the Civil Rights Act as well as a longtime ERA opponent, immediately rose in opposition. He predicted that compulsory military service for women, the decline of traditional family relationships, and the invalidation of rape laws and protective labor legislation would all follow from the adoption of legal sex equality. Rep. Martha Griffiths, Democrat of Michigan, a longtime advocate of women's rights, appealed to her colleagues to protect white women from employment discrimination. "I rise in support of the amendment," announced Griffiths, "because I feel as a white woman when this bill has passed . . . that white women will be last at the hiring gate." Eager to undermine the race discrimination provisions of

Title VII, Southern legislators chimed in to support Griffiths. Legislators warned that without the amendment, "the white women of this country would be drastically discriminated against in favor of a Negro woman."[60]

Rep. Edith Green, Democrat of Oregon, PCSW member, author of the Equal Pay Act, and longtime women's rights supporter, feared that an alliance between feminists and Southerners would derail the entire bill. Green declared, "I do not believe this is the time or place for this amendment . . . For every discrimination that has been made against a woman in this country there has been 10 times as much discrimination against the Negro of this country."[61] Reluctant to gamble on a "killer" amendment, Green could not join her female colleagues in their otherwise unanimous support of the sex provision.

Segregationist solicitude for the "White, Christian Woman of United States Origin" reflected the concerns of some NWP members who believed that the Civil Rights Act would subject white women to increasing discrimination. Nina Horton Avery, chairman of the Virginia Committee of the NWP, worried that the bill would "relegate white women of Christian religion to oblivion from every angle." She implored Congress "to prevent a mongrel race in the United States and . . . fight for the rights of white citizens in order that discriminations against them may be stopped."[62] In contrast, some NWP members viewed the civil rights movement as a valuable source of momentum.[63] Meta Heller wrote to Emma Guffey Miller that while she "would be happy to serve" on the NWP committee forming to safeguard women's interests in the Senate debate over the Civil Rights Act, she wanted

> to emphasize that I feel the Civil Rights Bill is terribly important. We all recognize, I think, that the Southerns [sic] tried to muddy the issue by suggesting Title VII of the Bill be amended to forbid discrimination on account of sex. In my opinion . . . today it is the negro [sic] women who will win for all of us equal rights. I only wish all women's organizations would get behind the civil rights movement, forgetting their prejudices for their own advancement.[64]

Pauli Murray cherished the same wish. The prevailing portrayal of the sex amendment as a favor to white women and a blow to black civil rights impelled Murray to reframe the provision as centrally concerned with the rights of African American women. When the sex amendment was in danger of failing in the Senate, Murray wrote a memorandum circulated among senators and White House officials, arguing that including sex was the only way to extend the benefits of Title VII to the group that most needed them: black women. In response to the argument that omitting the sex amendment would profit African Americans at white women's expense, Murray offered a very different vision: "What is more likely to happen . . . [is that] in accordance with the prevailing patterns of employment *both* Negro and white women will share a common fate of discrimination, since it is exceedingly difficult for a Negro woman to determine whether or not she is being discriminated against because of race or sex." In fact, Murray wrote, "Title VII without the 'sex' amendment would benefit Negro males primarily and thus offer genuine equality of opportunity to only *half* of the potential Negro work force."[65] Armed with these arguments, Murray and her allies succeeded in saving the "sex" amendment.[66]

The inclusion of sex alongside race in Title VII did not banish all racist arguments from the NWP's rhetorical arsenal in one fell swoop, but it prompted the NWP's leaders to reconsider their alliance with segregationists.[67] Once the NWP had won protection against sex discrimination, members were invested in the survival of the civil rights statute.[68] The recalcitrance of the newly formed Equal Employment Opportunity Commission (EEOC), which openly gave lower priority to sex discrimination claims than to race discrimination complaints, soon alerted feminists to the need for mobilization.[69] Feminists of all persuasions could unite behind women's right to be free from discriminatory hiring, wage, promotion, and firing practices.

Title VII created an unprecedented bond between struggles for racial justice and sex equality. In their 1965 article "Jane Crow and the Law: Sex Discrimination and Title VII of the Civil Rights Act of 1964," Pauli Murray and Mary Eastwood, a young Justice Department attorney who had served with the PCSW, endorsed a race-sex parallel and provided a template for analogical legal arguments under the Constitution and Title VII.[70] Privately, Murray worried that "[w]omen's groups [were] divided and disorganized."[71] She warned, "Unless we develop some fast coordinated action, we will lose the little we thought we gained."[72] Publicly, she hoped the civil rights movement could inspire a newly assertive feminist posture. She told the National Council of Women in October

1965: "It should not be necessary to have another March on Washington in order that there be equal job opportunities for all. But if this necessity should arise, I hope women will not flinch from the thought."[73]

Two or three years earlier, such revolutionary rhetoric might have led Miriam Holden to suspect nefarious NAACP plots to co-opt the women's rights movement. But intervening events had transformed Holden's opinion of Murray.[74] Now, she wrote to Alice Paul of Murray's "excellent" speech and her "objective and courageous position."[75] Murray's civil rights orientation was no longer anathema to NWP members; her dedication to the enforcement of Title VII dovetailed nicely with the group's own agenda.

Murray and her allies had succeeded in severing the opportunistic alliance between feminists and segregationists. Nevertheless, advocates for women's advancement still faced formidable challenges. The women's movement remained divided over the ERA and sex-specific protective labor legislation. No institutional structure existed to implement Murray's Fourteenth Amendment litigation strategy; her vision of an "NAACP for women" had yet to materialize. Public officials and journalists frequently characterized Title VII's sex discrimination provision as an irrelevant fluke. Even as women's advocates increasingly found common ground, they endured indifference, reluctance, and even outright hostility from the constituencies and decision makers whose support they needed to achieve the transformative changes they sought.

Pauli Murray and other female civil rights activists had long argued for women's inclusion in the public face of the civil rights leadership.[76] But they confronted a conventional wisdom among civil rights liberals that framed economic independence for African American women as a threat to racial equality. Liberals, policy makers, and social scientists assumed that black women's economic and political independence—or at least their household leadership—undermined family stability and African American progress.[77] In 1963, on the eve of the March on Washington, Murray declared: "[N]o civil rights campaign can be permanently successful which does not stand foursquare for *all* human rights." She went on to protest that Negro women "have had to bear the dual burden of 'Jim Crow' and 'Jane Crow'" only to "find that the 'second class equality' they have shared with Negro men is dissolving and that they are being frozen out of the positions of partnership in the struggle which they have earned by their courage, intelligence, militance, dedication, and ability."[78]

For their part, most civil rights leaders were at best equivocal. Many were outright dismissive. The reply of Whitney Young, executive director of the National Urban League, was unapologetic: "For the purposes of improving the stability of our Negro family life . . . , I would think that Negro women leaders . . . should make their primary goal the lifting of the social, economic and educational status of their men."[79] James Forman of the Student Nonviolent Coordinating Committee (SNCC) agreed with Murray that there could be no "successful 'revolution' if it is not completely dedicated to the equality of the sexes." But he qualified this bold statement by noting that several distinguished black women leaders had recently visited SNCC's Selma headquarters, and "learned a great deal." Equally annoying, he signed his letter, "One man—one vote."[80] Congress on Racial Equality (CORE) national director James Farmer called Murray's charge "essentially correct," but doubted "that discrimination against women in the civil rights movement is a matter of design in any but a few cases."[81]

Murray did not retreat: in November, she addressed the National Council of Negro Women (NCNW) on "the tendency to assign women to a secondary, ornamental or 'honoree' role." She called the reply from the March on Washington's officials to her entreaties "a typical response from an entrenched power group." She insisted that "the Negro woman can no longer postpone or subordinate the fight against discrimination because of sex to the civil rights struggle but must carry on both fights simultaneously."[82]

For feminists, the unprecedented legislative success of the mid-1960s offered an opportunity to build upon egalitarian enthusiasms, to turn abstract rights into concrete remedies not only for black men, but for women of all races. But if 1965 ushered in the Voting Rights Act and the repudiation of attempts to repeal Title VII, it also brought the flames of the Watts riots and the release of an intellectually incendiary document, Daniel Patrick Moynihan's *The Negro Family: The Case for National Action*. Moynihan drew on the work of sociologist E. Franklin Frazier, who had diagnosed in America's urban ghettos a vicious cycle of poverty and family instability. The Moynihan Report catalogued the symptoms of this decay: a quarter of marriages dissolved, a quarter of births illegitimate, a quarter of Negro families headed by females, and a "startling increase" in welfare dependency. Moynihan traced this "tangle of pathology" to the "matriarchal structure" of black communities.[83] According to Moynihan, the same family breakdown that left women without breadwinning husbands and children without fathers led almost inexorably to juvenile delinquency, crime, and violence.

The Moynihan Report's emphasis on "pathology" and its unflattering portrait of the "Negro Family" offended many activists.[84] However, the report's critique of "matriarchy" reinforced a liberal consensus that linked female household leadership and labor force participation with "emasculation," poverty, crime, and African American male unemployment.[85] A 1967 *Parade* article by Lloyd Shearer, "Negro Problem: Women Rule the Roost," exemplified the attitude feminists abhorred: "Unless and until the Negro family structure in America becomes a patriarchy instead of the matriarchy it now is, this country is not likely to enjoy social peace."[86] Catherine East, who had served in senior positions for various committees on the status of women since her involvement in the PCSW, called Shearer's article "the ugliest piece of racism parading under the guise of science" since the 1920s. The answer to the problems facing poor families, East insisted, was not merely to "cater to the Negro boy," as Shearer suggested. Instead, she urged policy makers to tackle the real problems underlying poverty, especially high rates of female as well as male unemployment; low wages; the unavailability of birth control, abortion, and day care facilities; inferior schools, and racial segregation.[87] Privately, East derided the Moynihan Report as "anti-negro and anti-feminist."[88] Rep. Martha Griffiths had a similar reaction: "It is high time to disperse the syrupy miasma flowing from the Moynihan Report that 'Negro women have it good' when the facts are just the opposite and produce detrimental effects on their economic progress."[89]

For many in the civil rights community, however, the focus on rehabilitating black manhood seemed long overdue. Moynihan's prescription for the ailing black family coincided with the rise of the masculinist Black Power movement and a growing conviction that racial unrest could be quelled only through growth in employment opportunities for black men.[90] The historian Deborah Gray White writes that "[b]y the middle of the 1960s," many black Americans "had supplanted the principle that a race could rise no higher than its women. . . . By the end of the decade, black Americans were endorsing the concept that the race could rise no higher than its men."[91] Even some who sympathized with the feminist critique saw the Moynihan Report's potential to bolster affirmative employment policies.[92]

By targeting matriarchy, the report supported a vision of equal employment opportunity that excluded black women—and women generally—not merely incidentally, but by design. Job training programs developed in its wake catered to men, often overlooking or explicitly limiting women's participation. For most of the 1960s, the EEOC gave short shrift to Title VII's sex discrimination prohibition. Early affirmative action efforts such as the Philadelphia Plan, which mandated goals and timetables for government contracts, similarly focused on placing African American men in jobs traditionally monopolized by white males.

Feminists of all races challenged Moynihan's conclusions and reactionary interpretations of his data. Murray argued that Moynihan did "a great disservice to the thousands of Negro women in the United States who have struggled to prepare themselves for employment in a limited job market which is not only highly competitive but which, historically, has severely restricted economic opportunities for women as well as Negroes." She worried that "the Negro males may be pitted against the Negro females in a highly competitive instead of a co-operative endeavor."[93]

The promotion of equal employment opportunity for black women became central to feminists' response to Moynihan.[94] Murray's friend and mentor Caroline Ware and National Council of Negro Women President Dorothy Height together wrote a widely circulated document entitled "To Fulfill the Rights of Negro Women in Disadvantaged Families." Ware and Height proposed alternative solutions to the problems of African American families in general and black women in particular. Height and Ware blamed black women's plight on a "lack of income" and on "discrimination," which they deemed "second only to poverty as a source of disadvantage." They wrote, "[I]t will profit [the Negro woman] little to be no longer blocked because of race but barred by sex from effective employment and citizen participation. For her, enforcement of Title VII . . . with respect to discrimination in employment on the ground of sex is as vital as its enforcement on the ground of race."[95]

Height and Ware's reference to "citizen participation" alongside "employment" reflected feminists' challenge to the exclusion of women from jury service. Jury service seemed an ideal vehicle for persuading civil rights advocates that the rights of women were integral to the achievement of racial justice. At the same time, the jury service issue held out the promise of vindication for Murray's Fourteenth Amendment litigation approach, an effort designed to transcend the ERA conflict and unite the women's movement. Together with equal employment opportunity, in the mid-1960s, jury service became the centerpiece of Murray's quest to place African American women and what would later be called the "intersection" between race and sex at the center of feminist legal advocacy.

In 1965, Gardenia White and several other African American women and men challenged the Lowndes County, Alabama jury that acquitted the men accused of killing civil rights activists Viola Liuzzo and Jonathan Daniels. In Alabama, as in Mississippi and South Carolina, the law excluded women of all races from jury service, while black men were kept off juries through de facto custom and extralegal violence.[96] The resulting case, *White v. Crook,* linked the civil rights and women's rights struggles, complete with what Fred Graham of the *New York Times* called the "all-purpose plaintiff—Negro women."[97] In 1961, Justice Harlan had written in *Hoyt v. Florida* that the exemption of women from jury service "in no way resembles [cases] involving race or color in which the circumstances . . . compel[led] a conclusion of purposeful discriminatory exclusions from jury service."[98] *White v. Crook* provided a stark and compelling opportunity to convince the Justices that sex discrimination and racial injustice went hand in hand.

White advanced feminist legal advocacy beyond *Hoyt* in several significant respects. *White* challenged the outright exclusion of women from jury service. The case involved a straightforward equal protection claim on behalf of the excluded potential jurors, rather than focusing on a criminal defendant's rights. *White* could unite the rights of women and African Americans in the annals of constitutional jurisprudence, or so Murray hoped. And the *White* case excited feminists on both sides of the ERA controversy, from NWP leaders to Women's Bureau officials.[99]

The plaintiffs' lawyers used a traditional tool of civil rights litigation, expert testimony, to support the link between women's rights and racial justice in jury service. Harvard psychologist Robert Coles, a prominent expert on the effects of segregation on white and black Southerners, established the historical similarities in legal disabilities between "women" and "Negroes," their common tendency to cope with inferior status through exaggerated deference and self-deprecation, and white women's greater "social sympathy" and "compassion" for African Americans— both perceived and actual.[100] The plaintiffs' brief elaborated these arguments, detailing the civil rights activism of white and black Southern women and emphasizing their propensity for nonviolent protest and the restoration of community harmony.[101]

The three-judge district court that convened to hear *White* included two men well known for their "heroic part in ending [racial] segregation."[102] Richard T. Rives, a native of Montgomery, Alabama, was one of the "Fifth Circuit Four" responsible for implementing *Brown v. Board of Education.* Frank M. Johnson, Jr., a liberal Republican descended from Alabama Unionists, had joined Rives in a 1956 decision that struck down segregated seating on Montgomery buses.[103] During the 1950s and 1960s, both men and their families endured threats of death and dismemberment from white Southerners opposed to racial integration.[104] Yet Rives and Clarence Allgood, the third member of the panel, did not relish tackling the issue of women's exclusion from juries. Rives initially failed to perceive the constitutional question at stake and hoped he and Allgood could "gracefully back out," leaving the case in Johnson's hands.[105] Only later did Rives realize that *Hoyt* had left open the question of whether the complete exclusion of women from jury service violated equal protection.[106]

Still, the plaintiffs' lawyers were optimistic. Kenyon called the brief— patched together by civil rights lawyer Chuck Morgan—a "mish-mash," with "bits and pieces about women all through the thing." But she also had "the feeling that, no matter how crazy the brief, we're going to win."[107] And win they did. In February 1966, the court ruled in favor of Gardenia White and her co-plaintiffs on sex as well as race discrimination grounds. The judges declared, "[T]he conclusion is inescapable that the complete exclusion of women from jury service in Alabama is arbitrary."[108] "Sound the tocsin!" exclaimed Marguerite Rawalt, lawyer and longtime ERA supporter. "A Federal Court has ruled that women are within the equal protection clause of the 14th amendment!"[109] A euphoric Mary Eastwood called the result "far better than I had dared hope for. It's the most important thing to happen to women since the Nineteenth Amendment. (At least)."[110] Kenyon wrote effusively: "Other victories will follow. But this one turned the key in the lock. Like the Civil Rights Boys when the *Brown* decision was handed down in 1954, 'I could cry.'"[111]

White v. Crook provided a singular opportunity, at once offering a chance to demonstrate the interdependence of the civil rights and women's causes, a test of Murray's Fourteenth Amendment alternative to the ERA, and a vehicle for uniting the women's movement. Murray told ERA proponent Alma Lutz, "[W]e differ not so much in our objectives as in our strategy. It is just possible that through court interpretation the Equal Rights Amendment will be written into the Constitution." The *White* litigation, Murray added, "just may be the opening we have been looking for."[112] She wrote to Rawalt: "I conceive of *White v. Crook* as the *Brown v. Board of Education* for women in this country. . . . [W]hile the Supreme Court has not yet spoken, it is unthinkable that it could say any less."[113]

Ironically, Gardenia White lost her chance to join Linda Brown in the annals of constitutional history in large part because Richmond Flowers, Alabama's attorney general and 1966 Democratic primary opponent of First Lady Lurleen Wallace, was among the few white Southern politicians who courted black votes before federal legislation and local activism produced substantial numbers of black voters.[114] It soon became clear that the state of Alabama would not appeal the *White* ruling and that the Supreme Court would not consider the jury exclusion question.[115]

The momentum generated by *White v. Crook* did spur the ACLU toward a more active role in women's rights advocacy.[116] Murray and Kenyon argued—to their sometimes skeptical male colleagues as well as to the courts—there was "an integral relation between the exclusion of women and exclusion of Negroes [from jury service]."[117] They overcame civil rights leaders' objections to the inclusion of sex in the proposed federal jury legislation and their arguments became a mainstay of official ACLU statements.[118] But the jury service cases never became the "women's *Brown v. Board*," and they failed to unite civil rights and women's rights in Supreme Court jurisprudence as Murray had hoped. Instead, many feminists moved one step closer to the conclusion that an ERA might be necessary after all.

Now, feminists refocused their efforts on employment discrimination, where litigation subtly reshaped the relationship between race and sex equality. The National Organization for Women (NOW) was founded in 1966, conceived as an "NAACP for women" and dedicated to the enforcement of Title VII. The cast of characters involved in litigating and

strategizing about the late 1960s feminist legal docket included government employees like Mary Eastwood, Catherine East, and Caruthers
Gholsen Berger; "retired" attorney and longtime ERA proponent Marguerite Rawalt; feminist attorneys Sylvia Roberts and Sylvia Ellison;
and civil rights lawyers Phineas Indritz and Philip Hirschkop. They
handled the cases with few resources during a contentious and unstable
period for the various national women's organizations with which they
were associated.[119]

During the late 1960s, feminist lawyers drew heavily upon the analogical arguments Murray and her allies had developed. Some of their
cases were controversial within the women's advocacy community because they directly or indirectly challenged protective labor laws. Convincing courts that differentiating between employees on the basis of sex
often harmed rather than "protected" women was an uphill battle, particularly when some longtime advocates for women and for workers
generally remained unconvinced. Analogies to race helped feminists to
frame their clients' challenges to protective laws as part of a larger
struggle against segregation and inequality.

In March 1966, when Thelma Bowe, Georgianna "Sue" Sellers, and
several other women filed a lawsuit against Colgate Palmolive, they
protested a discriminatory seniority system and the outright exclusion of
women from the company's most lucrative jobs. Colgate Palmolive defended its practices, arguing that it was only complying with state
weight-lifting restrictions for women.[120] But the litigation highlighted
how those laws effectively disqualified all women from most of the best
jobs and their attendant benefits. Lorena Weeks's case against Southern
Bell and Leah Rosenfeld's suit against Southern Pacific Railroad, both
filed in May of 1966, also used Title VII to challenge employer practices
that denied women job opportunities in the name of compliance with
state protective laws. Southern Bell defended its practice of excluding
women from the position of "switchman" on the ground that Georgia's
law restricting the weight a woman could be required to lift rendered sex
a "bona fide occupational qualification" (BFOQ) for the job.[121] Southern Pacific argued that women could be categorically denied the position of agent-telegrapher on similar grounds.[122]

Aviation worker Velma Mengelkoch's suit threatened protective labor laws more directly. In seeking to enjoin enforcement of a state
statute limiting the number of hours women could work, Mengelkoch's

challenge implicated the Fourteenth Amendment, not just Title VII.[123] Caroline Ware wrote in February 1967 that *Mengelkoch* was interpreted in some quarters as an indication that NOW was "just a continuation of the old 'equal rights' faction," indifferent to the plight of working women.[124] Although she was acutely aware of these internal tensions, Ware's friend and protégée Pauli Murray supported the *Mengelkoch* litigation.[125] Murray thought *Mengelkoch* could give feminism a working-class face and at the same time expand women's constitutional rights. She and Catherine East hoped that the case could help women's advocates move beyond their disagreements once and for all.[126]

NOW embraced *Mengelkoch,* predicting that the case "may well result in a landmark decision in civil rights for women comparable to the historic decision of *Brown v. Board of Education.*"[127] Marguerite Rawalt took over the case in early 1967, writing her motions and briefs on a shoestring budget with the help of NOW's Legal Committee. A longtime advocate of women's rights, Rawalt had retired from over thirty years of service as an attorney with the Bureau of Internal Revenue in 1965. The only pro-ERA member of the PCSW, Rawalt served as president of the National Association of Women Lawyers and the National Federation of Business and Professional Women and was the first female head of the Federal Bar Association. By her own admission, Rawalt was a relatively recent convert to the strategy of modeling feminist legal arguments on those of the African American civil rights movement.[128] Initially, Rawalt had been suspicious of Murray's approach, but she admired Murray's support for including sex in Title VII, and by 1966 she agreed that bringing cases under the Fourteenth Amendment as well as working for the ERA was the wisest course of action.[129]

Rawalt eagerly took up the cause of Velma Mengelkoch, a widow with three children and the unofficial spokeswoman for female employees at the Anaheim Autonetics Plant. Mengelkoch challenged California laws prohibiting women from working more than eight hours per day or lifting more than twenty-five pounds. She testified before a state employment committee in 1966, "Those of us here today are all heads of households. The law restricts our ability to work overtime but nobody allows us to pay less rent, or get meat any cheaper, or pay less income tax."[130] Mengelkoch and her coworkers argued that their inability to work overtime limited their income and excluded them from more lucrative and desirable positions within the company. The *Orange County*

Register reported in October 1966 that the case was "expected to go all the way to the Supreme Court."[131]

NOW's amicus brief in *Mengelkoch* urged the court to reject arguments that "women are more easily fatigued than men, that they are less stable emotionally, that their attendance on jobs is not as good, that they take more sick leave, that they are more likely to be temporary workers, that they do not need to work, that they should be home with their children, that they are distracting to men working on the same job." These were "[g]eneralizations as to the inferiority of women," and like those about "Negro children, are unacceptable in the eyes of the law." Indeed, just as some counseled "gradualism" with respect to the "efforts of Negro citizens to attain equality," so too did "armchair generals" recommend "patience" to women "on such grounds as that 'the time is not right' or that public opinion and sociological change will eventually give women all they deserve." But women, NOW suggested, needed special protection from employment hazards about as much as black children required protection from equal, integrated education. The challenged California statute was a "Jane Crow law," and the "doctrine of special treatment for women, like the misguided doctrine of 'separate but equal' treatment for Negroes, must now be discarded." The brief proclaimed: "Not since *Brown v. Board of Education* has a case raised more substantial constitutional issues."[132]

NOW made such dramatic claims in an effort to convene a three-judge district court whose decision could be appealed directly to the Supreme Court. To the dismay of Rawalt and her colleagues, however, the court ruled that the issue presented in *Mengelkoch* was indistinguishable from earlier cases in which courts had upheld protective labor laws. The bottom line: no "substantial constitutional question."[133]

Mengelkoch's supporters responded by arguing that women-only protective labor laws had become outdated and counterproductive. Technological changes, they said, rendered physical differences between men and women irrelevant. Moreover, challenges to protective labor laws in the early twentieth century were initiated by employers seeking to invalidate protective laws by asserting women's freedom of contract; now, women themselves brought suit to vindicate their own rights.[134] Back then, sex-specific protective laws were the only weapon workers could wield against exploitative working conditions, since the Court had invalidated regulations of male employees' hours and wages. In contrast, feminists argued: "[T]oday equal opportunity and freedom from restrictions for women as well as for racial, ethnic, or religious groups is considered part of human rights." Passage of Title VII, they claimed, made clear that Congress "recognized that women, regardless of race, were subjected to invidious employment discrimination comparable to that inflicted upon racial minorities."[135]

Many judges initially resisted feminists' parallels between race and sex. District of Indiana Chief Judge William E. Steckler, a Truman appointee with a strong civil rights record, flatly rejected the *Colgate* plaintiffs' arguments. In 1967, Steckler declared bluntly, "Sex, under the Civil Rights Act of 1964, is not to be equated with race."[136] A federal district court in Georgia ruled that state protective laws made sex a BFOQ for the position of switchman, and that Southern Bell's refusal to consider Lorena Weeks—or any other woman—for such jobs did not violate Title VII.[137] But NOW lawyers pressed forward. The EEOC joined in their appeal of *Colgate* to the Seventh Circuit, supporting feminists' call for a narrow interpretation of Title VII's BFOQ exception. The NOW brief emphasized the analogy to race as well as the larger constitutional questions implicated in rules restricting women's employment options.[138] The NOW lawyers eventually succeeded in their Title VII suit against Colgate Palmolive, but in 1968 the Supreme Court rejected Mengelkoch's constitutional appeal and sent the case back to the Ninth Circuit.[139] Feminists' aspiration to bring a "women's *Brown v. Board*" to the Court had been dashed again.

The analogy between race and sex discrimination had been carefully developed by Murray to highlight the interconnections between racial justice and sex equality. Now, feminists often described sex and race inequality as parallel, rather than intersecting phenomena.[140] While lawyers like Rawalt were happy to capitalize upon friendly race precedents, they did not prize the connections that were central to Murray's race-sex analogy and overall constitutional strategy. But race-sex parallels nevertheless served an important purpose, reframing apparently benign "protections" as unjust, discriminatory, and contrary to the spirit of the civil rights revolution.

After enduring "a kind of fateful exclusion from the inner circle of civil rights activities," feminism felt like home to Pauli Murray. In early 1966, she wrote exultantly to Mary Eastwood: "[O]ur involvement in advancing the status of women gives us meaning and focus to our lives. . . .

[H]aving an intellect and an equalitarian point of view has been almost a handicap to me in finding a place in the civil rights struggle, as if it were a threat to male colleagues. No one, however, can deny me the right to speak out on behalf of women. Hooray for our side!"[141] Later that year, Murray helped to found NOW. She hoped the new organization could avoid the divisive battles of the past.[142]

Feminist support for the ERA swayed in the balance in 1967 when NOW established a committee to study the constitutional rights of women.[143] The committee included several longtime ERA supporters, among them Alma Lutz and Marguerite Rawalt, as well as Mary Eastwood, who had come to believe that feminists should pursue a new amendment. Other members, such as civil rights lawyer Phineas Indritz, had misgivings triggered by continued opposition from labor unions and civil rights groups. Protective labor legislation remained an especially thorny issue for women union leaders, many of whom now believed in the desirability of an ERA but had yet to convince their male colleagues.[144]

The NOW committee debated several proposals, including at least two "Human Rights Amendments." One would have combined an ERA-like prohibition of sex discrimination with protection for abortion and a ban on all state and federal funding for private entities that discriminated on the basis of race or national origin. Another would have prohibited "discrimination against any person based upon age, color, economic status, national origin, political belief, race, religion, sex, social status or any other non-merit factor," and would have applied "not only to the United States or any State but also to private action."[145]

These Human Rights Amendment proposals linked women's equality with both African American civil rights and reproductive freedom. Neither had historically been associated with ERA advocacy. But just when the NWP was becoming increasingly obsolete and irrelevant, Alice Paul and her compatriots intervened to stymie even the tiniest changes to the ERA's language. When Betty Friedan proposed a much more modest change—that the words "equal treatment" be substituted for the phrase "equality of rights under the law"—Paul quickly quashed this modest "New Amendment for a New Era" initiative.[146]

NWP's steadfast insistence on retaining the old ERA language reflected its members' distrust of NOW's more expansive agenda. NOW was relatively mainstream on the spectrum of late 1960s feminism, but to the NWP—now composed primarily of much older women, some of whom were veterans of the suffrage struggle—NOW was full of young upstarts with radical ideas.[147] Miriam Holden wrote to an NWP colleague in February 1967 of the need to "disassociate ourselves from the current wave of activity" concerning "problems of sexual or psychological supremacy." Holden feared that "[t]he idea of 'equal rights' . . . [had] been debased," and that the new women's movement was producing a "mass fear that American women are seeking to pre-empt the masculine role in our society. . . . [O]ur Amendment," she insisted, "is aimed solely at remedying the *legal* disabilities of American women."[148]

Eastwood was quite sympathetic to the more radical agenda of younger NOW members. But she nevertheless respected Paul's vehement opposition to deviating from the old ERA language. Whether it was pragmatism, inertia, or Eastwood's desire for her elders' approval that won the day, Eastwood concluded that NOW should work in concert with the NWP and other pro-ERA groups.[149] At the same time, NOW came under increasing pressure from other activists to endorse the existing language of the ERA. In the fall of 1967, NOW's Washington, D.C. chapter passed a resolution giving unequivocal support to the amendment.[150]

At NOW's second annual conference in November, organizers convened a special all-conference discussion of the ERA and abortion, the two most contentious issues facing the young organization.[151] The ERA debate was long and vigorous. UAW representatives Dorothy Haener and Caroline Davis requested that NOW grant them more time to convince labor leaders of the ERA's merits, while Indritz warned that a new amendment had no chance of passing Congress and urged instead the continued pursuit of litigation under the Fourteenth Amendment.[152]

Murray assumed her time-honored mediating role.[153] In place of a resolution committing NOW to immediate support of the ERA, she proposed allowing local NOW chapters seven months to choose between three alternatives: endorse the ERA as is, endorse an alternative amendment with different wording, or incorporate the ERA into a general Human Rights Amendment. As the conference minutes recorded, "much discussion followed," but Murray mustered only fifteen votes, while eighty-two voted for NOW's immediate endorsement of the ERA.[154]

With NOW's embrace of the ERA, feminists had taken a momentous step. But the price was high. Several labor union women resigned, including Dorothy Haener, who wrote: "I mourn, almost as though it were a human thing, for this organization whose birth . . . gave such high hope and promise of being a vehicle for men and women, as well as interested organizations from all strat[a] of society to unite in seeking common goals in a civil rights movement for women."[155] Murray, arguably the organization's strongest voice for collaboration with other civil rights causes, left the conference "deeply disillusioned."[156] Three days later, she wrote an anguished letter to NOW cofounder Kay Clarenbach, predicting that a single-minded focus on the ERA would confine the movement "almost solely to 'women's rights' without strong bonds with other movements toward human rights" and "might develop into a 'head-on collision' with Black civil rights and other struggles." Murray felt that concentrating on the amendment in light of other groups' reluctance betrayed her own identity as well as her aspirations for the feminist movement. Murray told Clarenbach of her "inability to be fragmented into Negro at one time, woman at another, or worker at another." She left the conference, she said, feeling "like a stranger in my own household . . . passé, old, and declassed."[157] Although Murray remained in close touch with NOW activists, she decided to pursue her feminist legal agenda—including, eventually, explicit support for the ERA—within the ACLU's more expansive organization.

In choosing to endorse the old ERA, NOW rejected alternative formulations that stressed other forms of inequality, extended beyond formal state action, and guaranteed reproductive freedom.[158] Instead, NOW replicated the NWP's vision of women's equality, in isolation from racial and other forms of discrimination and separate from reproductive rights. NOW did not dissociate itself from abortion rights—far from it. Indeed, the 1967 conference also resoundingly endorsed women's reproductive freedom and called for the repeal of laws criminalizing abortion.[159] But NOW's rejection of alternative amendments that incorporated reproductive freedom suggested that constitutional equality and reproductive rights would be separate enterprises.[160]

At the same time, the idea that Fourteenth Amendment litigation and agitation for a constitutional amendment were complementary gained momentum. Eastwood, still an attorney for the Department of Justice as well as one of NOW's primary legal strategists, promoted this dual constitutional strategy:[161]

> As a matter of tactics, even if the ERA fails to pass, vigorously pushing for it will show women are demanding equal rights and responsi-

bilities under the law by the most drastic legal means possible—a constitutional amendment. The effect, provided we make clear we think [the] 14th *properly interpreted* should give women [the] same unqualified protection, would be to improve our chances of winning 14th amendment cases.[162]

By 1968, the dual strategy was the more-or-less official position of NOW.[163] Even the NWP thawed, as Caruthers Gholsen Berger suggested that the group should reconsider the Fourteenth Amendment's potential. "The ERA," she declared, "need not *compete* with the 14th amendment."[164]

Murray remained an active member of the ACLU Equality Committee.[165] Indeed, her personal disappointment with the 1967 NOW conference barely interrupted her strategizing: she predicted that her estrangement from NOW and its pro-ERA stance would help her to convince the ACLU to support litigation efforts like *Mengelkoch, Weeks,* and *Colgate-Palmolive*.[166] But the male-dominated ACLU leadership prioritized black male empowerment in the mid-1960s, leaving women's concerns for later resolution.[167] They also feared that opposing protective legislation for women would undermine the ACLU's relationship with labor organizations.[168] Kenyon had long been frustrated with the slow pace of change in attitudes toward women's rights: "I know exactly how the Black Panthers feel," she said, "ignored, passed over, segregated (intellectually at least), and frustrated until they are ready to kill."[169] Kenyon's commitment to the Fourteenth Amendment approach—which predated Murray's—outpaced her opposition to the ERA, and as the two enterprises appeared increasingly compatible, she gradually embraced the dual strategy.[170]

Before 1970, Murray, Kenyon, and their allies had been thwarted in their efforts to make sweeping changes in ACLU policy.[171] But in 1969, the EEOC interpreted Title VII to prohibit protective legislation for women only, removing one of the last barriers to liberal support for an ERA.[172] As feminist groups coalesced around the ERA, Murray and Kenyon openly endorsed the amendment. In March 1970, with the ERA before Congress, Murray wrote forcefully to "urge as strongly as I can that ACLU *not* testify in opposition."[173] Murray and Kenyon expressed concern that President Richard Nixon would make good on his promise to pack the Court with "strict constructionists." Moreover, now that feminists were mobilizing behind the ERA, Murray believed that a universalist human rights approach required civil rights organizations to join them.[174]

Kenyon, too, was ready to declare her support for the ERA. "We still approve of the XIV Amendment approach," Kenyon and Murray wrote in a memorandum to the ACLU Board. "I think we all do. But in spite of heroic efforts on the part of women as well as of ACLU, the Supreme Court has consistently rejected us as having no place under it. . . . There comes a time when you cannot wait any longer, when you must find new tools for the tools that have failed you," the memo declared. "This I believe is such a time."[175] Six days later, the ACLU Board endorsed the ERA.[176] Women's Bureau head Esther Peterson publicly embraced the ERA the following year.[177] Feminists now agreed that the constitutional change they sought could and should be pursued through a dual strategy.[178]

By 1970, feminists spoke a common language. In hearings on sex discrimination, the formerly skeptical Rep. Edith Green pressed the race–sex analogy relentlessly.[179] When Congress debated the ERA, the amendment's allies routinely contrasted the courts' commitment to racial equality with its dilatory approach to laws that discriminated against women. They insisted that sex inequality deserved the same treatment as racial injustice. They often contended that women's inferiority was, if anything, more deeply ingrained in American law and culture than racial inequality. ERA supporters were fond of quoting Rep. Shirley Chisholm's declaration: "[I]n the political world, I have been far oftener discriminated against because I am a woman than because I am black."[180] ERA-friendly lawmakers like the African American Rep. John Conyers urged witnesses testifying before Congress to consider whether race and sex were analogous. Most complied readily, though some warned that comparing injustices might divide rather than unite disadvantaged groups.[181]

Supporters of the ERA generally acknowledged that differences between race and sex would dictate divergent approaches in some areas. For instance, while racially segregated bathrooms, dormitories, and military barracks seemed quintessentially unconstitutional, proponents argued that concerns about sexual privacy supported separate living facilities for men and women. Where women's or men's "unique physical characteristics" made sex-neutral laws impractical—in areas such as childbearing or sperm donation—ERA proponents allowed for slightly less rigorous judicial scrutiny.[182]

On the other hand, ERA supporters were concerned that even the stringent standards of judicial scrutiny developed for racial classifications would not be rigorous enough to overcome judicial propensities to accept supposedly "benign" or "protective" sex classifications. The ERA would require even stricter review, they claimed. Yale Law Professor Thomas Emerson and the feminist students who wrote the definitive law review treatment of the ERA maintained that the amendment would mandate an "absolute prohibition" on sex-based legal classifications.[183]

Opponents of the ERA countered that sex-neutral laws would produce ridiculous outcomes. Harvard Law Professor Paul Freund argued that the "moral dimensions of the concept of equality are clearly not the same in the two cases [of race and sex]."[184] The primary congressional opponent of the ERA, North Carolina senator Sam Ervin, cited Freund's analysis frequently and drew on his stature as a respected liberal legal scholar.[185] Sex-segregated educational options, athletic teams, bathrooms, and dormitories, Freund argued, remained legitimate, despite the wholesale constitutional rejection of Jim Crow. Equal participation by women in the military, he and others suggested, would require a fundamental overhaul of the armed services far beyond what successful racial integration had required two decades earlier. Freund predicted that the ERA, by analogy to the constitutional prohibition on racial classification in marriage laws, might lead same-sex couples to demand the right to marry and adopt children.[186] ERA opponents rejected the premise now embraced across the feminist community—that sex and race discrimination were similar enough to warrant comparable constitutional treatment.

The role of "reasoning from race" had evolved in the years since Murray and her allies had revitalized the strategy in the early 1960s. When Murray proposed the Fourteenth Amendment approach to the PCSW, her race-sex analogy served the dual purpose of uniting feminists divided over the ERA and protective laws and integrating feminist advocacy into a larger civil rights agenda. Reasoning from race did not necessarily mean embracing formal equality or nondifferentiation in all circumstances; rather, Murray's "functional" analysis seemed to offer a middle ground between the uncompromising position of the NWP and the reluctance of other advocates to view all sex-based differentiation as constitutionally problematic. As it turned out, achieving consensus within a divided women's movement entailed leaving behind the more expansive visions of equality embodied in the "Human Rights Amendments." Instead, feminists embraced the text forged by an older generation with narrower aspirations.

When Flo Kennedy compared "women" and "Negroes" in 1946, she hoped that analogies between race and sex could foster collaboration among often-divided and diffuse subordinated groups. Murray used her position as a "Negro woman" to disarm skeptics in the civil rights community and reframe the fight against sex discrimination as an integral component of African American progress. Murray and her feminist allies went on to stress black female empowerment as the solution to African American poverty and urban unrest. The southern jury service cases provided an unrealized opportunity to unite the causes of civil rights and women's rights under a single banner carried by black women.

Yet reasoning from race did not necessarily link the two movements closest to Murray's heart. Transformed into legal arguments, race-sex analogies could be abstract and distancing. Advocates could urge that sex be treated like race for legal purposes without acknowledging how race and sex inequality were intertwined, either in law or in the lives of women of color. Nor could reasoning from race succeed in any form without the answering embrace of the civil rights and legal establishments feminists ultimately sought to persuade.

2

"WOMEN AND MINORITIES"

In 1970, NOW President Aileen Hernandez asked Merrillee Dolan, head of the organization's task force on Women and Poverty, to write a "critical analysis" of the Moynihan Report. "So many of his damaging notions have formed the basis of the federal policies which either ignore women altogether or actually worsen their circumstances," Hernandez lamented.[1] She wanted Dolan to focus not on black family structure, but on "women in poverty," and how government antipoverty programs promoted "*man*power training" and jobs for men at women's expense.[2] Dolan's widely circulated critique castigated Moynihan for recommending that African Americans emulate white couples' "equalitarian" relationships. "If 'equalitarian' means that each sex performs *expected* tasks . . . according to sex . . . with the male holding the economic strings and therefore power over the female whose job is housecleaning, babysitting, and providing sex services, then slavery based on race could also be called 'equalitarian,'" Dolan wrote.[3]

By 1970, feminists had embraced a legal strategy based on an analogy between race and sex discrimination. But they still faced skepticism about the urgency of combating sex-based inequality. Five years after its release, the Moynihan Report cast a long shadow over feminists' aspirations. Restoring male breadwinners to African American households was the only way to stem poverty and social disorder, said leading liberals. In their eyes, equal employment opportunity for women threatened racial progress. These doubters prompted a small but influential cadre of African American feminists to argue that economic independence for black women was the key to family stability and racial equality. Their distinctive brand of reasoning from race spotlighted intersections between race and sex inequality, promoted alliances between the civil rights and feminist movements, and placed black women at the center of both struggles.

Over the next few years, feminists' legal victories undercut the male breadwinner/female homemaker model as a basis for public policy. And feminists succeeded in expanding civil rights to include "women" alongside racial minorities. The experience and example of African American women proved useful in legitimating feminist demands. But for civil rights advocates and EEOC lawyers, feminists were attractive coalition partners in part because of their ability to mobilize white women, a large and potentially powerful constituency. The imperatives of political and legal advocacy impelled feminists to make increasingly abstract and universal claims about women generally. As "women and minorities" became an established category in the American political lexicon, the law compared but did not connect race and sex inequality. Judges broke "women" and "minorities" into separate and distinct categories, framing race and sex as parallel rather than intertwined. As a result, race–sex analogies later bore much of the blame for obscuring the intersections between race and sex in the law and in the lives of women of color.

In retrospect, reasoning from race also seemed inadequate to confront the disadvantages women suffered because of their childbearing capacity. After all, there was no racial analogue to pregnancy. But in the early 1970s, reasoning from race and combating pregnancy discrimination under the equal protection clause appeared perfectly compatible. Indeed, although some judges initially balked, feminists enjoyed considerable success in persuading courts to treat pregnancy discrimination as sex discrimination. Reasoning from race did not inevitably foreclose the inclusive and expansive conception of equality feminists sought.

Feminists saw evidence of Moynihan's influence everywhere in the early 1970s. A NOW study warned that the "effect of Moynihan's report is still a widely proliferating theory that the aspirations of all women, black and white, are inimical to the black cause." Another pamphlet cited a Labor Department official's recommendation "that the sex provision of Title VII be repealed, that the Federal government be made the employer of last resort for all men with families, and that men be placed in charge of all government programs for the disadvantaged, since 'placing these (disadvantaged) younger men under dominant women will only increase their long-run psychological disabilities.'"[4] White women's labor force participation joined "matriarchy" in black families as a widely perceived threat to African American progress.

Lax enforcement of anti-discrimination laws dogged women's advocates. Although they made progress within the EEOC, feminists railed against continued foot-dragging. Other federal agencies required almost constant prodding from NOW to include women in their affirmative action programs.[5] NOW leader Ann Scott complained in 1971, "Our efforts have been aimed at both the [Office of Federal Contract Compliance] and the EEOC, neither of which is doing much of anything for anyone, and even less for women."[6] Old debates over how to prioritize the pursuits of race and sex equality resurfaced as civil rights advocates and feminists fought over limited government resources. When NOW argued that the U.S. Civil Rights Commission's jurisdiction should expand to include sex discrimination, Frankie Muse Freeman, a former NAACP lawyer and the first female member of the Commission, cautioned that "without a substantial increase in its resources[, the Commission] could lose its momentum, and its competence in the area of discrimination based on race, color, and national origin could be dissipated."[7]

Skepticism about the women's movement persisted within the black community.[8] Some black women chided white feminists for eschewing middle-class lifestyles that were unavailable to many African Americans. Almena Lomax, a journalist and divorced mother of six, charged that "women's lib" was nothing but a "frivolous bid for attention by the most privileged and coddled women in the world. . . . [W]e have yearned after the status [of] wives and mothers, able to devote our attention to the care of our families and homes, which Women's Lib would chuck overboard."[9] Others worried that competition from white women would endanger already scarce job opportunities for African American men. As Enola Maxwell, an Oakland settlement house chaplain, declared in

1972, "We want to get some of those white women back in the home and our Black men into those jobs and off the streets."[10]

Other African American women rejected arguments that black women's independence could only come at black men's expense, but they suspected that white feminists would be fickle partners in challenging the power structure. An anonymous black woman told the feminist publication *Off Our Backs* in 1971 that "much of the ideology of Women's Liberation is plagiarism."[11] Novelist Toni Morrison observed that African American women didn't "want to be used again to help somebody"—in this case, white women—"gain power—a power that is carefully kept out of their hands."[12]

Even civil rights activists with feminist sympathies often perceived "women's libbers" as focused on sexual conflict to the detriment of bread-and-butter economic issues. Coretta Scott King said feminists "spen[t] too much time talking about sex and marital contracts and not enough about tokenism of both black and white women and equal pay for equal work."[13] The day after feminists demonstrated en masse in a "Strike for Equality" in 1970, Bayard Rustin criticized their limited vision: "What is wrong with [feminists'] demands"—free abortions, 24-hour day care, and equal educational and employment opportunities—"is that they don't go far enough." Without demands for socialized medicine, an overhaul of public education, and full employment, Rustin argued, feminism would "become just another middle class foray into limited social reform."[14]

Pauli Murray saw feminists' relative moderation as pragmatism rather than weakness, however. She compared the Strike for Equality to the 1963 March on Washington and scolded Rustin for his "backhanded" support of "legitimate demands of the human rights revolution."[15] Defending NOW and its larger goals, Murray challenged Rustin to bring NOW "closer to the Negro rights movement." She urged: "We need you, just as you need us; the only difference between now and the past is that we are determined to be accepted as partners and equals."[16]

The late 1960s had been a tumultuous period for the nation, and for Murray. Student protests rocked universities, including Brandeis, where Murray now taught. She recoiled at the "radical turnabout in racial consciousness" that Black Power represented. Murray later recalled the "excruciating anguish" she felt when "convulsions of Negro student rebellion spread like contagious madness." She found herself occupying "a no man's land between the whites and the blacks, belonging wholly to neither, yet irrevocably tied to both."[17] Having labored long and hard for recognition as an individual and for relationships across lines of color, gender, and culture, she found the younger generation's challenge to the ideal of integration deeply unsettling.

Comparing Black Power to women's liberation helped Murray understand the "strident" rhetoric and separationist ethos she found so painful. When a young friend urged her to "substitute the words 'women,' 'women's consciousness,' and 'women's liberation' for 'black'" she saw that her "barely disguised hostility toward the Black Revolution was in reality my feminist resentment of the crude sexism I perceived in many . . . male leaders." As Murray later explained, "The early 1970s found me responding alternately to the competing demands of the black movement and the women's movement, often taking the lonely (and unpopular) position of calling for a broad, inclusive expression of feminism at a time when many prominent Negro women felt impelled to subordinate their claims as women to what they believed to be the overriding factor of 'restoration of the black male to his lost manhood.'"[18] Murray persevered in promoting her vision of "indivisible human rights," resisting attempts to fracture her identity as a "Negro woman."

In the early 1970s, an increasingly influential group of African American feminists joined Murray in championing the virtues of interracial feminist alliances. For these women, connections between race and sex discrimination, between "blacks" and "women," and between the civil rights and feminist movements, went beyond abstractions or political expediency. They believed that the struggles for racial justice and feminism could be complementary and mutually reinforcing. Frequently invoking parallels between sex and race, they developed a distinctive response to the prevalent view that a gendered division of family labor remained an essential ingredient of racial progress.[19]

Like Murray, these feminists had strong and abiding ties to other social movements. Aileen Clarke Hernandez, the daughter of Jamaican immigrants and a graduate of Howard University, worked as a labor organizer and served on California's Fair Employment Practices Commission in the early 1960s. President Lyndon Johnson appointed Hernandez to the EEOC in 1965, where, she recalled, "The message came through clearly that the Commission's priority was race discrimination—and apparently only as it related to Black men."[20] In 1966 Hernandez resigned in frustration, declaring her intention to "create an alliance between the civil rights and women's rights movements."[21]

As President of NOW in the early 1970s, Hernandez fought against sex-segregated job advertising, for EEOC enforcement of Title VII, and for the inclusion of women in affirmative action programs.[22] Press coverage frequently commented on her habit of comparing sexism to racism.[23] "[T]he attitude that holds race and sex discrimination as mutually exclusive," she said, was "both short-sighted and self-defeating. Without equally vigorous enforcement against sex discrimination, the Federal Government tacitly encourages employers to continue discrimination on every other one of the prohibited bases."[24] Hernandez encouraged her colleagues to take an expansive view of the feminist agenda and its relationship to other movements, including but not limited to racial justice. In 1971, for instance, she supported a NOW resolution declaring that lesbian rights were women's rights and protested the NOW Legal Defense Fund's decision to decline a case brought by a lesbian mother threatened with losing custody of her children.[25]

Eleanor Holmes Norton, a Yale Law School graduate and Murray protégé, belonged to a new generation of feminists.[26] As an ACLU attorney in the 1960s, Norton represented activists ranging from the Mississippi Freedom Democratic Party to George Wallace and the National States Rights Party. In 1970, Mayor John Lindsay named Norton chair of the New York City Commission on Human Rights. Norton immediately convened a series of "Open Hearings on Women's Rights," which brought together a diverse group of feminist leaders and members of the public to discuss everything from abortion to the obstacles facing welfare mothers and domestic workers.[27] Over the next several years, she became a respected voice in anti-discrimination law and policy.

Like Murray and Hernandez, Norton regularly relied on comparisons between race and sex. In doing so, she used differences as well as similarities to her advantage. "I don't for a moment believe that women have suffered the same kind of injustices that blacks have," she said in 1971. "But still, many of the psychological and economic problems are the same."[28] Indeed, to Norton, the challenge of achieving sex equality had no parallel, not even in the struggle for racial justice. "Basic as would be the changes" wrought by racial equality, she said, "they would change society, not civilization as sexual equality would."[29]

Feminists like Murray, Norton, and Hernandez were uniquely situated to mediate between the civil rights and women's movements. All were determined to recast feminism and antiracism as equally important components of a larger human rights struggle. All sought coalitions between black and white women at a time when such alliances remained highly controversial within the African American community. The race-sex parallels they promoted were part of a larger theory of racial progress that rejected the emulation of an idealized patriarchal family structure. Hernandez and Norton brought Murray's philosophy to elite feminist and legal organizations and even government agencies. Rep. Shirley Chisholm of New York, the first African American woman to serve in Congress, promoted similar ideas in the political arena.[30]

With a mixture of careful diplomacy and dogged persistence, these women built interracial feminist coalitions and strengthened ties between male-dominated civil rights organizations and the women's movement. Hernandez spearheaded a Minority Women's Task Force within NOW. She frequently held the predominantly white organization accountable to the women of color and poor women NOW was often charged with ignoring.[31] Norton chided women's organizations at a national conference on employment opportunity in 1971: "Unless the women's movement begins to amass some record so that the women who now don't relate see some concrete reasons to relate, they will grow at too slow a rate to effect social change."[32] Both women frequently reminded well-intentioned white feminists that expanding their base of support required more than lip service.

These feminists also spoke forcefully to African American women. When younger black women dismissed the women's movement as white, middle-class, and irrelevant, Murray called on women of all races to "recognize the common moral roots of our social evils of which racism and sexism are symptoms."[33] Hernandez tried to convince African Americans of their stake in feminism. She cofounded Black Women Organized for Action in 1973 and worked closely with other women of color within NOW.[34] Without interracial coalitions, Norton argued, women could not enforce antidiscrimination laws, fund free universal child care, or eliminate disparities in everything from Social Security to the military. At the first conference of the National Black Feminist Organization (NBFO), the *New York Times* reported, "When some of the women expressed doubts about being aligned with the white women's liberation movement, because they though it 'frivolous' or believed that white women had contributed to discrimination toward blacks, [Norton] admonished them and said black women would have to form a coalition with white women's groups and with other organizations to get any legislation passed."[35]

African American feminists needed a theory that reconciled women's empowerment with racial progress if they were to build alliances with white feminists and the black civil rights movement simultaneously. They built upon the work of women like Murray to portray gender equality as a prerequisite to racial advancement. Norton urged black couples to "pioneer in establishing new male-female relationships around two careers."[36] Her influential 1970 essay, "For Sadie and Maude," argued that African American women had much to teach white women about overcoming gender hierarchy. Rather than modeling the black family on white patriarchy, Norton argued, African Americans should embrace strong and equal male-female partnerships.[37] She told *New York Times* reporter Charlayne Hunter in 1970, "The black woman already has a rough equality which came into existence out of necessity and is now ingrained in the black life style. [T]hat gives the black family very much of a head start on egalitarian family life."[38] Norton predicted that "fortified by her uncommon experience as co-breadwinner in the family, the black woman can be expected to move . . . into far wider participation in business and in all higher-paying occupations—quite possibly in advance of white women."[39] The Moynihan Report associated black women's independence with "pathology" and family instability; Norton saw it as salutary.

Norton's views were shared by many feminists in the upper echelons of politics and the professions.[40] Former Howard Law School dean and diplomat Patricia Roberts Harris said in 1971, "Despite assertions to the contrary, black women did not make black men second-class citizens. Whites did that." In fact, Harris argued, "Black women have a life experience of equality with men to protect, and it is one to be proud of."[41] As Murray put it, "People who blame our troubles on 'Negro matriarchy' are ignoring a source of strength in Negro women that ought to be available to white women, too."[42] In 1973, Caroline Bird described Murray as a "true integrationist," who "would like to see black women use their psychic freedoms to pioneer egalitarian marriages which can serve as models for young people of both sexes and races."[43]

Each of these women was a "pioneer" of sorts in family life as well as in public pursuits. Norton and Harris strove for egalitarian marriages in their own lives: both, in the 1970s, were married to professional men supportive of their wives' aspirations.[44] Norton declared in 1971, "My husband is the answer to a woman's dream—a strong, completely secure male, unthreatened by women who want to improve themselves outside the home."[45] Norton juggled challenging family and work responsibilities: when tapped to head the New York City Human Rights Commission at age 32, she was pregnant with the first of two children and suffering from severe morning sickness.[46] Murray grew up surrounded by strong women, and her 1947 essay, "Why Negro Girls Stay Single," explored the dilemmas facing well-educated black women seeking mates.[47] Murray and Hernandez both married and divorced early, and later enjoyed intense personal and professional partnerships with other women. Ultimately, the male breadwinner/female homemaker model threatened all that these women had built for themselves, their families, and the black community more generally.

These advocates used race-sex analogies strategically, arguing that women's demands for equal educational and employment opportunity were just and legitimate, integral rather than antithetical to racial justice. They did not uncritically posit parallels between race and sex, "women" and "minorities." Hernandez, for one, regularly recognized and articulated the limitations of the race-sex analogy.[48] Norton urged feminists to overcome their reflexive reliance on simple parallels between race and sex, civil rights and women's rights. "Analogies to other forms of inequality often confuse rather than enlighten," she suggested in 1971. "Subtlety of analysis . . . has too often eluded the [women's] movement."[49]

Black feminists outside of government and the legal community tended to be far more skeptical of race-sex comparisons and of interracial alliances.[50] In her influential essay, "Double Jeopardy: To Be Black and Female," the black socialist feminist Frances Beale described the "white women's liberation movement [as] basically middle-class." She noted its "extremely anti-male tone," arguing that "the main emphasis of Black women must be to combat the capitalist, racist exploitation of Black people."[51] In a 1970 article in *Black Scholar,* Linda LaRue put it more bluntly: "[A]ny attempt to analogize black oppression with the plight of the American white woman has the validity of comparing the neck of a hanging man with the hands of an amateur mountain climber with rope burns." She scorned "what common literature addresses as the 'common oppression' of blacks and women" as a "tasty abstraction designed purposely or inadvertently to draw validity and seriousness to the women's movement through a universality of plight."[52] Some white feminists agreed. Catharine Stimpson, a young white professor of English, criticized race-sex analogies for "exploit[ing] the passion, ambition, and vigor of the black movement," for "evad[ing], in the rhetorical haze, the harsh fact of white women's racism," and for precluding an independent feminist identity.[53]

Murray, Norton, Hernandez, and Harris were not inherently at cross-purposes with their critical counterparts. All shared revulsion at the Moynihan Report's approach to racial progress and championed the empowerment of black women.[54] Feminist legal advocacy, as distinguished from the larger "women's liberation" movement, emphasized issues like economic opportunity that African American feminists agreed should be high priorities on the progressive agenda, even if they disagreed on the relative merits of reform and revolution.[55]

Why, then, did African American feminist lawyers and policy makers invoke the same race-sex parallels that so infuriated other activists? At a time when most civil rights leaders, not to mention government officials, saw feminism and black progress as mutually exclusive, to model arguments for women's rights on the case for racial justice was both subversive and savvy. Reasoning from race allowed black feminists to invoke paradigms already accepted by the civil rights and legal establishments and to highlight the benefits of allying themselves with a numerous and potentially powerful constituency—white women.

In turn, white feminists used analogies between race and sex and alliances with black women to gain credibility among civil rights advocates.[56] In 1971, the new NOW President Wilma Scott Heide promised to "reach out to other human rights activists" and "develop models of compliance so that we needn't compete for scarce resources."[57] She later told NOW members, "[M]y black and brown sisters and brothers can no more afford the 'feminine mystique' lifestyle than can I." Heide declared, "It's time we get together as women of all races and minority men and educate ourselves and each other on the interrelationships of racism and sexism."[58] When Ruth Bader Ginsburg lobbied for the inclusion of girls in Princeton's newly established summer engineering program for disadvantaged youth, she faced objections from liberals who argued that the educational and employment opportunities of young black men should be the focus of limited resources. Exasperated, Ginsburg sent local ACLU official Jameson Doig copies of Murray's and Norton's essays on black women and requested Norton's personal intervention.[59] Ms. Magazine editor and NBFO co-founder Margaret Sloan remarked in 1973 that black women's involvement in feminist organizations "len[t] credibility to the women's liberation movement which . . . was not being taken seriously . . . as a 'political and economic revolutionary force.'"[60]

Many civil rights advocates remained wary of white feminists. As African American columnist Kermit Scott explained in 1971, white women were "already part of the system," adding leverage that could make alliances fruitful "when our self interest and our goals intersect." On the other hand, he wrote, "one should recognize that within a racist society there are certain basic definitions which separate people . . . beyond their immediate grievances in the power structure."[61] Making "women and minorities" a viable political category required that the perceived benefits of coalition outweigh the costs.[62]

Developments in the law helped to persuade civil rights advocates of their stake in feminists' success. In September 1966, Ida B. Phillips, who earned $45.00 a week as a waitress at Donut Dinette, applied for a position as an assembly trainee at a Martin-Marietta steel plant in Orlando, Florida. Phillips, who had seven children aged three to fifteen, would earn $2.25 an hour and benefits at the plant. There was no question that women could and did do the job, which involved fitting a steel part into a computer system programmed to produce missiles. But a receptionist told Phillips that the company would not consider hiring a mother with young children.[63]

Phillips was white, but her plight as a working mother resembled that of many African American women. The NAACP Legal Defense Fund (LDF) took Ida Phillips's case, and women's organizations and the EEOC intervened on her side. Civil rights advocates recognized that unfavorable rulings in sex discrimination cases could easily spill over into race discrimination law. Accordingly, Phillips's supporters used a race-sex analogy to connect Phillips to all Title VII litigants, especially African Americans. As the EEOC's brief put it, "One could not convince [a]

Negro being denied the job . . . that the consequences of the pre-school age children disqualification are any less discriminatory against him because of race by demonstrating that other Negroes have met this admittedly disparate requirement."[64]

To the lower courts, Martin-Marietta's refusal to hire women with preschool-aged children seemed quite reasonable. Fifth Circuit Judge Lewis R. Morgan wrote that only "discrimination based solely on one of the categories, i.e., in the case of sex; women vis-à-vis men" violated Title VII. He could not imagine that Congress meant "to exclude absolutely any consideration of the differences between the normal relationships of working fathers and working mothers to their pre-school-age children, and to require that an employer treat the two exactly alike." Morgan concluded: "The common experience of Congressmen is surely not so far removed from that of mankind in general as to warrant our attributing to them such an irrational purpose."[65]

Phillips's petition for reconsideration of her case was denied, but Chief Judge John R. Brown, a staunch advocate of civil rights for African Americans, wrote in dissent. "The case is simple," he insisted. "The distinguishing factor seems to be motherhood versus fatherhood. The question then arises: Is this sex-related? To the simple query the answer is just as simple: Nobody—and this includes Judges, Solomonic or life tenured—has yet seen a male mother."[66]

Lower courts had considered other Title VII sex discrimination cases, but *Phillips v. Martin-Marietta* was the first to reach the Supreme Court. The federal government's amicus brief, signed by Solicitor General Erwin Griswold, supported Phillips, asserting that there was no "textual basis" for treating sex and race discrimination differently under Title VII.[67] In fact, the bona fide occupational qualification (BFOQ) defense allowed employers to assert that being a man (or a woman) was a BFOQ for a given job, even though they could never make whiteness an occupational prerequisite. Feminists and their allies therefore had to explain why courts should not take a more lenient approach to sex discrimination than to race discrimination.

In arguing for a narrow interpretation of the BFOQ exception, feminists framed Martin-Marietta's policy as a threat to all minority workers. Amici curiae briefs warned that upholding Martin-Marietta's policy would allow employers to impose similar restrictions on racial and religious minorities. NOW and Human Rights for Women cautioned that if

Martin-Marietta could discriminate against women with young children, "then Catholics with more than two children can be discriminated against, blacks can be required to pass a special stringent test to qualify for a job, and Spanish-surnamed Americans can be required to have PhD's in English."[68] A brief from the ACLU, signed by Pauli Murray and Dorothy Kenyon among others, similarly stressed how a loss for Ida Phillips could spell the end of effective remedies for race discrimination.[69]

Phillips's supporters also emphasized the policy's disproportionate impact on black women. The LDF's brief maintained that the "primary adverse impact" of Martin-Marietta's policy was "on blacks," since "[m]ore than twice as many non-white mothers as white mothers" were "heads of families."[70] The government connected the case to the Nixon administration's goal of welfare reform—painting the lower court decision as "contrary to the federal policy of encouraging unemployed women with pre-school age children to seek gainful employment as an alternative to welfare payments."[71] Equal employment opportunity, the brief implied, dovetailed nicely with fiscal conservatism as well as liberal feminism. But such arguments also echoed African American feminists' claims that jobs for women would advance rather than impede economic progress for black families.

Phillips was the Supreme Court's first women's rights case since *Hoyt v. Florida* had declared women "the center of home and family life." The oral argument caused feminists to wonder whether a decade of advocacy had made any difference. One low point came when Chief Justice Warren E. Burger remarked:[72] "The Department of Justice, I am sure, doesn't have any male secretaries. . . . They hire women secretaries because they are better and you hire women assembly people because they are better and you make the distinction between women who have small children and women who don't."[73] Burger's matter-of-fact ratification of what feminists saw as blatant sex discrimination horrified advocates. The Women's Equity Action League (WEAL)'s Bernice Sandler told Pauli Murray, "We have a long way to go."[74]

In the end, the Court's opinion in *Phillips* said very little. A per curiam decision sent the case back to the lower court for further development of the record, but left open the question whether the employer could show that its policy satisfied the BFOQ exception.[75] The Justices' internal correspondence confirms that their ruling was intentionally enigmatic. Justice Harry A. Blackmun "[got] the feeling" that the lower court's reasoning was "unsound," though he thought that "discrimination [not] to hire a woman with pre-school age children has some rationality behind it."[76] Later, he wrote to the Chief Justice, "I feel that the less we say by way of explanation, the better."[77] Burger agreed, revising an early draft to avoid the "risk [of] saying too much too cryptically."[78]

In some ways, *Phillips* symbolized the distance between feminists' aspirations and reality. The Court's opinion was hardly a ringing endorsement of women's equal employment opportunity. Still, *Phillips* provided some cause for optimism. The federal government solidly backed Phillips and argued for a narrow interpretation of the BFOQ exception. Civil rights icon Justice Thurgood Marshall took a strong feminist stand in his concurrence, declaring, "[T]he Court has fallen into the trap of assuming that the Act permits ancient canards about the proper role of women to be a basis for discrimination."[79] And perhaps most importantly, feminists had successfully framed court rulings that condoned sex discrimination as a threat to civil rights litigation generally.

Feminists used the Phillips case to make common cause with the civil rights movement. When Nixon nominated Fifth Circuit Judge G. Harrold Carswell to the Supreme Court in 1970, Betty Friedan joined civil rights leaders in condemning Carswell's "blindness" toward sexism as well as racism, citing his vote against Ida Phillips.[80] Carswell's eventual defeat was due primarily to his reputation for mediocrity and tolerance for racial prejudice, but the feminist civil-rights alliance that helped to scuttle his nomination was unprecedented.

Feminists' headway with civil rights advocates stemmed not only from Title VII's linkage of race and sex but also from the dawning recognition of women's potential political power. By the early 1970s, the women's movement was ascendant, and traditional civil rights organizations were on the defensive. At the first meeting of the National Women's Political Caucus (NWPC) in the summer of 1971, veteran civil rights leader Fannie Lou Hamer proposed an alliance with feminists to buoy the civil rights movement's waning political fortunes: "Let's hook up these minorities and make one hell of a majority!" she told a cheering crowd.[81] NAACP leader Roy Wilkins joined in. Just two years earlier, Wilkins had declared, "Biologically, [women] ought to have children and stay home. I can't help it if God made them that way and not to run General Motors."[82] Now, he praised feminists and predicted that "[r]acism, a persistent and pervasive disease, will get a rough ride from the ladies" of the

NWPC. Wilkins turned white women's greater success in the courts as well as the job market into a source of solidarity. "If the women and minority groups combine their power," he wrote, the dividends "could be astronomical."[83] A few months later, NOW leaders sparred with Wilkins over the decision of the Leadership Conference on Civil Rights (LCCR) to honor two congressional opponents of the ERA. But out of the controversy came a committee on women's rights and before long, the LCCR's endorsement of the ERA.[84]

Such coalitions, fraught and fragile as they were, grew as women flexed their political muscles on a national stage.[85] Efforts to strengthen the EEOC's authority failed in the late 1960s, but in the 1970s, feminists and civil rights advocates together championed extending the EEOC's jurisdiction to educational institutions and state and local governments.[86] As Congress debated the amendments to Title VII, gone were jokes about the fairer sex and female ditchdiggers, replaced by earnest declarations about the menace of sex discrimination. Gone too were strange-bedfellow coalitions between segregationist Southern Democrats, feminists, and female Republican legislators. Recently elected feminist congresswomen Bella Abzug and Shirley Chisholm of New York reminded their colleagues of the "double discrimination" suffered by "minority women."[87] A House report declared that "women's rights are not judicial divertissements," and that sex discrimination was "to be accorded the same degree of social concern given to any type of unlawful discrimination."[88] EEOC chair William H. Brown III testified to the "[striking] similarities between race and sex discrimination."[89] Women's organizations' early interactions with the EEOC had evolved from picketing and protest to face-to-face meetings, personal correspondence, and "follow-through." NOW president Heide recalled that by the end of 1973, when Brown left the EEOC, he "had gotten the message."[90]

A confluence of factors produced this turnaround. Within the EEOC, feminists Sonia Pressman and Susan Deller Ross, a protégé of Murray and Norton at the ACLU, prodded their male colleagues to take women's rights seriously.[91] The assiduous promotion of feminists' agenda by NOW leaders also paid dividends.[92] For established civil rights groups vulnerable to the Nixon administration's political calculations, the women's movement represented an increasingly powerful constituency that the administration could not afford to ignore.[93] And EEOC lawyers and staff had self-interested as well as altruistic motives.

Oral historian Sylvia Danovitch observes, "[S]ome male attorneys may
not have taken sex discrimination seriously, but there was a natural cor-
rective: the younger lawyers eager to make their 'name.'"[94] Sex discrimination now seemed like an exciting new field rather than a frivolous
afterthought. And cases like *Phillips v. Martin-Marietta* underscored how
unfavorable rulings in sex discrimination cases could threaten civil rights
precedents.

By the early 1970s, feminist and civil rights organizations collaborated openly. In one local action that went national, women's groups
banded together with African Americans in the Minneapolis-St. Paul
area. In 1971, representatives of the Minneapolis Urban League, the St.
Paul Urban League, and NOW's Minnesota chapter issued a joint statement condemning discriminatory practices by General Mills, Inc. (GMI)
as "a primary factor in the economic oppression of *women and minorities.*" They described how the two movements had "joined forces" to
demand that GMI adopt new hiring goals and timetables. NOW of
Minnesota filed a class action lawsuit against the company on behalf of
women and minority men in July 1972. In August, the National Urban
League (NUL) initiated a selective buying campaign against GMI, which
the National Boards of NOW and WEAL joined. The groups charged
that "General Mills practices double discrimination against black
women, who are kept on the lowest rung of the ladder of opportunity."[95] Internal NOW documents framed cooperation with NUL as an
effort "[t]o show unity of women and minorities in their opposition of
the odious sex and race discrimination."[96] NOW and NUL called for a
nationwide "girlcott" of GMI products for Thanksgiving week of 1972,
using the slogan "Betty Crocker is an Aunt Tom!"[97]

Feminist and civil rights advocates cooperated in lawsuits against
DuPont, Hughes Tool, Firestone Tire, and the Big Three automakers.[98]
Most famously, concerted pressure from civil rights and feminist groups
produced a sweeping consent decree that settled the discrimination
claims of female and minority male workers at the nation's largest private
employer, AT&T. The suit took aim at the occupational segregation uncovered by Phyllis Wallace, an African American economist.[99] While the
case began primarily as a race discrimination suit, feminists pushed the
EEOC to promote what the formerly skeptical Commission lawyer
David Copus called "the really revolutionary view" of "institutionalized
sex discrimination" as "espoused by the National Organization for

Women." The AT&T settlement prompted the *New York Times* to declare the case a "benchmark in the gradual shift of equal employment opportunity from its status as a predominantly 'black' issue to a 'women's issue.'"[100] Fifteen thousand workers received back pay; thirteen thousand were women. Hiring goals for women included about 40 percent of "inside" craft jobs and about 20 percent of "outside" jobs, positions from which women previously had been excluded.[101] References to "women and minorities" had become commonplace.[102]

In the early 1970s, NOW leaders often emphasized how the government's failure to address sex discrimination harmed minority women.[103] NOW pressed for changes to federal contract compliance forms, which initially did not require employers to supply statistics on women by race, or on racial minorities by sex. The forms did permit employers to double-count black women by listing them in both the racial minority and female categories, but, as NOW officials noted, "did not require that companies pay them two salaries," effectively depriving minority communities of additional jobs and pay.[104] NOW's Ann London Scott told a congressional committee that the AT&T settlement highlighted the need to "simultaneously attack . . . systemic discrimination against females, blacks, and Spanish-surnamed Americans," lest minority women continue to suffer a "disproportionate handicap" and lest legal remedies be unevenly and ineffectually enforced.[105]

But putting a white face on feminists' agenda increasingly seemed expedient, especially given white women's potential electoral power. Employment policies and practices that targeted single mothers affected a wide swath of women, and universalizing their appeal could broaden feminists' constituency and defuse troubling stereotypes about "welfare mothers." Like Ida Phillips, other white women challenged job training programs that explicitly favored male job seekers, trained women for inferior positions, and focused on job categories that excluded women.[106] The plight of white or racially non-specific "women" increasingly dominated feminists' political lobbying as well as their litigation strategy. A 1972 NOW critique of Nixon's welfare reform proposals opened with the story of a white woman suddenly impoverished by divorce. "Is it misleading to introduce a critique of welfare with an example of a white middle-class woman and her children?" the authors of NOW's Senate testimony asked. "We think not."[107]

Aileen Hernandez herself felt torn between the universalist approach

that emphasized commonalities between black and white, male and female, and a more particularistic view that focused on minority women's
interests. In her request to Merrillee Dolan for a critique of the Moynihan Report and its impact on poor women, Hernandez had instructed:
"Don't write about blacks; instead write about women in poverty and
how the ideas of Moynihan have permeated the poverty programs' *man*-
power training (e.g., WIN [Work Incentive Program]) and what that
means for women in poverty."[108] Hernandez hoped to influence a white
audience. But broadening the appeal of reform could diffuse its impact
on those most in need. And even offering black professional couples'
egalitarian marriages as a model for white families obscured how such
marriages remained beyond the reach of many poor women. In testimony before the California Legislature in 1974, Hernandez quoted a
young black poet's words to white women activists, concluding with the
line, "We share all of *your* problems, *we* share few of mine."[109] African
American feminists' triumph would prove double-edged.

Reasoning from race followed a similar trajectory in constitutional
law.[110] For most of the 1960s, feminists had limited success in convincing courts to accept any analogy between race and sex. In the early
1970s, courts increasingly proved willing to reason from race. But the
partial incorporation of race-sex parallels into law had unexpected consequences for feminist legal strategy and for the values that Pauli Murray
and other pioneers of reasoning from race held dear.

Early setbacks in cases like *Mengelkoch* (see Chapter 1) did not deter
feminists for long. They redeployed the language of civil rights when
Alice de Rivera, a thirteen-year-old from Brooklyn with top scores in
mathematics, sued for admission to the prestigious all-male Stuyvesant
High School in New York City in 1969. Her supporters compared the
school district's policy to the "separate but equal" standard established in
Plessy v. Ferguson and de Rivera's plea to that of Linda Brown of *Brown v.
Board*. All-male elite public schools made girls "second-class citizens,"
they said.[111] Separate education for male and female students was, like
racial segregation, "inherently unequal."[112] DeRivera's lawyers relied on
old chestnuts, including the PCSW report, the Murray-Eastwood Jane
Crow article, and Myrdal's observations about the parallels between

"women" and "Negroes."[113] Feminist advocate Catherine East compared the New York policy to Southern states' exclusion of women and black men from juries, noting the irony of white men's support for racial integration in the South and their blindness to sex discrimination on their own doorstep. New York City Board of Education member John Doar had once assisted James Meredith in his quest to integrate the University of Mississippi, East reminded the mayor.[114]

Support from lawyers and judges with civil rights experience or sympathies grew steadily. Judge John Sandifer "seemed to be very sympathetic" to de Rivera's claim, as East reported to Women's Bureau chief Elizabeth Duncan Koontz. "He is a Negro judge who appreciated the relationship to the *Brown* case."[115] Sandifer "made life difficult for the corporation counsel," which, under Mayor John Lindsay, had committed itself to racial justice.[116] Feminists' strategy paid off. When a ruling in de Rivera's favor appeared likely, the Board of Education reversed itself and voted to admit her to Stuyvesant.[117]

Around the same time, JoAnne Kirstein and several other Virginia women challenged the University of Virginia's male-only admissions policy with the help of attorney Philip Hirschkop. Just four years out of law school, Hirschkop was an up-and-coming litigator.[118] He and his partner, Bernard Cohen, were renowned for their representation of an interracial couple arrested for violating Virginia's antimiscegenation law; they took *Loving v. Virginia* all the way to the Supreme Court in 1967.

Kirstein was the first of several important women's rights cases tried before federal district court Judge Robert Merhige, Jr. Born in Brooklyn of Lebanese ancestry, Merhige graduated from the University of Richmond's law school and, after serving in World War II, returned to the Confederacy's former capital to establish himself as a hard-charging trial attorney. President Johnson appointed him to the bench in 1967, and less than two weeks into his tenure, Merhige presided over the high-profile and controversial trial of Black Panther H. Rap Brown, whom Hirschkop helped represent.

In *Kirstein*, Hirschkop relied heavily on an analogy between sex and race segregation. He exchanged numerous letters and documents with East, Murray, Dorothy Kenyon, Pressman, Phineas Indritz, and attorneys in the ACLU's national office. Hirschkop's brief drew on all of the foundational sources explicating the race-sex analogy. Judge Merhige's initial ruling reflected an acceptance of this approach: "If racial segregation in State supported institutions is a denial of the due process of law guaranteed by the Constitution, as indeed it is, then the allegations . . . [are] indeed a patent denial of due process and equal treatment required by law."[119] A three-judge district court went on to declare in 1970 that the exclusion of women from the college violated equal protection, but the court declined "to go further and to hold that Virginia may not operate any educational institution separated according to the sexes."[120] In other words, sex-segregated education might not, like racial segregation, be "inherently unequal." Hirschkop was disappointed. "While we managed to desegregate the University of Virginia, which is what we set out to do, I had hoped for more," he wrote. "At any rate, we must accept our victories."[121]

Feminists found more to celebrate in a decision of the California Supreme Court in May 1971, the first to declare sex, like race, a "suspect classification" subject to "strict scrutiny." Justice Raymond E. Peters's opinion in *Sail'er Inn v. Kirby* overturned a liquor licensing law that banned female bartenders.[122] Echoing the amicus brief of Berkeley law professor and sex discrimination expert Herma Hill Kay (whose protégé Wendy Webster Williams was Peters's law clerk), Peters stressed that "[s]ex, like race and lineage, is an immutable trait, a status into which the class members are locked by the accident of birth." He wrote: "Laws which disable women from full participation in the political, business and economic arenas are often characterized as 'protective' and beneficial. Those same laws applied to racial or ethnic minorities would readily be recognized as invidious and impermissible. The pedestal upon which women have been placed has all too often, upon closer inspection, been revealed as a cage."[123] *Kirby* was the first time a court accepted the parallel between race and sex as a matter of legal doctrine, accompanied by a sustained focus on the similarities between racial and sex-based legal subjugation.

Wendy Williams's role in *Kirby* reflected the changing demographics of the American legal elite.[124] Though scholars and observers disagree over the degree of clerks' influence on judicial decision making, it seems clear that clerks played an increasingly active role in internal court deliberations during the second half of the twentieth century.[125] In the 1970s, law school graduates included more than a handful of women for the first time. Slowly but surely, their perspectives and those of the first male clerks to have professional contact with significant numbers of female classmates filtered through to judges.

Six months after *Kirby,* the Supreme Court heard a case that feminists hoped would transform the law of sex discrimination at the federal level.[126] Sally Reed, who had lost her only child to suicide, challenged an Idaho law that automatically designated her estranged husband Cecil as their son's estate administrator because he was a man. Ruth Bader Ginsburg, scholar and budding women's rights expert, helped draft Mrs. Reed's brief to the Supreme Court.[127]

Ginsburg, who had been appointed to the Rutgers faculty in 1963, was the twentieth woman ever to hold a law professorship in the United States. At first, Ginsburg had steered clear of the heady world of politics and activism, focusing instead on comparative law and civil procedure. In 1968, when a group of female law students asked her to teach a course on women and the law, Ginsburg began studying and, eventually, transforming, women's legal status.[128] One of her colleagues at Rutgers later recalled that, after reading Simone de Beauvoir's *The Second Sex,* Ginsburg was a "changed woman": "There was a passion that all of a sudden gripped her."[129] Ginsburg enjoyed an egalitarian marriage to tax attorney Martin Ginsburg, although Martin's battle with cancer and the demands of raising two children while completing law school and launching her career as a professor made for a sometimes harrowing juggle of work and family responsibilities.[130] By 1970, women's rights had become virtually a full-time pursuit for Ginsburg. She developed courses, wrote articles, and delivered speeches on women and the law; helped her students found a feminist law journal; and dove deeper into litigation through the ACLU.[131]

In *Reed,* Ginsburg translated the analogical arguments that Pauli Murray had proposed almost a decade earlier into a document that would become known as the "grandmother brief." The ACLU's brief argued that all sex-based legal distinctions were, like race-based distinctions, inherently suspect.[132] The brief asserted that sex and race were both "congenital, unalterable trait[s] of birth," characterized courts' unwillingness to recognize the injustice of sex discrimination as a mistake comparable to the *Plessy* decision, and drew the familiar parallel between slavery and women's status at common law. Feminists also tackled the myth that women's lives had historically been filled with privilege. "[N]o pedestal marks the place occupied by most women," the brief asserted, going on to quote Sojourner Truth.[133] Other amicus briefs joined the

ACLU in drawing upon the race–sex analogy, flooding the Court with entreaties to consider sex and race discrimination as similar and equivalent harms prohibited by the Fourteenth Amendment.[134]

Ginsburg and her colleagues hoped *Reed* would convince the Court of the inherent injustice of sex-based legal classifications. ACLU legal director Melvin Wulf browbeat allies who did not prioritize the argument for strict scrutiny of sex-based classifications.[135] He also attempted, unsuccessfully, to wrest the case away from Allen Derr, Sally Reed's personal attorney, and to draft Eleanor Holmes Norton to present oral arguments in the Supreme Court.[136] With her formidable intellect and impeccable civil rights and feminist credentials, Norton seemed the perfect person to argue that the Justices should treat sex like race. As Wulf feared he would, Derr stumbled in opening with what was supposed to be a parallel to *Brown v. Board of Education,* stammering something about "colored people" that caused supporters to cringe.[137]

In the end, a unanimous but cryptic ruling authored by Chief Justice Warren E. Burger held that administrative convenience was an insufficient justification for classifying individuals on the basis of sex.[138] Wulf and other feminists criticized the Court's "bland and very narrow opinion."[139] Pauli Murray hoped that "[t]he pressure for ERA [would] force the Court to take the additional steps." But given Nixon's appointment of three apparent conservatives (Burger, Harry Blackmun, and Lewis F. Powell) to replace liberals Earl Warren, Abe Fortas, and Hugo Black, and especially the President's recent nomination of William H. Rehnquist to fill Harlan's seat, Murray "shudder[ed] to think what the Court might do. Anyway," she concluded, "we have taken a baby step."[140]

Baby steps were, in a sense, exactly what Ginsburg had in mind. She hoped to do for sex discrimination what Thurgood Marshall and the NAACP Legal Defense Fund had done for racial segregation: gradually enlighten the Court "one case at a time, step by step."[141] Ginsburg said publicly that she was "delighted with the [*Reed*] decision."[142] She was acutely aware that women had a tough row to hoe in arguing for the application of the equal protection clause to sex discrimination. Feminists were appealing allies for embattled civil rights advocates in part because of women's potential electoral power. But as a majority of the population, women were not, like African Americans, a "discrete and insular minority" of the sort that the Court had seen as requiring protection in the political process. And the framers of the Fourteenth Amendment,

Ginsburg acknowledged, had never intended to grant equal rights to women. In the early 1970s, reasoning from race served Ginsburg's cautious radicalism well: the law of race discrimination grounded feminist claims in legal precedent. At the same time, characterizing sex-based classifications as similar to racial distinctions boldly reframed as invidious what many had long considered benign.

Feminists knew that some of the most intractable discrimination against women occurred in realms where the prescribed social implications of physical differences—reproductive capacity chief among them—constrained women's participation in economic and political life. Accordingly, combating discrimination based on pregnancy ranked among feminists' foremost priorities. Women's "unique physical characteristics" later seemed to have doomed feminist efforts to reason from race because reproductive differences between men and women had no clear racial analogue. Reliance on a constitutional analogy to race did not, however, foreclose a vision of sex equality that acknowledged reproductive rights as central. As *Reed* was making its way to the Supreme Court, lawsuits by female employees successfully charged that policies prescribing mandatory leaves of absence or termination on the basis of pregnancy unconstitutionally discriminated against women as women.

Many feminists considered the disadvantages facing pregnant women to be "the greatest single case of sex discrimination in employment," in the words of ACLU Women's Rights Project (WRP) coordinator Brenda Feigen Fasteau.[143] In the early 1970s, pregnancy discrimination cases against school districts and government agencies appeared around the country. In Austin, Mary Ellen Schattman challenged the Texas Employment Commission's policy prohibiting employees from working for two months prior to childbirth. In Cleveland, junior high school teachers Jo Carol LaFleur and Ann Elizabeth Nelson sought to invalidate a regulation prohibiting teachers from teaching their classes past the fourth month of pregnancy. In Chesterfield County, Virginia, high school social studies teacher Susan Cohen protested a similar regulation requiring pregnant instructors to take a leave of absence at the end of their fifth month. And in California, Air Force nurse Captain Susan Struck argued that the military's policy mandating discharge of any officer who gave birth while in the service violated her constitutional rights.

Differential treatment of women and men on the basis of women's childbearing capacity still seemed natural and inevitable to many judges. In May 1971, Judge James C. Connell upheld the Cleveland school district's mandatory leave policy as reasonable given the school board's weighty interest in preventing "sudden disruption of the students' classroom program due to an unforeseen complication in the teacher's condition."[144] Schattman's equal protection claim was also rejected by the Fifth Circuit, which found that because men and women were not "similarly situated" when it came to pregnancy regulations, Schattman could take no refuge in the equal protection clause.[145]

Susan Cohen fared better with Judge Merhige. Since presiding over the Kirstein case less than two years earlier, Merhige's desegregation of the Richmond schools had prompted death threats and personal ostracism. Merhige's dog was shot and killed, a cottage on his property burned, and his family sent abroad for their own safety.[146] Meanwhile, Merhige's court earned the moniker "rocket docket" in recognition of the speed with which its judges dispatched complex litigation.

Philip Hirschkop, by now a familiar presence in Merhige's courtroom, represented Cohen. Once again, he drew on the feminist legal network, including expert testimony from Catherine East refuting the school district's contention that pregnant workers missed an unusual amount of work.[147] Merhige responded, holding that pregnancy should be treated like any other temporary disability. He invalidated the mandatory leave policy on the seventeenth anniversary of *Brown,* noting that "pregnancy, though unique to women, is like other medical conditions, [so] the failure to treat it as such amounts to discrimination which is without rational basis."[148]

Meanwhile, the ACLU had what Ruth Bader Ginsburg believed was an ideal case to showcase the injustices visited upon pregnant workers and to establish sex equality as the primary constitutional justification for women's reproductive autonomy. Captain Susan Struck was on active duty in Vietnam when she became pregnant. Military regulations required her immediate dismissal. The only way for Struck to avoid summary discharge under the rules was to end her pregnancy. Unmarried and Roman Catholic, Struck felt compelled by her religious beliefs to carry the pregnancy to term and place her child for adoption. Struck's choice—end her pregnancy or her military career—gave her case a particularly gripping quality. She could argue that the rule infringed upon her right to privacy and autonomy in deciding whether or not to pro- create, and upon the free exercise of her religion, which proscribed abortion. But framing the case as an equal protection violation first and foremost could propel the law of sex equality doctrine beyond the re- quirement that women and men be "similarly situated" before judges could find a constitutional violation.

Captain Struck's constitutional claims failed in the lower courts, at least initially. Federal district court Judge William Goodwin granted the military's motion to dismiss, and the Ninth Circuit affirmed. The appel- late court dismissed her equal protection claim in little more than a para- graph. Judge J. Warren Madden wrote: "[A] relevant physical difference between males and females justifies their separate classification for some purposes, and avoids the problem of a denial of Equal Protection of the Law." He concluded: "the two sexes are not fungible."[149]

Struck's request for a rehearing was denied, but two of the judges, Benjamin C. Duniway and the only female member of the court, Shirley Hufstedler, supported her petition.[150] Judge Duniway stressed that the Supreme Court decision in *Reed v. Reed* had changed the relevant law: "It is not enough to say that there are physical differences between men and women, or that men and women are not fungible. . . . The question is, in view of the general obligation to treat the sexes alike established in *Reed,* whether there is a rational basis for the special and unique treatment of pregnancy, embodied in the regulation. I can find none."[151] Duniway even adopted the rhetoric of racial analogy, remarking, "I cannot believe that any of my colleagues would hesitate for a moment to strike down a regulation stating that no person of African ancestry can be commis- sioned, or one stating that all such persons now holding commissions shall be discharged. In principle, this case is no different." Why, Judge Duni- way inquired, "should a female officer whose infant is adopted lose her commission . . . and a male officer whose infant is adopted keep his? Why should a female officer who aborts her child keep her commission, and a female officer who delivers her child forfeit her commission? Why should a female officer who has a baby forfeit her career . . . ?"[152]

These were exactly the questions Struck and her lawyers hoped the Supreme Court would ask. When her petition for certiorari was granted, Ginsburg and her colleagues seized upon Duniway's dissent and a small but growing body of precedent suggesting that regulations that disadvantaged pregnant workers constituted harmful discrimination on the basis of sex. In addition to *Reed,* they could call upon a recent Fourth Circuit panel decision in *Cohen,* upholding Judge Merhige's decision to invalidate the Virginia school district's mandatory discharge rule.[153]

Apart from their equal protection claim, Struck's attorneys maintained that the military regulations violated her "right to privacy in the conduct of her personal life." But they framed this privacy argument, too, in terms of equality and a feminist conception of freedom. The regulations, they argued, reflected traditional assumptions about women's proper roles: "The discriminatory treatment required by the challenged regulation . . . reflects the discredited notion that a woman who becomes pregnant is not fit for duty, but should be confined at home to await childbirth and thereafter devote herself to child care." This "outmoded standard" violated the right to privacy established in earlier cases that invalidated restrictions on the sale and distribution of contraceptives.[154] Those opinions, however, had not invoked women's freedom to order their lives in nontraditional ways; rather, they had emphasized marital privacy and individual autonomy. The *Struck* brief, in contrast, stressed how mandatory discharge for pregnancy limited women's freedoms, but not men's.[155]

To Ginsburg's lasting disappointment, the *Struck* case was remanded and dismissed as moot not long after she and her colleagues completed their brief on the merits.[156] The Air Force dropped discharge proceedings against Struck under pressure from Solicitor General Erwin Griswold, who reportedly "told subordinates he could never win the suit."[157] Similar claims, including Air Force officer Mary Gutierrez's suit in Washington, D.C., also fizzled when the Air Force retained Gutierrez and waived the discharge of a third officer after a federal court in Colorado held that the policy violated substantive due process.[158] Over the next several years, the Armed Forces reconsidered their policies on pregnant service members; by the time the Second Circuit held in 1976 that such discharges were unconstitutional, most of the challenged regulations had been revised or repealed.[159]

Meanwhile, lower courts increasingly vindicated feminist claims that imposing employment restrictions on women because they were pregnant constituted sex discrimination, pure and simple. In July 1972, the Sixth Circuit overturned the district court's ruling in *LaFleur,* the Cleveland high school teacher's case, finding the mandatory discharge policy "a rule which is inherently based upon a classification by sex": arbitrary, overbroad, and unreasonable. Judge George Clifton Edwards, Jr., singled out the school district's reference to "pointing, giggling and . . . snide remarks" by students as particularly irrelevant: "Basic rights such as those involved in the employment relationship and other citizenship responsibilities cannot be made to yield to embarrassment."[160]

Some judges even connected rules penalizing pregnant women with other laws, policies, and practices that stifled women's opportunities in the name of motherhood. In 1972, Judge Constance Baker Motley, a veteran civil rights attorney and one of the first African American women to serve on the federal bench, allowed a class action suit to proceed on behalf of women affected by New York City's mandatory maternity leave policy. She wrote, "It is true, as plaintiffs claim, that equal rights for women is an idea whose time has come."[161] Ohio federal Judge Carl Rubin emphasized the unfairness of "stereotyp[ing]" all women as incapacitated by pregnancy, calling such assumptions a "manifestation of cultural sex role conditioning" that should not be allowed to "redound to [women's] economic or professional detriment." Noting that "[s]exual stereotypes are no less invidious than racial or religious ones," Rubin declared that "[a]ny rule by an employer that seeks to deal with all pregnant employees in an identical fashion is dehumanizing to the individual women involved and is by its very nature arbitrary and discriminatory."[162]

To be sure, significant disagreement remained about the status of pregnancy-based distinctions. The Fourth Circuit sitting en banc reversed Hirschkop's victory in the *Cohen* case. Judge Clement Haynesworth, President Nixon's first unsuccessful Supreme Court nominee, had dissented from the panel's ruling and now wrote for the full court: "Only women become pregnant; only women become mothers. But Mrs. Cohen's leap from those physical facts to the conclusion that any regulation of pregnancy and maternity is an invidious classification by sex is merely simplistic." Haynesworth and his colleagues saw "pregnancy and maternity" as "sui generis." Unlike employees of different races, women and men differed in essential ways that were the product of "no manmade law or regulation."[163]

But this narrow conception of sex equality increasingly became the minority position in the early 1970s. Courts' acceptance of feminist arguments that pregnancy discrimination was sex discrimination per se suggested that equal protection jurisprudence might not succumb to a cramped version of reasoning from race. These cases also held out hope for a constitutional linkage between women's reproductive freedom and sex equality. And around the same time, feminists were beginning to argue successfully that restrictions on abortion amounted to a denial of equal protection to women, based on sex.[164]

As of 1973, it remained to be seen how the Supreme Court would resolve the relationship between reproductive rights and sex equality.[165] In retrospect, the Court's opinions in *Roe v. Wade,* the landmark challenge to laws criminalizing abortion, suggested that the Justices did not see reproductive freedom as constitutionally intertwined with women's rights cases. Feminist lawyers in *Roe* made a number of constitutional arguments in terms of sex equality, including equal protection claims.[166] But Justice Blackmun's opinion for the Court grounded the abortion right in privacy and due process. He emphasized physicians' prerogatives rather than women's liberty, establishing what Ginsburg would later characterize as "a medically approved autonomy idea, to the exclusion of a constitutionally based sex-equality perspective."[167]

Feminists greeted *Roe* with a mixture of relief and euphoria, despite misgivings about Blackmun's reasoning.[168] Rhonda Copelon, a feminist lawyer at the Center for Constitutional Rights, expressed hope that the specificity of Blackmun's opinion—criticized as illegitimate judicial legislation by many constitutional scholars—would augur speedy enforcement of *Roe,* in contrast to the Court's dilatory approach in *Brown.* Her colleague Janice Goodman saw "parallels between *Brown* and the abortion decision even more so than between *Brown* and *Reed* because the abortion decision goes to the guts of the women's struggle . . . just like the right to equal and integrated education did for Blacks."[169] Feminists recognized that *Roe* was only partially "responsive to [their] women's rights arguments," but as Copelon put it, the decision "could have been horrendous."[170]

Observers would later lament the shortcomings of race-sex analogies in exposing and combating discrimination against women on the basis of their "unique" childbearing capacity. But feminists' early success in making sex equality arguments against pregnancy discrimination and abortion restrictions suggests that the separation of reproductive freedom from sex equality was far from inevitable. In 1973, the federal government's brief in Jo Carol LaFleur's case proclaimed: "That only women become pregnant is no more an answer to a claim of sex discrimination than was the fact that only Chinese wore pigtails a defense to the charge that an ordinance banning them . . . worked a racial or ethnic discrimination."[171] Reasoning from race did not preclude an interpretation of equal protection that included women's freedom to make reproductive choices without forfeiting their livelihoods.

In the spring of 1973, a new generation of feminist lawyers gathered at a Ford Foundation-sponsored conference for "Equal Rights Advocates," where they debated the relevance of the civil rights model to the women's movement. Some, like Stanford law professor and Pauli Murray protégé Barbara Allen Babcock, favored the kind of national coordination the NAACP LDF had provided for race equality litigation.[172] Others, including Murray's Jane Crow coauthor Mary Eastwood, were ambivalent or downright hostile to centralizing decision making and resources. The mostly thirty- and forty-something attorneys also discussed the wisdom of including lesbian rights on the feminist agenda, with Sylvia Roberts and Kathleen Peratis speaking in favor and Ginsburg urging her colleagues to tread cautiously in litigating politically fraught issues.

Pauli Murray encouraged the group to learn from the black civil rights movement. In 1938, she recalled, Thurgood Marshall had declined to use her race-based rejection by the University of North Carolina as a test case. "Even though I was very disappointed," she said, "I can see now that the decision was appropriate." Like civil rights lawyers, feminists "should develop a number of criteria for taking cases—not merely whether the issue is feminist or not," she argued.[173] Murray encouraged her compatriots to develop "collective wisdom on which issues to press" in order to avoid making bad law. Peratis and others saw "a value in the lunatic fringe." "The two," Murray posited, "are not mutually exclusive."[174]

Murray was the elder stateswoman of the Equal Rights Advocates conference: at sixty-three, she had been a civil rights activist since before many of the other participants were born. Dorothy Kenyon had succumbed to cancer the year before, just short of her eighty-fourth birthday. Of the thirty-four women who planned to attend, only Marguerite Rawalt, seventy-eight, was more senior than Murray, and an illness caused Rawalt to miss the conference.[175] Murray was also the only non-white participant in the meeting, as she gently reminded her colleagues.

She emphasized the importance of "cultivating black women lawyers and litigants," arguing one last time for an "integral relationship" between race and sex discrimination.[176]

January 22, 1973, was the day the Court handed down *Roe v. Wade*, former President Lyndon B. Johnson died of a heart attack, and Nixon announced a cease-fire in Vietnam. Pauli Murray recalled it primarily as her dear friend Renee Barlow's fifty-ninth birthday and the day Barlow began a risky new treatment for her brain tumor. Barlow passed away one month later. Her death inspired in Murray "an urgency to complete my mission on earth in the days left to me."[177] Murray still believed, "in the tradition of the late Dr. Martin Luther King" that "the core of our troubles—alienation because of race and sex, political corruption, economic dislocation, senseless violence—is in the moral and spiritual realm."[178] Murray felt "increasingly inadequate as both a lawyer and a teacher" in addressing these problems. At age 63, she left the Brandeis faculty, entering divinity school at the General Theological Seminary. The fact that women had yet to be ordained as Episcopal priests only deepened her determination to fulfill her spiritual calling to unite all human rights.[179]

In one of her final public speaking engagements before entering the seminary, Murray spoke to a racially diverse audience at George Washington University of "understandable" alienation among "younger militant women of color" and of the need to "reduce mistrust" and "rebuild bridges between white women and black women." Murray called upon the "New Feminism" to embrace "the cause of Black Liberation [as] part of its own cause and carr[y] the moral battle into every white home in this country."[180] Murray would now do her part as a priest and liberation theologian, using religion rather than law to unite the two causes closest to her heart.

Two days after Murray's GW speech, the Supreme Court decided *Frontiero v. Richardson*, which marked the apex of race-sex analogies in constitutional law.[181] Sharron Frontiero, a twenty-three-year-old Air Force lieutenant, had discovered in 1969 that military servicewomen, but not servicemen, were required to prove their spouse's dependency in order to receive a housing allowance or spousal medical benefits. Sharron's husband Joseph, a junior at nearby Huntingdon College, could not show that he relied on his wife for more than half of his income, largely because of veterans' benefits he received as a result of his own military service. When Frontiero saw her first post-wedding paycheck as a physical therapist at Maxwell Air Force Base hospital in Alabama, she "thought it was a mistake. I set out to correct it," she later recalled, "and that's when the trouble started." As she navigated the military bureaucracy, Frontiero said, "I had people telling me, 'You're lucky we let you into the military at all.' And then I got mad."[182] She found a civil rights lawyer in Montgomery, and filed suit in federal district court.

Frontiero highlighted what Ruth Bader Ginsburg called "double-edged" discrimination. By assuming that men were primary breadwinners with economically dependent wives, the military denied benefits to men married to servicewomen. Moreover, these sex-based legal classifications devalued the economic contributions of married women, who received fewer benefits for their families. Such schemes, feminists argued, created incentives for families to conform to a male breadwinner/female homemaker model.

Even for lawyers and judges steeped in civil rights law, the notion that allocating government benefits differently to husbands and wives constituted sex discrimination did not come easily. The Frontieros, represented by Joseph J. Levin, Jr. and Morris Dees, Montgomery lawyers and founders of the Southern Poverty Law Center (SPLC), presented their case to a three-judge district court in Alabama that included Richard Rives and Frank M. Johnson, Jr., the authors of the jury service decision *White v. Crook* (see Chapter 1). Since then, Johnson had written another landmark sex discrimination opinion. Ruling for Lorena Weeks in her challenge to Southern Bell's refusal to hire women as switchmen, Johnson declared that Title VII "vests individual women with the power to decide whether or not to take on unromantic tasks."[183]

In *Frontiero*, Johnson's clerk Jack Billings urged the judge to declare sex a suspect classification, drafting an opinion that analogized sex to race and applied strict scrutiny to the statute.[184] After the Supreme Court decided *Reed* without addressing whether sex-based classifications were suspect, Johnson discarded this bold draft. But he did believe that *Reed* rejected administrative convenience as an insufficient justification for laws that discriminated on the basis of sex. Rives and Judge Frank H. McFadden did not see the challenged statute as differentiating primarily on the basis of sex, however. Nor did they interpret *Reed* as signaling a sea change in constitutional law. In the end, Rives and McFadden upheld the law, while Johnson based his dissent on *Reed,* without expressing any view about whether sex should be a suspect classification.[185]

Once the Frontieros appealed their case to the Supreme Court, the ACLU WRP clashed with the SPLC over substance and strategy. The SPLC's Chuck Abernathy thought it best to keep a "Nixonian low profile," given the "Burger Justices' preoccupation with decisions which would have a revolutionary impact on the courts (if not the law)."[186] As in *Reed,* the WRP urged that the case should be argued by a female attorney—Ginsburg—but Levin and Dees had decided to argue the case themselves.[187] In the end, the WRP filed an amicus brief, and Ginsburg was afforded time to present its arguments to the Court.[188]

The Supreme Court's deliberations and opinions in *Frontiero* displayed the advantages and pitfalls of feminists' race-sex analogies.[189] After Justice William O. Douglas assigned the Court's opinion to Justice William J. Brennan, Jr., the Justices' deliberations centered on whether to take the more radical step of declaring sex suspect. Brennan, an Eisenhower appointee who joined the Court in 1956, had become a liberal leader on the Court. He had, however, voted with the majority in *Hoyt v. Florida* and remained hesitant to hire a female law clerk well into the 1970s.[190] But as Ginsburg and Wendy Webster Williams later wrote, "When women's voices joined with those of African Americans seeking justice and equality, Justice Brennan was poised to listen."[191]

Brennan initially drafted an opinion striking down the benefits scheme under *Reed,* but then lobbied his colleagues to declare sex "suspect." Marshall had already expressed his view that *Reed* had applied something more than rational basis review, and Justice Byron R. White agreed, adding that he believed congressional approval of the ERA meant that sex classifications were suspect "whether the amendment is adopted or not."[192] Justice William O. Douglas embraced Brennan's position, adding that "[f]or purposes of employment I think the discrimination [against women] is as invidious and purposeful as that directed against blacks and aliens."[193] In contrast, Justice Lewis F. Powell, Jr. saw "no reason to consider" the issue and cited the ERA's pendency before state legislatures as cause for caution.[194] Justice Potter Stewart agreed with Powell and suggested that Brennan characterize the challenged statute as "invidious discrimination," which he called "an equal protection standard to which all could repair."[195] Brennan replied that he saw

ERA ratification as a "lost cause," and envisioned *Frontiero* as an opportunity to reach the same result.[196]

Brennan's *Frontiero* opinion stressed the nation's "long and unfortunate history of sex discrimination," which he compared to racial subjugation: "[T]hroughout much of the 19th century the position of women in our society was, in many respects, comparable to that of blacks under the pre–Civil War slave codes. Neither slaves nor women could hold office, serve on juries, or bring suit in their own names, and married women traditionally were denied the legal capacity to hold or convey property or to serve as legal guardians of their own children."[197] He wrote that "sex, like race and national origin, is an immutable characteristic determined solely by the accident of birth." Unlike "physical disability" or "intelligence," sex—like race—"frequently bears no relation to ability to perform or contribute to society."[198]

Brennan's new draft declared sex suspect and called for strict scrutiny of sex classifications. But he remained one Justice short of a majority. Blackmun's clerk James Ziglar hoped to convince the Justice to join Brennan's opinion. Ziglar believed that *Frontiero* could "head-off" the ERA, which he thought too extreme. He called Brennan's new draft "the best of both worlds"—strong enough to preempt an ERA and flexible enough to permit some sex classifications—but he did not convince Blackmun.[199] Although Blackmun had authored *Roe v. Wade* just months earlier, he remained skeptical of Ginsburg and her arguments about gender roles and stereotypes.[200] In the end, Stewart concurred in the judgment only, and Justice Powell wrote a concurrence, joined by Burger and Blackmun, arguing that the ERA's pendency militated against a more expansive interpretation of the Equal Protection Clause.[201] Powell charged that the Brennan opinion attempted "to pre-empt by judicial action a major political decision."[202]

Frontiero exemplified the paradoxes of feminist legal advocacy circa 1973.[203] On the one hand, feminists seemed well on their way to transforming the law of sex equality. Although she had not secured a majority for the sex-as-suspect analysis, Ginsburg declared victory, calling Brennan's opinion "a joy to read."[204] Whatever standard of review the various Justices applied, all but Rehnquist agreed that the government could no longer promote the male breadwinner/female homemaker model at the expense of families who eschewed traditional gender roles.[205] In the lower courts, the tide seemed to have turned in favor of seeing pregnancy discrimination as an equal protection violation. Congress had not only ratified the ERA but passed unprecedented legislative protections against sex discrimination and decriminalized abortion.[206]

But feminists' success in the courts also undermined arguments for an ERA.[207] As Powell's concurrence vividly demonstrated, the ERA's pendency provided a rationale for judges who were reluctant to analogize sex to race. Brennan's failure to secure a majority gave reluctant courts a reason not to strike down sex-discriminatory laws. At the same time, the plurality's embrace of strict scrutiny in *Frontiero* made the ERA seem less necessary.[208] As the initial wave of ratifications ebbed, some in the women's movement began to share Justice Brennan's doubts about the ERA's eventual success.[209]

By 1973, antidiscrimination law incorporated analogies between race and sex to an unprecedented degree. Analogies provided a common language and strategy for feminist legal activism. They helped to convince skeptical civil rights advocates of the benefits of coalition and to persuade legal decision makers to see sex inequality as a problem worthy of disapprobation and remediation. African American feminists reasoned from race as part of a larger effort to resist the imposition of patriarchal family structure as a panacea for poverty and racial inequality.

But for all of its benefits, the analogy-based strategy proved double-edged. Powell's refusal to join Brennan's opinion may have had as much to do with his deep and enduring reluctance to endorse parallels between race and sex discrimination as with his desire to defer to democratic processes. During the *Frontiero* deliberations, he wrote to Brennan: "I may add that I see no analogy between the type of 'discrimination' which the black race suffered and that now asserted with respect to women."[210] In another memorandum, he noted that "[w]omen certainly have not been treated as being fungible with men (thank God!). Yet, the reasons for different treatment have in no way resembled the purposeful and invidious discrimination directed against blacks and aliens."[211]

Brennan's opinion listed the ways that sex discrimination resembled race discrimination to justify heightened judicial scrutiny. But such a list of qualifying attributes—immutability, visibility, political powerlessness—could as easily constrain as expand the equal protection clause's scope and applicability to other disadvantaged groups. And because Brennan justified the application of strict scrutiny to sex-based classifications on the basis of a parallel between race and sex as categories, his opinion could be read to imply that sex discrimination violated the equal protection guarantee only when it resembled discrimination based on race.[212]

Finally, Brennan's comparison of race and sex erased the intersections between race and sex that underpinned Pauli Murray's constitutional strategy.[213] When she proposed the equal protection litigation approach a decade earlier, Murray's primary objective had been the unification of civil rights and feminist movements. Her analogical arguments reflected her recognition of the interconnections as well as the parallels between race and sex inequality. Brennan's *Frontiero* plurality opinion lacked this grounding, abstractly equating "women" and "blacks." *Frontiero* was the first in a line of cases in which white couples insisted upon their right to adopt nontraditional gender roles without penalty. Though these couples had followed the advice of African American feminists like Murray and Norton, the roots of their challenges to the male breadwinner/female homemaker model in African American history and activism barely surfaced in legal briefs and remained completely submerged in court opinions. In retrospect, 1973 was both the high-water mark of race-sex parallelism and a moment suffused with hints of the hazards that lay ahead.

3

RECESSION, REACTION, RETRENCHMENT

Reasoning from race had just begun to pay dividends when economic and political upheaval threatened to obliterate the hard-won gains of "women and minorities." The recession of 1974–1975 deepened resistance to aggressive enforcement of equal employment policies. Amid mass layoffs, white male workers clung to seniority systems, their last remnant of job security.[1] African Americans and white women protested the adverse impact of last-hired-first-fired rules. "The polarization effect cannot be underestimated," declared Eleanor Holmes Norton from her civil rights post in New York, where budget cuts eliminated one-third to one-half of city jobs held by white women and people of color.[2] Aileen Hernandez warned her NOW colleagues that affirmative action and other remedies for discrimination would "be very much under fire in the years ahead."[3] Norton and Hernandez were right. The politics of scarcity fractured the already fragile Democratic coalition, which had depended upon economic prosperity and tenuous interregional and interracial alliances.

These tensions helped conservatives reframe the civil rights revolution as too much, too fast.[4] Opposition to government intervention in race relations swelled in the 1970s. Controversies over busing to achieve school desegregation roiled American communities.[5] Rapid turnover in personnel and mounting case backlogs plagued the EEOC between 1974 and 1977. Nixon's appointees to the Supreme Court, while perhaps not as consistently conservative as feminists had feared, backed away from the Warren Court tradition of liberal innovation.[6] Legal scholar Alan David Freeman identified 1974 as the year when "colorblindness" overtook antidiscrimination law, as courts attempted "to make the problem of racial discrimination go away by announcing that it [had] been solved."[7] Conservatives now embraced the idea that law and policy should ignore race. Even some civil rights sympathizers feared that taking race and sex into account in allocating jobs and educational opportunities would interfere with the individual rights liberals had worked so hard to establish.[8]

The efficacy of reasoning from race depended upon a robust conception of civil rights. Analogies to race became increasingly problematic as Americans entertained second thoughts about remedying racial injustice. And to those who were skeptical of federal judges and bureaucrats, comparisons between sex and race were more alarming than inspirational. To many more, such parallels seemed inaccurate. Feminists struggled to paint sex discrimination as worthy of redress when the obstacles women faced appeared to be different in nature and magnitude from racial injustice. But differences between race and sex—and between men and women—did not dictate the law's response to inequality. Rather, they provided an opening to resist the expansion of civil rights.

Even as they promoted parallels between race and sex, feminists recognized differences between them. "Women," as a group, did not face the same hurdles as "minorities"; race and sex discrimination did not take identical forms; poor and black women confronted obstacles that privileged white women were spared. Ruth Bader Ginsburg wrote in 1975 that "generators of race and sex discrimination are often different. Neither ghettoized minorities nor women are well served by lumping their problems in the economic sector together for all purposes."[9] Commentators noted many other distinctions: women constituted a majority of the population, in contrast to the "discrete and insular minorities" the law had recognized as deserving special solicitude under the equal protection clause.[10] Women were distributed evenly throughout the population, sharing the socioeconomic status and resources of their male peers. As one author explained, "[M]inorities form hereditary social and economic communities, characteristically poor; women do not form a community and represent every social class."[11] Whereas respectable discourse now viewed racial differences as superficial and socially constructed, women's ability to give birth remained an enduring distinction between the sexes. Discrimination against women, many believed, was less hateful and more subtle than prejudice directed at racial minorities. Legal philosopher Richard Wasserstrom wrote, "Women are both put on a pedestal and deemed not fully developed persons. . . . [S]exual ideology . . . does not unambiguously proclaim the lesser value attached to being female."[12] And legal remedies like the Fourteenth Amendment and the Civil Rights Act of 1964 made African Americans, not women, their intended target.

But each of these differences between race and sex, "women" and "minorities," could cut both ways. If existing laws intended to combat race discrimination did not ensure women's equality, feminists reasoned, all the more reason to extend their reach or give women their "own" constitutional amendment. The subordinating consequences of reproductive differences between men and women made the quest for sex equality more, not less, urgent to feminists. If sexism's greater subtlety rendered it "more deeply embedded in the culture" and "harder to eradicate," then rigorous judicial scrutiny and expansive remedies might be all the more necessary.[13] Women's diffusion throughout the population arguably made organizing collective action for feminist goals more difficult and thus worthier of legal support. Even white women's relative privilege could be spun to feminist advantage. The underrepresentation of minority groups in jobs and universities could be blamed on systemic economic inequality. But, as Norton put it, "Women are not, as a group, disadvantaged; thus it is impossible to explain their subservient status in the work place except by virtue of discrimination."[14] If women started out with essentially the same tools as men, then unequal outcomes must be the result of bias.

The political valence of similarities and differences between race and sex proved malleable. As feminists soon discovered, their opponents too could use the associations between race and sex equality, "women" and "minorities," to strategic advantage. In the second half of the 1970s, conservatives exploited race-sex analogies to new ends, no one more skillfully than Phyllis Stewart Schlafly.

After a rigorous but traditional education at Sacred Heart Academy in St. Louis, financed by her mother's hard-earned wages, Stewart turned down a full scholarship to a local Catholic women's college, enrolling instead at Washington University in 1941. Stewart earned her way through college by working eight-hour night shifts testing firearms in a munitions factory. Columbia, Radcliffe, and Wellesley all offered her financial aid for graduate study; she chose Radcliffe, and she so impressed her professors that one offered to sponsor her application to Harvard Law School. The fact that Harvard did not admit women in the mid-1940s apparently did not deter Stewart, but the steep cost of legal education did. She headed to Washington to seek a job in the federal government. Eventually, Stewart found work in the private sector with the American Enterprise Association, the precursor to the American Enterprise Institute, and her career in conservative politics was underway.

During the next several decades, Stewart married attorney Fred Schlafly and moved to Illinois; wrote *A Choice, Not an Echo* (1964), the book that helped launch Barry Goldwater's presidential candidacy; ran for Congress twice; became a voice for anticommunism and aggressive nuclear preparedness, and against détente with the Soviet Union; and earned a law degree. Eventually, she led a movement that transformed the Republican Party. Her career achievements would have been the envy of any feminist. Although she trumpeted the importance of a sexual division of labor in the home, with authority vested by God in the husband, hers was a remarkably egalitarian marriage to a man who supported and encouraged her activism. Despite a rigorous schedule of public speaking, writing, and traveling, Schlafly raised six children and taught each of them to read, a feat she touted as her most cherished accomplishment.[15] Schlafly spent much of the 1970s in an all-out effort to defeat the ERA, part of a wide-ranging crusade against feminism and liberalism. Schlafly disseminated her political and legal views in her syndicated columns, in publications like the *Phyllis Schlafly Report,* and in her best-selling 1977 book, *The Power of the Positive Woman.*

For Schlafly, the race-sex analogy became a convenient shorthand for everything that was wrong with the ERA, and with feminism more generally. Schlafly's model "Positive Woman" "reject[ed] the argument that sex discrimination should be treated the same as race discrimination." Schlafly asserted: "There is vastly more difference between a man and a woman than there is between a black and a white, and it is nonsense to adopt a legal and bureaucratic attitude that pretends that those differences do not exist."[16] Schlafly predicted that the consequences of reasoning from race would be dire. In the early days of the ERA ratification debates, she pointed to Paul Freund's analysis of the race-sex parallel's more controversial potential ramifications, including the integration of athletic teams, restrooms, and prison facilities. Freund's work revealed "that there is no logical or legal basis for the court deciding differently in the matter of sex from their decisions in the matter of race," she emphasized.[17] Later, Schlafly warned: "The surest way to predict what the ultimate effect of ERA will be is to ask yourself the question: 'Are we permitted to make this difference or separation based on race?' If your answer is 'no,' then— if ERA is ratified—you will not be permitted to make the same difference or separation based on sex."[18]

Conservatives also exploited the growing linkages between race and sex in their opposition to affirmative action in education and employment. In the 1970s, the affirmative action debate centered primarily on race. But a number of commentators focused their criticism on affirmative action for women, which allowed them access to arguments less available to critics who concentrated on race.[19] Both economic and cultural conservatives argued that sex differences in employment were based on women's voluntary decision to prioritize domestic life over wage work. A 1975 *Labor Law Journal* article by management professors Butler Shaffer and J. Brad Chapman contended that "hiring quotas" threatened "to emasculate the concept of employment relationships founded upon the freely expressed wills and agreement of the parties and to reinstitute status as a primary factor." They asserted that any post–Civil Rights Act disparities between male and female employment were "as much the product of employment preferences of women as they are of employers' male chauvinism." It was unfair, Shaffer and Chapman argued, to punish an employer "for simply responding to a condition for which he [was] not responsible" by imposing upon him a remedy that was "not even reflective of the choices of the supposed beneficiaries of such quotas." Such policies, they wrote, were sure to backfire, creating a vicious cycle of "male resentment" and "female disenchantment."[20]

Free-market critics like Shaffer and Chapman did not necessarily deny the persistence of gender inequality, but they argued instead that its roots were in the home, rather than in workplace or public policies. The prominent black conservative economist Thomas Sowell, for instance, attributed women's shifting labor market fortunes to changing demographics rather than to the success of equal employment policies. As Sowell told it, after the Second World War, as women married earlier and bore more children, their participation in gainful employment declined; subsequently, as those trends reversed themselves, women began to catch up with men. The end of the baby boom, not antidiscrimination laws or affirmative action, was responsible for women moving toward greater equality in the workplace, Sowell argued. "A much stronger case can be made that career women are discriminated against in the home, where they are expected to carry most of the domestic burdens, regardless of their jobs," he wrote in 1976.[21] "Such a situation may not be just," Sowell acknowledged, "but it does not result . . . from employer discrimination."[22] Affirmative action for women, in Sowell's eyes, was a solution in search of a problem.

Cultural traditionalists like Schlafly went further, excoriating affirmative action for women as a threat to the American family and its traditional division of labor. Schlafly recognized immediately how feminists' race-sex parallels endangered the male breadwinner/female homemaker model. Schlafly chastised "women's libbers" for "trying to make wives and mothers unhappy with their career" by convincing them that they were "'second-class citizens' and 'abject slaves.'" In an oft-repeated formulation, Schlafly wrote: "Women's libbers are promoting free sex instead of the 'slavery' of marriage. They are promoting Federal 'day care centers' for babies instead of homes. They are promoting abortions instead of families."[23] Schlafly professed to believe in equal opportunity for women and men—indeed, her own life was a striking testament to women's limitless potential.[24] She stood up for conservative women's "vital political role."[25] But Schlafly denounced equal employment laws and the activists who promoted them, charging that they undermined the political economy of the family. "Under women's lib demands today, employers are being forced to hire and train an inexperienced single girl with no dependents, in order to achieve some enforced quota, rather than a more qualified married man with one to eight dependents," she complained in 1975.[26] Schlafly criticized Department of Health, Education, and Welfare (HEW) regulations that prohibited schools and colleges from giving preference to an employment applicant who was "the head of household or principal wage earner in such employee's or applicant's family unit," contending that such rules were "part of the militant women's lib attack on the family as the basic unit of our society."[27] In her view, the government should affirmatively promote a traditional family structure.

Schlafly inverted feminists' arguments for affirmative action. She maintained that breadwinning men and traditional families were the true victims of discrimination. Rules prohibiting employers from considering sex and marital status meant "clear and cruel discrimination . . . against a husband and father trying to support his family," she wrote. Schlafly urged Congress to amend Title VII "to authorize employers to give job preference in hiring and promotions, and retentions during layoffs, to the . . . Principal Wage Earner in each family."[28] She complained that affirmative action for "women and minorities" infringed on "a husband's right and ability to fulfill his role as provider," and constituted an assault "against the right of his wife to be a full-time homemaker." Giving employment preferences to breadwinners would "encourage homemakers to stay in the home, rather than competing in the labor market for the scarce available jobs."[29]

Women, Schlafly argued, should be grateful to serve spouses rather than employers. "If you complain about servitude to a husband, servitude to a boss will be more intolerable," she warned. "The women's liberation movement to the contrary, there *are* male and female roles," she insisted. "If marriage is to be a successful institution, it must likewise have an ultimate decision maker, and that is the husband."[30]

According to Schlafly, workplace gender integration was partly to blame for the demise of sexual morality and marital fidelity. She quoted an unnamed police chief as saying: "After we put 11 women on the street, three of the four married women among them subsequently filed for divorce, and four of the men who had been teamed with women also started divorce proceedings. . . . If you put two women together in a squad car, they fight. If you put male and female together from 8:00pm to 4:00am, they fornicate." Schlafly wrote, "Not only is a fireman's work beyond the physical strength of nearly all women, but the work pattern of firemen, involving long hours of living, working, and sleeping together, makes a sex-integrated fire department incompatible with community morals and customs."[31] Adultery, illegitimacy, and broken homes were the inevitable result of affirmative action, she contended.[32]

Schlafly's critique focused on sex-based rather than race-based policies. It would have been difficult for Schlafly to argue that affirmative action for African American men undermined the breadwinner/homemaker model, or that Hispanic men should or did choose lower-paying jobs because they wished instead to fulfill domestic responsibilities. The possibilities for interracial sex in integrated work settings were more likely targets of conservative reaction, but mainstream activists generally avoided such lightning rods.[33] It was easier to argue that women were physically weaker than men, that they voluntarily chose low-paying, low-status jobs, and that their entrance into the workplace would disrupt sexual mores than it would have been to contend the same for men of color. Focusing on affirmative action for women allowed cultural conservatives—particularly women—to make arguments against cultural change that were no longer acceptable when deployed against racial integration.[34]

Critics of affirmative action exploited the association between race and sex even as they rejected attempts to equate the two categories. Schlafly often referred to remedial policies that covered both women and minority men, without distinguishing between them. She derided the AT&T consent decree "forced on the telephone company by the federal courts" for "establish[ing] 'goals,' 'intermediate targets,' and 'timetables' under which the employer [was] forced to override every other value (including qualifications, seniority, and number of dependents) in order to achieve its 'affirmative-action' quota for women."[35] She condemned HEW regulations, declaring, "We reject the theories of 'reverse discrimination' and 'group rights.' It does no good for the woman who may have been discriminated against 25 years ago to know that an unqualified woman today receives preferential treatment at the expense of a qualified man. Only the vindictive radical would support such a policy of revenge."[36] Schlafly often let readers draw their own conclusions, mentioning "minorities" in passing, if at all.[37]

In an inversion of feminists' arguments that equal access to jobs and training would help women to achieve economic independence and self-sufficiency, Schlafly associated equal employment opportunity with a rise in welfare dependency. Job preferences, she said, meant that "[m]ore people go on welfare, which in turn increases the taxes that all of us must pay."[38] But when she mentioned race explicitly, Schlafly usually cited others. In a typical reference, she quoted another (unnamed) commentator: "Women's Lib and the ERA will only promote a labor market dominated by double income families, most of whom will be white, and the welfare rolls will be bloated with more and more no-income families, most of whom will be black. The result will be untenable for all thinking people."[39]

Ironically, cultural conservative arguments against affirmative action for women resembled the Moynihan model that influenced so many liberals in the 1960s and 1970s. In Schlafly's narrative, the beleaguered man was presumably white and opposed to government intervention. In Moynihan's account of a decade earlier, the burden of female empowerment rested on the shoulders of African American men, who had a prior claim on government assistance. Nevertheless, the moral of these stories was similar: equal employment and affirmative action for women threatened to emasculate men and to unfairly penalize spouses who conformed to traditional gender roles. According to cultural conservatives, these roles were the only means of maintaining economic security for white families. Liberals of an earlier era saw affirmative action for African American men as crucial to restoring stability in Americans' public and private lives; in the 1970s, conservatives regarded all affirmative action as a threat to family survival.[40]

In many conservatives' accounts, the civil rights revolution was a sobering cautionary tale, not a source of inspiration. Schlafly described deeply contested race precedents in matter-of-fact terms but condemned their applications to sex-based laws and practices: "The courts have held that racial equality does not permit the individual to have the freedom of choice between all-white schools, all-black schools, and mixed schools. Are we not going to say that equality of the sexes does not permit us to have freedom of choice between boys' schools, girls' schools and coed schools?"[41] Such formulations traded simultaneously on opposition to racial integration and on the intuition that single-sex schooling differed fundamentally from Jim Crow.

Schlafly recast criticism of the civil rights revolution as antifeminist critique. She warned in 1976: "Practically every pro-ERA lawyer states—even boasts!—that ERA will impose a national standard which will apply the same strict standard to sex as we now apply to race. . . . The agitating women's lib lawyers (in NOW, ACLU, EEOC, and HEW) are following the exact same pattern of bureaucratic regulation and court litigation as the 'civil rights' lawyers have done."[42] The analogy was damning indeed, since the ERA's foes held federal courts responsible for nearly all of America's social ills. Civil rights rulings in the areas of "forced busing," "reverse discrimination," "states' rights," and the rights of criminal defendants, as well as abortion, school prayer, and national security foreshadowed expansive judicial interpretations of the ERA.[43] James J. Kilpatrick, who had been a prominent defender of racial segregation, made a similar point in a 1974 anti-ERA essay: "More than a century later, the courts still are finding meanings in the 14th [Amendment] that its framers and ratifiers never knew they put there."[44] Kilpatrick's readers knew what he meant.

Conservatives viewed the resemblance between the ERA and the Reconstruction Amendments as a harbinger of doom. Feminists and their supporters had modeled the ERA's enforcement clause on virtually identical provisions contained in the Fourteenth, Fifteenth, and Nineteenth Amendments.[45] Conservatives cited the same landmark civil rights cases that liberals celebrated to bolster their claim that the ERA would mandate even more intrusive federal encroachments on states' rights. The ERA, Schlafly predicted, "will transfer into the hands of the Federal Government the last remaining aspects of our life that it does not already control."[46] *Runyon v. McCrary* (1976), for instance, barred private schools from discriminating on the basis of race. Schlafly reprinted the decision in her newsletter and warned: "If ERA applies the *Runyon v. McCrary* rule to sex, no private school will be permitted to bar any pupil on the basis of sex; all private schools will be compelled to go coed—probably with 'affirmative action' ordered by HEW."[47]

Perhaps most damning, Schlafly warned that reasoning from race would lead down a slippery slope toward "homosexual rights."[48] Taken to its logical conclusion, she said, "equal rights on account of sex" led inexorably to the enfranchisement of "homosexuals," "arrogant lesbians," and "perverts." Echoing Freund's suggestion during congressional hearings on the ERA, she noted: "It is precisely 'on account of sex' that a state now denies a marriage license to a man and a man, or a woman and a woman."[49] Schlafly cautioned that "[a] homosexual who wants to be a teacher could argue persuasively that to deny him a school job would be discrimination 'on account of sex.'" And she predicted that "ERA will probably require police and fire departments to hire and promote homosexuals, or face charges that the departments are discriminating 'on account of sex.'"[50] Schlafly peppered her anti-ERA polemics with references to "militant" and "arrogant" lesbians. She maintained that pro-ERA groups like NOW were "*for* pro-lesbian legislation so that perverts will have the same legal rights as husbands and wives, such as the right to get marriage licenses, to file joint income tax returns, and to adopt children."[51] Schlafly was prescient, although many of the gay rights arguments she foreshadowed did not become prominent until decades later. In the meantime, gun-shy ERA proponents usually denied that the amendment would mandate same-sex marriage, rejecting the view that gay rights inevitably followed from sex equality.[52] Schlafly's race-sex analogies not only countered feminism, but shaped its contours.[53]

Schlafly's hyperbolic rhetoric should not obscure how her anti-feminist advocacy reflected larger cultural and political trends in the 1970s. Many Americans perceived both the civil rights and sexual revolutions as deeply threatening. Many more likely found changes in gender roles and family structures unsettling.[54] Feminists did not always own the radical implications of their vision of sex equality; by giving voice to those who embraced or clung to traditional gender hierarchies, Schlafly helped to define feminism's image in the public mind.[55] More subtly, her legal and political arguments adroitly exploited connections between race, sex, and sexuality augured by the rise of "women and minorities." In an increasingly conservative climate, feminists' carefully constructed link between civil rights and women's rights became a liability as well as an asset.

In the decades before 1970, feminists who opposed the ERA had emphasized the threat posed by the amendment to protective labor legislation for women, legislation that conservatives disliked. After most liberals, including labor movement advocates and nearly all feminists, turned against sex-specific protective laws, conservative opponents of the ERA did an about-face and lamented their demise. By the mid-1970s, opponents had reframed the threat posed by feminism. Now, they condemned equal rights and championed the traditional prerogatives of women's economic dependence—namely a husband's financial support and fidelity. At the same time, they extolled the sex-based advantages enjoyed by modern women. As Schlafly was fond of saying, "Of all the classes of people who ever lived, the American woman is the most privileged."[56] She and her allies rejected the notion that women should receive special consideration outside the sphere of home and family. From their perspective, "job preferences" for women constituted "reverse discrimination" that undermined the foundations of American society.

To feminists, opposition to sex-differentiating protective labor legislation and support for affirmative action in employment seemed perfectly compatible. When protective laws did not overtly exclude women, they perpetuated stereotypes that kept women out of higher-paying jobs. Affirmative action, in contrast, challenged outdated notions about women's natural proclivities and capacities, and helped women break into traditionally male occupations.[57]

But if superficially benign laws were often just discrimination in disguise, then how could judges tell a "true" affirmative action policy from yet another oppressive measure? And how could the arguments feminists made against laws giving special "benefits" to women also shield affirmative action for women and for racial minorities? Legal and political developments intensified these quandaries. Challenges to race-based remedies appeared alongside lawsuits attacking "benign" sex classifications, forcing feminists to articulate not only the differences between programs that ameliorated injustice and those that perpetuated inequality, but also the distinctions between race and sex discrimination as social phenomena.

The latent conflict reached a crisis point in the Supreme Court's 1973–1974 term. In *DeFunis v. Odegaard,* Marco DeFunis, a Sephardic Jewish applicant rejected by the University of Washington Law School, attacked that institution's affirmative action policy as unlawful race discrimination. In *Kahn v. Shevin,* Mel Kahn, a Florida widower, challenged a state property tax exemption for widows (but not widowers) on sex discrimination grounds.[58]

The *Kahn* case came as an unwelcome surprise to Ruth Bader Ginsburg and the ACLU Women's Rights Project (WRP). *Kahn* did not involve the kind of "double-edged discrimination" that Ginsburg liked to showcase. Unlike the military benefits scheme challenged in *Frontiero,* the damage to women under Florida's statute was attenuated. Denying benefits to the dependent spouses of servicewomen degraded women's breadwinning capacity and denied their husbands benefits; depriving widowers of a property tax exemption did not impinge upon women's ability to provide for their husbands.

Once *Kahn* reached the Court, the WRP argued that to presume widows were in need of financial assistance perpetuated sex stereotypes. Ginsburg did not believe *Kahn* was a good case on which to stake the WRP's fight for strict scrutiny; by her own account, she "trie[d] to fudge" on the issue of what standard of judicial review should apply.[59] Ironically, the WRP found itself on the receiving end of a lecture about women's unequal economic status and prospects: "Although women make up an ever-increasing portion of the work force, they are still far behind in obtaining equality of economic opportunity," Florida's lawyers argued, accusing the plaintiff of downplaying women's economic disadvantages.[60] Ginsburg hoped for a reprieve until the end, declaring to a friend, "I'll give you a gold medal if you can suggest any route other than equal protection for widower Kahn."[61]

Compounding Ginsburg's dismay, *DeFunis* was argued the same week.[62] She feared that *DeFunis* would lead the Justices to see Florida's property tax exemption as a permissible remedial measure analogous to affirmative action. Conversely, *Kahn* had the potential to undermine arguments for "true" affirmative action: if Mel Kahn's lawyers proved too much, the Court might conclude that all distinctions based on sex (or race) were impermissible, even if intended to combat discrimination.[63] The WRP's briefs in *Kahn* were careful not to close the door on legitimate remedial measures.[64] But Ginsburg warned that solicitude for benign race classifications should not spill over into sex equality law. "Thus far," she observed at oral argument, "this Court has applied the label 'suspect classification' only in opinions involving discrimination hostile to groups not dominant in society." But, she cautioned, "a one-way approach in sex discrimination cases would be fraught with danger for women, because of the historic tendency of jurists to rationalize any special treatment of women as benignly in their favor."[65]

Ginsburg's concern about the juxtaposition of *Kahn* and *DeFunis* turned out to be well-founded. The Court issued its decisions in the two cases on consecutive days in April 1974.[66] Justice William O. Douglas wrote for the majority in *Kahn* that the widows' tax exemption rested upon a desire to compensate women for the economic disadvantages they suffered, particularly after losing a spouse. He distinguished the policy challenged in *Frontiero* as hurting rather than helping women, and noted: "Gender has never been rejected as an impermissible classification in all instances." Perhaps most jarringly, Douglas cited the original "Brandeis brief" in *Muller v. Oregon* (1908) for its emphasis on how "the special physical structure of women has a bearing on the 'conditions under which she should be permitted to toil.' "[67] Brennan's dissent agreed that laws designed to ameliorate economic discrimination against women were permissible and necessary, but contended that Florida's law did not meet the "narrowly tailored" element of strict scrutiny analysis—a standard that Douglas now implicitly abandoned.[68]

Justice White's dissent criticized the assumption that all widows were more economically disadvantaged than all widowers as resting upon the stereotype that all widows "have been occupied as housewife, mother, and homemaker and are not immediately prepared for employment." White did not find Florida's remedial justification a "credible explanation," given that wealthy widows received the exemption but needy widowers did not.[69] To Ginsburg, White was "the only one with complete integrity," though she had "some sympathy with Brennan and Marshall in their effort to avoid conflict with their probable position in *DeFunis*."[70] In the end, the Court dismissed *DeFunis* as moot over a dissent from Douglas that questioned the compatibility of race-based affirmative action with individual rights under the equal protection clause.

Douglas's opinion in *Kahn*, Ginsburg fumed, was "a disgrace from every point of view."[71] "It is galling," Ginsburg wrote to a fellow lawyer, "that Douglas sees women as appropriate objects of benign dispensation (ranked with the blind and the totally disabled) when he should know that there is no surer way to keep them down than to perpetuate that brand of chivalry. His *DeFunis* dissent indicates he would regard such a 'favor' for blacks (where the same earnings gap can be demonstrated) as 'invidious.' "[72] In the end, Ginsburg's initial assessment seemed correct: *Kahn* was "the wrong case brought to the Court at the wrong time."[73] *DeFunis*, on the other hand, had struck "a sensitive nerve," as Ginsburg wrote shortly after the Court's dismissal of the case. She concluded: "It demonstrates why sex discrimination can't be lumped together with discrimination against historically disadvantaged minority groups."[74]

Kahn and *DeFunis* highlighted the limitations of reasoning from race in the mid-1970s. Mel Kahn's surprise appearance as a sex discrimination plaintiff demonstrated that despite Ginsburg's efforts to present hand-picked constitutional sex equality cases to the Court in careful sequence, feminists could not maintain the kind of litigation monopoly that made the NAACP LDF such an appealing institutional model. Inopportune cases like *Kahn* sprang up locally to thwart Ginsburg's plans. Furthermore, civil rights and feminist advocates faced the same increasingly conservative political climate, but at different junctures in their movements' evolution. Feminists supported affirmative action for white women and people of color, but they had yet to vanquish what they believed to be paternalistic and damaging laws disguised as protection. At a time when race-based affirmative action was coming under increasing attack, arguments that sex-based classifications should be forbidden threatened to undermine the potential for coalitions between civil rights and feminist advocates. If feminists appeared to endorse sex-blindness, they might subvert civil rights leaders' efforts to counteract the rise of colorblindness. Feminists began to qualify their reliance on a constitutional race-sex parallel.

Pregnancy lacked a clear racial analogue. But discrimination based on women's reproductive capacity went to the very heart of the feminist agenda. Its centrality to women's subordination made challenges to pregnancy-based discrimination the perfect candidates for a landmark constitutional ruling. Before 1974, feminists persuaded many courts to recognize pregnancy discrimination as unconstitutional (see Chapter 2). But some of the legal decision makers they hoped to convince still viewed pregnancy as an exception to the equal protection paradigm.

When the Court was deciding whether to hear Susan Cohen and Jo Carol LaFleur's challenges to their school districts' policies forcing teachers to go on leave early in pregnancy, it looked as if the Justices might avoid the constitutional issue by waiting for a statutory case under Title VII. The EEOC had issued new regulations in 1972 declaring that policies discriminating against pregnant women violated Title VII. And now that Title VII applied to public employers, future school boards might be expected to adjust their policies to bring them into line with the EEOC's guidelines. Powell clerk Bill Kelly thought that pregnancy cases were "obviously" different from other sex equality cases and therefore "bad vehicles for the development of sex discrimination law."[75] But the Court granted certiorari to consider both the Cleveland and Virginia policies shortly before handing down its decision in *Frontiero*.

The threshold question in both *Cohen* and *LaFleur* was whether mandatory maternity leave created a sex-based classification, and if so, whether that classification should be subject to heightened scrutiny under the equal protection clause. Powell, who had concurred separately in *Frontiero* just a few months earlier, retained his "firm opinion" that sex should not be a "suspect" classification. In his notes on the pregnant teachers' cases, he wrote: "Whatever may be said about the past (and this can be 'plenty'), I should think it would be offensive to the women's lib movement today to bracket them—in terms of their political and social influence and ability to assure their own equal rights—with minorities, aliens, and indigents."[76]

In *Frontiero,* Powell had privately expressed his qualms about parallels between race and sex, but publicly couched his objections in terms of respect for legislative processes. With the ERA's ratification still pending, Powell had argued, the Court should not reach out to impose strict scrutiny. In September 1973, his clerk, Jack Owens, informed him that the ERA was "in deep political trouble." The amendment's pendency, therefore, no longer seemed the best rationale for treating sex and race differently. Instead, the clerk advised Powell to air his objections to the "powerful analogies" between sex and race. The point of making race "suspect" was to allow minority groups to overcome their "lack of numbers or disenfranchisement," Owens argued. As a majority of the population, women had it "within their power to overcome this evil."[77] Emphasizing political process would allow Powell to avoid several minefields. He would not need to posit inherent biological differences between men and women, to minimize the deleterious effects of sex discrimination, or to pass judgment on the male breadwinner/female homemaker model.[78]

Blackmun offered another way out. Instead of viewing the mandatory maternity leave policies as sex-based classifications, the Court could characterize them as distinguishing "between those who are disqualified to teach for reasons of pregnancy and those who are disqualified for other medically indicated reasons," in which case they would be subject only to rational basis review.[79] This approach would still protect Cohen and LaFleur, he reasoned. "It is easy to say initially that any regulation that relates to pregnancy is automatically and per se sex discriminatory," Blackmun wrote privately. "I am not at all certain that this is necessarily so."[80] The Court could avoid what Owens called "difficult analytical question[s]" associated with sex discrimination analysis by treating the leave policy as a traditional equal protection violation that lacked a rational basis, and the Justices seemed poised to do just that.[81]

Then Justice Potter Stewart changed the terms of the debate. Along with Powell and Blackmun, Stewart was often at the ideological center of the Court, a position that offered the "swing" Justices considerable influence over reasoning as well as outcomes. Though *Cohen* and *LaFleur* had been briefed and argued as equal protection cases, Stewart preferred to see them as due process cases. He argued that the school boards had violated the teachers' due process rights by creating an "irrebuttable presumption" of inability to teach after the fourth or fifth month of pregnancy.[82]

Stewart's approach became the opinion for the Court. "The words sex discrimination are nowhere mentioned, believe it or not," marveled Blackmun's clerk upon reading Stewart's draft.[83] Powell wrote a concurrence, maintaining that the case should be decided on equal protection grounds without reaching the questions of whether "sex-based classifications invoke strict judicial scrutiny" and "whether these regulations involve sex classifications at all."[84] The Court had sidestepped the central question of whether discrimination based on pregnancy was sex discrimination under the equal protection clause.[85]

Not for long. In *Aiello v. Hansen* (later *Geduldig v. Aiello*), female plaintiffs challenged a California Unemployment Insurance Code provision that exempted pregnancy from the state's disability insurance program until 28 days after the pregnancy's end.[86] Carolyn Aiello, a self-supporting hairdresser, had suffered an ectopic pregnancy. Augustina "Sally" Armendariz, the sole financial provider for herself, her husband, and her infant son, was ordered by her doctors to cease her work as a secretary for several weeks in order to recover from a miscarriage. Jacquelyn Jaramillo, who experienced a normal pregnancy and delivery, also supported her family while her husband finished school. None of the women could collect benefits under California's policy.[87]

Calling the exclusion of pregnancy from disability benefits sex discrimination posed a fundamental challenge to the male breadwinner/ female homemaker model.[88] Offering benefits to pregnant workers meant treating women as individual economic actors and primary breadwinners. A *Wall Street Journal* editorial warned that pregnancy benefits for workers would "further weaken the family unit." The editors argued that California's policy could not be discriminatory, since "procreation is in fact a joint venture of both man and woman," a "planned, joyous process" the burden of which was born by families, not individual women. Single women did bear the financial consequences of pregnancy alone, the editors acknowledged. But they doubted whether "full sexual equality implies that women should have economic protection for bearing children out of wedlock."[89] Others worried that rampant "population growth" would result from "eliminat[ing] . . . one of the significant deterrents to pregnancy—loss of wages," as one South Carolina attorney put it.[90] Some supporters of pregnancy benefits countered that protecting women from discrimination would result in net savings for the state. One "Married, Working Mother of Four" scoffed at the notion that pregnancy discrimination was fiscally prudent. "[N]ot paying these mothers and making them lose their jobs or seniority more often than not will add them to the welfare rolls."[91] The pregnancy cases involved not only the future of sex equality doctrine, but the ongoing struggle over equal employment and its implications for family structure and political economy.

Wendy Webster Williams, the young feminist lawyer in Northern California who represented the plaintiffs in *Geduldig,* had already contributed to the nascent feminist constitutional canon when she drafted the *Sail'er Inn v. Kirby* decision as a clerk to California Chief Justice Raymond Peters in 1971.[92] Since her clerkship, Williams had won a poverty law fellowship and launched her career as a feminist litigator. Williams saw the California case as an opportunity to tackle a prevalent form of discrimination against women and to advance the constitutional jurisprudence of sex equality more generally.[93]

At first, it seemed that the plaintiffs could capitalize on the momentum generated by feminists' recent court victories. In May 1973, two weeks after *Frontiero,* a three-judge district court ruled 2–1 that California's policy violated the equal protection clause. Judge Alfonso J. Zirpoli held that pregnant women must be treated as individuals, not as a group that would inevitably make large and unwieldy insurance claims. Zirpoli wrote: "Sexual stereotypes are no less invidious than racial or religious ones. Any rule by an employer that seeks to deal with all pregnant employees in an identical fashion is dehumanizing . . . and is by its very nature arbitrary and discriminatory." If the state wished to limit the size of insurance claims, Zirpoli maintained, the equal protection guarantee required that it do so directly, rather than using pregnancy as a proxy.[94] In dissent, Judge Spencer Williams contended that "it is exceedingly difficult to talk about equality of treatment between the sexes when pregnancy is involved."[95] In his view, women's reproductive capacity defied assimilation to an equality paradigm premised on comparing "similarly situated" individuals.

The plaintiffs' brief to the Supreme Court challenged such arguments, maintaining that pregnancy's status as a "unique physical characteristic" of women made an equality analysis even more essential. "At the core of the historical discrimination against women," recognized by the plurality in *Frontiero*, "are what were then considered to be the 'unique' differences between men and women, particularly pregnancy and the maternal role long considered inseparable from it." *Geduldig* was the perfect case, the plaintiffs argued, for the Court to recognize sex as suspect. Their brief stressed the "recent and growing recognition that gender discrimination is as pervasive and costly to society and its disadvantaged members as racial discrimination and requires the same affirmative and stringent measures to eradicate it."[96]

Whereas some judges viewed pregnancy as "sui generis," Justice Blackmun saw it as all too typical in its disproportionate impact on women. Blackmun worried that holding California's scheme unconstitutionally discriminatory would mean that all laws would be measured by their impact on particular groups: "[W]e would never come to an end in this kind of analysis," he cautioned privately.[97] Blackmun drafted a concurrence that he would never file, emphasizing that to him, *Geduldig* was "not a sex discrimination case," but rather "an insurance case and no more." Although "[o]ne race, one sex, residents of a particular geographic area, may run a greater statistical risk of disease and injury than another," Blackmun wrote, "surely, all need not be identical in susceptibility, or be treated exactly alike for purposes of insurance coverage in order to satisfy the demands of . . . equal protection."[98] If all such disparate burdens triggered equal protection scrutiny, no insurance plan would be safe from challenge.

To Blackmun's clerk, Robert Richter, the Justice's position was untenable. "Your response . . . that there are other diseases that only occur to one race or one sex, appears to beg the question," he wrote bluntly. "Presumably, the state would be hard put to argue that a sickle cell anemia exclusion was likewise reasonable." Instead, Richter argued, "The concept of sex discrimination is that there are no inherent differences between men and women that would permit the state to make classifications based on sex. Here, however, the argument can be made that there is an extremely relevant and inherent difference (the ability to bear children) and the classification is directly related to this trait." Richter wasn't sure he agreed with this analysis, but he "believe[d] a solid majority of the Ct agrees with it."[99] In order to rule for California, Richter said, the Justices would have to explain why the race paradigm simply could not be applied to pregnancy.

California's lawyers couched many of their arguments in terms that drew on the same intuition: that the pregnancy challenges were inherently different from race discrimination cases. They argued that the Court had found the mandatory maternity leave policies attacked in *LaFleur* to violate due process rather than equal protection because of "the unique nature of pregnancy-related absences from work."[100] They predicted that fiscal constraints might force California to discontinue disability benefits altogether if required to include pregnancy.[101] In any event, the state argued, the benefits scheme could not be discriminatory, because overall, female workers did not receive less in benefits than male workers.

Justice Stewart's majority opinion in *Geduldig* made his earlier private arguments against equal protection for pregnant women part of constitutional jurisprudence. California's insurance scheme, Stewart noted, "divides potential recipients into two groups—pregnant women and non-pregnant persons. While the first group is exclusively female, the second includes members of both sexes." In a footnote, he wrote that "[w]hile it is true that only women can become pregnant it does not follow that every legislative classification concerning pregnancy is a sex-based classification like those considered in *Reed* . . . and *Frontiero*."[102] Since men could not give birth, and women did not necessarily become or remain pregnant, discrimination based on pregnancy was not necessarily sex discrimination. California's disability scheme therefore was subject to the least stringent level of review, rational basis analysis.

Brennan dissented vehemently from this view. He would have analyzed the disability program under the equal protection clause. He wrote: "[B]y singling out for less favorable treatment a gender-linked disability peculiar to women, the State has created a double standard for disability compensation. . . . Such dissimilar treatment of men and women, on the basis of physical characteristics inextricably linked to one sex, inevitably constitutes sex discrimination."[103] Whereas District Judge Zirpoli had stressed the violation of women's right to be treated as individuals, Brennan emphasized that the law treated women as a group differently from men.

Feminists were chagrined and outraged by the majority's ruling. Criticism of *Geduldig* became a "cottage industry" during the following decade.[104] Ginsburg condemned *Geduldig*'s "terrible implications," warning that "[f]or a working woman, particularly a poor one . . . this case could influence her to have an abortion."[105] As she had done in *Struck,* Ginsburg linked reproductive decision making to the disadvantages pregnant women confronted in the workplace. But *Geduldig* divorced reproductive autonomy from sex equality. By denying that pregnancy-based disadvantage offended the equal protection clause, the Court severed the link that feminists had so carefully forged.

At the same time, antifeminists used what Phyllis Schlafly called the "abortion-ERA connection" to discredit both reproductive rights and the ERA.[106] Antiabortion activists warned that the amendment would enshrine reproductive rights in the constitution for all time. Feminists, wrote Schlafly, "support ERA as the essential step in establishing abortion as an act that is constitutionally and psychologically normal."[107] As one NOW officer saw it in 1973, "The Right-to-Lifers and anti-ERA forces are by and large the same people (and money) and are anxious to tie the two issues together through their usual tactic—hysteria."[108] Many feminists tried to counter these arguments by disentangling, in rhetoric and strategy, the issues of sex equality and abortion rights. A 1973 NOW strategy paper suggested that members in unratified states would "want to concentrate efforts on the E.R.A. and not confuse the two issues" and that opponents were "trying to connect them to defeat the E.R.A."[109] Many ERA proponents insisted that the amendment would have no impact on abortion. In the process, they also undercut the argument that abortion restrictions violated the equal protection clause or state constitutional equality guarantees.[110]

Geduldig seemed to epitomize the race-sex analogy's limits. Berkeley law student Katharine Bartlett observed in her critique of the decision: "Where sex discrimination finds easy parallels to race discrimination . . . courts tend to recognize the discrimination. . . . Where the resemblance to race discrimination is not so clear . . . meaningful review is sparing and unpredictable."[111] How much of their reluctance to see pregnancy discrimination as sex discrimination stemmed from judges' doubts about the race-sex analogy's accuracy is impossible to measure. In any event, the requirement that sex inequality resemble racial injustice in order to invoke legal protection provided a convenient rationale for containing the rights revolution.

*   *   *

In some ways, sex-segregated education seemed like an ideal setting to
call on a parallel to race. School segregation had been the paradigmatic
form of unconstitutional race discrimination, the foundation on which
civil rights lawyers and judges built modern equal protection jurisprudence. In the late 1960s, feminists had successfully used analogies between race- and sex-based exclusion to compel the admission of women
to Stuyvesant High School and the University of Virginia. Feminists
hoped that judges sensitized to civil rights claims could recognize the
harm to girls and young women of exclusion from prestigious educational institutions.

But sex segregation had been neither as pervasive nor as controversial as racial segregation in American public education. Although coeducation had become the norm at all levels, single-sex exceptions
(especially girls' schools and women's colleges) remained relatively untouched by the stigma of injustice that now attached to racial segregation. As feminist lawyers discovered, arguing that sex segregation was like
racial segregation was a risky strategy. Many judges simply did not see
single-sex education—or even the exclusion of girls and women from
prestigious schools—in the same light as Jim Crow.

In *Vorchheimer v. School District of Philadelphia,* a white female student
challenged her exclusion from Central High School, a venerable all-male
Philadelphia institution.[112] Susan Vorchheimer's class action lawsuit
against the Philadelphia school district deliberately echoed the concerns
animating *Brown.* She argued that Girls' High, Central's counterpart and
the only "academic" high school open to female students, offered an inferior and less prestigious education. Represented by local attorney and
Girls' alumna Sharon Wallis, Vorchheimer asserted that the "sexual segregation of Philadelphia's academic high schools imposes upon female
students a badge of inferiority, teaching them expressly and by example
that they are not qualified to compete with male students in academic
pursuits."[113] Vorchheimer testified before federal district court Judge
Clarence C. Newcomer that she feared psychological damage and
material harm if she attended Girls' rather than Central.[114] Wallis also
pointed to Central's long and distinguished history, its large private en-
dowment, and its record of producing alumni who assumed local and

national leadership positions. Girls', on the other hand, was less prestigious, its alumni "less influential," and its educational program "traditionally suffered from sexual stereotyping attributing lower career
aspirations to women."[115] In contrast to the social science evidence in
Brown, though, Wallis presented no expert data on the effects of sex segregation on girls. The school district called two experts to testify about
the purported educational benefits of single-sex education.

Judge Newcomer was not persuaded by Wallis's analogy to *Brown* or
by the school district's assertion of single-sex education's merits. Instead,
the judge held that the substantially equal education offered by the two
schools took the case "out of the realm of *Brown v. Board of Education*"—
even though *Brown* had famously declared even "separate-but-equal" to
be "inherently unequal."[116] Newcomer explicitly rejected Wallis's argument that the exclusion of girls from Central High created a feeling of inferiority in female students, noting that even if the much-criticized
sociological evidence cited in *Brown* was legitimate, the plaintiff had not
presented any evidence of psychological detriment here. Instead, Newcomer found that no legitimate educational objectives justified Central's
refusal to admit girls. If the district's true purpose was to protect girls from
the disadvantages of coeducation, then all of Philadelphia's schools should
be sex-segregated, he argued. "[M]ales, and not females, are the intended
beneficiaries of defendants' exclusionary policy," he concluded.[117]

Like the lower court, the Third Circuit rejected the plaintiff's analogy to racial segregation. But the panel's majority concluded that the
Supreme Court's new sex discrimination jurisprudence could not sustain
Susan Vorchheimer's claim. Judge Joseph F. Weis, Jr. wrote for the court
that the "substantial equality" of Central and Girls' High Schools meant
that no special scrutiny was necessary. And the school district had presented "sufficient evidence to establish that a legitimate educational policy may be served by utilizing single-sex high schools." Significantly,
Weis suggested that the intent underlying the maintenance of single-sex
schools was of primary importance. Although sex separation "has limited acceptance on its merits," the judge wrote, "it does have its basis in
a theory of equal benefit and not discriminatory denial."[118] Unlike racial
segregation, the majority asserted, single-sex education was born of benign intentions.

Dissenting Judge John J. Gibbons compared the majority's reasoning
to *Plessy v. Ferguson,* the infamous 1896 case upholding racial segregation

in public transportation.[119] The majority had emphasized that Susan Vorchheimer had chosen an "academic" high school over other available educational alternatives. Gibbons retorted: "It was 'voluntary,' but only in the same sense that Mr. Plessy voluntarily chose to ride the train in Louisiana. The train Vorchheimer wants to ride is that of a rigorous academic program among her intellectual peers. Philadelphia, like the state of Louisiana in 1896, offers the service but only if Vorchheimer is willing to submit to segregation. Her choice, like Plessy's, is to submit to that segregation or refrain from availing herself of the service."[120] It was the first and last time in the Vorchheimer litigation that a judge accepted the race-sex parallel.

The legal briefs filed by feminists in *Vorchheimer* led some scholars to surmise that Ruth Bader Ginsburg and the WRP pursued a full-blown parallel between race and sex segregation, using *Brown* as a model.[121] In fact, Ginsburg's papers reveal that she recognized the strategic pitfalls of such an approach. Framing the *Vorchheimer* case as a replay of *Brown,* she anticipated, could be interpreted as a broad-based attack on single-sex education as inherently unequal in all circumstances—a position the Supreme Court was unlikely to embrace. Ginsburg's Women's Rights Project was anxious to avoid the bold parallel embraced by Judge Gibbons's dissent.

But disagreements over strategy undermined the collaboration between Vorchheimer's attorney, Sharon Wallis, and the WRP. At first, it seemed the lawyers had "agree[d] that separate and unequal [was] the position [they] should push."[122] The problems began with Wallis's draft petition for certiorari, which Ginsburg thought "overplay[ed] the sex/race analogy" and got "into hot water" over whether schools that excluded whites or men were constitutionally problematic. Deficiencies in the factual record also dismayed WRP lawyers.[123] A strong brief from the Philadelphia school district "convince[d]" Ginsburg that the WRP was right to proceed cautiously. The school district refuted the race parallel and emphasized the possibly fatal consequences for single-sex education if the plaintiffs prevailed. "Now," Ginsburg wrote to her colleagues, "we must go even further to make it plain that our class seeks no 'sweeping' change, leaves 'the system' intact, and 'freedom of choice' an open question."[124] But the WRP lost control over Vorchheimer's reply brief in the ensuing tussle with Wallis.[125]

Before the WRP and Wallis parted ways, Ginsburg drafted her own reply brief, which contrasted with Wallis's eventual submission to the Court in its treatment of the race analogy, among other issues of form and substance. In the end, Wallis's brief quoted extensively from *Brown*, including the decision's "inherently unequal" language, even though she disclaimed any contention "that gender based classifications in education are totally analogous to those based on race." Ginsburg's draft, instead, assured the Justices that Vorchheimer was not "assert[ing] that single-sex schools are per se impermissible." Rather, Ginsburg focused on the history of single-sex elite education in Philadelphia, arguing that "reservation of Central to young men has deep roots in 'sexist concepts once and still prevalent about women.'" The policy "simply perpetuat[ed] the gender line drawn in 1836" and reinscribed in the 1890s when feminists failed in their effort to move women into "intransigent" "male bastions" and instead were forced to settle for separate and inferior schools.[126] Ginsburg's reply brief never reached the Court in an official capacity, but she did distribute the document to a number of interested parties, including *New York Times* reporter Lesley Oelsner, Assistant Attorney General Drew Days, and Jerry Lynch, Ginsburg's former student and a law clerk to Justice William Brennan.[127]

Records of the Court's deliberations suggest that Ginsburg's concerns were warranted. With Justice William Rehnquist sidelined by chronic back pain, Sharon Wallis made her argument to only eight of the nine Justices. After the Justices' first conference, Lynch was optimistic about the plaintiff's prospects: four members of the Court—Brennan, Potter Stewart, Thurgood Marshall, and Lewis Powell—"agreed that while the findings of the district court regarding the equality of the boys' and girls' schools were somewhat ambiguous, they could and should be read to mean that the schools were not in fact of equal prestige and quality." Three Justices—Harry Blackmun, John Paul Stevens, and Chief Justice Warren Burger—"found that the two schools were substantially equivalent, that complete equality was unnecessary, and that the state should have freedom to experiment." These three would therefore vote to affirm the Third Circuit's judgment. Justice Byron White felt the factual record on inequalities between the boys' and girls' schools was insufficiently developed, and he thus tentatively voted to remand the case for further fact-finding.[128]

By the Justices' second conference vote, however, Chief Justice

Burger was concerned that the Court would find itself split 4–4 on *Vorchheimer*.[129] "In my view," he wrote, "action by an equally divided Court would be open to valid criticism as an institutional failure to meet our obligations."[130] Therefore, Burger told his colleagues, his preference would be to canvass Justice Rehnquist's view. Alternatively, the case could be reargued in the presence of all nine Justices. "Obviously," Burger declared, "we did not take this case to evaluate findings against the record but only to decide whether gender separated equal schools are 'inherently unequal,' and that issue should neither be evaded nor delayed."[131]

Defining the issue presented by *Vorchheimer* this broadly was exactly the pitfall Ginsburg and her WRP colleagues had sought to avoid.[132] If Burger could frame *Vorchheimer* as a question of whether separate but equal was "inherently unequal" in the context of single-sex education, he was assured victory. And Burger could safely call for reargument, knowing that Rehnquist would almost certainly vote with him. Burger did not convince five of his colleagues to vote for reargument, so the resulting 4–4 split meant that the Third Circuit's ruling against Vorchheimer would stand.[133] The Chief Justice wrote to Blackmun that he was resigned to the inconclusive result: "[U]ntil the Court gives me two votes as in ancient English law when a court is equally divided, I find it difficult to cope with four unregenerate, unreconstructed 'rebels'! In which case I conduct as orderly a retreat as possible."[134]

The Court's capriciousness was the real problem, according to critics. WRP director Kathleen Willert Peratis complained that "[e]very case seems to be decided on its own facts, depending on how the Court felt that day," and Ginsburg agreed that "the Court is not giving courts and lawyers the guidance" they needed.[135] Ginsburg reflected later that perhaps the sex segregation issue had reached the Court too soon, without the "generation of litigation" that had laid the groundwork for *Brown*.[136] *Vorchheimer* had not showcased a well-developed factual and social science record comparable to that presented in *Brown*. That evidentiary deficiency, as Ginsburg's comments suggest, might have been preventable.

But feminists' strategic dilemma was more difficult to overcome. If sex segregation had to look just like racial segregation to be recognized as a constitutional harm, the battle was over before it had begun. Comparisons to racial discrimination prompted some judges to see discrimination against women behind apparently benign differentiation. For others, the analogy was unconvincing, or even a mandate to ignore sex inequality that did not resemble ill-intentioned race discrimination.

"How far can one push the analogy between sex and race?" wondered African American attorney and professor Inez Smith Reid in 1975. In feminists' demands for constitutional change, she saw a "vicious clash of competing interests." By demanding "suspect class" status for women, Reid charged, feminists endangered equal protection for racial minorities. The analogy also begged the question, "Would Black women be considered women, or Blacks?" Either way, feminists' litigation record made Reid pessimistic about the prospects for meaningful change under the equal protection clause.[137]

Reid's critique focused on the Constitution, but Title VII seemed to offer a more promising way to highlight the interconnections between race and sex and to unite the interests of "women and minorities." After all, in 1964, Murray had successfully argued that including sex discrimination in Title VII was integral to African Americans' rights. Without protection for women, she emphasized, "one-half of the Negro population" would be left out. Black women used Title VII in the mid-to-late 1960s to apply for jobs in textile mills long monopolized by white female workers.[138] In other words, black women could and did use Title VII's prohibition of racial discrimination to break into "women's" jobs.

But African American women faced more formidable legal obstacles when they sought access to jobs off limits because of race *and* sex. Emma DeGraffenreid's case against General Motors later became a classic example of judges' blindness to how race and sex discrimination operated in tandem to thwart equal employment.[139] Prior to 1970, GM employed few female workers at its St. Louis plant. The company cited Missouri's protective labor laws, which prohibited women from working more than nine hours per day and kept them away from heavy machinery. Before 1970, a small number of white women worked in the "cushion room," making automobile seats and upholstery, but no black women held these positions. In the early 1970s, GM finally began to hire black women, who made up about one-fifth of the St. Louis metropolitan population.

The economic downturn erased those gains almost immediately. By August 1974, all of the plant's black female workers had been laid off, save the janitor.[140] Five of those workers, Emma DeGraffenreid, Brenda Hines, Alberta Chapman, Brenda Hollis, and Patricia Bell, filed a complaint with the EEOC, alleging that GM's "last hired–first fired" seniority policy violated Title VII. The Supreme Court had not yet addressed this issue, but lower courts had held that seniority policies could be invalid under Title VII if they perpetuated past patterns of discrimination against "women" or "minorities."

Represented by the NAACP Legal Defense Fund, the plaintiffs filed suit in federal district court in 1975. Judge H. Kenneth Wangelin, a Nixon appointee, issued a ruling the following year. Wangelin could not tell "whether or not the plaintiffs [were] seeking relief from racial discrimination, or sex discrimination." In any case, he believed that plaintiffs "should not be allowed to combine statutory remedies to create a new 'super-remedy'" and so he examined the suit "to see if it state[d] a cause of action for race discrimination, sex discrimination, or alternatively either, but not a combination of both."

Wangelin quickly disposed of the sex discrimination claim by citing Missouri's protective law, noting that GM had hired female employees "for a number of years prior to the enactment of the Civil Rights Act of 1964." The judge did not mention that the women hired prior to 1964 were all white, nor that they were confined to a small subset of available jobs in the plant. DeGraffenreid's coworkers said that GM's exclusion of black women from its assembly plant had deterred them from applying for employment until the early 1970s. DeGraffenreid herself had applied for a job with GM in 1968 and been rejected; she tried again, this time successfully, in June 1973, and was laid off six months later.[141] Wangelin dismissed the other plaintiffs' claim that they would have applied for positions at GM were it not for the employer's discriminatory policies as nothing more than "conclusory allegations."[142]

Wangelin did recognize the plaintiffs' race discrimination claim, but he ruled that the women should join another pending race discrimination class action against GM. He rejected the LDF's argument that *DeGraffenreid* must proceed as a separate suit, given the additional element of sex discrimination. A dozen years after Murray and her allies argued for including sex discrimination in Title VII precisely *because* black women would be left unprotected by a statute that covered race but not sex, Wangelin wrote, "the legislative history surrounding Title VII does not indicate that the goal of the statute was to create a new classification of 'black women' who would have greater standing than, for example, a black male. The prospect of the creation of new classes of protected minorities, governed only by the mathematical principles of permutation and combination, clearly raises the prospect of opening the hackneyed Pandora's box."[143]

On appeal, the EEOC supported the LDF's position. "Of all the readily identifiable groups against whom discrimination is directed, black women have traditionally suffered the severest economic deprivation," the EEOC brief stated. The district court's position meant that "black women will be allowed to aspire to parity with one depressed and victimized group of their choosing. They may either seek equality with white women by suing to end race discrimination or seek equality with black men by suing to end sex discrimination."[144] As scholars of intersectionality would later lament, *DeGraffenreid* meant that black women could only seek redress to the extent that either black men or white women experienced discrimination of similar nature and magnitude. Wangelin's opinion did not contemplate the possibility that black women might suffer from discrimination at the intersection of race and sex.

Judge Wangelin allowed Emma DeGraffenreid and her coplaintiffs to join their black male counterparts' suit, but in 1977, the Supreme Court upended the emerging lower court consensus that seniority systems that perpetuated past discrimination violated Title VII. In *Teamsters v. United States*, the Court held that a facially neutral seniority system would only run afoul of the law if the *intent* behind it was discriminatory.[145] *Teamsters* mooted the seniority issue in *DeGraffenreid*, since the plaintiffs had not alleged that GM's seniority system was the product of discriminatory intent.[146]

This focus on intent was emblematic of a shift in the Court's jurisprudence at mid-decade. In 1976, the Justices also had applied an intent requirement to constitutional equal protection claims in *Washington v. Davis*. In *Davis*, African American plaintiffs unsuccessfully challenged the use of a written test that disproportionately excluded black applicants from employment with the District of Columbia police department.[147] Reporter Carol Falk observed several months later, "[F]or some time, the Court has been handing down rulings that . . . would have made it difficult, if not impossible, to win many of the crucial civil rights cases of the 1950s and 1960s."[148]

Race-sex analogies foundered not because they were inherently flawed, but because their success as a legal strategy depended upon political and economic conditions that did not survive the upheavals of the mid-1970s. Reasoning from race became less useful to feminists as race precedents—and American political culture—became more conservative. Skeptical judges and other legal decision makers made race analogies compulsory in order to justify their refusal to recognize women's discrimination claims. To rescue reasoning from race, feminists would have to redefine race and sex equality, and reshape the relationship between them.

4

REASONING FROM SEX

When she heard that the East Cleveland police department was accepting applications from prospective officers, Cuyahoga Community College student Elizabeth Smith decided to put her law enforcement coursework to use. But at 5'5" and 136 pounds, Smith did not meet the department's requirement that officers be at least 5'8" and weigh 150 pounds. She obtained a court order and took the required written test anyway. When her score did not meet the cutoff for eligibility, city officials told Smith she could not retake the exam. With the help of feminist attorneys at the recently established Women's Law Fund, she brought a class action lawsuit against the city of East Cleveland. Smith, an African American woman, argued both race and sex discrimination. She won in federal district court: Judge Thomas Lambros ruled in 1973 that the police department's written test discriminated against African Americans and that the height and weight requirements disproportionately excluded women in violation of the equal protection clause and other civil rights laws.[1]

As Smith's lawsuit underscores, colorblindness was not the only vision available to feminists and civil rights advocates in the 1970s. Many individual women and men, grassroots organizations, lawyers, and government officials argued that formal equality could not magically erase centuries of discrimination and injustice. Employers, they noted, often replaced overt racial segregation and exclusion with "neutral" employment requirements that nonetheless put minority workers at a disadvantage in hiring, firing, and promotional decisions. Recruitment efforts frequently bypassed communities of color altogether. Despite some gains, occupational segregation was alive and well, and not only in the South.

To overcome these more stubborn obstacles, advocates turned to two legal concepts: effects-based or "disparate impact" analysis and a variety of policies known collectively as affirmative action. Disparate impact attacked facially neutral employment practices that had a disproportionate effect on disadvantaged groups. Affirmative action encompassed a range of remedies across the fields of employment, government contracting, and education that proponents considered necessary to overcome past and present discrimination and disadvantage.

Feminists in the 1970s did not only pursue "formal equality" that focused on winning "equal treatment" for women and men; they also turned to more expansive theories of equality. At first, they often framed their claims in terms of equal treatment. But feminists soon found, as had their counterparts in civil rights advocacy, that formal equality did not remedy lingering patterns of discrimination and inequality. Feminists used theories developed in race cases to tackle sex inequality. At the same time, it became increasingly clear that race and sex discrimination doctrines were intertwined in complicated ways. Feminists and their judicial allies found themselves manning the barricades in defense of embattled race precedents even as they tried to expand the universe of remediable sex discrimination and disadvantage.

The promise of disparate impact theory lay in its potential to attack structural, clandestine, and inadvertent discrimination by focusing on the effects of employer policies rather than on discriminatory purpose or intent. Beginning with *Griggs v. Duke Power Company* (1971), courts applied Title VII to practices that disproportionately affected racial minorities. *Griggs* challenged personnel tests and other employment requirements that a North Carolina company instituted after Title VII outlawed overt racial segregation and exclusion. The Supreme Court held for the first time that the Civil Rights Act "proscribes not only overt discrimination but also practices that are fair in form, but discriminatory in operation."[2] Feminist and civil rights advocates hoped that *Griggs* would help them to combat entrenched patterns of exclusion and underrepresentation.

Feminists embraced disparate impact in the years after *Griggs*. Women plaintiffs like Elizabeth Smith challenged height and weight requirements imposed by law enforcement departments. Feminists also recognized the potential of disparate impact to fight policies that placed working women at a disadvantage because of their family responsibilities. As National Association of Women Lawyers president NettaBell Girard Larson put it in 1972, women required "protection against indirect, covert, or unconscious sex discrimination under the guise of functional classification," especially employment policies that penalized caregivers.[3] Although *Griggs* was a Title VII case, advocates hoped courts would extend the disparate impact principle beyond employment to constitutional cases of all kinds.

It was not initially apparent that pregnancy discrimination litigation would rely on disparate impact. After all, Elizabeth Smith's own attorney, Jane Picker, took Jo Carol LaFleur's cases against mandatory maternity leave all the way to the Supreme Court by arguing primarily that discrimination against pregnant women was simply sex discrimination.[4] To feminists, discrimination based on pregnancy did not seem neutral at all. At first, it looked like feminists would be able to persuade courts to see pregnancy discrimination as "based on sex," or sex discrimination "per se" (see Chapter 2). But many judges considered pregnancy "sui generis" and therefore outside the realm of equality law altogether. As a result, feminists fell back on *Griggs'* "effects-based" or "results"-oriented model. In doing so, they entered an intricate doctrinal battle with profound implications for both sex and race equality law.

After *Geduldig v. Aiello* (1974) denied women constitutional protection from pregnancy discrimination (see Chapter 3), feminist lawyers turned to Title VII. The EEOC had interpreted Title VII to cover pregnancy discrimination, and several cases were already moving through the lower courts. One such case was *Gilbert v. General Electric*, where women, represented by Ruth Weyand and Winn Newman of the International Union of Electrical, Mechanical and Radio Workers (IUE), challenged General Electric (GE)'s exclusion of pregnancy from employee disability benefits.[5] In legal terms, GE's policy was the private sector mirror image of the California disability scheme attacked in *Geduldig*.

The trial judge in *Gilbert*, Robert Merhige of the Eastern District of Virginia, had a feminist-friendly record: he had required the admission of women to the University of Virginia in 1969, and in 1972 he had recognized Susan Cohen's claim that mandatory maternity leave for teachers violated the equal protection clause.[6] In *Gilbert,* Merhige again ruled for the plaintiffs: "While pregnancy is unique to women, parenthood is common to both sexes, yet under G.E.'s policy, it is only their female employees who must, if they wish to avoid a total loss of company induced income, forego the right and privilege of this natural state. . . . That such is discriminatory by reason of sex is self-evident." Merhige rejected GE's contention that pregnancy was voluntary and thus distinguishable from other temporarily disabling conditions. Congress could not have intended that women "forego [their] fundamental right . . . to bear children, as a condition . . . of employment free of discrimination," he wrote.[7]

To Merhige, pregnancy discrimination was sex discrimination, pure and simple. But the Supreme Court decided *Geduldig* two months after Merhige's ruling.[8] Plaintiffs and their allies continued to make the per se sex discrimination argument in the wake of *Geduldig.* But they also relied increasingly on the effect-based analysis pioneered in race cases. On this view, because they had a disproportionate impact on women's employment opportunities, practices that disadvantaged pregnant workers violated Title VII, and perhaps even the equal protection clause, even if they were not explicitly "based on sex."

Before *Geduldig,* feminists had more to gain from arguing that pregnancy discrimination was per se sex-based—prohibited by both Title VII and the equal protection clause.[9] After *Geduldig* undermined this approach, *Griggs* provided an increasingly attractive—and essential—alternative. In 1975, Diane Zimmerman, a student of Ruth Bader Ginsburg at Columbia Law School, identified in the diverse and often cryptic pre-*Geduldig* opinions striking down pregnancy exclusions the "use of an effect analysis." Courts recognized how policies penalizing pregnancy in the workplace contributed to "the overall second-class status of the employed female."[10] That same year, Elisabeth Rindskopf and Kathleen Peratis tackled "Pregnancy Discrimination as a Sex Discrimination Issue" in the *Women's Rights Law Reporter.* They maintained that disparate impact analysis could be applied to pregnancy classifications under the ERA.[11]

In June 1975, the Fourth Circuit upheld Judge Merhige's decision in *Gilbert,* citing *Griggs.*[12] Feminists continued to argue that pregnancy discrimination was sex discrimination per se, and part of a larger pattern of bolstering male breadwinners and their nonworking wives at the expense of female workers. Peratis and Rindskopf expressed optimism that

Geduldig would not reverse "all of Title VII pregnancy law," such that the per se sex discrimination argument might survive under the statute.[13]

Feminist lawyers and their allies offered several alternative theories of disparate impact when GE appealed *Gilbert* to the Supreme Court.[14] The ACLU Women's Rights Project (WRP) argued that because only women could become pregnant, no further showing of impact was necessary.[15] Gilbert's own lawyers enumerated several ways in which GE's policy disproportionately harmed women. Since disability benefits were part of employees' compensation package, excluding pregnancy meant women as a group received less compensation than men. A pregnant woman would be under "economic pressure to hide her disability and continue to work" or "might be forced into a lower-paying job." Male employees, on the other hand, were "free to embark on any course of conduct involving either voluntary or involuntary disability," including vacations, hair transplants, rhinoplasty, drunkenness, and even dangerous criminal activity, and still receive compensation.[16] Relying on disparate impact impelled feminists to spell out explicitly what seemed obvious to them: excluding pregnancy from coverage created barriers to equal employment and reproductive choice that men would never confront.

Feminists' renewed emphasis on disparate impact arguments was less a change in the nature of the equality advocates sought than a reassessment of the legal arguments that could succeed in the Supreme Court. Like the disparate impact argument, feminists' contention that pregnancy discrimination was per se sex discrimination itself took sex equality law beyond formal equality, which emphasized the need for men and women to be "similarly situated" before equal protection analysis applied. In other words, disparate impact analysis gave feminists another way to argue what they had been arguing all along: that women's childbearing capacity should not redound to their disadvantage as workers and citizens, and the fact that only women could become pregnant made pregnancy discrimination more, not less, of an issue central to sex equality.

In June 1976, the Supreme Court dealt disparate impact theory a severe blow. In *Washington v. Davis,* the Justices upheld an employment test for District of Columbia police officers, despite its disproportionate impact on African American job applicants. The Court held that discriminatory intent was necessary to establish an equal protection violation.[17] A policy's impact was relevant to proving intent, the majority said, but not enough by itself to run afoul of the Constitution.

The Court's retreat from disparate impact under the equal protection clause gave employers hope for a similar retrenchment under Title VII. GE wanted the Court to limit *Griggs* to the denial of jobs and promotions, not fringe benefits that were "merely incidents of a job." In case that broader argument failed, they also worked hard to distinguish pregnancy from race discrimination. Race and sex discrimination were different, GE contended, and the law treated them differently.[18] Little legislative history on Title VII's sex discrimination provision existed.[19] Moreover, employers warned, a decision for pregnant employees could spill over into the race context and beyond: "The necessary implication of the 'disparate effect' argument is that the only disabilities for which an employer can lawfully refuse to provide protection are those which the sexes, and races, and ethnic groups, experience in roughly equal percentages. Such a conclusion would stand Title VII on its head."[20]

The Justices and their clerks immediately recognized that *Gilbert* could become a referendum on *Griggs*. Powell's initial inclination was to find a Title VII violation, based on a disparate impact theory. His conference notes cited "*Griggs*—the impact here is on women." Stewart had similar instincts: Powell's notes indicate that Stewart found *Griggs* "persuasive" authority, *Geduldig* "relevant," and "no case . . . controlling." To Stewart, *Gilbert* was an "extremely close case."[21] Brennan, Marshall, and Stevens voted to affirm the Fourth Circuit; White, Rehnquist, and Chief Justice Burger voted to reverse.[22]

For the Justices who initially voted to uphold GE's policy, *Geduldig* was persuasive authority. Law clerk Donna Murasky tried to convince Blackmun otherwise. Murasky's own experience taught her that "much of discrimination against women [had] its basis in the childbearing function that they perform." She told Blackmun about law firm interviewers who peppered her with questions about her reproductive plans—questions that male applicants never faced. Murasky concluded that GE's policy could not be reconciled with the "two broad principles" underpinning Title VII—the removal of "artificial barriers" to the advancement of "blacks and women" in the workplace, and the idea that "an impact, and not a motivation analysis is proper." In short, Murasky wrote, "if those discriminations are not . . . prohibited by Title VII, I have no idea why Congress bothered to include the sex discrimination provision of the Act."[23]

Blackmun disagreed with Murasky, writing on her memo, "Donna overstates." But he remained torn. Blackmun thought the *Geduldig* precedent was "powerful." On the other hand, he wrote, "I have always felt that *Geduldig* involved a bit of strong-arming in typical P[otter] S[tewart] fashion." Blackmun called GE's argument that private employers should not be subject to stricter standards than the Constitution required of public employers "almost unanswerable." He was bothered by the fact that the GE coverage did not include pregnancy-related complications, yet also worried that a "decision adverse to GE will prompt management to do away with disability income plans" altogether. Title VII's legislative history was ambiguous, though Blackmun acknowledged: "If impact is critical under Title VII, then under the *Griggs* decision it certainly is critical here." Overall, he was "inclined to reverse" and rule for GE, but he noted that there were "potent factors the other way" and that he "could be persuaded in that direction."[24]

Unlike Murasky, law clerk William Block did not attempt such persuasion. In Block's view, GE's insurance scheme was discriminatory only if it meant that female employees received less in overall benefits than their male counterparts.[25] In other words, only the "bottom line" mattered. The plaintiffs had not shown that women received less compensation overall than men from GE. But neither had GE demonstrated that women and men had actually received equal compensation. If the burden of proof were placed on the employer, then the plaintiffs could still prevail. But if the burden was on the plaintiffs, they would lose.

Like Block, Powell clerk Gene Comey homed in on the burden of proof question, but he emphasized the political stakes of the case: "[O]ne way to reach the 'women win' result would be to say that a Title VII case IS made out simply by showing that an employer refuses to cover a disability unique to one sex." Then the employer could still prevail by showing that women and men received the same net benefits from the policy. "Placing the burden of proof on women is the most logical approach," he noted, "[b]ut placing that burden on the employer is the approach most likely to convince women that the Court is sensitive to claims of sex discrimination." Comey concluded, "To the extent the Court is concerned about its press, this latter approach has some appeal." Justice Powell wrote in the margin: "We shouldn't be."[26]

Powell and Stewart eventually voted to uphold GE's policy. Stewart apparently had decided that his opinion in *Geduldig* required him to conclude that pregnancy-based discrimination was not sex-based discrimination under Title VII any more than it was under the equal protection clause. White agreed, citing the women's failure to meet their burden of proof: as Powell summarized White's remarks, "If women are arguing 'effect,' they have failed to make a case."[27] In the end, Blackmun, too, voted to reverse, giving GE a six-Justice majority.

Once the per se sex discrimination argument had failed to win a majority, *Griggs* became the primary battlefield on which *Gilbert* would be fought. Chief Justice Burger assigned the majority opinion to Justice Rehnquist, the Court's most conservative member. As a clerk to Justice Robert Jackson during the Court's consideration of *Brown*, Rehnquist had written a memo supporting the "separate but equal" mandate of *Plessy v. Ferguson,* though he later denied that the memo reflected his own views. While advising the Goldwater campaign, he recommended that the Arizona senator oppose the Civil Rights Act of 1964.[28] As a Phoenix lawyer and Republican Party official in the mid-to-late 1960s, Rehnquist was "an outspoken opponent of liberal legislative initiatives such as busing to achieve school integration."[29] In a 1970 internal Justice Department memorandum, then-Assistant Attorney General Rehnquist had condemned the ERA as seeking "nothing less than the sharp reduction in importance of the family unit, with the eventual elimination of that unit by no means improbable." Rehnquist could "not help thinking that there is also present somewhere in [the pro-ERA] movement a virtually fanatical desire to obscure not only legal differentiation between men and women, but insofar as possible, physical distinctions between the sexes."[30] In 1973, he had been the lone dissenter in *Frontiero v. Richardson,* which extended spousal benefits to husbands as well as wives of military personnel.[31]

Rehnquist's first draft of *Gilbert* disturbed his colleagues and their clerks. His treatment of *Griggs* and the disparate impact question was the major point of contention. Clerk Diane Wood wrote to Justice Blackmun, "Although I do not favor the result reached by Justice Rehnquist in his proposed opinion, I like even less the way he reaches that result. Specifically," she worried, "the opinion suggests that *Griggs* . . . may no longer be good law. . . . The holding, as I understood it, was to be that the women have not shown discriminatory effect (i.e. that their net benefits are less). Justice Rehnquist's opinion, however, attempts to hold that even proof of effect is no longer sufficient." Wood read Rehnquist's draft as "effectively overrul[ing] *Griggs sub silentio.*"[32]

Wood did not convince Blackmun to change his mind about the

outcome of the case. Powell's chambers, worried about the impact of Rehnquist's draft on *Griggs,* did suggest several changes, which were "largely adopted" in Rehnquist's second draft.[33] Blackmun's clerks remained concerned, however, that Rehnquist was trying to "rule in dicta that Title VII goes no further than the Fourteenth Amendment . . . thus overruling *Griggs.*"[34] Block recommended that Blackmun propose several changes to Rehnquist that he believed would mitigate the implied dilution of *Griggs.* After an exchange with Rehnquist's clerk, Block was hopeful that Rehnquist would make the changes in order to "get a court."[35] But Rehnquist rejected all of Blackmun's proposed revisions.[36]

Rehnquist did not disguise his desire to contain disparate impact analysis. Brief concurrences by Blackmun and Stewart attempted to shore up *Griggs.*[37] Dissenters Brennan and Marshall vehemently rebutted *Gilbert's* holding that GE's policy of excluding pregnancy from coverage was "not a gender-based discrimination at all" and castigated the majority's "unexplained and inexplicable implications" about the reach of *Griggs.*[38]

Reaction among feminists was even more critical. Ginsburg called *Gilbert* a "disaster."[39] Ruth Weyand deemed it "the most disastrous court decision on women in the last 50 years."[40] Susan Deller Ross charged that the decision "legalized sex discrimination." Ross, who as a lawyer for the EEOC had helped to draft the commission's pregnancy discrimination guidelines, worried that the decision meant employers could "treat pregnant women as harshly as they like—firing them, refusing to hire them and forcing them to take long, unpaid leaves of absence."[41] The Justices who voted with the majority also heard from irate citizens. Marian F. Sabetny-Dzvonik of Venice, California, wrote to Blackmun: "Your decision is an insult to all women and evidence of your antediluvian philosophy. . . . When will you rule that businesses may deny work to Blacks because of sickle-cell anemia and to Jews because of Tay-Sachs?" Alexander Buchman of Los Angeles called the ruling "[d]egrading, demeaning, injurious, contemptible."[42] Press coverage was predictably mixed: the *New York Times* condemned the decision as typifying rightward drift on the Court, while the *Wall Street Journal* praised the majority for recognizing that "[m]en and women are biologically different, and no man-made law is likely to bring about much change in that."[43]

To feminists, the decision perpetuated the *Geduldig* view that pregnancy discrimination was not sex discrimination, despite its status as the "cornerstone of all sex discrimination in the employment sphere," as feminist attorney Marcia Greenberger put it.[44] Less visible but perhaps even more worrisome, *Gilbert* might insulate from attack policies that disproportionately harmed women.[45] Feminists fought back on two fronts: first, by attempting to limit *Gilbert's* reach through litigation; and second, by lobbying for proposed legislation explicitly designed to overturn it.

The next disparate impact case to reach the Supreme Court, *Dothard v. Rawlinson,* was not about pregnancy, but it did bear on the future of *Griggs.* Southern Poverty Law Center attorney Pamela Horowitz met Dianne "Kim" Rawlinson in a Montgomery, Alabama hair salon in 1974. Rawlinson was washing hair despite her college degree in correctional psychology because she could not meet Alabama's height and weight requirements for prison guards.[46] Rawlinson challenged the requirements with Horowitz's help, and the lower court, which included Judges Richard Rives and Frank Johnson, found that they violated Title VII. The court also invalidated a policy that banned women altogether from certain prison guard positions that involved inmate contact.

The stakes of *Dothard* were high: the case could determine both the fate of disparate impact and its application to sex discrimination. On appeal to the Supreme Court, Alabama used Rehnquist's opinion in *Gilbert* to argue that *Griggs* should not apply.[47] The state also attacked the district court's reliance on general population statistics as proof of disparate impact. Burger clerk Alex Kozinski agreed that the court should have examined the characteristics of applicants. "It stands to reason . . . that the position of prison guard is not particularly attractive to women and that a relatively small percentage of women apply for the position," he argued.[48] Burger himself wrote to Stewart: "Given the vulnerable position of a prison guard who must patrol in the midst of hundreds of inmates, without a weapon, the *appearance* of strength would seem to be as important a characteristic as possession of actual strength."[49]

After oral argument, at least four Justices were skeptical of the district court's decision. Burger thought the height and weight requirements were "per se reasonable," according to Powell's notes, while White and Blackmun agreed with Kozinski that data about the height and weight of women who applied for prison guard jobs would be necessary to shift the burden of proof to the defendants. Rehnquist also saw the plaintiffs' statistics as "too weak." Brennan, Marshall, and Stevens were inclined to affirm the district court on both points. Stewart and Powell believed that the height and weight requirements should be invalidated but that the ban on women for the inmate-contact guard positions was justified. Both emphasized that the Court's rulings should be "narrow."[50] Their view ultimately prevailed.

Dothard's result contained an apparent contradiction: the Court reasoned from race in applying *Griggs* to the height and weight requirements, but in upholding the prison guard bona fide occupational qualification (BFOQ) defense, the majority implicitly ratified social as well as statutory differences between race and sex. Stewart's opinion for the majority rejected out of hand Alabama's argument that national population statistics should not be sufficient to establish a prima facie case of discrimination. After all, Stewart noted, "otherwise qualified people might be discouraged from applying because of a self-recognized inability to meet the very standards challenged as being discriminatory." Under Title VII, the state could still have defended the height and weight requirements by showing that they were "consistent with business necessity," but it had not done so. The height and weight requirements therefore failed to satisfy Title VII.

In contrast, Stewart's opinion upheld sex as a BFOQ for some prison positions, though only as an "extremely narrow exception to the general prohibition of discrimination on the basis of sex." Calling the "environment in Alabama's penitentiaries" a "peculiarly inhospitable one for human beings of whatever sex," Stewart said that "it would be an oversimplification" to label the challenged regulation "an exercise in 'romantic paternalism.'" The majority maintained that prison security itself was "at stake" in *Dothard*. "A woman's relative ability to maintain order . . . could be directly reduced by her womanhood."[51] Justice Marshall's partial dissent charged the majority with promoting "ancient canards about the proper role of women."[52]

Both sides had reason to emphasize the limitations of *Dothard*. Marshall concluded his opinion by expressing relief that "the Court's decision" on the BFOQ issue was "carefully limited to the facts before it."[53] In a footnote, Stewart noted that "Alabama's penitentiaries are evidently not typical," and that in many maximum security all-male prisons female guards had been used effectively.[54] At the conservative end of the spectrum, Justice Rehnquist's concurrence sought to limit the reach of the Court's disparate impact analysis. Rehnquist emphasized the weakness of

Alabama's case, making clear that a stronger defense would have convinced him.[55]

Kathleen Peratis described the BFOQ ruling as "worrisome," but Ginsburg characterized *Dothard* as "on the whole . . . a plus in terms of this court."[56] *Dothard* was a case of extremes. The use of applicant data instead of general population statistics would have been particularly distortive. The defendants' case was unusually weak and poorly argued. The Alabama prison system had been declared—ironically, by Frank Johnson himself—to be in an unconstitutional state of chaos. Thus *Dothard* was not "a vehicle for sweeping writing," as one clerk put it.[57] Especially given the potential for retrenchment demonstrated in Rehnquist's concurrence, *Dothard* was significant because it confirmed *Griggs*'s applicability to sex discrimination and applied a robust version of disparate impact analysis.[58]

So *Griggs* was safe, for the time being, at least as applied to employment tests. But feminists still worried about the future of disparate impact claims in pregnancy cases as *Nashville Gas Company v. Satty* wound its way to the Supreme Court. Nora Satty, a clerk in the Nashville Gas Company's accounting department, became pregnant in 1972 after more than three years on the job. She gave birth in January 1973, the day after the Supreme Court decided *Roe v. Wade*. Seven weeks later—once her employer's mandatory maternity leave period had elapsed—she tried to return to work. The Company had eliminated Satty's previous position, so she bid on three open permanent positions. Company policy eliminated Satty's accumulated job-bidding seniority because of her pregnancy leave, so newer employees jumped ahead of her in line. Nashville Gas gave Satty a temporary assignment at lower pay, but had nothing to offer her when the six-week job ended.[59]

Satty's challenge prevailed in the lower courts, before *Gilbert* came down. The *Gilbert* plaintiffs had not been able to show to the Court's satisfaction that the overall benefits women received under GE's disability insurance policy were inferior to the benefits collected by men. In contrast, Satty's lawyers had a credible way to demonstrate that female employees at Nashville Gas suffered a net loss because they were forced to forfeit job-bidding seniority. Unlike the plan upheld in *Gilbert,* no cost savings resulted from Nashville Gas's policy, and eliminating the discrimination would not give women "extra compensation."[60] Feminists also argued that the policies' "devastating" and "inevitable" impact on women demonstrated the company's discriminatory intent. The AFL-CIO's brief charged that the policies were based on the "gender-related stereotype" that "a woman who gives birth to a child will want to, and ought to, remain at home with the infant for a substantial length of time, even though she is physically able to return to work."[61]

The Justices unanimously accepted the disparate impact argument against Nashville Gas Company's seniority policy. Rehnquist's draft won the relieved assent of Brennan's clerk, Steven Reiss. Reiss wrote to his boss, "I think we have reason to be pleased with the opinion since it is far more positive in its general tone and import than we had reason to expect it would be."[62] Rehnquist distinguished *Gilbert* on two grounds. First, he differentiated between "benefits" and "burdens": in *Satty,* the employer "imposed on women a substantial burden that men need not suffer." Second, Rehnquist categorized *Gilbert* and *Satty* as arising under different provisions of Title VII.[63] To Justice Stevens, these distinctions seemed "illusory." He surmised that the difference between actionable and noncognizable pregnancy discrimination "may be pragmatically expressed in terms of whether the employer has a policy which adversely affects a woman beyond the term of her pregnancy leave"—in other words, "long after pregnancy itself is all but a memory."[64]

Stevens's blunt appraisal of *Gilbert* and *Satty* offered the greatest clarity, but although some of his colleagues were sympathetic to his approach, they preferred more oblique interpretations. Clerk Miles Ruthberg recommended to Marshall that he avoid signing on to Stevens's concurrence: "JPS' [John Paul Stevens] opinion characterizes *Gilbert* even more broadly than WHR [William H. Rehnquist] himself does. If WHR's distinction of *Gilbert* is somewhat thin, so much the better; it will be that much easier to distinguish."[65] Powell, too, made his own concurrence deliberately opaque. He returned clerk Sam Estreicher's draft "chopped up a bit," describing himself as "fuzzing the analysis deliberately."[66] Rather than referring directly to "disparate impact" or "discriminatory effect," Powell chose to discuss "discrimination in 'compensation.'"[67] Brennan and Marshall joined his concurrence, apparently agreeing that the less explicitly said about the majority's approach to *Griggs,* the better.

Ironically, the very swing Justices who provided the deciding votes against recognizing pregnancy discrimination as per se sex discrimination remained vigilant in their defense of *Griggs.* Feminists, with the help of Blackmun, Stewart, and Powell, successfully staved off Rehnquist's attempts to demolish disparate impact altogether.

Feminist reaction to *Satty* was mixed. NOW Legal Defense Fund director Phyllis Segal "deplored" the Court's refusal to revisit *Gilbert,* but called the protection against loss of seniority "an important victory for the women's movement." Though she acknowledged that the Court had "cut back on the worst implications of *Gilbert,*"[68] Susan Deller Ross called the ruling "confused."[69] Journalist Carol Falk remarked perceptively that civil rights and women's advocates "may well find they're better off with a bit of fuzziness, if the court continues to show signs of limiting the principles that were responsible for so many victories against job discrimination."[70]

Confusion and uncertainty could be useful in another way—as an argument for legislation to overturn *Gilbert.* In his initial memo on *Gilbert,* Justice Blackmun wrote of his ambivalence about the proper resolution of the case, "There is one comfort, and that is that Congress may cure the situation if our guess is not in accord with their desire." Labor and women's groups formed a coalition called the Campaign to End Discrimination Against Pregnant Workers (CEDAPW) immediately after *Gilbert* came down, and began seeking congressional repudiation of the ruling.[71] One week later, the ACLU and the Pennsylvania Commission for Women convened a strategy meeting in Philadelphia, which was attended by more than forty lawyers, lobbyists, and legislators.[72] The group met shortly thereafter with congressional leaders in Washington to draft new legislation. If they were not successful, union lawyer Elizabeth Neumeier declared, the law would return women to "the days of 'barefoot and pregnant.'"[73] Susan Deller Ross warned that unless Congress acted, Title VII would be "dead for women workers, whatever their race or national origin."[74]

The campaign for protection against pregnancy discrimination invoked women's right to equal treatment with men, but it also entertained broader visions of social support for parents. Journalist Letty Cottin Pogrebin noted in 1977 that "one of the most entrenched male supremacist assumptions is that woman's work is unimportant . . . and, most of all, secondary to a woman's reproductive capacity."[75] She wrote, "If men could get pregnant, maternity benefits would be as sacrosanct as the G.I. Bill." Erica Black Grubb and Andrea Hricko observed that *Gilbert* "raise[d] . . . broader social questions about who is responsible for the propagation of the race." Rather than penalizing women workers for bearing children, they argued, policy makers should emulate other Western governments by offering "liberal maternity and paternity leave, providing free or inexpensive day-care centers for children of working parents, and enforcing the rights of women to retain seniority and other benefits when returning to work after childbirth."[76]

CEDAPW appealed to fiscal and social conservatives too. They argued that if the law was not changed, "women—especially low-income women—will be discouraged from carrying their pregnancy to term," that "[w]ithout the mother's salary, it will be more difficult for many parents to provide their new babies with proper nutrition and health care." Even more alarming, "[p]regnant women and women with young babies may be forced to go on welfare."[77] Proponents of new legislation frequently cited the plight of Sherrie O'Steen, a young mother and GE employee forced to stop working and denied disability benefits when she became pregnant. After her husband abandoned them, O'Steen and her two-year-old daughter lived in rural Virginia without heat or electricity, surviving on cold sandwiches and water.[78] Supporters sold pregnancy legislation not merely as an antidiscrimination measure, but as essential to the well-being of women and their families.

The Pregnancy Discrimination Act (PDA) and subsequent state legislation providing additional benefits for pregnant employees famously sparked a debate among feminists about whether "equal treatment" or "special treatment" was the most appropriate approach to pregnancy in the workplace.[79] The focus on this controversy has obscured an equally important question raised by the PDA: whether disparate impact claims could be brought on behalf of pregnant women. For example, would having no sick leave policy, or offering employees only a very short sick leave period, violate the law?

The top priority of the PDA proponents was to overturn *Gilbert* and make pregnancy discrimination sex discrimination per se; they did not focus on the disparate impact question in lobbying for the legislation. The resulting law's text and legislative history proved susceptible to multiple interpretations. The first clause of the PDA revised Title VII's definition of "sex" to include pregnancy and related conditions, which suggested that existing Title VII law (including disparate impact) should apply. As a House committee report put it, "[T]he bill defines sex discrimination . . . to include these physiological occurrences peculiar to women; it does not change the application of title VII to sex discrimination in any other way."[80] In the PDA's official legislative history, the most direct reference to disparate impact implied that the Act was designed to make resorting to disparate impact arguments less necessary, rather than to undermine such claims.[81] A Senate conference report indicated that the bill would "insure that favorable decisions such as the decision with regard to seniority in the *Satty* case [would] be preserved."[82] PDA supporters frequently endorsed the EEOC guidelines, which included disparate impact as well as per se claims of pregnancy discrimination, as "rightly implement[ing]" Title VII's sex discrimination prohibition.[83]

On the other hand, the legislative history also contained assurances from PDA proponents that the bill would not mandate particular benefits for pregnant workers—or even any benefits at all if they were not already available to nonpregnant employees. Lawmakers referred to "equality of treatment" as the standard.[84] At the same time, though, proponents did not foreclose the possibility that employers could voluntarily provide benefits to pregnant employees that were not available to other temporarily disabled workers, implying that the PDA was not a pure prohibition on differentiating between pregnant and nonpregnant employees. On this view, the PDA only precluded distinctions that negatively affected pregnant women.[85]

Disparate impact remained crucial to employment equality for pregnant women in the eyes of many feminist lawyers. Attorney and professor Nancy Erickson wrote shortly after the PDA's passage that "the outward structure of [the PDA], as of Title VII as a whole, is conservative. Employers must simply treat women, and blacks and other minorities, the way they treat white males. If certain benefits are not extended to men, they need not be extended to women. Yet, women are not men manqué, and to think that equality can be achieved in this way is erroneous." The PDA "will settle some of the major problems of pregnancy discrimination," Erickson concluded, "but it leaves others untouched. We must continue to develop theories to overcome these, which tend to be the thorniest problems of all."[86]

But just as disparate impact seemed poised for an unlikely renaissance in pregnancy discrimination cases, the PDA—one of feminists' greatest legislative triumphs—inadvertently threatened the legal basis for a claim with potentially much greater bite. In the coming years, many courts would take a narrow view of disparate impact in pregnancy

discrimination cases, rejecting women's challenges to employer policies—like the denial of leave to all workers—that made childbearing and
employment incompatible for women.[87] These decisions, together with
the noisier equal treatment/special treatment debate of the 1980s, obscured the ways in which feminists reached beyond formal equality and
helped to save disparate impact in the 1970s.

To Ruth Bader Ginsburg, the "most stubborn obstacle to equal opportunity for women" was their "customary responsibility for household management." In a 1975 article, "Gender and the Constitution," she declared
that "above all else, the home-work gap must be confronted." Her prescription: "man must join woman at the center of family life, and government must step in to assist both of them during the years when they have
small children." To that end, Ginsburg argued, the government and employers should provide job and income security for childbearing workers
and quality child care options for working men and women of all income
levels.[88] Only then would the male breadwinner/female homemaker assumptions that underlay discrimination finally begin to fade.

Feminists had long sought government support for child care in order to enable women's full participation in the workplace. They encoun-
tered fierce resistance from social conservatives, whose opposition led
President Nixon to veto the most ambitious child care legislation passed
by Congress in the early 1970s.[89] Feminists continued to campaign for
legislation, but also pursued voluntary maternity leave and child care
provision as part of affirmative action plans in public and private sector
employment.[90] For instance, NOW's "model affirmative action program" listed "child care" and opportunities for "part-time work" as key
affirmative action remedies for women.[91]

Feminists also supported more conventional forms of affirmative action for "women and minorities." Even their constitutional litigation
strategy, often perceived as calling for sex-blindness, reached beyond the
equal-treatment model. But before they could transcend formal equality,
advocates first had to convince judges to distinguish between "benign"
classifications that often harmed women and "genuine affirmative action" intended to overcome the effects of discrimination.

Ruth Bader Ginsburg hoped that *Weinberger v. Wiesenfeld*—the "first
gender discrimination case that she would control from start to finish"—

would put her constitutional litigation agenda back on track after disappointing Supreme Court decisions in *Kahn v. Shevin* and *Geduldig v. Aiello*.[92] Paula Wiesenfeld, a schoolteacher who earned substantially more than her husband, died in childbirth. After her death, Paula's widower, Stephen, had trouble finding adequate child care and reduced his own work hours to care for their son, Jason. He challenged his ineligibility for Social Security survivors' benefits that were available to widows but not widowers.[93] At oral argument, Ginsburg cast the challenged provision as "law-reinforced sex-role pigeon-holing defended as a remedy."[94] *Wiesenfeld* was Ginsburg's "ideal" case, because the facts allowed the WRP "to cast men in the role of being good parents" and to endorse "the care of two loving parents, rather than just one."[95] The case highlighted discrimination against men who served as family caregivers, as well as against female breadwinners.

Ginsburg fought an uphill battle. At first, *Wiesenfeld* struck many as "a comparatively easy case," as law clerk Richard Blumenthal, a protégé of Daniel Patrick Moynihan, wrote to Blackmun.[96] The Court had just upheld a tax exemption for widows in *Kahn v. Shevin*. "Working women, to be sure, are disadvantaged" by the denial of survivors' benefits to their spouses, Blumenthal admitted. Even so, "widows with children are far more likely to need such benefits than widowers."[97] Blackmun was initially inclined to uphold the law, as were Burger and Rehnquist.[98] Powell saw the problem with devaluing working women's contributions by denying benefits to their widowers, but he disapproved of fathers who stayed home with their children. Julia "Penny" Clark, who was Powell's first female law clerk, speculated that such fathers were "a small class, no doubt." Powell responded, "I would hope so—though the ever-increasing welfare rolls even in prosperous times suggest a high level of indolence."[99] Clark recommended striking down the classification, but it was "a close and difficult case" for Powell.[100] Powell's concurring opinion reflected his misgivings about recognizing fathers' right to care for children.[101]

In the end, though, the vote for Stephen Wiesenfeld was unanimous, and a majority embraced Ginsburg's arguments.[102] Writing for the Court, Brennan emphasized that "such a gender-based generalization cannot suffice to justify the denigration . . . of women who do work and whose earnings contribute significantly to their families' support." The opinion also stressed the difficulties that Stephen Wiesenfeld would have faced as a parent caring for his children alone: "It is no less important for a child to be cared for by its sole surviving parent when that parent is male rather than female," Brennan wrote. "[T]o the extent that women who work when they have sole responsibility for children encounter special problems, it would seem that men with sole responsibility for children will encounter the same child-care related problems."[103] Ironically, the opinion's drafter, Marsha Berzon, had "almost lost her chance" to work with Brennan because of his enduring reluctance to hire a woman.[104]

For feminists, *Wiesenfeld* was a triumph.[105] Brennan's opinion seemed to signal the demise of the male breadwinner/female homemaker model as a valid basis for allocating government benefits. Still, sex equality law remained in flux. After Justice William O. Douglas's retirement in 1975, only three members of the Court were on record as supporting strict scrutiny, and Douglas's replacement, John Paul Stevens, had attracted opposition from feminists during his confirmation hearings.[106] *Kahn* and *Schlesinger v. Ballard* (1975), in which the Court upheld different promotion requirements for military servicemen and women, suggested that some "benign" sex classifications were still permissible.[107]

In 1976, the Court clarified the standard of review applicable to sex-based classifications. *Craig v. Boren* challenged an Oklahoma law that allowed eighteen-year-old girls to purchase low-alcohol beer while boys had to be twenty-one. Young men, the state argued, were more likely to have alcohol-related accidents. The "near-beer" case struck many as "silly," but it did raise the question of whether the government could rely on statistical differences between males and females to classify based on sex. In *Craig,* the Court established "intermediate scrutiny"—a standard somewhere between rational basis review and strict scrutiny—for sex classifications. A sex-based distinction would have to be "substantially related" to the achievement of "important governmental objectives," wrote Brennan for the majority.[108] Blackmun welcomed the intermediate standard; he had long hoped to establish such a "middle-tier" for sex classifications. Other Justices, including Burger and Powell, were less enthusiastic.[109] Perhaps sensing his colleagues' increasing ambivalence about sex equality cases, Brennan used *Craig* to consolidate what gains he could—as Powell's clerk put it, to "make hay while the sun is shining."[110]

But the Court still had not explained how to tell the difference between sex-based classifications that harmed women and those that promoted sex equality. *Califano v. Goldfarb,* argued the same day as *Craig,* challenged another Social Security survivors' benefit. All widows but only widowers who had received at least one-half of their financial support from their wives were eligible. Ginsburg charged that the benefit scheme favored traditional families over "egalitarian union[s] in which man depends on woman fully as much as woman depends on man." The case, she wrote, "presents a textbook example of the insidious discrimination . . . of laws that treat men as the breadwinners that count."[111] For the swing Justices, though, *Goldfarb* was a very close case.[112] Stewart, Blackmun, Powell, and Stevens all worried that the Court had "gone too far" in sex discrimination cases."[113] And unlike Stephen Wiesenfeld, Leon Goldfarb had the opportunity to prove his dependency and receive benefits.

Ginsburg approached the oral argument in *Goldfarb* warily, worried that the Justices would not see the challenged law as harmful to wage-earning women. Dependent widowers were not left in the cold by the challenged law, and widows received a benefit regardless of need. Further complicating matters, race-based affirmative action was before the Court again. Ginsburg did not want to take a position that would endanger either affirmative action or sex equality law. Sure enough, Justice Stevens tried three times to ask her whether laws discriminating against men should be judged by the same standard as those that harmed women.[114] Ginsburg skirted the question. "With preferential program issues in the wings . . . I tried to avoid treading on that territory," she explained a few days later.[115] She worried that cases like *Goldfarb* would "jeopardiz[e] the forward movement we might generate in sex discrimination cases more clearly entailing an adverse impact on women."[116]

In the end, Brennan could only muster a four-Justice plurality for his opinion striking down the sex classification, with Stevens providing the fifth vote in a concurring opinion.[117] *Goldfarb* was an important victory, especially given its significant price tag. But the case reflected both confusion and dissension among the Justices about whether and when sex-based distinctions were harmful to women.[118]

Greater clarity came just three weeks later in an unlikely case, *Califano v. Webster*. Will Webster, representing himself, had challenged an obscure provision that gave women a slight advantage over men in calculating their average wages for purposes of receiving Social Security benefits.[119] A federal district court ruled in Webster's favor, and the government appealed. The Court decided the case without briefing or oral arguments.[120] As Brennan law clerk Jerry Lynch, who had been a student of Ginsburg's, put it in a letter to his former professor two days after the ruling, "Somewhat oddly, the Court has seen fit to synthesize its cases on gender discrimination purportedly 'beneficial' to women by means of a summary reversal. . . . [T]he job was done without benefit of briefing, and I suspect that to the extent the Court really believes what the opinion says, it may be of considerable importance."[121] Lynch himself had drafted the *Webster* per curiam opinion, and he described his delicate balancing act in *Webster* as an effort "to confine legitimate 'benign' discrimination pretty narrowly, throwing in a plug for absolute equality . . . and yet preserving the possibility that truly compensatory programs can be clearly identified."[122] The opinion distinguished cases like *Kahn* and *Webster,* in which the challenged law served the "permissible" goal of "redressing our society's longstanding disparate treatment of women," from instances like *Frontiero, Goldfarb,* and *Wiesenfeld,* in which "the classifications in fact penalized women wage earners." In *Webster,* the Court said, the legislative history made "clear that the differing treatment of men and women . . . was deliberately enacted to compensate for the particular economic disabilities suffered by women."[123] Ginsburg praised her student's "fine" work. "Had I been assigned the task, I could not have done better," she declared.[124]

Webster enabled a new strategy: whereas feminists had once reasoned from race in sex cases, now they reasoned from sex to argue in favor of race-based affirmative action. Over the next several months, the Justices considered a high-profile challenge to U.C. Davis Medical School's affirmative action program. In *Regents of the University of California v. Bakke,* Allan Bakke, a white man, challenged an admissions policy that set aside a certain percentage of slots for students of color as a violation of his civil rights. *Webster* provided "a framework for the Court's decision [in *Bakke*]," Ginsburg explained in a series of law review articles, speeches, and letters to the editor. "The program assailed in *Bakke* . . . surely does not coincide with historic role-typing nourished by race-based animus." Instead, she argued, the Court's description of the *Webster* statute was equally applicable to *Bakke:* "'the only discernible purpose' of the program [was] to redress 'society's longstanding disparate treatment' of [racial minorities]. And in operation, the special admissions arrangement serves 'directly to remedy some part of the effect of past discrimination,'" as the Court put it in *Webster.*[125]

Sex equality law now had many advantages as a template for evaluating race-based affirmative action. Allan Bakke and other "reverse discrimination" plaintiffs decried affirmative action as unfairly burdening white men. Using *Webster* as a model could shift the inquiry away from the burden imposed upon white applicants by affirmative action. In the sex equality cases, the Court showed little concern about "benign" discrimination's effect on men; rather, they asked whether women were helped or harmed. *Webster* also stressed that the impetus for the challenged law should be the result of a deliberate effort to advance the status of women, rather than an "accidental byproduct" of outdated stereotypes. Since race-based affirmative action programs tended to be the result of recent, considered, and well-intentioned efforts at remediation, *Webster*'s focus on the process and purpose of enactment bolstered their legitimacy. *Webster* posed as the key question whether an affirmative action program helped beneficiaries to transcend traditional, oppressive roles.

Moreover, *Webster* asserted that generalized societal discrimination justified sex-conscious remedies, a controversial proposition in the debate over race-conscious programs. This ability to respond to societal discrimination at the most general level was highly relevant to cases like *Bakke*, where the challenged affirmative action program was a response not to intentional discrimination or segregation, but to the more diffuse effects of societal disadvantage. When considering laws favoring women, the Justices seemed willing to let this background assumption of inequality go virtually unquestioned. The conservative Justices were more, not less, inclined to acknowledge women's comparative disadvantage. After years of being told that sex discrimination paled in comparison to racial oppression, feminists now inhabited a constitutional climate friendlier to the anti-subordination claims of women than to those of racial minorities.[126]

Yet the race-sex analogy continued to hold potential dividends for sex equality jurisprudence; reasoning from sex to extend intermediate scrutiny to race-based affirmative action could imply a reciprocal borrowing of strict scrutiny for sex as well as race. The convergence of race and sex equality doctrine, so problematic in the period before *Webster*, now appeared both promising and possible.

Feminists were not alone in appreciating *Webster*'s potential. Amici curiae in *Bakke* used the sex equality cases to argue for the applicability of intermediate, rather than strict, scrutiny to race-based affirmative action programs.[127] One brief identified what Justice Stevens later labeled an "anomalous result": if the courts applied strict scrutiny to race-based affirmative action, they would erect a higher barrier to remedial programs for racial minorities than for women.[128] *Webster* also proved useful to the Carter administration in *Bakke*.[129] The government used *Webster* to demonstrate the Court's willingness to accept remedial programs designed to overcome generalized discrimination.[130] At the same time, *Webster* suggested a limiting principle: classifications based on race or sex might be permissible in some circumstances but not others. The emerging sex equality doctrine acknowledged and even highlighted the difficulties of line-drawing, but still offered a way to distinguish between beneficial and detrimental classifications.

Webster's justifications for affirmative action were not new; they were deeply rooted in the advocacy, scholarship, and jurisprudence of antiracism.[131] But the *Webster/Bakke* juxtaposition made possible an unprecedented convergence of race and sex equality doctrine. In the past, commentators who argued for affirmative action based on race had paid almost no attention to sex discrimination.[132] Feminists looked to race equality doctrine as a source of universal equal protection principles. Now, however, the analogy's promise ran in reverse: race-based affirmative action policies, under fire in an increasingly conservative political climate, stood to gain from a parallel with sex classifications.[133]

The *Bakke* case produced more amicus briefs than any Court case to date. Powell clerk Bob Comfort's seventy-page memo to the Justice concluded that the main issue in the case was the standard of review applicable to U.C. Davis Medical School's admissions policy. Comfort responded to affirmative action supporters' argument for intermediate rather than strict scrutiny by identifying a crucial distinction: "With respect to sex, there are only two categories to be compared, men and women. . . . Therefore, the class-wide questions of who has been hurt and who will be burdened are simple." But for racial and ethnic minorities, the picture was more and more complex: "The prejudice faced by every distinct racial and ethnic group entering this country makes each a potential candidate for compensatory legislation." Further, Comfort argued, "[i]n a melting pot country, race and ethnicity have a peculiar capacity to inflame which other distinctions lack." Powell wrote in the margin: "Good answer to possible reliance on 'sex' classifications not being subjected to strict scrutiny."[134]

Meanwhile, Brennan's chambers drafted what he hoped would be the opinion for the Court in *Bakke*, relying heavily on an analogy to the sex equality cases. Those cases established that benign distinctions deserved heightened scrutiny primarily because of their potential to stigmatize women and minorities. Intermediate scrutiny would guard against such abuses without precluding all affirmative action.[135] In a memorandum to his colleagues, Brennan emphasized that the Court's prime concern was "stigma, insult, badge of inferiority," as epitomized by cases that condemned "'old notions' that demean[ed] women by denying them any place in the 'world of ideas' and [the Court's] rejection of 'traditional ways of thinking' that assume all members of the female sex to be dependents." Brennan wrote: "I should think the propriety of [*Webster's*] approach follows *a fortiori* in the case of reliance on race to address past racial discrimination."[136]

But Powell had never accepted a full-blown parallel between race and sex, and he was loath to do so now.[137] As it had been before, Powell's was again the deciding vote in *Bakke*. Five Justices—Powell, Brennan, Marshall, White, and Blackmun—agreed that U.C. Davis could take race into account in making admissions decisions; four Justices—Stevens, Rehnquist, Burger, and Stewart—concluded that the university's policy violated the Civil Rights Act; Justice Powell found the program constitutionally invalid. Powell was the only Justice to concur in both elements of the Court's holding, which upheld the constitutionality of taking race into account but struck down U.C. Davis's particular vehicle for doing so. His became the Court's opinion.[138]

Just as he had resisted reasoning from race in earlier cases, Powell rejected reasoning from sex in *Bakke*. Sex-based classifications were different from racial ones in two salient ways, he asserted. First, sex-based distinctions were "less likely to create the analytical and practical problems present in preferential programs premised on racial or ethnic criteria." In questions of gender, he wrote, "there are only two possible classifications. The incidence of the burdens imposed by preferential classifications is clear." But "[m]ore importantly," wrote Powell, "the perception of racial classifications as inherently odious stems from a lengthy and tragic history that gender-based classifications do not share. In sum," he concluded, "the Court has never viewed such classification as inherently suspect or as comparable to racial or ethnic classifications for the purpose of equal protection analysis."[139] Race and sex discrimination were not of the same magnitude or social abhorrence. Strict rather than intermediate scrutiny was therefore appropriate for all race classification, even when used to help rather than hurt disadvantaged minorities.[140]

Many liberals and moderates greeted *Bakke* as a Solomonic balancing act that preserved affirmative action while invalidating the type of remedy that most troubled its critics—the quota.[141] But feminists challenged Powell's distinction between race and sex. In a 1979 article, feminist attorney Nancy Gertner refuted the Justice's claim that the Court was more competent to distinguish between the invidiousness or benignity of sex-based than race-based classifications. Gertner argued that "courts have experienced difficulties in defining sex discrimination . . . which they never experienced in defining race discrimination."[142] Feminists also attacked the contention that sex discrimination lacked a "lengthy and tragic history." Indeed, as Ginsburg emphasized, the Court itself had recognized such a history on several occasions.[143] Ginsburg acknowledged that the analogy between race and sex was imperfect, but regretted that Powell had not "indicate[d] sharper perception of similarities, as well as the differences, in our society's manifestations of race and sex discrimination."[144] Gertner added that the "greatest tragedy of sex discrimination may well be its relative subtlety." She explained: "[E]ven today sex discrimination, and particularly sex stereotypes, are not recognized as discrimination." Indeed, Gertner argued that this problem of recognition militated in favor of greater, not lesser scrutiny for gender-based affirmative action.[145]

Bakke marked a turning point in equality jurisprudence and in the affirmative action debate more generally. Powell's opinion rejected not merely the applicability of the less stringent standard of review developed in sex equality doctrine to race cases. He also sidelined a more capacious conceptualization of discrimination's meaning, effects, and remediation. Recognizing enduring structural barriers to women's advancement might have helped legal decision makers see that racial minorities still faced obstacles that formal equality could not remedy. But by placing race and sex equality jurisprudence on separate paths, *Bakke* undermined these connections.

Before the Southern Poverty Law Center (SPLC)'s Pamela Horowitz met Dianne "Kim" Rawlinson in a Montgomery beauty salon, the Center was already representing Brenda Mieth in her attempt to become the first female state trooper in Alabama. When Mieth, an "A" student in criminal justice and an award-winning Pentagon secretary, learned that she was ineligible for a state trooper position, she requested an interview with Colonel E. C. Dothard, the department's director. Dothard told Mieth that she could not take the state trooper examination because she did not meet the height (5'9") and weight requirements. Dothard added that he believed the job was too dangerous for women. He made Mieth an honorary state trooper at the conclusion of the interview.[146]

Mieth was not appeased by Dothard's "courtly gesture," particularly after she applied for other law enforcement positions in Alabama, Virginia, and Maryland and turned up nothing.[147] She knew that Dothard did not enforce the height and weight minimums uniformly—men who did not meet them had been hired as state troopers. Mieth filed a class action suit against Alabama on behalf of all female prospective applicants.

Judges Richard Rives and Frank Johnson did not find *Mieth v. Dothard* a difficult case. "[A]lmost no women" could meet the height and weight requirements, and none had ever been hired as an Alabama state trooper. Dothard testified that he worried about women being "assigned to the rural areas of our state. . . . [A] trooper is supposed to be able to protect other people . . . and I just feel like they could not do the job out there by themselves."[148] This evidence prompted the judges to find intentional discrimination in violation of the equal protection clause.[149] Women, the court declared, "do not need protectors; they are capable of deciding whether it is in their best interest to take unromantic or dangerous jobs." The court gave the state thirty days to initiate a recruitment program targeted at women.[150]

Colonel Dothard and his colleagues were dismayed. In a press release, Dothard predicted: "[T]he public will suffer from this decision. We can hire women and treat them equally, but, can they protect the public?" Captain John Henderson feared for the future of state law enforcement. "There is no way around it," he told the *Daily Ledger,* "The admission of women to the trooper force could cause morale as well as moral problems." He worried that night shift assignments involving male and female partners could, as the newspaper put it, "cause family problems for both troopers," and anticipated an "increase in the use of guns," presumably due to women's physical weakness. Sgt. C. T. Stewart expressed similar concerns to the Selma Rotary Club, emphasizing that male and female troopers would be "out in the field all hours of the night," creating "domestic problems." The Troy *Messenger* editorialized, "It's not a matter of principal [sic], rather it is a matter of reality that

leads Dothard to un-welcome women to the state police force." The editors concluded on an ominous note: "While there are women who
want . . . the notoriety of being among the first to be Troopers one
wonders if they have thought how proud they would be to also be the
First Alabama State Trooper to be raped, or the first woman Trooper to
wash out."[151]

Nevertheless, a Department of Public Safety (DPS) press release was
accompanied by a picture of a smiling Dianne Baylor, a department secretary, modeling a trooper uniform. A new recruitment pamphlet featured a picture of Baylor, who was white, standing alongside an African
American man wearing a strained expression and a trooper uniform. The
two stood beside a patrol car with a grinning white male trooper in the
driver's seat. The *Alabama Journal* reported that the department's hasty efforts to develop recruitment materials caused a commotion: one of the
secretaries asked to pose for a pamphlet withdrew after her boyfriend
"got mad at her," and Baylor "had to wear a wig over her long, blonde
locks to meet hair requirements"—not to mention the tailoring challenges posed by uniforms made for men. Radio recruitment spots
warned, "It isn't an easy job and it is one in which you will be judged on
your own merits." SPLC attorney John L. Carroll sounded cautiously
triumphant, however, when he told the Montgomery *Advertiser* that he
expected the decision to be "used as a precedent by women across the
country" to challenge height and weight requirements.[152]

But almost two years after the court ordered the Alabama DPS to
grant female applicants equal access to state trooper positions, not a
single woman had begun work.[153] The culprit, according to SPLC attorneys, was Alabama's preference for military veterans, which granted five
additional points to all veterans who received an honorable discharge and
ten additional points to qualified veterans with service-related disabilities, or, if those disabilities rendered them unqualified, to their wives.[154]
SPLC attorneys went back to court in June 1978, arguing that the veterans' preference should be suspended. Several women had scored in the
top twenty-five on tests, but only one appeared in the top twenty-five
names on the employment register after veterans' preference points were
taken into account. Only 7.3 percent of female applicants earned veterans' points, compared with almost 41 percent of males. "[I]n effect," the
SPLC argued, Alabama "gives preference to males in hiring since so few
women until recently were able to serve in the armed forces."[155] Johnson
found the motion not "sufficiently germane to the sex discrimination

question that was originally presented in this case," noting in a letter to Judges Rives and Varner that the plaintiffs did "not attack the constitutionality of the Alabama Veterans' Preference Statute."[156]

Others did. Veterans' preferences could not be challenged under Title VII, as they were explicitly exempted from statutory coverage, but these preferences had become a focal point for feminists' constitutional disparate impact claims by the mid-1970s. Veterans' preferences took a variety of forms, from granting veterans additional points on civil service hiring and promotion exams (as Alabama's statute did) to giving an absolute preference to any veteran who so much as passed such exams (as was the case in Massachusetts and New Jersey).[157] Because women historically had been restricted to between 1 and 2 percent of the armed forces, veterans' preferences placed women at a distinct disadvantage in civil service employment. The ACLU Equality Committee had investigated the issue as early as 1971, commissioning a memo on the impact of veterans' preferences on equal employment opportunity. Peter Gregware suggested that the ACLU look for a test case. The Union's Massachusetts chapter eventually collaborated with the Boston law firm Ropes & Gray on just such a suit.[158] In 1972, NOW's annual conference excoriated the discriminatory impact of veterans' preferences on women workers.[159] By 1975, the U.S. Civil Rights Commission questioned the scope of these preferences and urged limits on their duration.[160] Veterans' preferences also came under fire from local women's organizations and state commissions on women's status in the mid-1970s.[161] Newspapers including the *New York Times* and *Los Angeles Times* sided with reformers. "Imagine the furor," a typical proreform editorial began, "if Americans discovered that women and minorities were being cheated out of chances at government jobs by a well-liked but exclusive club."[162]

Some feminist lawyers feared a backlash against reform, however, particularly as beleaguered veterans returned from Vietnam. When attorneys Sylvia Roberts and Marilyn Hall Patel suggested in 1973 that NOW initiate litigation against veterans' preferences, Legal vice president Judith Lonnquist demurred. "I do not think that it would be good public relations for NOW to file such litigation, nor do I think there is much ultimate likelihood of success," she wrote. Ginsburg was similarly hesitant.[163]

Veterans' groups lobbied vociferously against any rollback, proving that caution was warranted. Plaintiff Helen Feeney became the object of hateful, threatening mail when she challenged the veterans' preference in

Massachusetts.[164] In reality, most reform proposals called only for limits on preferences' duration or magnitude. But veterans' groups—often headed by veterans of World War II and Korea—exercised formidable political influence. When President Jimmy Carter proposed scaling back veterans' preferences as part of his ambitious civil service reform package, the Veterans of Foreign Wars (VFW), the American Legion, and other national organizations steadfastly opposed the reforms. Key Democratic power broker and California senator Alan Cranston declared veterans' preferences untouchable, notwithstanding the administration's concessions to recently discharged soldiers and to disabled veterans generally.[165]

The veterans' preference debate intersected with battles over affirmative action and race in ways that made feminist intervention potentially treacherous. Observers often noted the collision between "[e]qual opportunities for women and minorities" and "gratitude to America's fighting men."[166] Reformers pointed out that 98 percent of veterans were male, and 92 percent were white.[167] But veterans' groups countered that the most recent cohort of veterans was in fact disproportionately nonwhite, and accused reformers of seeking to curtail preferences just when minority men were in a position to benefit. In this way, they framed feminists' position as opposed to the interests of "minorities."[168] VFW head John Wasylik pointed to "minority leaders [who had] testified in favor of keeping the laws" intact "so that minorities [could] get a foot in the door of the federal job market."[169]

"Minorities" actually took a range of positions on veterans' preferences. National civil rights organizations largely supported the feminist position on the grounds that overall, lifetime preferences harmed nonwhite men and women. Indeed, federal employment figures cited by the Carter administration showed that in 1976 women held 2.8 percent of high-level (GS-16 through GS-18) positions, and minorities as a group fared only slightly better at 5 percent.[170] Veterans' groups could sometimes find support for their position from minority advocates, however, particularly when they framed preferences as important to recently returned veterans of color. For instance, in a fiery city council dispute over Los Angeles's veterans' preference scheme, the *Los Angeles Times* reported that "representatives of minority groups noted that the [extra] points [on the civil service exam] were of critical value to blacks and Chicanos because of the large percentage of unemployed among their numbers."[171] Allen K. Campbell, chair of the Civil Service Commission and a proponent of reform, emphasized that minority men still constituted a tiny percentage of the total veteran population, but many writers on the veterans' preference controversy noted the tensions.[172] As one observer put it, "The sentiment to abolish veterans' preference raises an interesting problem: What happens when *your* affirmative action program clashes with *my* affirmative action program?"[173]

Ironically, feminists had often cited veterans' preferences as a precedent for remedial benefits for "women and minorities." Wilma Scott Heide asked a NOW convention in 1973, "If veterans' preference is fair to aid those endangered or disadvantaged by national demands, are not women also disadvantaged by institutional sexism, minorities by racism, the poor by classism and all women endangered by childbirth and rape?"[174] Other defenders of affirmative action used the same tactic. Leroy Knox wrote to the *Philadelphia Tribune* in 1978, "The organized attacks against 'Affirmative Action' programs designed for the benefit of racial minorities . . . are discriminatory attacks." After all, he pointed out, the "affirmative action program for veterans of foreign wars is called 'Veterans' Preference.'"[175] Justice Blackmun's separate opinion in *Bakke* supporting U.C. Davis's affirmative action program had noted, "[G]overnmental preference has not been a stranger to our legal life," and listed veterans' preferences as his first example.[176]

If veterans' preferences really resembled affirmative action, then questioning their validity could undermine policies benefiting racial minorities and women. Reformers unconsciously echoed opponents of affirmative action when they argued that veterans' preferences undermined "merit"-based hiring. Mae M. Walterhouse, president of Federally Employed Women (FEW), said at a Senate hearing in 1978, "[W]omen have nothing to fear, and everything to gain, from institution of a true merit system in the Federal civil service," including the elimination of most veterans' preferences.[177] The Carter administration pointed to the moribund state of the federal bureaucracy, suggesting that reform served the goals of efficiency as well as equal opportunity. Feminist supporters of affirmative action tread carefully: many drew a distinction between legitimate compensatory policies and those that placed too heavy a burden on nonbeneficiaries. Columnist Ellen Goodman wrote, "Any government has a right, maybe even an obligation, to offer remedial help, affirmative action, to groups at a disadvantage in the job market for special reasons. A veteran who left his job to go to war deserves that help . . . But," she clarified, "there is a big difference between giving a healthy veteran a helping hand and giving him a chit for life—at the expense of the young, minorities, women and merit."[178]

Despite the hazardous racial politics of veterans' preferences, feminist lawyers hoped to use race precedents to challenge them.[179] For instance, in *Castro v. Beecher*, black and Spanish-surnamed applicants for jobs in the Boston police department had sued to end a variety of hiring practices on constitutional disparate impact grounds.[180] For female job-seekers challenging veterans' preferences, earlier cases like *Castro* provided promising ammunition. Esther Feinerman's suit against Pennsylvania, filed in 1972 after she received the second-highest score on the state's civil service exam but was passed over in favor of two lower-scoring veterans, used race precedents to argue disparate impact. But the court ruled against Feinerman and rejected her race analogy. Even if she had proven disparate impact, the judge said, a lower standard of scrutiny would apply anyway because hers was a sex discrimination case.[181]

Such defeats reinforced qualms about the likely outcome of challenges to veterans' preferences. Ginsburg had "counseled against further efforts" to overturn Massachusetts's preference.[182] But in March 1976, a three-judge federal district court struck down the Massachusetts law. "The practical effect of Veterans' Preference is clear," Judge Joseph L. Tauro wrote. It "absolutely and permanently forecloses, on average, 98% of this state's women from obtaining significant civil service appointments." Tauro held that "[i]n the context of the Fourteenth Amendment, '(t)he result, not the specific intent, is what matters.'"[183] Concurring Judge Levin Campbell emphasized the extreme nature of Massachusetts's preference.[184] In dissent, Judge Frank Murray argued that the challenge to the veterans' preference "presents an even less compelling claim for sex discrimination than [the pregnancy discrimination claim in] *Geduldig v. Aiello*, where only women were in the group burdened by the classification."[185]

The Supreme Court's decision in *Washington v. Davis* three months later posed an even more formidable doctrinal obstacle: plaintiffs now had to prove discriminatory intent in order to have a viable constitutional disparate impact claim. The Court remanded the Massachusetts case for reconsideration in light of *Davis*. Helen Feeney's lawyers argued that the dramatic disparate effects of the veterans' preference were eminently foreseeable and therefore "intentional" for purposes of constitutional analysis.[186] Again, a majority of the three-judge federal district court agreed.[187]

As *Feeney* headed to the Supreme Court, the political struggle over veterans' preferences wore on. Already under fire from veterans' groups, the Carter administration became embroiled in an internecine dispute over *Feeney.* The first point of contention concerned whether Solicitor General Wade McCree should file an amicus brief. If the SG supported Massachusetts, he would be in the awkward position of defending a more extreme veterans' preference scheme than the federal preference President Carter and the Civil Service Commission chair had already tried to overhaul. On the other hand, supporting Feeney or remaining neutral could call into question the administration's support for laws favoring veterans.[188] A veteran of World War II, an honors graduate of Harvard Law, and the first African American to serve on the U.S. Court of Appeals for the Sixth Circuit, McCree had argued for the federal government as amicus in the *Bakke* case.[189] On the advice of his deputies, Frank Easterbrook and William Bryson, McCree filed a brief that distinguished the federal veterans' preferences from the Massachusetts program, and defended both against Feeney's constitutional challenge.[190]

Feminists and their allies cried foul.[191] Several members of Congress signed a letter to the attorney general, Griffin Bell, demanding an explanation. Massachusetts governor Michael Dukakis sent a telegram urging Bell to withdraw the SG's brief.[192] After assistant attorneys general Barbara Babcock and Patricia Wald arranged a meeting between Bell and representatives of several women's organizations, Ruth Bader Ginsburg and NOW LDEF's Phyllis Segal wrote a memorandum to the AG criticizing the SG's brief. The brief, they protested, "treat[ed] *Feeney* as implicating a total assault on veterans' preference," rather than as a narrow challenge to an especially discriminatory scheme. Furthermore, the SG's brief advanced an excessively "stringent interpretation of the *Washington v. Davis* purpose requirement."[193] McCree and his deputies resisted feminist criticism, noting among other things that its discussion of *Washington v. Davis* had been vetted by the DOJ's Civil and Civil Rights Divisions.[194] But Wald and EEOC chair Eleanor Holmes Norton echoed their fellow feminists' objections to the SG's brief. Norton drafted a proposed supplemental brief to be filed by the SG.[195] Easterbrook and Bryson called these "gestures" a "costly sop" to "political pressure groups" that threatened both the DOJ's authority and its institutional credibility.[196] In the end, Easterbrook "reluctantly" endorsed what he believed to be the lesser of evils: Norton's brief was submitted on behalf of four agencies opposed to the SG's position—the EEOC, Office of Personnel Management, and the Labor and Defense Departments.[197]

Once again, feminists' fortunes depended upon how the Court would apply race discrimination precedents to policies affecting women. Powell's *Bakke* opinion perpetuated the Court's practice of using race-sex parallels when feminists wanted to distinguish between race and sex inequality but not when they worked to advocates' advantage. Recent cases unambiguously required a showing of discriminatory intent in constitutional disparate impact cases. Yet sex discrimination often rested on unspoken assumptions about gender roles, or "benign" protectionist rationales. When they adopted veterans' preferences, legislators were unlikely to have expressed any explicit intent to keep women out of the civil service.

The perils of reasoning from race increased as the law grew more conservative. Feeney's supporters could not avoid race precedents, but they could focus on the distinctive attributes of sex discrimination. Requiring proof of discriminatory motive "would be particularly inappropriate in sex discrimination cases," Feeney's lawyers argued, because "[t]he nature of invidious sex discrimination is not so much a desire to disadvantage or harm women for its own sake, but rather an overriding insensitivity or indifference to their legitimate interests based on 'outdated misconceptions concerning the role of females in the home rather than in the 'marketplace and world of ideas.'"[198] Because such stereotypes were so ingrained, "requiring proof of legislative intent to discriminate against women might leave many statutes intact," argued the brief submitted by several women's organizations. Indeed, that brief asserted, the Court had not required proof of intent to discriminate in earlier gender cases.[199]

The veterans' preference differed from the laws challenged in prior constitutional cases, however, in that it did not involve an overt sex-based classification. Opponents therefore emphasized that the preference's disparate impact on women stemmed directly from the government's own discrimination against women in the military. Because women had been excluded from most military jobs, few could achieve veteran status. The harmful effect on women was thus so inevitable that the Court should infer intent, Feeney's attorneys argued.[200] The feminist organizations' brief went further, arguing that "proof of intent should not be required" at all, because the preference "incorporates de jure discrimination and reflects deeply imbedded traditional notions about women."[201]

Feminists did not want the Court to require proof of discriminatory intent as they now did in race cases. But they did wish to reap the benefits of race precedents that used prior *de jure* discrimination as evidence of intent. Feminists accused the government of inconsistency: in school segregation cases, the United States had argued against a stringent intent requirement in order to remedy *de facto* segregation in northern school districts.[202] The women's organizations' brief also compared veterans' preferences to "the tying of current voter registration to prior voting eligibility," a policy whose unfairness to disenfranchised African Americans would be self-evident.[203]

Feminists could hardly have found a more entrenched sex-based distinction to challenge. To its defenders, the veterans' preference was easily distinguishable from other kinds of discrimination. Moreover, unlike racial segregation and disenfranchisement, the exclusion of women from many military jobs retained its legitimacy. To some, "discrimination" between men and women in the armed forces looked more like the ultimate benign dispensation. One irate veteran wrote to Helen Feeney, "Lady, it was the millions of men whose crosses are around the world . . . who were discriminated against. Where were the women in World War I, World War II, Korea, Vietnam . . . ? You and your ilk," he concluded, "want the benefits of war but not the *burdens*."[204]

Feeney's supporters also had to calibrate their arguments against Massachusetts's veterans' preference lest they contribute to the backlash against affirmative action. The Washington Legal Foundation (WLF), a conservative group usually opposed to affirmative action, argued that given the changing demographic composition of the military "one can no longer characterize the armed forces as a white, male preserve. Legislation aiding veterans, therefore, has an impact of aiding minorities and women." In short, the WLF argued, "Veterans preference may be in time, just another form of affirmative action."[205] *Newsweek* called *Feeney* "one of the most important affirmative-action cases since . . . *Bakke*" and characterized the feminists' complaint as one of "reverse discrimination."[206] In fact, feminists wanted to capitalize on *Bakke's* skepticism about "preferences" without fatally undermining government's ability to use race- and sex-conscious remedies for discrimination.[207] In the end, their briefs quoted Powell's invocation in *Bakke* of "the serious problems of justice connected with the idea of preference itself" and cited language in Brennan's *Bakke* opinion about the ideal of "individual merit or achievement."[208]

Once again, the analogy to race cut both ways. The swing Justices disliked veterans' preferences, but they were acutely aware that whatever the Court did in *Feeney* would affect race cases as well. Powell's "gut reaction" was that Massachusetts's veterans' preference could not "be sustained under modern gender-based discrimination analysis" given its "discriminatory impact." He drafted a separate concurrence, never filed, expressing his distaste for veterans' preferences as a matter of policy.[209] Blackmun, too, found the Massachusetts veterans' preference "extreme and annoying."[210] Both Justices had carefully preserved *Griggs* and Title VII's disparate impact theory even in cases where they ultimately rejected feminists' specific claims. But Blackmun and Powell remained wary of the application of disparate impact theory in constitutional cases, because it could potentially endanger any existing law or policy that had a disproportionate impact on a disadvantaged group. Powell did "not want to undercut or weaken the authority" of *Washington v. Davis* and other cases.[211] He also worried that feminists' argument about veterans' preferences "incorporating" prior discrimination against women in the military could spill over into race cases. The "incorporation" argument was "difficult . . . to cabin," clerk David Westin warned. "[U]ntil the last twenty years many Negroes were purposefully excluded from many colleges and universities. To say, however, that any distinction according to one's college education is therefore purposefully discriminatory would be absurd."[212] And Justice Stevens pointed out at oral argument that the incorporation argument potentially endangered all veterans' benefits, not just employment preferences.[213]

In the end, the Supreme Court rejected Feeney's challenge. Justice Stewart's opinion for the Court acknowledged that "[c]lassifications based upon gender, not unlike those based upon race, have traditionally been the touchstone for pervasive and often subtle discrimination," and that Massachusetts's absolute preference for veterans admittedly "operate[d] overwhelmingly to the advantage of males." "Race is the paradigm," Stewart wrote, and "[e]ven if a neutral law has a disproportionately adverse effect upon a racial minority, it is unconstitutional under the Equal Protection Clause only if that impact can be traced to a discriminatory purpose." So it was for laws imposing disproportionate disadvantages on women. Over protestations from dissenting Justices Brennan and Marshall—and, apparently, from Virginia "Ginny" Kerr, the clerk who drafted Stewart's opinion—the seven-Justice majority refused to read discriminatory intent into the Massachusetts legislature's choice to award an absolute preference to a veteran population that was only 1.8 percent female.[214] Worse, the majority opinion went beyond *Washington v. Davis,* defining discriminatory intent stringently—as undertaking a course of action in part " 'because of,' not merely 'in spite of,' its adverse effects upon an identifiable group."[215]

All observers seemed to agree with *New York Times* reporter Linda Greenhouse's characterization of *Feeney* as a "setback for the women's movement."[216] NOW President Eleanor Smeal called the decision "devastating."[217] Lynne Revo-Cohen of the advocacy group Federally Employed Women identified the "ultimate irony" of *Feeney:* "The number of reverse discrimination cases where men are claiming their rights are being denied by targets, goals and quotas for hiring women and minorities, highlights the inequity of the *Feeney* decision. Here we have a highly qualified woman competing for a job on *merit* alone, and the Supreme Court cuts her off at the knees!"[218]

Civil rights advocates worried that *Feeney* would spill over into constitutional race cases. Greenhouse predicted that the Court's "rigorous standard" for proving unconstitutional disparate impact would "influence the outcome of an array of equal-protection cases."[219] Indeed, liberal scholars would deride *Feeney's* insidious effects on the efficacy of equal protection for years to come.[220]

The Court had foiled feminists' attempts to reconstruct the relationship between race and sex equality law. Whereas they had once reasoned from race, feminists had begun to reason from sex, arguing that the seemingly unique aspects of sex discrimination could pave the way for a more expansive conception of civil rights generally. But perceived differences between race and sex classifications allowed the increasingly conservative majority to erect higher constitutional barriers to affirmative action in *Bakke.* And in *Feeney,* the allegedly greater subtlety of sex discrimination did not convince the Justices to depart from the stringent conception of intent developed in race cases. Ultimately, the Justices proved unwilling to reason from sex even as their vision of racial justice became increasingly narrow.

Feminists continued to win when they challenged laws that explicitly differentiated between men and women, however. Three weeks after *Feeney,* the Court unanimously endorsed such a challenge in *Califano v. Westcott.*

In *Westcott,* two couples from Massachusetts challenged a state Aid to Families with Dependent Children (AFDC) regulation providing benefits to households that included unemployed fathers but not unemployed mothers. The fact pattern was by now familiar. Cindy and William Westcott did not fit the stereotypical male breadwinner/female homemaker model. Cindy, through part-time jobs as a bookkeeper and chambermaid, had supported the family. When she lost her job, the Westcotts were ineligible for welfare benefits because William did not meet the requirement for "unemployed" status, since he had not worked recently.

Like the Frontieros, the Wiesenfelds, and the Goldfarbs, Cindy's family would have received benefits had she been a man. There was a difference, though, argued the government: whereas those earlier cases involved contribution-based social programs like Social Security or military service, AFDC was "a non-contributory program based on need." And the law targeted men quite deliberately, in an effort to "correct a flaw in the AFDC program, namely the program's tendency to induce unemployed fathers to desert so that their wives and children could become eligible for AFDC benefits."[221]

In 1967, when the law's fathers-only provision went into effect, the Moynihan Report's analysis still dominated welfare and employment policy. Now, a dozen years and as many constitutional sex equality cases later, the policy had little hope of survival.[222] Justice Blackmun's clerk, Thomas Merrill, called the appellants' argument that the law was not sex discriminatory "bordering on the frivolous," and declared, "It makes no more sense to reduce costs by providing no benefits to families headed by unemployed females than it does to reduce costs by providing no benefits to families headed by unemployed blacks or unemployed Puerto Ricans."[223] Even the more conservative Justices saw no way to uphold the law. At conference, Stewart voiced his disagreement with the precedents but nevertheless declared himself bound by them, and the part of the Court's opinion declaring an equal protection violation was, in the end, unanimous.[224]

The preceding dozen years of feminist advocacy had changed the reigning conception of how the law could regulate the division of labor within families.[225] Blackmun's opinion for the Court condemned the challenged provision as "part of the baggage of sexual stereotypes that presumes the father has the primary responsibility to provide a home and its essentials, while the mother is the center of the home and family life."[226] Ginsburg wrote to Stephen Wiesenfeld before the *Westcott* deci-

sion, "The Supreme Court is about to decide the most important fol-
low-up to your case. . . . It will be harder to win, because the context is
welfare rather than social security. But if it is a winner, I will be satisfied
that we have reached the end of the road, successfully, on explicit sex
lines within the law."[227] After the decision, she told law professor Gerald
Gunther that she was "elated about *Westcott.*" She continued: "Not a
peep, even from Rehnquist, on the sex discrimination issue. The 9–0
count means, I think, that for explicit classification by sex, all that is
missing from 'suspect' categorization is the seal."[228]

By the end of the 1970s, then, feminists had won in the subset of sex
equality cases involving "explicit classification by sex." The relative success
of these cases helps to account for feminists' subsequent reputation for
pursuing formal equality. Feminists' attempts to reformulate the race-sex
analogy did not fare as well, and were largely forgotten. As race precedents
became increasingly conservative, feminists tried to extend the greater
flexibility of sex equality jurisprudence to race-based affirmative action, to
apply effects-based disparate impact concepts developed in the race context to sex discrimination, and to expand the definition of constitutional
equality. These efforts were not wholesale failures. Feminists and their allies succeeded in saving *Griggs* from evisceration, and the Pregnancy Discrimination Act redefined statutory sex discrimination. Though Justice
Powell rejected reasoning from sex in *Bakke,* the Court preserved the possibility that affirmative action programs would survive constitutional
scrutiny. But feminists' efforts to preserve disparate impact and affirmative
action remained largely hidden, their reasoning from sex unrecognized.

Feminists' reputation for pursuing formal equality also grew out of
the relative invisibility of women of color in the constitutional sex
equality cases of the 1970s. Advocates persuaded the Supreme Court to
reject the male breadwinner/female homemaker model African American feminists had challenged in the wake of the Moynihan Report. But
they did so in cases that seemed far removed from the lives of many
women of color and their families. The constitutional cases that produced Supreme Court opinions often featured white husbands and wives
claiming spousal benefits. Even *Westcott,* a case about welfare—associated
in the public imagination with black single mothers—involved married
couples of unspecified racial background. And reasoning from sex, like
reasoning from race, did not always capture what Pauli Murray once
called the "conjunction" of race and sex.

5

LOST INTERSECTIONS

"I've never felt this way about a black chick before," Margaret Miller's supervisor said when he appeared uninvited on her doorstep. On her first day on the job, Maxine Munford's boss inquired whether "she would make love to a white man and if she would slap his face if he made a pass at her." Willie Ruth Hawkin's coworker remarked that he "wished slavery days would return so that he could sexually train her and she could be his bitch."[1] Such treatment may have been shocking, but it was nothing new. What was new in the 1970s was that workplace abuse had a name—harassment—and it would soon have a legal remedy: civil rights law. At first, black women who complained often were advised to file race discrimination claims against their employers.[2] But by the end of the decade, feminists had succeeded in defining sexual harassment as sex discrimination.

African American women played a pivotal role in transforming the definition of sex discrimination to include sexual harassment. Black plaintiffs brought many of the early cases. Government officials such as Eleanor Holmes Norton were among the first to recognize and combat sexual harassment.[3] Feminist scholars—most famously, Catharine MacKinnon—conceived sophisticated theories of sexual harassment that self-consciously and selectively invoked analogies to race.[4] Precedents from the law of racial harassment aided the lawyers who crafted legal arguments against sexual harassment.[5] Parallels to race helped judges to see sexual abuse of women in the workplace as discrimination based on sex.[6]

In a way, African American women were too successful in universalizing their experience: once women of all races could claim violation, the particular underpinnings of black women's claims were obscured. Race remained virtually invisible in most court opinions analyzing sexual harassment claims.[7] By 1980, when the EEOC issued sexual harassment guidelines for public comment, some advocates worried that policy makers had forgotten the roots of sexual harassment law in the experiences of black women. They insisted that for women of color, sexual harassment could not be separated from racial subordination.[8]

African American women's pioneering role and the prominent place of analogies to race in the development of sexual harassment law under Title VII are well known to scholars. Far less attention has been paid to similar patterns in constitutional cases. Supreme Court opinions in constitutional sex equality cases typically featured white plaintiffs and mentioned race as an abstract analogue to sex, if at all. The absence of intersections between race and sex in these decisions masks a historical reality: African American plaintiffs frequently brought groundbreaking constitutional sex equality claims, often in cases with prominent racial dimensions. From employment restrictions on unmarried mothers to sex-segregated education to jury service, equality claims emerged from contexts in which race and sex were inseparable. But as these claims moved through the courts, race faded from view, except as a comparator.

These largely forgotten cases relied on alternative visions of equality whose recovery alters our understanding of feminist legal advocacy in the 1970s.[9] Strands of activism and constitutional case law often viewed as distinct or divergent were in fact intertwined. Race and sex, reproduction, equality, and sexuality intersected in social reality and in feminist strategy long after these connections disappeared from constitutional doctrine. Recapturing this history reveals what has remained hidden, and helps to explain why.

In December 1972, twenty-two-year-old Katie Mae Andrews applied for a teacher's aide position in the Drew, Mississippi, public schools. Andrews was a local success story in the Mississippi Delta's Sunflower County: with help from her family and community, she had finished college after giving birth to child while still in her teens. She was overqualified for the teacher's aide job, which required only a high school diploma. Andrews hoped the position could launch her career in education. But Drew's new school superintendent, George F. Pettey, had banned the employment of unmarried mothers. On her application form, Andrews wrote that she was single and childless. The elementary instruction coordinator, Mrs. Fred McCorkle, discovered that Andrews had a young child and no husband, and denied her the job. Andrews lived with her parents, siblings, and child, a support network that made relocation impractical. Instead, she found factory work in nearby Cleveland, Mississippi.

Andrews did not take the rejection lying down. She refused to settle for a job that she could have obtained without even a high school degree and that paid a fraction of what she could earn as a teacher's aide. Twenty-year-old Drew High School graduate Lestine Rogers, who had worked as a teacher's aide the previous school year, and at least three other women also lost their jobs because they had "illegitimate" children. Andrews and Rogers found a young attorney, Charles Victor McTeer, who filed suit in federal district court, claiming unconstitutional discrimination. The case was set for trial in March 1973 before Chief Judge William C. Keady in nearby Greenville.

The Drew superintendent's rule was part of a larger backlash against civil rights. Andrews, Rogers, and the three other young women denied employment were African Americans. Administrators Pettey and McCorkle were white, as was the (married) woman McCorkle hired as a teacher's aide. White residents in Drew had stubbornly resisted desegregation. Pettey came to Drew from Tunica County, where his school board had used public monies to fund teachers and textbooks for private "segregation academies" to which whites decamped in the wake of court-ordered desegregation in 1970.[10] Like Tunica and many other school systems in the Mississippi Delta, Drew retained only a fraction of its white student body in the wake of desegregation. Despite a student population that was now 80 percent black, the percentage of white teachers and administrators rose. At the same time, the number of African American teachers and administrators, as well as local tax dollars devoted to public education, declined precipitously. Drew school board members, in fact, all sent their own children to segregated private schools.[11]

Southern states had long used morals regulation as a weapon in defense of white supremacy. Segregationists stoked fears of sexual disorder, "miscegenation," and "mongrelization" to beat back challenges to Jim Crow.[12] After *Brown,* "pupil placement" plans allowed school officials to preserve segregation through nominally race-neutral methods, including "moral" factors such as parents' marital status. States and localities often conditioned the receipt of government benefits like Aid to Dependent Children on similar factors.[13]

Threatening the livelihood of anyone who questioned white supremacy was a venerable tradition in the Mississippi Delta.[14] The heyday of grassroots civil rights organizing had passed, but the repression that accompanied its early stirrings was still fresh in the minds of Mississippi residents. By the early 1970s, resistance to African American advancement usually took less violent forms, but Drew High School's 1971 graduation was marred by the murder of graduating student Jo Etha Collier by inebriated white men. Many in the black community attributed the killing to tension over voter registration drives. The white principal of Drew High expressed regret at Collier's death, reportedly saying that she was "a good girl. She was a black student, but she was a good girl."[15]

Pettey's rule against hiring unmarried mothers followed the tradition of pursuing by superficially neutral means what could no longer be achieved by law. The burden of Superintendent Pettey's policy fell mainly on African American women. Young white women who became pregnant out of wedlock traditionally were sent to homes for unwed mothers and relinquished their children for adoption. Neither homes for unwed mothers nor adoption services included black women and their children in their clientele. African Americans expected to raise their "illegitimate" children, often with the help of extended family.[16] Knowledge about family planning and access to contraceptives remained limited in rural black communities and, in towns like Drew, recorded nonmarital births occurred almost exclusively among black women. Teaching in the black public schools had been one of the few professions open to African Americans, especially women, in the segregated South.[17] Pettey claimed to be concerned about a rise in "schoolgirl pregnancies" in Drew, arguing that unwed mothers were poor role models for children. But to Drew's black community, his rule was part and parcel of a campaign to forestall integration.

District Judge Keady seemed an unlikely champion of civil rights. The fifth child of an Irish saloonkeeper and a nurse with roots in the Southern plantation aristocracy, Keady had attended the Greenville, Mississippi, public schools and had married a kindergarten classmate. Born without a right forearm or hand, Keady excelled in athletics as well as academics. He decided early to be a lawyer, working his way through college and law school on scholarship to Washington University in St. Louis. After a brief stint in the Mississippi legislature during World War II, he returned to Greenville to practice law for the next twenty-odd years before his nomination to the bench by President Lyndon B. Johnson.

Keady was confirmed by the Senate on April 3, 1968; by the time he reached his home in Mississippi the next evening, Martin Luther King, Jr. was dead and the nation's capital in flames.[18] Less than two months later, the Supreme Court declared the minimal desegregation produced by "freedom of choice" plans unconstitutional in *Green v. New Kent County School Board*.[19] Keady later wrote, "Had I known the Green decision was just around the corner, my eagerness for the federal bench would have been considerably diminished."

The judge soon found himself under fire from all sides. The Justice Department and civil rights activists berated him for moving too slowly, local school boards resisted desegregation, and irate white Southerners assured him in "blunt letters" that they could not forgive betrayal by "a son of the Mississippi Delta."[20] During his early years on the bench, Keady developed a reputation as a strong supporter of civil rights protesters' First Amendment rights, and by the time of the Andrews hearings, he had declared the brutal conditions in Mississippi prisons unconstitutional.[21] Every pro–civil rights ruling he issued earned him an eruption of hate mail, but Keady strove to maintain cordial relationships with everyone from segregationist Senator James O. Eastland to NAACP leader Aaron Henry and the civil rights lawyers who—often successfully—argued cases before him. Keady's early attempts to follow higher courts' desegregation mandates reflected his conviction that requiring immediate integration, particularly in the elementary grades, would "devastate" the public school system. He often disagreed with the methods prescribed by the courts above, though not with the principle of ending segregation.[22]

Andrews's lawyer, Charles Victor McTeer, had just moved to Greenville in 1973. Orphaned in early childhood, McTeer was raised by his great-aunt in a black middle-class neighborhood of Baltimore. One of less than a dozen black students at Westminster College in Maryland, he pledged a previously all-white fraternity, but resigned in anger and dismay at his fraternity brothers' jubilant reaction to Dr. King's assassination. Shortly thereafter, McTeer spent his first summer in Mississippi. His admiration for Fannie Lou Hamer and other civil rights activists in the Delta moved McTeer to accept a scholarship to Rutgers in Newark, home of civil rights lawyer Arthur Kinoy. There, Morty Stavis, Kinoy's cofounder of the Center for Constitutional Rights (CCR), became McTeer's mentor. McTeer moved to the historically all-black town of Mound Bayou after his graduation from law school in 1972, thinking he would stay about a year. Soon he had his first client—Katie Mae Andrews.[23]

McTeer had been practicing law only a few months, and his opponents were seasoned defenders of Southern states and localities. The school district's attorney, Champ Terney, had served in the University of Mississippi's student government during convulsive battles over integration and had married the daughter of Senator Eastland. Terney now regularly represented Mississippi state officials. His expert witness, Ernest van den Haag, a prominent defender of racial segregation in the 1950s, had recently credited theories of genetic racial inferiority. Van den Haag's participation apparently secured the testimony of the social psychologist Kenneth B. Clark, whose "doll studies" were cited by the Supreme Court in Brown as evidence of the psychological harm of segregation. Van den Haag and Clark had clashed in court and in print before; now they testified by deposition from New York.

Most riveting was the live testimony of Fannie Lou Hamer, a native of Sunflower County. Long a crusader for voting rights, Hamer had become increasingly involved in campaigns for school desegregation and educational equity. In 1970, on the sixteenth anniversary of Brown, she had filed a class action suit challenging Sunflower County's failure to implement a recent court-ordered desegregation plan. Hamer headed a biracial committee whose proposals to protect the jobs of black teachers and administrators had been largely adopted by Judge Keady.[24] Now, Keady accepted her testimony over Terney's objection, holding that Hamer was qualified to speak as a representative of the black community in Sunflower County.[25]

The Andrews hearings showcased struggles over race, sex, sexuality, reproduction, employment, and morality. The school district defended Pettey's policy as a "common-sense" reaction to rising "schoolgirl pregnancies" in Drew. White school officials argued that school employees could not set a proper moral example for their pupils if they had children out of wedlock. Pettey, McCorkle, and other white witnesses denied that the policy was racially motivated. They admitted that the rule likely excluded more black applicants than white applicants, but they insisted that was not discriminatory. Instead, they argued, the policy was essential to support for public education. School administrator and education professor Hal Buchanan predicted an "uprising" among white parents if Pettey's policy were suspended.[26] Ruby Nell Stancil, a high school math teacher and twenty-two-year veteran of the Drew school system, confirmed that the remaining white students would leave the public schools if unwed mothers were allowed to teach.[27]

The plaintiffs and their lawyers framed the Pettey rule as discrimination disguised as morals regulation. In terms of raw numbers, they had a strong case. All five applicants denied jobs under the policy were African American women. Recorded nonmarital births occurred more than ten times as often among black as among white Mississippians. As many as 40 percent of African American students in Drew were born to unmarried parents.

It was even more difficult for the school district to maintain that Pettey's rule would affect men and women similarly. Pettey freely admitted that the policy would be almost impossible to enforce against unwed fathers. When it came to pregnancy, he noted, women, not men, were "stuck with the result." When asked how she knew that the only male teacher's aide in the elementary school did not have any illegitimate children, McCorkle replied, "He is married." Nevertheless, the school district insisted that the rule was race- and sex-neutral, that it applied to black and white, male and female alike.

Judge Keady certified Mrs. Hamer as an expert on black community morality, but her testimony became a lesson in race, gender, and political economy. She excoriated a policy that prevented young black women from achieving economic independence through education and gainful employment. "[W]e all agree," Mrs. Hamer told Terney, "that these young womens are not really on trial. You are trying all of us. Because when you say we are lifting ourselves up and you tell us to get off of welfare, then when peoples try to go to school to get off of welfare to support themselves, this is another way of knocking them down." Again and again, she emphasized the devastating impact Pettey's rule would have on young mothers trying to escape poverty and oppression. "You always tell us . . . we have got so many kids on the welfare roll, 'Why don't you get up and do something?' And then when we start doing something, 'You don't have any business being that high.'"[28]

Hamer steadfastly denied that African American culture encouraged or condoned "illegitimacy." Rather, she testified, the black community honored women like Andrews and Rogers for obtaining education and employment against all odds. She scoffed at the notion that extramarital sexual relations occurred more often among African Americans than among whites. Hamer had "worked for white people for years" and knew that the relative paucity of illegitimate children in white households did not reflect any greater sexual purity. If Pettey's rule truly applied to all school employees who had ever engaged in nonmarital sex, she said, "[w]hen you get back to Drew this evening, lock up the doors. There won't be any school." The fact that only black women suffered under Pettey's rule made the policy's underlying racial motivation obvious, Hamer contended.

The connection between *Andrews* and the civil rights struggle became still plainer when Mae Bertha Carter, an African American mother of thirteen whose lawsuit had desegregated the Drew school system, testified for the plaintiffs. The Carter family had braved violence, destitution, and ostracism to send eight children to the otherwise all-white Drew schools under a "freedom of choice" regime in the mid-1960s.[29] Mrs. Carter said that she knew Katie Mae Andrews as an upstanding citizen and would feel perfectly comfortable having Ms. Andrews teach her children.[30]

The presence of Hamer and Carter in the courtroom underscored the origins of *Andrews* in the struggle over school desegregation; the issue of sex discrimination became increasingly prominent as the case progressed. Kenneth B. Clark's deposition explained how the Pettey rule used the regulation of sex to subordinate women. What Hamer spoke of with blunt candor, Clark elaborated with the erudition of academic social science. Pettey's policy was part of "a long history of discrimination against females on matters of sex and sexual behavior . . . designed to subordinate females to an essentially inferior role, which the power of our society is mobilized to reinforce." Clark dispelled the notion that unwed parenthood was the result of mediocre moral character or even a greater propensity to engage in nonmarital sex: "[I]t has to do only with the degree of sophistication necessary to control the consequence" of sexual intercourse—that is, knowledge of and access to contraception. A teacher's unmarried parental status would not influence students to emulate such behavior, unless undue attention was drawn to that status—for instance, by a punitive policy like Pettey's, he argued. Clark concluded, "It is a dehumanizing rule in that it imposes upon human beings a stigma which to me is absolutely unnecessary."[31] He could have given similar testimony in a case involving white female plaintiffs, although by invoking the language of stigma and badges of inferiority, Clark called upon the vocabulary as well as the pedigree of the civil rights movement.

Clark's emphasis on women's subordination may have resulted from his consultation with feminists in New York. Recognizing the dual racial and gender implications of the case, McTeer used his CCR and Rutgers connections to solicit the assistance of feminist lawyers, including Rhonda Copelon and Nancy Stearns, CCR attorneys who taught in the Rutgers women's law clinic and had been deeply involved in reproductive rights litigation since before *Roe*. *Andrews* raised many of the issues in which CCR was already invested: sex discrimination, reproductive rights, and racial inequality. For the feminists of CCR, the case provided a rare opportunity to address the intersections between race, sex, and reproductive freedom in collaboration with colleagues whose primary allegiance was to the civil rights struggle. They also shared information with attorneys at the EEOC.

For the twenty-four-year-old McTeer, CCR and the EEOC provided valuable experience and resources. McTeer's legal career was in its infancy when Katie Mae Andrews approached him about taking her case. The complaint he drafted did not allege a Title VII violation, though it did contain several other constitutional and statutory claims, including discrimination based on "race, sex, and single-parent status" and a denial of the due process right of parents to raise their children without undue interference.[32]

Amicus briefs from CCR and the EEOC elaborated McTeer's arguments, drawing on the knowledge of repeat players in reproductive freedom and employment discrimination litigation. Andrews's supporters emphasized that unwed parents, male and female, shared responsibility for the conception of children out of wedlock. The Pettey rule, they said, penalized mothers for nurturing their children while rewarding fathers for abandoning their offspring. Such policies perpetuated age-old techniques of subordination, they argued, including the regulation of sexuality and restrictions on women's employment.

Andrews was not the first lawsuit to challenge employment rules that penalized unmarried mothers. Earlier cases, too, featured women of color claiming both race and sex discrimination. A 1968 suit filed by the NAACP LDF against Southwestern Bell, for instance, included claims that the employer's exclusion of "unwed mothers" violated Title VII's ban on race discrimination. Arkansas federal district court judge Jesse Smith Henley rejected the LDF's arguments. Heley said the fact that "more Negro women have illegitimate children than do white women" was "interesting sociologically," but he found a rule that "bears more heavily on an underprivileged ethnic or racial group" acceptable, so long as it is adopted "in good faith." Southwestern Bell had a "legitimate interest at least to a point in the sexual behavior of its employees and their morale while at work. A woman who has had an illegitimate child," he wrote, "can well have an upsetting effect on other employees." Even if it were true, as he put it, that "certain classes of Negroes have a different attitude toward extramarital sex than do most white people," Title VII did not "require an employer to conform his standards to the Negro attitude."[33]

Henley did not consider whether the prohibition on employing un-wed mothers might constitute sex discrimination. Over the next few years, others did. Rejected for a job as a telephone operator, an African American woman filed a race discrimination charge with the EEOC in 1970; the employer responded that she had not been hired because of her status as an unwed mother. The Commission found that because 80 percent of "illegitimate" births in the surrounding community were to "non-white females," the policy was racially discriminatory. Refusing to hire unwed mothers was also sex discrimination, the EEOC ruled. Even if the employer attempted to apply the "illegitimacy standard" to unwed fathers as well, the decision noted, "it's a wise employer indeed that knows which of its male applicants truthfully answered its illegitimacy inquiry." Thus the "foreseeable and certain impact of an illegitimacy standard . . . is to deprive females . . . of employment opportunities."[34]

Shortly after the Supreme Court approved the disparate impact theory in *Griggs* v. *Duke Power Company*, a Puerto Rican woman successfully sued the NYPD with the help of the Legal Aid Society after she was rejected for a job as school crossing guard. She had been disqualified on grounds of "character" because she was "the mother of eight children by five differ-ent fathers." Observing that Sofia Cirino was "Puerto Rican and poor," and that a quarter of births to Puerto Rican New Yorkers were "illegitimate," Judge Andrew Tyler ruled that Cirino's "life style is too prevalent in her community to reflect against her 'character.'" Cirino had a "glowing letter of reference" from her previous job as a substitute teacher's aide, and "[a]lthough . . . supported by Welfare," she "want[ed] to work, and does when work is available." Cirino's evident "competence and 'character'" made her exclusion "not only arbitrary, but illegal as discrimination . . . because of race and sex." Tyler wrote, citing *Griggs:* "If more Puerto Ricans have children out of wedlock than Caucasians, then a refusal of a position on that ground affects them more and is discriminatory. If the fact of children is more easily discovered about the mother who looks after them than the father who does not, then it is discriminatory against women."[35] Tyler's opinion anticipated many of the arguments Andrews's lawyers would later raise.

But schoolteachers had a tougher row to hoe than other employees challenging restrictions on the employment of unwed mothers. For one thing, until 1972, teachers usually had to rely on the Constitution, since Title VII did not yet apply to public employment. Moreover, teachers' traditional influence on children's moral development made such challenges especially sensitive. Courts usually afforded local school boards broad discretion to dismiss teachers on "moral" grounds, including unwed pregnancy and homosexuality.

Andrews's timing was fortuitous: she filed her suit at the peak of the law's efficacy for addressing equality claims. The Court was newly receptive to sex discrimination and abortion rights cases; legislative amendments made Title VII applicable to public school employment; and several lower courts had invalidated mandatory maternity leaves and other pregnancy-based discrimination under the equal protection clause. Some judges were recognizing race-based disparate impact claims under the Constitution as well as Title VII. In early March 1973, major setbacks—such as the Court's refusal to consider wealth-based classifications suspect and its declaration that pregnancy discrimination did not violate the equal protection clause—still lay in the future.[36]

Andrews's supporters tried to capitalize on the salutary constitutional developments of the previous two years. Practically speaking, they charged, the Pettey rule could not be applied equally to men and women: as CCR's brief put it, "[T]he father rarely admits his involvement or paternity, nor is it easily established," whereas a mother "is bound up in an inevitable biological and physical relationship to the

child . . . she . . . may have no alternative but to assume the social responsibility of rearing that child."[37] Recent sex equality decisions had established that it was impermissible to treat "similarly situated" men and
women differently. Here, Andrews's lawyers argued, men and women
"share[d] equally . . . whatever moral disability defendant attaches to
non-marital sexual relations and the parenting of an out-of-wedlock
child."[38] The plaintiffs also drew upon recent pregnancy discrimination
cases to support their contention that such sex-based classifications were
unconstitutional.

Even though McTeer had not brought a Title VII claim, the fluidity
of antidiscrimination law allowed the plaintiffs to draw on disparate impact analysis developed in statutory cases.[39] Given the "ten-to-one ratio
between out-of-wedlock children born to black and white women," the
policy's racially disparate impact was severe. Therefore, CCR argued, the
rule "comes under the ban on [facially neutral policies that] have the effect of disproportionately disqualifying or burdening blacks."[40]

The intersection of race and sex discrimination itself justified more
rigorous review of the Drew policy, CCR lawyers argued to Judge
Keady. The Pettey rule embodied a "conjunction of race and sex bias"
that should shift the burden to the school district to justify a "compelling
state interest" in the rule, CCR contended. The Supreme Court had not
established strict scrutiny as the proper standard of review for either sex-
based classifications or facially neutral policies with a racially disparate
impact. But in early 1973, such expansive interpretations of the equal
protection clause had not yet been foreclosed.

If the rule's dual race- and sex-discriminatory impact did not warrant the strictest scrutiny, CCR argued, then its impingement on reproductive freedom did.[41] Rhonda Copelon recalled, "We were doing a lot
of sex and reproductive rights cases, so the two aspects of feminist work,
which in a lot of places were separated, were really joined for us at
CCR."[42] The Supreme Court had just overturned blanket prohibitions
on abortion in *Roe v. Wade. Andrews* implicated the flip side of the abortion coin—the right to bear children without losing one's livelihood.
Copelon's colleague Jan Goodman explained, "We are arguing that all
women should have the freedom to choose . . . whatever the choice is,
to bear the child or to abort." As a CCR motion in *Andrews* put it, "Just
as employment could not be withdrawn or withheld from a woman who
exercised her fundamental right to abortion, so also for the woman who

exercised her fundamental right to procreate."[43] Ginsburg made similar arguments in Air Force nurse Susan Struck's challenge to military policies requiring the dismissal of pregnant service members around the same time.[44] Like Struck, Katie Mae Andrews had religious objections to abortion. She testified, "God put us here on earth and if it came up to that I feel that we should have them, you know. If we try to get rid of it, as most people do, that's killing it. Well, you know where we would wind up then."[45]

Moreover, for many African American women, the right to abortion seemed less pressing than an end to coercive measures of fertility control. Involuntary sterilization of African American women was rampant in Mississippi in the 1960s and 1970s; unnecessary hysterectomies became so common they were known locally as "Mississippi appendectomies." Fannie Lou Hamer estimated in 1964 that as many as 60 percent of the black women, married and unmarried, who entered Sunflower County Hospital, emerged with their "tubes tied." In the early 1960s, Mississippi legislators tried to pass a bill criminalizing illegitimate births among unmarried mothers receiving welfare; in lieu of jail, they proposed, women could "choose" to be sterilized.[46] In the 1970s, advocates at CCR and elsewhere worked to expose and oppose the use of federal dollars to fund coercive reproductive control measures around the country.[47]

Lawsuits to combat sterilization abuse foregrounded race discrimination and poverty rather than sex discrimination. In 1973, the Southern Poverty Law Center filed suit on behalf of Minnie Lee Relf, a twelve-year-old Alabama girl sterilized without her parents' consent.[48] Minnie Relf's lawyers did not make sex equality arguments; they relied primarily on the right to privacy in matters of family life and procreation culminating in *Roe v. Wade,* decided only a few months earlier.[49] But the Supreme Court was poised for a breakthrough in constitutional sex equality law. Shortly after the *Andrews* hearings, on May 14, 1973, the Court declared discrimination between husbands and wives in the allocation of military housing and medical benefits unconstitutional in *Frontiero v. Richardson.* McTeer quickly filed a supplemental memorandum of law arguing that sex was now a suspect classification. A few weeks later, Judge Keady ruled for Katie Mae Andrews and her compatriots.

Keady's opinion soundly rejected the school district's use of nonmarital childbirth as a proxy for immorality. "The unconstitutional vice . . . is that it conclusively presumes the parent's immorality or bad

moral character from the single fact of a child born out of wedlock."
Childbirth might or might not be voluntary, he stressed. Either way, extramarital sex should not permanently stain a mother's reputation. "A
person could live an impeccable life, yet be barred as unfit for employment for an event, whether the result of indiscretion or not, occurring
at any time in the past. In short," he wrote, "the rule leaves no consideration for the multitudinous circumstances under which illegitimate
childbirth may occur and which may have little, if any, bearing on the
parent's present moral worth."

Keady held that the Pettey rule was an irrational means to a dubious
end: "While obviously aimed at discouraging premarital sex relations,
the policy's effect," he noted, "is apt to encourage abortion." He called
the rule "mischievous and prejudicial" for requiring those who adminis-
tered the policy to "investigate" the parental status of school employees
and prospective applicants. "Where no stigma may have existed before,
such inquisitions by overzealous officialdom can rapidly create it," Keady
wrote. He held that the policy violated equal protection and due process
under the most lenient standard of rational basis review. And he offered
an alternative ground for his decision: that the policy's "essentially discriminatory effect . . . upon unmarried women is inescapable," rendering it a suspect classification of the sort condemned by a plurality of the
Supreme Court in *Frontiero*.[50]

The plaintiffs were overjoyed at Keady's strong language and at his
(admittedly questionable) interpretation of *Frontiero* as prescribing strict
scrutiny for sex-based classifications. "It was thrilling," Copelon later recalled, "he really got it. He could have said women are different, [preg-
nancy] shows on women and not on men, but he didn't, he really looked
at how the conduct being punished was the same for men and women."[51]

Some reacted less enthusiastically. One letter to the editor of the
Jackson *Clarion-Ledger* compared Keady to Hitler and opined that "for a
federal judge to order the tax paying workers of this state to subsidize
bastardry is the height of asininity."[52] A scathing column condemned
Keady for supporting the "Drew adulteresses" and endorsing "breeding
kids out of wedlock." A handwritten note to Keady personalized the
criticism further: "I don't think you are any better than these Heifers.
Decent white people should not have anything to do with you or your
family."[53] More moderate in tone was a letter signed by Frank Wallace
and H. V. Mahan: "[N]o Mississippi school board would hire a white un-

wed mother, so there can be no legitimate claim of discrimination when one refuses to hire a black unwed mother. . . . The best hope for all of us, including blacks, is that they move toward our standards, not we theirs."[54] Local reaction painted the case as being primarily about race and what some whites saw as the dire implications of desegregation for sexual morality.

In contrast, Keady's decision did not directly address the intersection of race, sex, and reproductive regulation. Although Keady mentioned the rule's exclusive application to black women, he did not base his decision on the policy's racial impact. He could have written virtually the same opinion in a case involving white plaintiffs. Keady discussed the unfairness of penalizing women harshly and indefinitely for giving birth to a child while unmarried and noted the rule's encouragement of abortion. But he did not rule on the plaintiffs' reproductive freedom arguments.

On appeal, CCR and the EEOC hoped to persuade the court to consider the race and reproductive freedom issues that had been so central to the *Andrews* hearings. But their request to participate in oral argument before the Fifth Circuit was denied.[55] In the end, the three-judge appellate panel affirmed Keady's ruling on traditional equal protection and due process grounds and expressly refused to endorse his application of strict scrutiny.[56] The school district's final appeal, to the Supreme Court, was feminists' last chance to raise the intersections of race and sex discrimination, equality and liberty, reproduction and employment.

The school district hoped to dodge such issues. The real question, lawyers for Mississippi argued, was whether "unwed parents of illegitimate children" were "constitutionally protected."[57] To the Supreme Court, the state stressed the Pettey rule's race- and sex-neutrality, and accused the plaintiffs of trading in racial stereotypes. Plaintiffs' expert Ronald Samuda had suggested that black and white Americans held fundamentally different values with respect to nonmarital childbearing. The school district's brief quipped, "[I]t is somewhat ironical that in 1975 plaintiffs who are members of the class which sued this school district to bring about total integration are now . . . asking this Court to turn back the clock and . . . treat the populace of the Drew school district as two separate and distinct cultural groups."[58]

This argument exposed one of the dilemmas facing opponents of the Pettey rule: they struggled to explain how the rule was racially discriminatory without suggesting that African American culture somehow encouraged or condoned "schoolgirl pregnancies." One of McTeer's submissions to Judge Keady had characterized the Pettey rule as "creat[ing] a preference for the white middle class values favoring contraception, abortion, and the pill, while penalizing the black community's reality of the matriarchal society, black unwed childbirth and childraising."[59] The CCR lawyers conducted extensive research, scouring everything from sociological studies of black family life to Mississippi illegitimacy statutes, from Myrdal's *An American Dilemma* to Hawthorne's *The Scarlet Letter*.[60] Their arguments drew on social science literature that characterized the "matriarchal" family structure as a "fundamentally positive survival mechanism," as the brief put it. "It was the deliberate conscious policy of the slaveholder to dispute and prevent marriage and cohesiveness among Blacks," CCR argued. Recent laws and government policies "perpetuated this centrifugal pressure on poor, largely Black families." Aid to Families with Dependent Children, for instance, created a "family-splitting incentive." This historical context revealed that the school district's policy could "[not] be separated from its roots in the most vicious legal discrimination imaginable."[61]

The plaintiffs also faced a delicate task in making constitutional race discrimination arguments. Much had changed since 1973, when Andrews filed suit. Then, it seemed possible that courts would allow disparate impact claims under the equal protection clause as well as Title VII. The controversy over disparate impact had deepened by early 1976, when *Andrews* was argued. The Court had already agreed to consider whether disparate impact analysis applied in constitutional cases.[62] Andrews's supporters were careful to assure the Justices that they need not resolve this difficult question in *Andrews*. They emphasized the "inevitable" impact of the Pettey rule primarily on African American women and the "fundamental rights" denied them.[63] In case disparate impact was not enough, Andrews's lawyers highlighted evidence that the policy was part of a larger pattern of intentional racial discrimination.

Despite its prominence in his courtroom, Judge Keady's opinion said little about race, and the Fifth Circuit opinion offered even less. The plaintiffs tried to reintroduce the issue by underscoring how recently school desegregation had taken place. They described Pettey's involvement in "perpetuating racial segregation in the Tunica County school system," and reprinted in footnotes earlier statements by the school district's expert, Ernest van den Haag, suggesting that African Americans might be genetically inferior to whites.[64]

After submitting their main brief to the Court, Andrews's lawyers found what they hoped would be their smoking gun. In August 1973, the plaintiffs in Mae Bertha Carter's suit against the Drew school district had challenged faculty hiring and recruitment policies; the defendants' answer revealed that only 47 percent of teachers in the district were black in the 1973–1974 school year, compared with 67 percent in 1969–1970. After court-ordered desegregation in 1970, "the ranks of black faculty were decimated, while white faculty increased."[65] In 1976, Andrews's lawyers argued in a supplemental brief that "Mr. Pettey's rule, adopted during a period of 'whitening' of the faculty, was in fact a race-based classification, both in purpose and impact."[66] By amassing additional circumstantial evidence of racial discrimination, Andrews's attorneys hoped to persuade the Court that Pettey's ban on unwed mothers disfavored African Americans by design.

Emerging contradictions and persistent uncertainties in constitutional sex equality law also complicated feminists' task. By early 1976, the Court had backed away from making sex a suspect classification but had not yet settled on a standard of review. And the Justices had sent mixed signals about whether sex equality principles applied in cases involving reproductive differences between women and men. In 1971, the Court had invalidated the denial of custody to unmarried fathers without a hearing, suggesting that the law no longer considered unwed fathers automatically irrelevant to their children's lives.[67] But the 1974 decision in *Geduldig v. Aiello* upheld the exclusion of pregnancy from California's disability benefits program, implying that where pregnancy was concerned, the government could leave women "stuck with the result" without violating the equal protection clause.[68]

Feminists tried to nudge sex equality law forward while assuring the Court that existing precedents supported their position. A brief from the ACLU Women's Rights Project (WRP) and Equal Rights Advocates, signed by lawyers including Ruth Bader Ginsburg and Wendy Webster Williams, declared that Pettey's rule "presents an unwarranted return to the times during which stigmatization of unwed mothers was a tool, along with forced pregnancy, compulsory marriage and deprivation of birth control information, by which women were kept in their legal and societal place."[69] *Andrews* thus reflected "the historical and legal reasons

for holding that sex, like race, should be viewed as a suspect category."
But the Court need not revisit the question of strict scrutiny for sex-
based classifications, the brief argued. Singling out unwed mothers while
sparing fathers was not even rationally related to the school district's
stated goal of providing role models to impressionable students.[70]

Andrews's supporters also sought to capitalize on the Court's newly
critical, if somewhat inconsistent, attitude toward classifications based on
illegitimacy.[71] In the early 1970s, equal protection challenges invalidated
laws that treated nonmarital children differently from marital children
with respect to, for example, the right to sue for the wrongful death of a
parent, or to claim survivors' benefits, welfare funds, or child support.[72]
The Pettey rule, Andrews's lawyers argued, encouraged parents to abandon their children and burdened "mother and child as a family unit."
The policy stigmatized nonmarital children and sentenced them to almost certain poverty, an amicus brief from the Child Welfare League of
America stressed. These arguments were familiar from earlier cases
where antipoverty and civil rights lawyers focused on children's rights in
challenging classifications based on illegitimacy.

The lawyers in *Andrews* broke new ground, however, in linking
illegitimacy-based classifications with both race and sex discrimination.
Classifications based on illegitimacy had long intersected with sex and
race inequality, but court decisions failed to address these connections.[73]
"This is the first case," CCR's *Andrews* brief declared, "wherein the
Court is squarely presented with the inherently discriminatory impact
on women of an illegitimacy classification." In practice, they said, the
policy forced unmarried mothers to sacrifice their careers, depend on
welfare, or move to another jurisdiction far from their families and support systems. CCR's briefs also linked penalties for illegitimacy to racial
discrimination against schoolchildren whose parents were unmarried.
Andrews's lawyers invoked *Brown's* language about stigma: "[T]he
School District perpetuates the precise evil repudiated by this Court in
[*Brown*], namely, the branding of these Black students with a badge of
inferiority."[74]

The CCR lawyers continued to argue that the Pettey rule violated
women's freedom to procreate. In the years before and since Katie Mae
Andrews filed her lawsuit, Copelon and her colleagues fought to ensure
poor women's access to abortion. CCR also collaborated with the Committee to End Sterilization Abuse (CESA) to advance the right to bear

children as well as the right not to do so.[75] In early 1970s lawsuits, feminists argued that discharging pregnant women or forcing them to take unpaid mandatory leave impermissibly required them to choose between motherhood and gainful employment.[76] But the Court had largely ignored feminists' invitation to fuse reproductive freedom and sex equality in this way. When *Andrews* reached the Supreme Court, CCR renewed the argument that local officials could not "condition employment upon a willingness and ability to avoid pregnancy by effective contraception or to terminate a pregnancy by abortion."[77]

Andrews presented the Court with issues that intersected frequently in the lives of poor Americans, but infrequently in constitutional jurisprudence. The plaintiffs pressed their novel argument for applying a higher level of scrutiny to the Pettey policy. Andrews's brief cited the "unusual confluence of fundamental rights and interests" implicated in the case, which, they argued, merited particularly rigorous review. They framed the challenged policy's position at the intersection of race, sex, privacy, procreation, and liberty as itself worthy of special scrutiny. The Court's decision to hear the case seemed to ratify Copelon's later observation that "[i]t was a time when the more rights and discriminations you could throw at the court, the more likely you would get into the Supreme Court."[78]

The clerk who reviewed Andrews's petition for certiorari recommended hearing the case, as he thought the question of whether the policy had a rational basis was "close." His assessment turned out to be an accurate reflection of the split among the Justices. Six members of the Court voted to hear the case, with Brennan, Marshall, and Powell in the minority, preferring to let the lower court ruling stand. Once cert was granted, these three Justices were also inclined to affirm on the merits. So was Blackmun, at first. Brennan and Marshall argued that the policy was sex discrimination, pure and simple. Powell had doubts about the lower courts' reasoning, but believed the result was probably sound.[79] Burger, White, and Rehnquist wanted to reverse. To them, the rule's flaws were a matter of policy within the prerogatives of a school board and superintendent.

Although the Justices disagreed profoundly on the merits of the case, many of them were far from eager to wade into the murky waters of disparate impact analysis, the scope of reproductive rights and privacy, and the relationship between illegitimacy classifications, racial oppression, and sex discrimination. As the National Education Association (NEA)'s amicus brief put it, the Andrews case "bristle[d] with constitutional issues of broad importance," all of them thorny.[80]

Powell's instincts (and his clerks) told him that the policy was constitutionally infirm. But he despaired of finding an analytical framework that did not lead to uncomfortable doctrinal forays.[81] He apparently agreed with clerk Carl Schenker's assessment that "the constitutional questions lurking around this case [were] . . . very difficult." Not only did the case implicate disparate impact theory, it "pose[d] serious questions about the scope of the right to privacy and the legitimacy of the State's proselytizing for traditional moral values."[82] Schenker thought it might be possible to construct an "appropriately narrow" rule "to prevent school teachers from encouraging anti-establishment moral behavior." But in *Andrews,* he wrote, "a yahoo promulgated a ridiculously overinclusive rule just because he didn't like having unwed parents around the school." Schenker concluded, "I think the Court should be wary about getting dragged into this case."[83]

Meanwhile, Blackmun's notes on the case, recorded prior to oral argument, evince some sympathy for the superintendent. Pettey "thought this was one way to attack the problem [of schoolgirl pregnancies] which obviously bothered him," Blackmun wrote. He doubted that the rule's disproportionate impact on African Americans was determinative: "Well, here we are in the middle of a small Southern town with a distinct concern for the increase in schoolgirl pregnancies and with a statistical record of illegitimate births among Negroes being 13 to 14 times greater than among whites. . . . Naturally enough, a rule such as this would have greater impact upon Negroes. . . . Should that fact, however, in and of itself nullify a rule such as this? It strikes me as . . . bootstrapping." He acknowledged "the destruction of the black family over the years," and that "[b]irth control is less available to the Negro for reasons of education and finances." But, he felt, "the situation is a difficult one and a very present problem." Blackmun apparently had not familiarized himself with the parties' racial identities or the fraught recent history of desegregation in the district. He "wonder[ed]" whether the superintendent was "Negro or white."

Blackmun resisted feminists' interpretation of the case as raising questions of sex discrimination. He characterized the ACLU's submission as "one of the those extreme briefs going back 50 or 60 years and citing some of the sex bias literature of that day in order to show that what is done in this day is unjustifiable." The Fifth Circuit's approach— finding a lack of a rational relationship between means and ends under traditional equal protection analysis—seemed best to Blackmun. Despite his misgivings about feminists' more ambitious claims, he "doubt[ed]" whether there was "any alternative than to affirm."[84]

But by the time of oral arguments, Blackmun had changed his mind. Blackmun's notes described McTeer as a "large N, light suit, outrageous, emotional," while Copelon he characterized as a "NY Ms." More substantively, Blackmun credited the school district's argument that it was only required to justify its action with respect to Andrews and Rogers, since the lawsuit was not a class action. The arguments on Andrews's side, on the other hand, were "no help." Blackmun wrote, "This is a rational conn[ection] for me," and reiterated his determination to "avoid [a] sex-based" ruling. Pettey's rule was "perhaps too broad, but not for the plaintiffs."[85] At conference, Blackmun indicated that if the Court reached the merits, he would vote to reverse.

By that point, though, the chances that the Court would reach the merits were slim. The NEA and the Solicitor General's office urged the Court to dismiss the appeal as improvidently granted—a "DIG," in Court terminology. New Title IX regulations issued by the Department of Health, Education, and Welfare in July 1975, three months after the Court granted cert in *Andrews,* prohibited public schools from making "pre-admission inquir[ies] as to the marital status of an applicant." They also banned "discriminat[ing] against or "exclud[ing] from employment any employee or applicant for employment on the basis of pregnancy, childbirth, false pregnancy, termination of pregnancy, or recovery therefrom," unless the employer could show that "such action [was] essential to successful operation of the employment function concerned."[86] These new regulations also incorporated a disparate impact standard similar to Title VII's.[87] Now that Title VII applied to public employers, including school districts, rules like Pettey's would almost certainly be vulnerable to disparate impact attack. "There can be no doubt," argued the NEA brief, that the Drew rule had "a significantly disproportionate impact on females and blacks."[88] Thus the school district would have to defend its policy against the stringent business necessity standard. A short memorandum for the United States as amicus curiae supported the NEA's position that the regulations "diminishe[d] the need for resolving the broad constitutional issues presented by the parties."[89]

The Justices greeted these invitations to dismiss with palpable relief. At conference, Chief Justice Burger supported the solicitor general's recommendation to DIG the case. Stewart and Powell agreed enthusiastically, and Brennan and Marshall seemed receptive. Stevens, who had joined the Court since the grant of certiorari, said he would affirm on the merits. But he also said he was not opposed to a DIG, although he noted that such a dismissal would imply that the case was indeed about sex discrimination. White and Rehnquist expressed concern about a DIG, apparently for this reason.[90] In the end, the Justices agreed to dismiss the case in a one-line order, without explanation. This resolution made sense to the Justices who would affirm the lower courts, because it let stand the ruling below. Those torn about the merits or uncomfortable choosing an analytical framework avoided a decision altogether. And for the Justices who would reverse on the merits, a cryptic DIG did little lasting harm.

The Court's dismissal of *Andrews* meant that the case would remain outside the feminist canon, little known even among legal scholars. Yet *Andrews* brought together strands of feminist and civil rights advocacy often understood as separate, presenting opportunities for constitutional innovation thought to have been foreclosed before the mid-1970s. The case generated close collaborations between civil rights and feminist lawyers and activists at a time when the two movements often pursued divergent priorities. Many of the canonical constitutional sex equality cases featured white plaintiffs who sought to equalize the benefits of marriage. In contrast, *Andrews* placed African American women's experience at the center of feminist legal advocacy. *Andrews* highlighted a plight common in poor communities of color: young unmarried women trying to escape from poverty and support their children.

Andrews was a rare, if not unique, constitutional sex equality case that underscored the meaning of reproductive freedom for poor women of color. The case complemented resistance to fertility control measures that targeted poor African American and Latina women. Fannie Lou Hamer had spoken out about involuntary sterilization, including her own nonconsensual hysterectomy, since the 1960s. By the mid-1970s, advocates for poor and minority women had begun to transform feminists' conception of reproductive freedom. The feminists of CCR collaborated with other activists in New York to combat sterilization abuse at the same time that they fought measures to limit federal Medicaid funding for abortion.[91] Through *Andrews,* they sought to incorporate into constitutional equal protection law a version of reproductive freedom that encompassed women's choice to have children as well as not to have them.

Andrews also exposed connections between nonmarital childbearing and race and sex inequality that earlier cases had largely suppressed. Some early challenges to welfare policies that policed single mothers' relationships with men or excluded illegitimate families from benefits included race discrimination claims, as did some challenges to laws that overtly discriminated against nonmarital children. But a combination of discouraging court decisions and strategic calculations by civil rights and antipoverty lawyers muted these lines of attack. Neither the welfare nor the illegitimacy cases characterized the challenged policies as sex discrimination, and they remained disconnected from feminist legal advocacy.[92] *Andrews* framed as unconstitutional race and sex discrimination what Hamer and others saw as the hypocritical practice of restricting black unwed mothers' employment, even as policy makers lamented growing welfare dependency.

The history of *Andrews* suggests that efforts to forge a constitutional link between reproductive rights and sex equality under the equal protection clause survived well beyond Ginsburg's failed attempt to bring Susan Struck's case against the Air Force's pregnancy discharge policy to the Supreme Court in 1972. Even after Court decisions such as *Roe v. Wade, Cleveland Board of Education v. LaFleur,* and *Geduldig v. Aiello* separated reproductive freedom from equal protection/sex equality law, feminists continued to press arguments that connected reproductive autonomy with women's economic citizenship.

And unlike previous pregnancy discrimination cases, *Andrews* unapologetically defended the rights of unmarried women to combine motherhood with gainful employment in a profession that prized moral rectitude. In that way, *Andrews* reached beyond the rights claimed by teachers like Jo Carol LaFleur, who fought school districts' mandatory maternity leave policies. Like Susan Struck's case, Katie Mae Andrews's challenge highlighted the relationship between reproductive freedom and sex equality, as well as the right of an unmarried woman to choose not to terminate an unplanned pregnancy. But Struck placed her child for adoption and sought to continue her military career; Andrews claimed the right to gainful employment *and* motherhood—without marriage.

Antidiscrimination statutes and regulations saved the Supreme Court from confronting the constitutional issues that confounded the Justices in *Andrews*. These laws applied to women and men of all races. Many of the employment discrimination cases brought by unmarried mothers in the mid-1970s and beyond did not implicate race discrimination, but instead featured sex discrimination and due process claims.[93] This proved to be a common pattern in sex equality law. Early cases, brought by people of color, framed either as race discrimination or as race and sex discrimination claims, often evolved into "pure" sex discrimination claims in later iterations, hiding their roots in racial justice movements.

Sex-segregated schooling is another little-known example of how race loomed large in early sex equality cases, but then faded away.[94] Even before the Supreme Court's decision in *Brown v. Board of Education,* sex segregation surfaced as a palliative for white Southerners' fears that racially mixed schools would lead to "mongrelization." This dread of "social equality," and especially interracial marriage, motivated many observers to suggest sex separation as a solution to the desegregation dilemma. *New York Times* columnist Arthur Krock wrote in 1956, "Apprehension that [the] steady expansion of . . . interbreeding would be the result of propinquity in mixed schools of adolescents is the basic cause of the Southern resistance." Therefore, he asserted, "the suggestion of separation by sexes goes to the heart of the controversy" over school desegregation.[95] "Not even the present [C]ourt can call it unconstitutional," boasted one sex separation enthusiast.[96] Southern politicians embraced the idea that school districts compelled to integrate should be free to separate boys and girls; several states enacted separate schools legislation in the mid-to-late 1950s.

When the federal government finally began to enforce racial desegregation in the 1960s, a number of Southern school districts turned to sex "separation." Some federal district court judges upheld such schemes in the hope that white parents would keep their children and their tax dollars in racially integrated public schools. In 1969, for instance, Judge Keady adopted what he later described as an "ingenuous" plan to separate boys and girls in the Coffeeville, Mississippi, schools. As Keady put it, "[T]he philosophy of teaching young people on a basis of separation by sex is respectable and has behind it a certain wisdom of the ages."[97] Whereas overt racial segregation had been largely discredited, at least among policy elites, most Americans did not see separating boys and girls in school as sex discrimination before the 1970s. Otherwise coeducational public schools almost invariably offered sex-specific courses in "shop" and home economics. Single-sex private schools retained an aura of prestige and refinement.

But as Keady and others soon discovered, to many African Americans, sex segregation was insulting, especially when accompanied by other measures designed to evade meaningful desegregation and to remove black teachers and administrators from their jobs. In many school districts, including Coffeeville, black students and their families boycotted the public schools and local merchants in protest of sex segregation. African Americans also mounted legal challenges to such plans, calling them "racial segregation by subterfuge."[98] These lawsuits prompted the Fifth Circuit to conclude that sex separation was unconstitutional if "racially motivated," but valid if based on "legitimate educational purposes." Some judges, including Keady, retreated from sex separation plans in the wake of African American protest, but others allowed school districts to present evidence refuting the charge of "racial motivation."[99]

The first challenges argued that sex separation was just repackaged race discrimination. Though no one doubted that sex separation was intended as an antidote to fears of "amalgamation," the "educational purposes" exception allowed school districts to develop seemingly race-neutral rationales for separating the sexes. But these supporting pedagogical theories violated emerging anti-sex discrimination norms. Southern school districts claimed that sex separation plans accommodated sex differences in learning styles and curricular interests. They argued that separation enhanced male student leadership, reduced demoralizing competition from females, and allowed efficient expenditure of school funds, avoiding the "needless duplication" of sex-specific resources and facilities like science labs, wood shops, and athletic arenas. Last but not least, they touted separation as a way to minimize the distractions and discipline problems caused by adolescent cross-sex contact.[100]

Opponents of sex segregation had a whole world of new legal theories and precedents to rely on when local ACLU attorney Jack Peebles filed a complaint on behalf of Kenlee Helwig and other plaintiffs in Jefferson Parish, Louisiana, in 1974.[101] In Jefferson Parish, as in other Southern school districts that adopted sex segregation during this period, concerns about "race-mixing" were just below the surface. The parish was among several suburbs of New Orleans that segregated its high schools by sex in the early 1960s in anticipation of desegregation, though initially none occurred. In 1965, a lawsuit forced an all-girls' public high school to admit twenty African American students. In 1969, federal Judge Herbert Christenberry approved a school board desegregation plan that preserved single-sex education in the parish, prompting African American students to demonstrate and feminists to investigate. Interviews conducted by local NOW members in late 1969 confirmed that the superintendent "in general, approved of mixing the sexes" but believed "unequivocally . . . that separation was necessary to accomplish racial integration." The superintendent remained convinced that "white parents would not accept the integration of the races and the mixing of sexes at the high school level at the same time," and warned of a "massive pull-out of white pupils" should coeducation accompany racial integration.[102] Plans to convert to coeducation prompted outcry over the projected expense and unspecified "discipline problems," with references to boys as "animals that would destroy the girls' schools." One local observer remarked, "[P]eople are not so much concerned with how much in the red the system may be, but how much black is in the system."[103]

Unlike previous challengers, the *Helwig* plaintiffs described sex segregation primarily as *sex* discrimination against girls. The sex equality revolution of the early 1970s had produced new rhetorical and legal weapons against sex separation. A 1970 law review note by law student Robert Barnett, "The Constitutionality of Sex Separation in Racial Desegregation Plans," articulated "a parallel to the harms found in race separation." Barnett relied on the usual suspects in legal and social science literature— Blanche Crozier, Pauli Murray, Gunnar Myrdal, Helen Meyer Hacker, and Ashley Montagu.[104] By 1974, Helwig's supporters could also cite Justice Brennan's endorsement of a race-sex analogy in *Frontiero v. Richardson*. Rather than asserting that sex segregation was merely "racial segregation by subterfuge," the plaintiffs in *Helwig* contended that sex segregation was *like* racial segregation, inflicting harms on girls comparable to those imposed on black children by Jim Crow. Expert witness Tulane professor Melvin Gruwell testified that purportedly "separate but equal" single-sex schools were not just materially unequal, but "inherently discriminatory toward women," inculcating feelings of inferiority in girls and ill-preparing them to interact and compete with men.

This account of sex segregation's harm appeared frequently in feminist legal literature of the mid-to-late 1970s. The American Friends Service Committee's 1977 report on Title IX implementation in Southern public schools devoted a chapter to single-sex public schools that drew an extended "parallel between racial and sex segregation." The authors emphasized the disparities at single-sex schools in two Louisiana parishes and in Amite County, Mississippi, and drew on interviews where "[f]emale students . . . repeatedly expressed feelings of vague inferiority, unease at their segregated status, and apprehension about the future." Quoting the *Helwig* briefs, the report called sex separation a "badge of inferiority which must be borne by women," and concluded, "Separate can never be equal."[105]

Calling sex segregation sex discrimination offered many advantages to feminists. Now that courts required race-neutral justifications for sex segregation, school districts relied instead on "legitimate educational purposes" that were much more vulnerable to charges of sex discrimination. Arguments about sex segregation's harm to girls also gave white women a stake in eradicating the practice. Separate schools for boys and girls seemed like a benign arrangement with a whiff of prestige; sex separation in Southern schools notorious for perpetuating racial oppression cast such arrangements in a more disturbing light. Cases like *Helwig* offered a compelling factual context that resonated with judges and others who were already sympathetic to civil rights.

But sex separation in the context of school desegregation intertwined race, sex, and sexual mores in ways that defied a legal doctrine bifurcated into the discrete categories of race and sex discrimination. Many African Americans perceived sex segregation as an affront to their dignity—as a remnant of Jim Crow, not merely its analogue. As C. J. Duckworth of the Mississippi Teachers' Association put it in 1970, "Sex segregation is a damned clear way of telling our people that they are inferior to whites." Everyone understood that the "real motive" of sex segregation was, as school officials admitted to the *Wall Street Journal* in 1970, "[t]o keep black boys from white girls."[106] In other words, sex segregation was self-evidently a form of morals regulation designed to safeguard white supremacy by limiting interracial social and sexual access.

Feminists' frequent focus on harm to girls also overshadowed sex separation's other detrimental impacts. Undoubtedly in many school districts, girls bore the brunt of sex-specific offerings that confined them to stereotypically female pursuits and afforded paltry resources in areas like science, shop, and sports. But African Americans also perceived sex segregation as insulting and harmful to boys and to the black community generally. American racial mythology had long cast black males in the role of sexual predator, and sex segregation's roots in white fears of "race-mixing" therefore stigmatized black boys in particular. Many school districts converted the formerly all-black and inevitably inferior facilities into boys' schools, and the formerly all-white campuses into girls' schools. As Taylor County, Georgia principal Jerry Partain put it, "In the South, we have always been very protective of our women."[107] Many African Americans thus perceived sex segregation in schools as sexualized racial insult, not just as sex discrimination against girls or boys.

The focus on sex discrimination amplified conversations about what constituted "healthy" social and sexual interaction among schoolchildren and masked their racial undertones. When justifying sex separation, school officials often cited the lack of "distractions" in single-sex environments. To some degree, these theories provided a race-neutral way to express the concerns that had animated sex separation in the first place. Proponents of coeducation such as Kenlee Helwig's mother responded that their children had scant "opportunity . . . to meet persons of the opposite sex in socially acceptable situations." Children in sex-segregated schools, she cautioned, were likely to "latch on to the first person they meet," leading to "early marriages and tragic unplanned pregnancies."[108] Others warned that single-sex schools were hotbeds of homosexuality. *Helwig* plaintiffs' expert Melvin Gruwell testified that "lack of association with the opposite sex is one of the two basic sources for homosexuality" and that more than two-thirds of "cases of homosexuality" reported by Louisiana high school principals "came from sex-separated schools."[109] Black parents in Amite County "sounded a special alarm about the tendency of boys to homosexuality" in the sex-segregated schools.[110]

The relationship between sex segregation and white supremacy was complex. For some officials and community leaders, sex separation seemed like a pragmatic solution to the problem of "white flight." If single-sex schools could prevent a mass exodus of white students and withdrawal of tax revenues, they might save public education and ease the way to racial integration. Many African American communities reacted to sex segregation with suspicion and hostility, especially when it left the public schools with mostly black students, few resources, and white administrators and school boards. But sex segregation enjoyed some qualified success. In Taylor County, Georgia, for instance, white students and tax dollars remained, and the school district retained black teachers and administrators in the sex-segregated, racially integrated schools. The black principal of the boys' high school, Albert O'Bryant, told the *Christian Science Monitor* in 1972 that while sex segregation "left something to be desired," it "seemed to minimize the problems some people have adjusting" to racial desegregation.[111] White and black students alike expressed dissatisfaction with single-sex education, but sex segregation remained in effect in Taylor County until 1978.

Once again, a statute saved the courts from resolving the constitutional questions presented by sex separation in desegregating Southern schools. After years of silence during which judges failed to rule on pending lawsuits challenging sex segregation, the Fifth Circuit decided in 1977 that the Amite County, Mississippi, plan violated an obscure provision of the Equal Educational Opportunity Act of 1974.[112] The act was primarily an anti-busing statute, but it also banned school assignments based on sex as well as race.[113] Sex separation in school desegregation plans thus not only evaded the Supreme Court's notice but escaped constitutional review altogether.

Recovering these cases reveals a social reality that bears little resemblance to the simple analogies between sex and racial segregation that dominated legal discourse about single-sex education. High-profile constitutional cases, such as Joanne Kirstein's successful attempt to convert the University of Virginia to coeducation and Susan Vorchheimer's unsuccessful bid to attend Philadelphia's Central High, featured white female plaintiffs challenging their exclusion from academically prestigious all-male institutions. These women framed their claims as analogous to—but quite separate from—those of African Americans seeking admission to all-white schools. Such abstract parallels failed to capture the intertwined relationship of sex segregation and white supremacy, or the harm of sex separation as perceived by many African Americans.

But the story told here also sheds light on the appeal of sex discrimination arguments in cases that began as challenges to racially discriminatory practices. As courts banned racially-motivated policies, school officials defended sex segregation on grounds that had traditionally raised no constitutional alarm: sex differences. But they did so at a historical moment when feminists had begun to succeed—largely through reasoning from race—in undermining the very sex stereotypes on which the school districts' justifications rested. Sex equality law gave plaintiffs and their lawyers new tools with which to fight old battles, as well as the benefits—and costs—of expanding the civil rights constituency to include white women.

Neither the unwed teachers' lawsuits nor the school sex segregation cases produced a Supreme Court decision. Cases involving women's exclusion or exemption from jury service did, offering hints of how rich and complicated intersections between race and sex were lost in the process of bringing cases to the Court. Pauli Murray had advanced 1960s cases like *White v. Crook* as the best hope for advocates and legal decision makers to recognize how the civil rights and feminist causes were intertwined (see Chapter 1). But when the Court finally resolved the constitutionality of exempting women from jury service in the mid-to-late 1970s, its decisions elided both the equal protection question and the intersections between race and sex so central to earlier feminist advocacy.[114]

Hoyt v. Florida, the Court's 1961 decision upholding Florida's exemption of women from jury service was infamous among feminists for Justice Harlan's assertion that women remained "the center of home and family life." The Court in *Hoyt* also pointedly distinguished the case from instances of racial exclusion: "This case in no way resembles those involving race or color in which the circumstances shown were found by this Court to compel a conclusion of purposeful discriminatory exclusions from jury service," Harlan wrote. "There is present here neither the unfortunate atmosphere of ethnic or racial prejudice which underlay the situations depicted in those cases, nor the long course of discriminatory administrative practice which the statistical showing in each of them evinced."[115] Gwendolyn Hoyt, her husband, and all participants in the jury selection process were white; race entered the case only by analogy.

The Supreme Court issued its first pronouncement on women and jury service since *Hoyt* in a 1975 case called *Taylor v. Louisiana.*[116] Billy Taylor, a white man, convicted by a Louisiana court for his role in a

crime that involved rape, robbery, and the kidnapping of two women
and a child, challenged his conviction on the ground that the jury convened to decide his fate included not a single woman.[117] Taylor argued
that Louisiana's exemption for women violated his Sixth Amendment
right to a jury composed of a "fair cross-section of the community," and
eight members of the Court agreed.[118]

Race did not play a prominent role in Justice White's opinion except
as a source of jury exclusion precedents and parallels. The *Taylor* majority relied on a then-recent 1972 case in which a white defendant successfully challenged the exclusion of African Americans from the jury that
convicted him.[119] Reasoning by analogy, Justice White concluded that
Taylor could challenge a jury composed only of men. Similarly, the 1979
Court decision invalidating Missouri's jury service exemption system did
not refer to the interplay of race and sex, even though the defendant,
Billy Duren, was black.[120]

The Court's opinions in these cases betrayed little if any recognition
of the race-sex interrelationships that had been so central to Murray's
and Kenyon's 1960s campaign for jury service equality. In *White v. Crook*
(see Chapter 1), African American women and men challenged their exclusion from a jury that acquitted the accused murderers of two civil
rights activists in 1965. In Mississippi, around the same time, Lillie Willis,
chairwoman of the local chapter of the Mississippi Freedom Democratic Party, questioned the exclusion of women and black men from the
jury pool in Sharkey County. According to a complaint filed in federal
court, Mrs. Willis faced charges of perjury and forgery in connection
with her mother's attempt to register to vote.[121] Eleanor Holmes Norton, then twenty-eight and less than two years out of Yale Law School,
helped to draft a brief arguing that Mississippi's statutory exclusion of
women from jury service was "arbitrary and unreasonable," given
women's increasing participation in public life and the historical parallels
between their status and that of black citizens.[122]

The Willis family paid a steep price for its activism. On Thanksgiving Day, 1965, Jennie Joyce Willis, the plaintiff's thirteen-year-old
daughter, was shot in the face as she stood outside her home in Anguilla.
Jennie was a civil rights leader in her own right—she had attempted to
register for seventh grade in the all-white Rolling Fork elementary
school earlier that fall. She lost her right eye as a result of the shooting.
Her lawyer, Alvin Bronstein of the Lawyers' Constitutional Defense

Committee, told the *Washington Post* that the bullet was apparently meant for her mother, in retaliation for her lawsuit challenging women's jury exclusion.[123] After arguing *Willis* before an unsympathetic court, Bronstein predicted that the Supreme Court would soon rule on sex discrimination in jury service.[124] But Lillie Willis's challenge never produced a lower court ruling, much less an edict from the Supreme Court. The charges against Willis were eventually dropped, and the Mississippi legislature repealed the sex-based exclusion in 1968.[125]

The Court missed another opportunity to tackle the relationship between race and sex in jury service when Claude Alexander appealed his conviction for aggravated rape in 1971.[126] Alexander, a young black man, had been sentenced by an all-white, all-male Louisiana jury to life in prison for sexually assaulting a young white woman in front of her boyfriend. *Alexander v. Louisiana* was just one of many cases in the late 1960s and early 1970s that challenged the exclusion or disproportionate underrepresentation of African Americans on Southern juries. Alexander's lawyers also challenged the dearth of women on the jury that convicted their client; Louisiana, like many states, exempted women from jury service unless they took steps to opt in. *Alexander* reached the Supreme Court around the same time as Sally Reed's challenge to Idaho's preference for male estate administrators. To feminists, *Alexander* presented an opportunity not only to reconsider *Hoyt* but to argue that sex classifications should be subject to strict scrutiny. An amicus brief from ERA sponsor Senator Birch Bayh and the National Federation of Business and Professional Women submitted in both *Reed v. Reed* and *Alexander* did just that.[127]

Justice White based his first draft opinion for the Court on race discrimination alone.[128] Disposing of the case in this manner would allow the Court to avoid *Hoyt* and the thorny question of how classifications based on sex should fare under the equal protection clause. Clerk George Frampton wrote to Blackmun that he was "surprised and disappointed that the ladies have lost out with Justice White," arguing that "the women have a good case, the issue should be faced, and an opinion can be written."[129] He urged Blackmun to consider writing a concurrence raising the sex discrimination issue, but it was Douglas who ultimately did so. Douglas's first draft declared that Louisiana's exemption of women from jury service "betrays a view of woman's role which cannot withstand scrutiny under modern standards."[130] The "rationale underlying" Louisiana's scheme was "the same" as that advanced by the concurring Justice Bradley almost a century earlier in Myra Bradwell's challenge to Illinois's ban on women lawyers: that "[t]he natural and proper timidity and delicacy which belongs to the female sex evidently unfits it for many of the occupations of civil life."[131] Douglas emphasized that, in practice, Louisiana's exemption eliminated virtually all women from service. In that way, the case was not unlike *White v. Crook*, where a lower federal court had overturned Alabama's de jure exclusion of women.[132]

But the rights of women seemed far more tangential in cases like *Alexander*. Claude Alexander, unlike Gardenia White and Lillie Willis, was no civil rights hero, but an unsympathetic convicted rapist. Alexander argued that an all–male jury could not be fair in a case involving a female victim. Not surprisingly, his lawyers expressed no underlying theory of the relationship between race and sex discrimination in jury service—another contrast to *White* and *Willis*. In *White*, Murray and Kenyon had argued expressly that including women on Southern juries would mean verdicts friendlier to the civil rights cause. In *Alexander*, Blackmun wondered, "[W]ould women favor or disfavor a man accused of rape under these circumstances?"[133] At oral argument, Alexander's attorney was asked this very question, and suggested that he might like "to have a black woman on the jury . . . to bring insight into this kind of situation."[134] For his part, the district attorney defended the clerk in charge of jury procedures.[135] At one point he quipped, "I like to think of myself as representing 21 million women who are for the Lib Movement, that is the liberty to make their own choice as to whether they should serve or not."[136]

Alexander was a less attractive vehicle for feminists' aspirations than earlier jury service cases, which had involved equality claims on behalf of women. It was harder to see how a male criminal defendant could claim that the exclusion of female jurors violated his right to equal protection.[137] In the end, the Court avoided this problem by deciding the case on the grounds of race discrimination and due process: Louisiana had deprived a black man of a jury that reflected a racial cross section of the community.

The Court's dodge of the sex discrimination issue in *Alexander* disappointed feminists, but they turned quickly to *Healy v. Edwards*. *Healy*, as historian Linda Kerber has written, was a class action "consciously structured as a test case, and there was some humor in it." Marsha Healy was a Louisiana Civil Liberties Union (LCLU) board member who "saw an opportunity in a civil suit initiated by a woman who had purchased a defective home permanent that had caused all her hair to break off at the roots."[138] The plaintiffs were represented by attorneys from the LCLU with help from Ruth Bader Ginsburg and the WRP, who challenged the state's sex-based exemption as a denial of equal protection to three groups: female prospective jurors rendered second-class citizens by the assumption that their domestic responsibilities outweighed civic duty; men saddled with a greater jury service burden; and finally, civil litigants deprived of a representative jury.

At first, the feminist challenge met with rousing success.[139] A plurality of the Supreme Court had just declared sex a suspect classification in *Frontiero*. Judge Alvin Rubin, writing for a three-judge federal district court, concluded that *Hoyt* was no longer binding in light of recent legal and social developments. Ruling that Louisiana's jury system deprived "all litigants of Due Process of Law and . . . female litigants of their right to Equal Protection," Rubin declared in ringing terms, "[w]hen today's vibrant principle is obviously in conflict with yesterday's sterile precedent, trial courts need not follow the outgrown dogma."[140] Around the same time, Chief Judge Frank M. Johnson, Jr. ruled on a class action suit brought by the Southern Poverty Law Center, charging race, sex, and income discrimination. Without reconsidering *Hoyt*, Johnson found that the disproportionate exclusion of black men and all women from a jury pool was sex as well as race discrimination.[141]

Another case headed for the Supreme Court, *Stubblefield v. Tennessee*, "tightly linked women's jury service to matters of race."[142] Edna Stubblefield, a nineteen-year-old African American woman, was accused of murdering another young black woman in a small-town bar after an argument. According to witnesses, the two women quarreled over a disputed romance. A brief struggle ended after Stubblefield fatally severed an artery in the victim's neck with a knife. A Henry County jury convicted her of murder and sentenced her to twenty years in prison.[143] Stubblefield's court-appointed attorneys, Marvin P. Morton, Jr. and William R. Neese, took a keen interest in her case. Neese admitted at the time, "I didn't enter the practice of law to be a crusader, but it has apparently turned out that way."[144]

Stubblefield's lawyers argued that the systematic exclusion of black citizens from Henry County's jury rolls and Tennessee's exemption of women from jury service deprived black female defendants like their client of a fair trial. Their evidence of race discrimination included the appointment of the same grand jury foreman, a white man, since 1937. That was not enough to persuade the appellate court to reverse Stubblefield's conviction, although a concurring judge doubted the constitutionality of Tennessee's jury service exemption for women. "No good reason occurs to me why, in this age of expanding equality for women under law, the mature female citizen should not be represented as part of the cross section of the community comprising our juries," the judge wrote. He believed the evidence against Stubblefield was overwhelming, however, so he merely suggested that the state legislature revise the exemption.[145]

In early 1974, Stubblefield's plight came to the attention of Ginsburg and her WRP colleagues when Stubblefield's attorneys responded to an ACLU query seeking information about cases involving women's rights.[146] Ginsburg wrote immediately to inform the Tennessee counsel about the court's rejection of a similar policy in *Healy,* and to lay the groundwork for ACLU involvement in *Stubblefield.*[147]

Ginsburg worried that the lower court record on the extent of racial exclusion was relatively weak, and so initially she omitted it entirely. Neese perhaps sensed another concern: a repeat of *Alexander.*[148] He wrote, "My primary concern is with Ms. Stubblefield and while I recognize that if the issue of racial exclusion is properly raised, the court may never reach the [constitutionality of Tennessee's exemption for women]. We are of the opinion, however, that the exclusion of blacks from Henry County juries was well shown and documented and well raised and should be included in this appeal." He was determined to preserve the issue for the Court's consideration just in case.[149] As Ginsburg wrote later to one of her WRP collaborators, Kathleen Willert Peratis, "Our Tennessee friends want to include the black exclusion issue so I tossed something in."[150] Her submission noted that between 1961 and 1972, "2259 whites were called for jury duty as opposed to 47 blacks," and "only 21 women were called (only one of whom was black) but none actually served."[151]

Meanwhile, Ginsburg was hard at work on the centerpiece of the WRP's jury service agenda, *Healy v. Edwards,* but *Healy* had a competitor on the Court's docket—*Taylor v. Louisiana*. Both cases challenged Louisiana's jury service exemption for women but were otherwise strikingly different: *Taylor* involved a male criminal defendant challenging the absence of women from a jury that convicted him of serious crimes against women. *Healy* was an equal protection challenge brought on behalf of much more sympathetic parties—prospective jurors and civil litigants. Nevertheless, since both *Healy* and *Taylor* challenged the constitutionality of the same law, they would be argued and decided together.

Neither *Healy* nor *Taylor* directly involved questions of race discrimination except as a source of parallels and precedents. And the swing Justices continued to question the validity of a race-sex analogy, especially in the equal protection context. Blackmun believed it was "not necessary here, and perhaps not desirable, yet to take the position that sex classification is suspect." After oral arguments in the two cases, he declared himself ready to embrace a "middle-tier" standard. He worried, however, about implying that a jury service scheme's disparate impact on women would violate equal protection. Blackmun foresaw "the possibility of embarrassment in some future case where [disparate] effect would be emphasized."[152]

Powell rejected feminists' claim that the jury exemptions violated women's rights. "I do not view this as a sex discrimination case," he wrote of *Healy*. Clerk Julia "Penny" Clark told Powell, "An uncritical eye could find parallels between racial exclusion and exclusion of women."[153] But women, unlike blacks in earlier cases, were not excluded from jury service; the selection scheme merely made their service voluntary. According to Powell himself, the real question was whether "due process" or "fundamental fairness" required "civil jury panels to be representative of the community." Here, the analogy to race seemed more relevant. White criminal defendants already had the right to a racially representative jury pool; men plausibly had a parallel right to a sex-integrated pool.[154]

Of the jury selection cases before the Court in 1974–1975, only *Stubblefield* incorporated race- and sex-based exclusion, compelling equal protection and due process claims, and a defendant who embodied the intersection between sex and race. *Healy*, though devoid of any overt racial aspect, was a deliberately designed test case that cleanly presented a women's equal protection claim and avoided unsympathetic criminal defendants. In the end, though, Louisiana moved quickly to amend its state constitution, eliminating the jury service exemption for women and rendering *Healy* moot.

But *Taylor* did produce an opinion, in which the Supreme Court held Louisiana's exemption scheme unconstitutional and rejected *Hoyt's* depiction of women as "the center of home and family life." After Blackmun complained that the majority overruled *Hoyt* without saying so, White revised his majority opinion and acknowledged that *Hoyt* was no longer good law. "If it was ever the case that women were unqualified to sit on juries or were so situated that none of them should be required to perform jury service, that time has long since passed."[155] Feminists regretted that the Court did not acknowledge the denial of equal protection to women. Still, they greeted *Taylor* as a significant victory. A *Los Angeles Times* editorial headline proclaimed triumphantly: "The Court Views Women as People."[156]

But the jury service decisions gave short shrift to the broader questions raised by feminists about women's citizenship. Feminists attacked even facially sex-neutral jury service exemptions for individuals with responsibilities for the care or custody of children. In amicus briefs and law review articles, CCR lawyers argued that the same level of scrutiny should apply to these "apparently neutral rules" since they "relate[d] to traditionally female functions or attributes such as child rearing."[157] Moreover, they contended, if the Court confronted women's equal protection claims directly, relevant race precedents were available. In a 1970 case, the Court had proclaimed that "[p]eople excluded from juries because of their race are as much aggrieved as those indicted and tried by juries under a system of racial exclusion."[158] Similarly, CCR said, women's "opportunity to avoid jury duty" was not a "benefit" but rather "a more subtle badge of inferiority."[159]

And *Taylor* offered little solace to Edna Stubblefield. Neese wrote to Ginsburg shortly before the oral arguments in *Taylor* and *Healy* that the imprisoned "Mrs. Stubblefield [was] becoming anxious" about the status of her case. Ginsburg replied that she "wished Mrs. Stubblefield patience and fortitude," adding, "[b]efore Christmas she should know where she stands."[160] As it happened, although Mrs. Stubblefield had to wait for the new year, her fate was indeed sealed in a mid-December memo from White to his colleagues. Several of the Justices were adamant that *Taylor* should not apply retroactively, to prevent attacks on numerous criminal convictions. And White found Stubblefield's other arguments weak. Like

Ginsburg, he felt that "the statistics supporting [Stubblefield's] claim relating to the systematic exclusion of blacks [did] not make out much of a case."[161] The Court dismissed Stubblefield's appeal in a one-sentence order.[162]

As potential jurors, litigants, and defendants, black women suffered disproportionately from the confluence of race and sex discrimination in jury service. Feminists continued to press for recognition of these connections. In 1975, the same year *Taylor* came down, a young African American woman, Joan Little, killed a white prison guard she said was attempting to rape her. Feminists and civil rights activists decried the racial and sexual oppression embodied in Little's indictment for capital murder. Angela Davis called on people of color to "understand the connection between racism and sexism that [was] so strikingly manifested" in Little's case, and on white women to "grasp the issue of male supremacy in relationship to the racism and class bias which complicate and exacerbate it."[163] CCR assisted in Little's defense, winning a change of venue that led to her acquittal by a race- and sex-integrated jury. Little became a cause célèbre. But what Kenyon and Murray had described as the "integral relation" between civil rights and women's jury service never surfaced in court opinions, much less those issued by the Supreme Court.

Why did so many women's rights cases follow a similar trajectory? Each of the episodes recounted here had its own logic and contingent outcomes. But a pattern is discernible. Both the prominent role of race in so many of the successful early sex equality cases and its receding presence later call out for explanation.

The changing methodology of white supremacy helps to account for the prevalence of early sex equality cases that involved race. Once the American legal system no longer tolerated overt racial segregation and discrimination, maintaining African Americans' subordination required more subtle, ostensibly race-neutral policies. Many of those practices—like single-sex schools or the exclusion of unwed mothers from employment—exploited the temporal lag between civil rights triumphs and feminist gains. For a brief time after civil rights victories had driven race discrimination underground, what feminists were beginning to call sex discrimination remained relatively untouched by constitutional proscriptions. In that sense, the integral role of African Americans in bringing claims is not itself surprising. In the unwed mothers and school segregation cases, policies based on sex or "morality" affected black communities disproportionately and apparently proceeded from racial animus.[164] Jury service cases were even more integral to the larger civil rights movement. In these cases, "reasoning from race" was almost beside the point—the cases were as much or more about race than about sex. And black communities' involvement in civil rights may have made the courts seem a logical place to air their claims.

Judges' receptiveness was essential to success in early cases. And many of the judges who wrote the early sex equality decisions were sympathetic to civil rights claims. William Keady came to trust Fannie Lou Hamer through school desegregation litigation. Richard Rives and Frank M. Johnson, Jr. saw the de jure exclusion of women from jury service through the same lens through which they viewed the elimination of African American men from the jury rolls. Similarly, Fifth Circuit Chief Judge John R. Brown, who wrote the dissent adopted by Justice Marshall in Ida Phillips's challenge to Martin-Marietta's refusal to hire mothers of young children, had won recognition as one of the courageous "Fifth Circuit Four" who advanced black civil rights.[165] Spottswood Robinson, who wrote the first appellate decision upholding a sexual harassment claim, was a renowned civil rights lawyer, as was Constance Baker Motley, who decided several early sex equality cases.[166]

The backgrounds of many lawyers bringing early sex equality cases would also have been known to sympathetic judges. Several were handled by the NAACP LDF, others by the Southern Poverty Law Center, and still others by lawyers affiliated with the ACLU or the Lawyers' Constitutional Defense Committee. Philip Hirschkop litigated *Loving v. Virginia* and other civil rights cases before taking on the University of Virginia's exclusion of women and a challenge to mandatory pregnancy leave. The judge in Hirschkop's cases was Robert Merhige, known as the "most hated man in Richmond" during the early 1970s for his rulings desegregating Virginia public schools.[167]

Even in cases where race and sex intersected concretely, though, those connections often evaporated in court opinions. Legal process was partly to blame. The factual context of a case was both visible and relevant to a trial court judge, who heard directly from witnesses and decided based on a case in all of its messiness. Writing a legible judicial opinion meant imposing order on unwieldy facts. The judges hearing these cases may have absorbed much that was never expressed in formal opinions. On appeal, the issues were boiled down to their essence, with facts and context reduced to bare bones. By the time a case reached the Supreme Court, it had been filtered through judges as well as advocates' and amici curiae briefs. At each stage, legal claims became more abstract and disconnected from their factual context.

In many instances, the political branches of government addressed the problem, letting courts off the hook. In theory, judges must avoid constitutional questions when a case can be resolved on statutory grounds. And legislation and administrative regulation often outpaced constitutional decision making. The Equal Educational Opportunity Act of 1974 saved the Fifth Circuit from confronting the equal protection questions presented by the school sex segregation cases. The 1972 amendments to Title VII and Title IX regulations issued by Health, Education, and Welfare rescued the Supreme Court from deciding the unwed mothers' case. Mississippi repealed its exclusion of women from jury service, and Louisiana amended its state constitution. For a case to reach the Supreme Court, at least one party must appeal or petition for a writ of certiorari. In several cases, the losing parties decided not to pursue their cases further.

But the Justices' reaction to *Andrews* suggests that even if more intersectional cases had reached the Supreme Court, the Court might not have been receptive. Innovative arguments about disparate impact, reproductive freedom, and the convergence of fundamental rights and suspect classifications inspired more wariness than sympathy. As the Court became increasingly conservative on matters of race and poverty during the 1970s, reminding the Justices of links between race, sex, and economic inequality might have hurt rather than helped feminists' cause. Focusing on the single axis of sex discrimination made practical sense in a world where feminism seemed ascendant and civil rights advocates struggled to defend their gains.

Further, many of the intersectional cases involved not only race and sex, but questions of sexuality and morality. As feminists were well aware, this was dangerous cultural ground. Earlier, civil rights and antipoverty advocates had carefully framed cases involving single parents, illegitimacy, and welfare as implicating children's rights and needs. They often avoided emphasizing race or sex discrimination claims even in cases of severe sex- and race-based disparate impact.[168] CCR tried to break away from this more cautious approach. But Rhonda Copelon later recalled that some feminists believed that the unwed mothers' case was a "terrible" idea, that "get[ting] into lifestyle questions" too soon was a "mistake."[169] In hindsight, the same elements that made the case so attractive to the feminists of CCR may have backfired before a fundamentally conservative Court.

And some feminist strategists may have avoided presenting their cases as anything other than simple sex discrimination claims. If a case could be decided on race discrimination grounds, the Court was less likely to move sex equality law forward. When Ginsburg spoke of the Louisiana sex segregation case *Helwig v. Jefferson Parish* as the "case that could have been," she did not fully explain its special appeal. Part of her wistfulness likely stemmed from the factual record and expert testimony developed in the lower court. Minutes from WRP strategy sessions record that Ginsburg and her colleagues thought cases involving racially motivated sex segregation "bolster[ed] the[ir] legal case." The racial backdrop also enhanced "the Project's enthusiasm for litigation in this area."[170] *Helwig* may have overlapped with race and civil rights just enough to help the Court to see sex segregation as discriminatory, but not enough to derail a favorable ruling on general sex equality grounds.

Feminists also had strategic reasons to make more general claims of discrimination that applied to white women or to women generally, rather than just to women of color. Many feminist advocates were themselves white; even those who were not, recognized the political clout white women brought to the feminist cause. Moreover, the claims pioneered by women of color tackled policies and practices that potentially affected all women, regardless of race, though not necessarily in the same way. In crafting legislation and administrative guidelines, feminists had to generalize. As litigants seeking review by the Supreme Court, they universalized their claims to persuade the Justices of their cases' larger significance.

This whitewashing had consequences. Women of color often led the way in expanding the definition of sex discrimination. But frequently their pioneering work was forgotten. The prototypical sex discrimination plaintiffs of the 1970s were white men and women. In many instances, they sought legal entitlements based on marriage at the same time that marriage rates among poor women and women of color fell. The cases that produced Supreme Court decisions and established enduring sex equality precedents referred to racial inequality only by way of analogy. Sex equality rulings compared "women" and "blacks" or "race" and "sex" without acknowledging how these categories overlapped.

This case law obscures the full picture of feminist legal advocacy as well as the conditions that inspired feminist activism. Read together, these hidden histories reveal how much sex equality law owed to groundwork laid by women and men for whom race and sex discrimination were inseparable. The regulation of sex, sexuality, and "morals" functioned to maintain white supremacy long after overt race-based policies no longer passed constitutional muster. Women's quest for economic independence was inextricably linked with reproductive freedom and the right of unmarried mothers to gainful employment. The early jury service cases cast women's quest for equal citizenship as not merely a pale parallel to civil rights but as central to the enfranchisement of African Americans. Recovering these cases offers a glimpse of how law is made and what is lost along the way.

6

In 1977, an assertive and inclusive brand of feminism was in the air. As feminists gathered for the International Women's Year (IWY) national convention in Houston, they fought to dispel depictions of the women's movement as monochromatic, upper middle-class, and narrow in its aspirations. First Ladies Lady Bird Johnson, Betty Ford, and Rosalynn Carter joined women from across the nation and from all walks of life. Women of color asserted their place in the feminist movement, uniting for the first time on a national scale. Overwhelming majorities of conference delegates embraced the ERA, Medicaid funding for abortion, and lesbian rights.[1] The same year, an important statement by African American feminists in the Combahee River Collective argued for the inseparability of race, class, gender, and sexuality.[2]

The political climate, too, seemed promising. Democrats controlled the White House and Congress after eight years of Republican presidents and divided government. Jimmy Carter won with the support of African Americans as well as Southern whites. Congresswoman Barbara Jordan, who gave a keynote address at the IWY conference, had nominated Carter in a stirring speech at the 1976 Democratic National Convention. Carter promised he would be to women's rights what LBJ had been to civil rights; he pledged to appoint women to high office, to fight for ratification of the ERA, and to fund day care programs.[3]

Less than four years later, feminists were reeling. Carter's presidency had been a colossal disappointment, Ronald Reagan's victory in 1980 was an even more devastating blow. Reagan's triumph ushered in a civil rights counterrevolution that threatened to undercut the fragile advances "women and minorities" had won. Supreme Court decisions ratified a narrow vision of sex equality, and the ERA fizzled.

The new era proved far from an unmitigated catastrophe. As conservatives made antifeminism an important front in their battle for political supremacy, they helped to galvanize feminists and strengthen ties among advocates for women, people of color, and the poor. The first woman on the Court salvaged significant feminist constitutional gains. And the ERA's defeat proved liberating as well as demoralizing to advocates. Even so, by the early 1980s, the analogies between race and sex pioneered by African American feminists in the name of unity became the targets of scathing critique from a new generation that emphasized differences between men and women, and among women. Reasoning from race seemed like a substantive and strategic failure. But the reality was far more complicated.

"Does the women's movement compromise the struggle of minorities?" asked organizers of a conference on the future of affirmative action in 1976. The answer, said law professor Ralph Smith, was "[e]mphatically and unequivocally" yes. Even so, he argued, "some form of coalition is not only possible, but is necessary." The growing backlash against civil rights meant that "our only hope for a real slice of the pie is a united front which demands some meaningful concessions."[4]

The following year, feminists and civil rights advocates applauded Carter's appointment of Eleanor Holmes Norton, guardian of the often fragile civil rights-feminist coalition, to chair the EEOC.[5] As Richard Clarke wrote in a column published in several African American newspapers, "Mrs. Norton is a prime advocate for the two groups that need an effective EEOC most—blacks and women. . . . [I]n a movement that often seems shrill and easily sidetracked to peripheral issues, Mrs. Norton stands out as a model of effective feminist advocacy."[6] But no one envied the challenges she confronted.[7] Derided as a "bumbling bureaucratic abomination," the EEOC faced an enormous backlog of more than one hundred thousand cases, a demoralized staff, and a dysfunctional organizational structure.[8] Norton streamlined EEOC procedures and reduced the backlog. Her long-term objective, she announced, was to attack discrimination systemically through pattern or practice suits, the government's equivalent of class actions.[9]

Meanwhile, conservative opposition and judicial ambivalence dogged the embattled civil rights movement. A week before Norton joined the administration, the Supreme Court ruled in *United States v. Teamsters* that challengers to an employer's seniority system under Title VII must prove intentional discrimination.[10] The decision disrupted a delicate détente between labor and civil rights advocates, and NAACP General Counsel Nathaniel Jones charged: "[The Justices] just shoved the car in reverse and it's going backwards a mile a minute."[11] At the same time, the university affirmative action case *Regents of the University of California v. Bakke* was headed for the Supreme Court. One poll purported to show that 83 percent of Americans opposed "preferential treatment" for women and racial minorities. Court watchers believed "reverse discrimination" challenges could jeopardize the future of all affirmative action in education and employment.[12]

Three weeks after *Teamsters,* the Court ruled 6–3 that states could deny Medicaid funding for abortion. When a reporter asked Carter whether it was fair that "women who can afford to get an abortion can go ahead and have one and women who cannot afford to are precluded," Carter's answer dismayed feminists and antipoverty advocates. "Well, as you know," he said, "there are many things in life that are not fair, that wealthy people can afford and poor people can't."[13] Personal and religious opposition to abortion tempered Carter's nominal support for *Roe v. Wade* and strained relations between feminists and HEW secretary Joseph Califano. Feminists' anger at the Carter administration only grew in the coming years.

Challenges to affirmative action and abortion funding met very different fates by the end of the 1970s. In 1979, the Supreme Court affirmed that Title VII allowed private employers to undertake voluntary affirmative action programs. In contrast, the following year the Justices upheld the Hyde amendment, a ban on federal government funding for abortion, by a 5–4 vote. But the struggles over abortion funding and affirmative action in employment aligned the interests of feminists with those of poor women and people of color in ways that previous Court cases had not. The result was an increasingly robust coalition that operated in spite of the separation of race and sex in legal doctrine.

On the surface, *United Steelworkers v. Weber* appeared to be a case about race, not gender. Production worker and union steward Brian Weber brought a "reverse discrimination" claim against his employer, Kaiser Aluminum, in 1974. Under a collective bargaining agreement, Kaiser admitted an equal number of blacks and whites to a training program designed to integrate Kaiser's almost exclusively white skilled craft workforce. At Weber's plant, four white and five black men were chosen for the training opportunity. But although he had more seniority than two of the African American trainees, Weber was not among them.

Press coverage of the *Weber* case explored the class as well as the racial implications of affirmative action policies like Kaiser Aluminum's; one journalist called Weber a "blue-collar Allan Bakke."[14] Gender received far less media attention; although some commentators observed in passing that *Weber* would affect women, few devoted sustained attention to the subject. They seldom mentioned that the Kaiser plan included a 5 percent quota for women. The small size of its job training program allowed Kaiser to fill all thirteen slots with men during the first year while still meeting the company's affirmative action goals. As a result, Weber pled only race discrimination in his suit.[15]

But civil rights leaders and Kaiser Aluminum workers saw the *Weber* litigation as an opportunity to highlight sex as well as race discrimination, and to enlist the support of feminists. At an Affirmative Action Coordinating Center meeting in December 1978, attorney Denise Carty-Bennia chided women's organizations for their timidity in earlier affirmative action cases. A NOW LDEF representative avidly followed the ensuing discussion of conservatives' efforts to "pit minorities and women against each other," the "classism of white middle class women," and the "sexism of black men." She noted that "[w]omen's groups were singled out as inactive and unconcerned" about past affirmative action cases.[16] *Weber* would be different, said leaders of the Affirmative Action Task Force (AATF), which united more than fifty labor, civil rights, religious, and feminist organizations.[17] Spokespersons routinely referred to the *Weber* suit as both a "racist" and "sexist" assault on the gains of women and racial minorities and emphasized the need for affirmative action's beneficiaries and supporters to band together and fend off the attack.[18] Many of the anti–Weber coalition members signed onto a "Statement of Principles" that declared, "The remedies for discrimination against minorities and discrimination against women are inextricably linked."[19]

White women had a clearer stake in *Weber* than in earlier challenges to affirmative action in university admissions; the male monopoly over higher-waged blue-collar work persisted long after women poured into law and medical schools. A brief from several prominent feminist organizations argued that "women and blacks" faced "astonishingly similar" obstacles in the workplace and required similar remedies.[20] In this case, an analogy between race and sex served feminists well, since affirmative action in employment affected women of all races and socioeconomic groups.

African American workers also spotlighted past discrimination against women at the Kaiser Aluminum plant. They asked the Court to remand the case for further factual findings, and to allow "Black and women workers" to intervene in the litigation.[21] As they pointed out, none of the other parties had any interest in tracing the dearth of black and female workers at the Gramercy plant to its true cause—race and sex bias. Such evidence would undermine Weber's reverse discrimination claim, but neither the union nor the employer could risk the liability or bad publicity that admitting long-term discrimination would bring. Because they worried that the Court would not endorse an affirmative action plan without proof of past discrimination, the would-be interveners argued they could provide such proof themselves.

The black and female Kaiser workers lost the battle to present evidence of historical injustice, but they won the war to preserve affirmative action. Feminists and civil rights advocates rejoiced when a majority of Justices upheld Kaiser's job training program and ruled that Title VII permitted voluntary affirmative action without proof of past discrimination.[22] Norton, Ruth Bader Ginsburg, and others had argued all along that *Weber* exceeded *Bakke* in its importance for "women and minorities"; now they had a "clear, straightforward victory" for affirmative action in employment. Norton promised a relaxation of EEOC affirmative action guidelines, declaring, "If I were sitting in an organization looking to bring a reverse discrimination suit, I'd start looking for a better way to spend my money."[23]

The Court's opinions did not mention women at all, nor did they offer any hint of women's substantial stake in the outcome. *Weber* reinforced public perceptions that affirmative action was about race and, perhaps, class, but not gender. The decision vindicated the collaborative work of feminist, civil rights, and labor organizations; at the same time, affirmative action for women remained at the margins of legal discourse.

This one-dimensional treatment obscured the hard-won unity of civil rights and feminist advocates. On the other hand, it permitted the Court to avoid deciding whether affirmative action to bring women into traditionally male blue-collar jobs should happen at all. Sidestepping that question allowed Americans to grow accustomed to race-based affirmative action before grappling with *Weber's* implications for women.

The battle over abortion funding also linked the interests of feminists and civil rights advocates in an area where relations had been strained. In the early 1970s, many poor and minority women feared coercive fertility control measures like involuntary sterilization more than the denial of abortion services. When poor women did seek abortion, lack of funds more than legal restrictions stood in their way. As Linda LaRue put it in a blunt 1970 essay, "Tasteless analogies like abortion for oppressed middle-class and poor women" implied that all women could choose whether and when to give birth. The reality was, "middle-class women deciding when it is convenient to have children, while poor women decide the prudence of bringing into a world of already scarce resources, another mouth to feed."[24] Black feminists, including LaRue herself, defended abortion rights, notwithstanding charges that the movement was part of a genocidal plot against black families.[25] And white feminists in organizations like the Center for Constitutional Rights (CCR) had long been involved in challenging federal and state restrictions on government funding for abortion. But balancing the ability of middle-class women to limit their family size through abortion and voluntary sterilization with poor women's desire to make uncoerced reproductive choices required careful coalition work.[26]

The conservative campaign against abortion funding indirectly fostered alliances between civil rights and feminist advocates.[27] Antiabortion groups and politicians aimed to restrict access and get the government out of the business of funding abortion services. Conservative activists linked abortion with the ERA, accusing feminists of destroying traditional family life. Most of the time, ERA proponents insisted that the "ERA-Abortion Connection" was a figment of Phyllis Schlafly's imagination. The IWY platform was typical: "ERA *will NOT* have any impact on abortion laws."[28] *Roe* located abortion rights in the doctrine of privacy, said defenders, not sex equality. Decisions like *Geduldig v. Aiello* (1974), which had upheld pregnancy discrimination against a sex-based equal protection challenge, reinforced this strategy by separating reproduction from sex equality. Subsequently, scholars have suggested that feminists shied away from making sex equality arguments in abortion cases in the late 1970s for fear of crediting the "abortion-ERA connection." Rhonda Copelon recalled instead, "We didn't make the sex [equality] argument because we didn't think it would win."[29] Whatever their motivation, attorneys in abortion funding cases avoided locating reproductive freedom in the constitutional guarantee of equal protection for women vis-à-vis men.[30]

Instead, feminists argued that banning Medicaid funding of abortion services violated equal protection by impermissibly distinguishing *between* women. Rather than comparing men and women and referring to constitutional sex equality cases, lawyers compared different classes of women: poor and minority women versus affluent women, and women who chose abortion versus those who carried a pregnancy to term.[31] An amicus brief written by NYU Law professor Sylvia Law and veteran reproductive rights lawyer Harriet Pilpel argued that abortion funding restrictions contained "an invidious classification which effectively denies poor pregnant women their Constitutional right to privacy."[32] Another brief called abortion rights "a medical blessing to women," but lamented that "indigent women have yet to share the benefits enjoyed by women of means."[33] Sex discrimination arguments did appear in these briefs, but usually highlighted how poor and minority women bore the brunt of employment discrimination and thus would suffer the greatest harm from unwanted pregnancy.

Similar arguments dominated congressional debates over the Hyde amendment, which prohibited the use of most federal Medicaid funds for abortion services. Moderate Republican senator Bob Packwood of Oregon argued that the Hyde amendment "disproportionately discriminated against poor black women" and called it "the worst example of socially unjust legislation this Congress could ever hope to put into law."[34] Anti-abortion legislators cited African American and Latino constituents' opposition to abortion and called the unborn a "true minority." But African American Democratic Rep. Yvonne Braithwaite-Burke of California condemned the Hyde measure as the "forced childbearing amendment": "[W]e do not believe that young girls should be forced to have children. We do not believe in a society where no one is willing to feed those children after they have them. . . . [T]here are no adoptive homes available for little black girls and boys who are born in poverty."[35] The Congressional Black Caucus and the U.S. Commission on Civil Rights strongly opposed the Hyde amendment for similar reasons.

Abortion rights advocates suffered a stinging defeat when the Court upheld Connecticut's refusal to fund abortion services in *Maher v. Roe* (1977). But the dissenting Justices reinforced the connections between reproductive freedom, race, and economic justice. Brennan decried the majority's "distressing insensitivity to the plight of impoverished pregnant women."[36] Blackmun wrote, "For the individual woman concerned, indigent and financially helpless . . . the result is punitive and tragic." The majority's assumption that poor women could obtain abortions without government help was, he said, "disingenuous and alarming, almost reminiscent of: 'Let them eat cake.'"[37] Marshall's dissent was even more explicit and impassioned. He charged that withholding funds "brutally coerce[d] poor women to bear children whom society will scorn for every day of their lives."[38] Marshall emphasized the decision's "devastating impact on the lives of minority racial groups." He lamented the "[m]any thousands of unwanted minority and mixed-race children" who lived "blighted lives in foster homes, orphanages, and 'reform' schools," attended "second-rate segregated schools," and subsisted on meager welfare benefits.[39] Unmistakably aligning antiabortion advocacy with fiscal conservatism, he decried "the ethical bankruptcy of those who preach a 'right to life' that means, under present social policy, a bare existence in utter misery for so many poor women and their children."[40]

In 1980, New York Medicaid recipient Cora McRae's challenge to the Hyde amendment reached the Court.[41] Feminists, led by Rhonda Copelon and her CCR colleagues, hoped to persuade at least two Justices that the federal Hyde amendment differed from the state ban upheld in *Maher*. The prohibition upheld in *Maher* applied only to abortions that were not "medically necessary"; the Hyde amendment funded abortions only to save a woman's life. This difference provided one possible basis on which to distinguish the cases. Further, while the state rules denied funds for many elective procedures, the Hyde amendment singled out abortion as the only "medically necessary" procedure excluded from Medicaid coverage. These distinctions proved sufficient for Justice Stevens. As Powell paraphrased Stevens's comments at conference: "This [case] is different. Gov't has decided here to 'harm' a certain number of women."[42]

Feminists needed one more Justice. Powell agreed that the "most troublesome argument" was that the Hyde amendment "penalize[d]" women by saddling them with potentially severe health consequences they could have avoided by terminating their pregnancies. He saw the policy as "unwise and unfair," and declared, "If I were in Congress I would have voted *against* [the] Hyde amendment."[43] Ultimately, however, the question for Powell was whether the government's interest in potential life outweighed a woman's interest in preserving her health by ending her pregnancy. Such decisions, he thought, were best left to legislatures. This view prevailed in an opinion for five Justices authored by Justice Stewart.[44] Stewart's opinion emphasized that "it simply does not follow that a woman's freedom of choice carries with it a constitutional entitlement to the financial resources to avail herself of the full range of protected choices."[45]

To Justice Stevens, who had voted to uphold the state ban in *Maher*, the Hyde amendment was different. He condemned the amendment for "inflicting serious and long-lasting harm on impoverished women" in "an unjustifiable, and indeed blatant, violation of the sovereign's duty to govern impartially."[46] Feminists, too, condemned *McRae's* devastating impact on "poor women, black women, and teenagers." The ACLU decried the ruling as "a complete and cruel abandonment of the constitutional guarantee of equal justice."[47] In blocking government funding for abortion services, opponents of abortion had inadvertently married the interests of predominantly white middle-class and professional women to the concerns of poor and minority women.[48]

Feminists hoped to unite all women behind the ERA in similar fashion.[49] Women of color traditionally had an ambivalent relationship to the ERA. Before the 1960s, many of the amendment's most devoted champions had been indifferent or even hostile to African American civil rights. The passage of Title VII had finally divorced ERA supporters from their alliance with Southern segregationists; African American feminists such as Pauli Murray and the formerly skeptical civil rights commissioner Frankie M. Freeman argued passionately that the ERA was vitally important to black women; and civil rights groups eventually endorsed the amendment in the early 1970s. Public opinion polling in the 1970s and early 1980s showed that black women were more likely than their white counterparts to support the ERA.[50] Nevertheless, many feminists of color prioritized other struggles. The Black Women's Plan of Action, crafted during the 1977 IWY conference, mentioned the ERA, but only in the context of larger human rights priorities, calling for "[t]he right to equitable treatment under law to be construed as including the eradication of discrimination based upon race, color, ethnicity, sex, or creed and support of ERA *as part of this broad task*."[51] Proponents still confronted skepticism among prominent civil rights leaders about the feminist movement's genuine commitment to black women.[52]

In the late 1970s, ERA proponents tried to acknowledge and expand the contributions of communities of color to the ERA effort. On the advice of African American board chair Mary H. Futrell, the proratification group ERAmerica resolved in 1979 to "correct some of the past 'oversights' committed against ethnic groups who had been actively involved in ERA ratification efforts."[53] Pro-ERA minority organizations pledged to "put to rest the myth that this is a 'white women's rights issue'" and "give credibility to the ERA in the Multi-Cultural community."[54] Articles in *Essence* and *Black Scholar* sought to dispel the "confusion" generated by anti-ERA forces that "portray[ed] the women's liberation movement as the exclusive property of so-called middle-class, frustrated, bra-burning housewives."[55] Mobilization by African Americans grew urgent when ERA proponents targeted southern states.[56] Advocates in the ACLU's Southern Women's Rights Project hoped that interracial ERA activism would prove that the "climate of mutual suspicion between white feminists . . . and black women [was] perhaps starting to thaw."[57] Women of color remained wary; as the Women's Bureau's Minority Task Force on ERA put it in 1980, "We are willing to work as we have always done, but not for crumbs."[58]

Pro-ERA literature aimed at minority women often recycled arguments developed in the preceding decades. NOW's pamphlet "Minority Women and the ERA" explained, "The white patriarchy has established a set of unrealistic male and female roles in which man is the breadwinner, woman a dependent," and linked employment discrimination against minority women with poverty in communities of color.[59] Pamphlets titled *The Equal Rights Amendment: What Does It Mean to You?* and *The E.R.A. and the Black Community* quoted Martin Luther King, Jr., and black feminists such as Aileen Hernandez, urging "women and minority groups" to "realize that the same arguments are used against both to keep us at the bottom 'in our places.'"[60] ACLU WRP newsletters reprinted Pauli Murray's early 1970s writing.[61] Comparisons of the ERA to the Reconstruction Amendments appeared everywhere. Trying to persuade an audience committed to civil rights but uncertain about feminism, proponents reiterated that the "bond of common problems can be a tool for a bond of common action."[62]

But the sustained portrayal of feminism's opponents as enemies of civil and human rights generally was new. Many earlier ERA skeptics like Paul Freund and Ted Kennedy were liberal civil rights supporters, not right-wing extremists. The conservative reaction against the civil rights revolution prompted fractious allies to rally together against a threatening foe. "This right-wing movement [against ERA] is part of a broader campaign today," wrote two black feminists, "directed against the rights of not only women, but of blacks and other working people as well.[63] One pro-ERA brochure listed the NAACP, National Council of Negro Women, National Black Feminist Organization, and the U.S. Commission on Civil Rights and other respected civil rights organizations on one side of the ERA ledger, and the Ku Klux Klan, the John Birch Society, the Communist Party, and the Mormon Church on the other side.[64] A NOW brochure claimed: "These are the people who have bombed Black churches; seek to destroy Native American families; advocate exploitative foreign wars; want Spanish-speaking people deported. . . . [They] may change their names but are the same conservative and reactionary element American minorities have long struggled against."[65] Pro-ERA groups used similar tactics to win the support of black politicians and local organizations, with some success.[66]

It later seemed as if feminists had narrowed their focus to the ERA in the final years of the ratification struggle, at the expense of the broader goals articulated by the diverse IWY gathering.[67] ERA proponents' "outreach" efforts to African American communities may have been too little, too late: by the time they launched these initiatives on a broad scale, the amendment arguably had little chance of passage. Feminists did seek, albeit somewhat belatedly, to include interracial solidarity against a conservative insurgency in the panoply of meanings the ERA evoked. But the convergence of interests between feminism and civil rights that helped to build coalitions to defend affirmative action and abortion funding was less apparent in ERA advocacy.

For many African Americans, access to jobs seemed the most pressing concern that antidiscrimination law could address. The favorable holding on affirmative action in *Weber*, a Title VII case, suggested that this federal statute might be a more potent weapon against inequality than the Constitution. It remained unclear, however, whether Title VII would

THE LATE CIVIL RIGHTS ERA
197
t>

recognize the particular forms of discrimination experienced by women of color.

In 1980, the Fifth Circuit considered the claim by Dafro Jefferies that the Harris County Community Action Association (HCCAA) had not promoted her because she was a black woman and had retaliated against her after she attempted to expose discrimination within the antipoverty organization. The only court precedent directly on point was the 1976 case *DeGraffenreid v. General Motors* (see Chapter 3), where a judge refused to consider the "combined" race and sex discrimination claim of black female employees at a GM plant in St. Louis.[68] Similarly, the district court had dismissed Jefferies's claims in large part because her employer had promoted (male) African Americans and (white) women.[69]

Jefferies's prospects on appeal were more promising. The Fifth Circuit staff counsel who screened her case noted that "the lower court . . . did not address the crux of appellant's grievance: that, by being *both* black *and* female, she had been the victim of discrimination. Hypothetically, discrimination against black female employees could exist even where black males and white females had been fairly treated."[70] The appellate panel that heard her case seemed predisposed to sympathize with Jefferies: Judge Elbert Tuttle was one of the "Fifth Circuit Four" famous for enforcing desegregation; Irving Goldberg had authored a landmark racial harassment decision; and newcomer Carolyn Dineen Randall was one of an unprecedented number of women President Carter had appointed to the federal bench.

From a family of lawyers, Randall earned a degree summa cum laude from Smith College and graduated from Yale Law School in 1962. After a summer in the Department of Justice's prestigious Honors program, she had applied for a position with Houston's U.S. Attorney, who turned her away, "cheerfully confessing that he was not up to hiring a woman."[71] She prospered as a corporate securities lawyer until Carter's Merit Selection Committee identified her as a potential nominee; Randall, a Republican, became the second woman ever to sit on the Fifth Circuit.

In an apparent victory for Jefferies, the two elder judges, Tuttle and Goldberg, rejected the notion that plaintiffs could not sue for a "combination" of race and sex discrimination. The panel held that "[r]ecognition of black females as a distinct protected subgroup . . . is the only way to identify and remedy discrimination directed toward black females" and deemed "the fact that black males and white females are not subject to discrimination" wholly "irrelevant." The majority could not "condone a result which leaves black women without a viable Title VII remedy."[72]

Judge Randall, however, was not persuaded that "combination discrimination" violated Title VII.[73] She worried about "the novelty and difficulty of a combination discrimination claim and the serious ramifications that recognition of such a claim would have on the ways in which it would be both proved and defended against."[74] To Randall, the practical dilemmas associated with combined race-sex claims warranted caution.

The Jefferies case reflected the ambivalent state of antidiscrimination law in 1980. To be sure, the decision improved upon the earlier rejection of "combined" race and sex discrimination claims. But no one remembered that just fourteen years earlier, Pauli Murray had saved Title VII's sex discrimination prohibition by insisting it was essential to preserve the rights of "Negro women." Dafro Jefferies ultimately lost her case.[75] And Judge Randall's misgivings presaged the future of "combination" claims, which remained notoriously difficult to prove for decades to come.[76]

By the end of the 1970s, feminists were openly frustrated with Carter.[77] His promises to women clashed with his determination to balance the federal budget and reduce the size of government.[78] Carter removed Midge Costanza and Bella Abzug from prominent positions after they criticized his opposition to abortion funding and his reductions in other social programs, and he only campaigned actively for the ERA during the final months of his presidency. NOW President Eleanor Smeal lamented in March 1979 that Carter had "raised hopes and expectations that [had] not been met by actual performance."[79] NOW's executive board announced in December that it would oppose Carter's reelection. "Our feeling," said Smeal, "is that the women's movement is being taken for granted, and we think that . . . should stop."[80]

But feminists' other options looked grim. Some turned to independent hopeful John Anderson, the only presidential candidate to support both federal financing for abortion and ERA ratification.[81] For its part, the GOP had alienated feminists. Only 29 percent of Republican National Convention delegates in 1980 were women, fewer than in 1972 or 1976, and the party withdrew its endorsement of the ERA after four decades of support.[82] Republican feminists openly criticized their party's platform and its candidate.[83] In October, delegates to

NOW's national convention rescinded the organization's opposition to Carter's reelection, but were unable to reach consensus on an endorsement. They could agree, however, "to condemn Mr. Reagan and to picket him and his running mate . . . at all possible appearances."[84]

Feminists saw Reagan's victory in 1980 as a "catastrophic defeat," in Smeal's words. Phyllis Schlafly declared that she was "on top of the world."[85] Republicans regained the White House after only four years in exile; they also defeated nine incumbent Democratic senators and won three open seats to take over the Senate for the first time since 1954. ERA champion Birch Bayh of Indiana was ousted by Dan Quayle, and feminist Elizabeth Holtzman lost narrowly to Republican Alphonse D'Amato in the New York Senate race.[86]

Conservatives quickly launched assaults on the "excesses" of the civil rights revolution. Emboldened supporters of antiabortion and school prayer constitutional amendments now controlled the presidency and the Senate. Reproductive rights, affirmative action, and the EEOC's sexual harassment guidelines seemed likely casualties of the counterrevolution. Reagan's transition team called for drastic cuts for the already cash-strapped EEOC and tried to exempt most federal contractors from affirmative action guidelines. Clarence Thomas, part of a young crop of "black conservatives," took over the EEOC's reins from Eleanor Holmes Norton. Republican senator Orrin Hatch of Utah, now the chairman of the Senate Committee on Labor and Human Resources, held hearings on affirmative action and sex discrimination in the workplace that discredited private remedial efforts and government involvement in antidiscrimination enforcement. The White House announced that Vice President George Bush would head an initiative to reconsider the "efficiency" of antidiscrimination laws.[87]

In the Reagan era, reasoning from race grew even more perilous. Colorblindness had gained ground in 1970s race discrimination jurisprudence. Relying on a race discrimination paradigm, therefore, increasingly meant arguing that women and men should be treated as similarly situated individuals. The swing Justices had been willing, albeit somewhat reluctant, to accept this premise in cases involving assumptions about women's economic dependence on men. In the 1970s, Ruth Bader Ginsburg and her allies carefully chose cases involving "double-edged discrimination," often the denial of benefits to married couples who did not conform to the traditional male breadwinner/female homemaker model. In those cases, male plaintiffs successfully argued that they—and their wives—should not be penalized for failing to conform to stereotypes about appropriate sex roles. The Court had a more difficult time seeing sex discrimination in pregnancy cases, even though the harm to women in those cases seemed self-evident to feminists.

The limited control feminists had exerted over the constitutional sex equality docket evaporated in the early 1980s. The Supreme Court increasingly considered issues that, like the pregnancy cases, involved entrenched physiological and social differences between men and women. But the cases that reached the Court were not handpicked by feminists to showcase how sex-based classifications harmed women. They therefore proved susceptible both to arguments about the enduring nature of sex differences and to charges that a victory for feminists would be a defeat for women.

The Court's first Reagan-era sex equality rulings confirmed feminists' worst fears. In *Michael M. v. Superior Court of Sonoma County,* a teenager charged with statutory rape challenged a California law that penalized underage males but not underage females for engaging in nonmarital sexual intercourse. Making rape laws sex-neutral was not high on feminists' agenda. Women's advocates were troubled by the sex-based distinction and the California Supreme Court decision upholding it, however. The state of California defended the penalty as an antidote to teenage pregnancy, but critics believed that the law stereotyped boys as sexual aggressors and girls as passive victims. The Women's Legal Defense Fund called the sex-based distinction a "remnant of what [the Court] has called 'romantic paternalism.'"[88]

In *Michael M.,* the Justices split over the outcome as well as the proper standard of review for the sex-based statutory rape law. According to Powell's conference notes, Chief Justice Burger considered the state's interest in preventing unwed pregnancy "substantial," and thought that the classification had "a rational basis." Rehnquist agreed, calling it an "easy case." Stewart said that because "males and females *are* different," the equal protection clause was "not applicable." Brennan argued that the heightened judicial scrutiny applicable to sex-based classifications under *Craig v. Boren* (1976) required the Court to strike down the distinction. White and Marshall concurred. Stevens believed that "whatever standard is applied the law is irrational."[89] Blackmun and Powell agreed with Brennan that *Craig* mandated intermediate scrutiny, but nevertheless voted to uphold the law.

Despite majority support for applying intermediate scrutiny, Rehnquist's draft opinion for the Court appeared to back away from the standard feminists had worked so hard to establish. Law clerk Susan Lahne lobbied Blackmun to oppose or at least amend Rehnquist's draft. When her entreaties to preserve a robust sex equality principle proved unavailing, she appealed to Blackmun's fervent belief in *Roe v. Wade:* "[I]n discussing the evils of teenage pregnancy, the opinion lists abortions as among the results the state legitimately seeks to inhibit," she wrote.[90] Prompted by Lahne's memo, Blackmun decided to rethink his position. He left open several possibilities, including joining Rehnquist's opinion, writing a separate concurrence, or even joining the dissent. He summarized each of his "problems" with the draft, which tracked Lahne's objections. Blackmun knew that his vote would likely control the outcome.[91] Encouraged, Lahne wrote, "I hope you will forgive me yet again haranguing you . . . Yet, I cannot escape the strength of my feeling about how this case should be resolved."[92] In the end, however, Blackmun wrote a separate opinion but concurred in the Court's judgment.[93]

Powell's clerks made even less headway than Blackmun's did in convincing their boss of the statute's constitutional infirmity. Greg Morgan's bench memo accepted for the sake of argument that preventing teen pregnancy was the statute's "actual purpose" but argued that the sex-based distinction was unconstitutional under *Craig.* When Morgan asserted that the same purpose could be served by a gender-neutral statute, Powell queried, "Is this realistic?" Powell agreed with California lawmakers that "as a general matter, young males [were] less likely than young females to take seriously the risk of pregnancy."[94] Powell wrote: "I would have thought . . . that since only women become pregnant they may be classified differently from men. . . . [T]he experience of mankind strongly suggests that men tend to be the aggressors in the sex act, and lack the inhibition vs. pregnancy that usually—certainly before the 'pill'—most women possess."[95] Powell signed onto Rehnquist's opinion: "Although I am not enthusiastic about some of the language, I can live with this—I think."[96]

The final Rehnquist opinion in *Michael M.* limited heightened scrutiny in cases where biological differences between men and women underlay differential treatment.[97] Stewart's concurrence explicitly distinguished between race and sex: "[D]etrimental racial classifications by government always violate the Constitution . . . so far as the Constitution is concerned, people of different races are always similarly situated." But, he wrote, "there are differences between males and females that the Constitution necessarily recognizes. In this case we deal with the most basic of these differences: females can become pregnant . . . males cannot."[98]

Such nods to colorblindness in a sex equality case suggested the Justice's desire to narrow permissible remedies for race as well as sex discrimination. Stewart's concurrence also contained what Blackmun clerk Lahne characterized as "plainly a poke at the recent affirmative action cases." Stewart cited the dissent in a recent decision upholding a race-based set-aside, as well as *Brown v. Board of Education* and the dissent in *Plessy v. Ferguson*. Blackmun wrote in the margin of Lahne's memo, "If I join, have this stricken."[99] He did not, and it was not.[100]

Feminists worried that *Michael M.*'s more lenient standard of review would spill over into a much higher-profile case, *Rostker v. Goldberg,* a challenge to military draft registration for men only. Initiated not by feminists, but by men who protested their own subjection to conscription, *Rostker* was argued the day after the Court decided *Michael M.* The sex discrimination claim was just one of several arguments in a series of challenges to the draft, but it became the only ground for appeal to the Supreme Court.[101]

Fighting for women's right to be drafted into military service was antithetical to many feminists' pacifist leanings as well as their political instincts.[102] As ACLU executive director Ira Glasser explained the motivation behind the case, "Our purpose is to invalidate draft registration for everyone, not expand it to anyone. . . . We have no more interest in having women drafted than in having men drafted."[103] By 1981, ERA supporters generally agreed that the amendment would subject women to the draft and to military service on the same basis as men.[104] ERA opponents routinely cited "women in combat" as a primary reason to reject the amendment.[105] NOW officer Muriel Fox therefore wondered whether the organization should sign on to an amicus brief in *Rostker:* "[T]hough we might devoutly wish ACLU to win the suit we might perhaps not want anti-ERA people [to] say we're trying to get women included in draft registration."[106]

The lower court decision striking down the all-male draft stoked anxiety among feminists despite their agreement with the outcome. For ERA proponents, *Rostker* threatened a fatal backlash against the badly weakened amendment. On the other hand, some feminists thought a favorable decision in *Rostker* could defuse the threat posed by an ERA. "[I]f we have a situation whereby the ERA will cause the drafting of women, then the ERA is in trouble even more than it is now," wrote NOW's Virginia Watkins.[107] Moreover, a ruling upholding the all-male draft would exclude women from a fundamental responsibility of citizenship.

Ultimately, most feminists felt they could not remain neutral in a case with potentially wide-ranging ramifications for women's rights under the equal protection clause. They strategized about how to frame the harm of draft exclusion. Watkins perceived "a degree of power in being 'wanted' by the government for a draft." She noted, "Draft resistance and Conscientious Objection played an important political role during the Viet Nam war. I would like to see . . . women having that power." She and others also hoped that Congress would be less likely to reinstate military conscription if it meant drafting women as well as men. They debated how much to emphasize the ways secondary status in the military deprived women of opportunities to learn self-defense.[108] Sociologist Cynthia Epstein advised women's groups to focus on the societal benefits of women's military participation, such as the increased availability of highly-trained workers and leaders.[109]

Feminist lawyers fell back on race-sex parallels, comparing the all-male draft to racial segregation of the armed forces. Exempting women from military obligations, NOW's brief insisted, "excludes women from the compulsory involvement in the community's survival that is perceived as entitling people to lead it and to derive from it the full rights and privileges of citizenship." Similar assumptions about black men had undergirded segregation in the military, but racial integration improved military preparedness and race relations more generally. So it would be for women, NOW contended.[110] The ACLU's brief warned that upholding the all-male draft would set "a dangerous and open-ended precedent," potentially validating anew racial classifications by the military.[111]

Rostker was "the Stalingrad of all sex discrimination cases," said one reporter.[112] The Court was sure to take a case of such "fundamental importance" and "national interest."[113] The future of sex equality law swayed in the balance. After the oral arguments, the Justices disagreed over the appropriate standard of review. Burger favored the rational basis test.[114] Brennan argued that the only real question was whether the exclusion of women was "substantially related" to military preparedness, an undeniably vital government interest but one that he believed was not actually at stake in this case. The registration of women, Brennan believed, would "cause no problem." Marshall thought the lower court "entirely right" that women [could] do anything men [could] do in [the] armed services." Stewart, Powell, and Blackmun voted to uphold the all-male draft.[115] White did as well, but more tentatively. Stevens agreed with the majority, contending, "[G]ender is different from race—in some gender cases it made no sense to treat men and women differently. In other cases, men and women *are* different." Rehnquist likewise insisted, "[W]omen and men are not similarly situated in Armed Services and can't be."[116]

The Court's ultimate support of the all-male draft dismayed feminists, but the Justices' correspondence suggests that the *Rostker* opinion could have been far more detrimental to their cause. Brennan intimated after the conference discussion that his vote might be winnable, prompting Rehnquist to write the decision narrowly. Clerk Paul Smith wrote to Powell: "Justice Rehnquist's clerk mentioned that they wrote this opinion as moderately as possible in order to increase their chances of getting Justice Brennan's vote. They may well have succeeded."[117] In the end, Brennan and White both joined Marshall in dissent, but Brennan's strategic move may have mitigated the damage to sex equality law.

Powell's mind had been made up almost from the start; he simply could not see women and men as similarly situated with respect to military service or family life. He found Smith's memos urging the inclusion of women in the draft "helpful, but not persuasive enough to convince me."[118] Powell had many concerns about the challenge to all-male draft registration.[119] "[S]ocietal interests . . . rooted in the history of our civilization, recognizing that women *are* different (thank goodness!)," he said, "and in some contexts need and should receive protections never traditionally accorded to men."[120] His clerk argued that the "tangible problems with drafting women—involving pregnancy, child care, the family in general . . . [were] present to a large degree when men are drafted as well." Powell replied, *"No."*[121] He also worried about forcing equality norms on military decision making.[122] Basic training, separate housing, overseas duty, and service in different types of units "[could] *be litigated by men and women,"* he wrote in red ink in his notes.[123]

Powell—usually a moderate counterpoint to Rehnquist's harder-line conservatism—lamented Rehnquist's temperate language in *Rostker*. Privately, Powell called Rehnquist's first draft "an 'over-kill' type of opinion that seems *timid* and *self-conscious* in its *repetitive* reliance on [the] duty to de-fer."[124] In Rehnquist's second draft, he said, "the word 'deference' is used with revolting frequency." He continued, "Congress would have been irresponsible to have included women in the registration/draft law. We already have an army that probably cannot fight." Powell concluded, "Although I view this as a weak and almost apologetic opinion, I'll join."[125]

Powell was far more polite in his correspondence with Rehnquist, but urged him to discuss the reasons behind the "'policy' against women in combat," including the "unprecedented strains on family life" that drafting women would produce.[126] Rehnquist replied that he had made "a conscious decision" to omit the argument made in a Schlafly-sponsored amicus brief that "women have different roles in family life and in society than men," doubting that view could command a majority.[127] Instead, Rehnquist focused on the draft law's voluminous legislative history delineating exactly why Congress believed women should not be required to register. Under such circumstances, he concluded, "[t]he Constitution requires that Congress treat similarly situated persons similarly, not that it engage in gestures of superficial equality."[128] For the purposes of draft registration, the majority said, "[m]en and women, because of the combat restrictions on women, [were] simply not similarly situated."[129]

Feminists did not know that they had dodged a bullet. They worried that the "majority's rationale signaled a retreat" from heightened scrutiny for sex classifications.[130] To dissenters Marshall and Brennan, the majority had "place[d] its imprimatur" on "one of the most potent remaining public expressions of" what Marshall had earlier labeled "ancient canards about the proper role of women."[131] The majority, Marshall wrote, seemed to treat the case as not involving sex discrimination at all.[132]

The statutory rape and military draft cases highlighted the way that race equality law had been reduced to a mandate to treat "similarly situated" individuals the same. For those who did not believe that men and women were "similarly situated," their differences justified many forms of differential treatment. Blacks and whites must be identical in the eyes of the law, but "real," "natural," or "physiological" sex differences were a different matter altogether. More subtly, these cases revealed the Court's increasingly cramped conception of race equality law. Now the law of equal protection was blind not only to color but to the persistence of material inequality. Race precedents provided few tools for feminists to address what they now called women's "subordination."[133]

Michael M. and *Rostker* thus presented feminists with no-win situations. Reasoning from race now meant arguing for formal equality. Arguments in favor of subjecting women to liability for statutory rape, or to military conscription, played directly into the hands of antifeminists. They had long warned that legal equality would "liberate" women to be raped with impunity, torn from their children and forced into the workforce, or worse, into military combat. Statutory rape laws could help prosecutors convict perpetrators in cases with insufficient evidence of force, potentially providing for more vigorous enforcement of laws against sexual assault. Ordinarily pacifist feminists might have been willing to gamble that drafting women would help to transform the military and limit Congress's willingness to reinstate the draft or deploy military force. But the risk that women's assimilation into the armed forces would be just that—assimilation—seemed high. And even if equal treatment with men in the military were desirable, it was hardly guaranteed. Feminists themselves argued that few if any women would perform the most dangerous combat duties in an effort to mitigate the threat posed by a nondiscriminatory draft.

Although favorable rulings in *Michael M.* and *Rostker* might not have significantly advanced feminists' cause, defeat proved no less demoralizing.[134] Smeal called *Rostker* an indication of "a political tide [that was] essentially putting women back in their traditional place." She worried that ideas about women's incapacity would "work their way into discussions of lower wage scales for women, and into other forms of discrimination."[135] Schlafly was jubilant at the reaffirmation of traditional sex roles that both cases represented. She commented: "The American people want different roles for men and women in the armed forces of this country. . . . It's perfectly obvious that if ERA were in the Constitution, the decision would have gone the other way."[136] Feminist lawyers told the *New York Times* that they thought the Court would have applied the same reasoning even if the ERA had been ratified.[137] These contradictions reflected feminists' predicament: on the one hand, decisions like *Rostker* and *Michael M.* strengthened feminists' case that an ERA was necessary to guarantee women true equality with men.[138] On the other hand, many feminists still worried about associating the ERA with sex-neutral rape laws or drafting women.

Four days after the *Rostker* decision and exactly one year before the amendment's ratification deadline, ERA proponents rallied on New

York City's Fifth Avenue. Betty Friedan declared, "[T]he ERA is more important than it ever was. If we ever had any illusion that we didn't really need it . . . that illusion was destroyed by the Supreme Court last week." But she also acknowledged, "It's going to take a miracle to get it." The *New York Times* noted that "despite the balloons, the music, and many brave words, the prevailing tone was both urgent and worried." Schlafly called a press conference of her own, declaring the ERA a "lost cause."[139] After a five-year period in which only one state had ratified the ERA and five had attempted to rescind their ratification, most feminists recognized that victory would likely elude them.

The contrast between feminists' hopefulness at the beginning of the Carter administration and their despair at Reagan's rise masked some important continuities. Reagan's election cemented coalitions between civil rights and feminist advocates that had been nurtured by the conservative reactions to affirmative action and abortion rights in the second half of the 1970s. In the months following the 1980 elections, the ACLU, NOW, and the NAACP reported unprecedented surges in membership and donations. "Forget your differences," labor leader William Robertson exhorted civil rights, civil liberties, labor, and feminist groups gathered in December 1980 for an "emergency" meeting to address the right-wing threat. "We don't have the luxury of dividing ourselves over single issues any longer."[140] The Reagan administration's hostility to civil rights and feminism horrified activists, but it also galvanized them.

Some civil rights measures proved remarkably resilient. Then–EEOC staffer Anita Hill later recalled that commission Chair Clarence Thomas followed her recommendation not to rescind the commission's embattled sexual harassment guidelines.[141] The Supreme Court eventually recognized sexual harassment claims and extended *Weber* to uphold sex-based affirmative action in the waning days of the Reagan era.[142]

And the Reagan administration did throw feminists an occasional bone. Carter had appointed record numbers of women to positions of power and influence within his administration, as well as an unprecedented contingent of "women and minority" judges—including Ruth Bader Ginsburg, who was confirmed to the D.C. Circuit court in 1980. But the lack of vacancies during his presidency denied Carter a Supreme Court appointment. Reagan did not emulate Carter by raising feminists' expectations on any other subject, but he did pledge to nominate a woman to the Court. When Potter Stewart retired in 1981, Reagan surprised everyone by choosing Sandra Day O'Connor, a state judge and former legislator unknown outside her home state of Arizona.

O'Connor's positions on abortion and women's rights alarmed social conservatives. Her views on *Roe v. Wade* were far too ambiguous for those who wanted a solidly "pro-life" nominee.[143] The National Right to Life Committee and the Moral Majority opposed her nomination.[144] One antiabortion activist quipped, "We've been sold out."[145] As a state legislator, O'Connor had supported equal pay for equal work, opposed sex-specific labor legislation, and sought more equitable marriage and divorce laws.[146] She had urged the U.S. senators from Arizona to vote for the ERA and had spoken on the amendment's behalf in the state legislature. O'Connor's support for the ERA ebbed as the amendment became increasingly controversial, exemplifying what her biographer later recognized as a commitment only to winning causes.[147] Nevertheless, conservative strategist Richard Viguerie warned, "Mrs. O'Connor's support of the ERA suggests that she might follow the path of judicial activism set by the Warren Court."[148]

NOW hailed O'Connor's nomination as "a victory for women's rights," even though few saw her as an active feminist.[149] But "after all," as *Los Angeles Times* reporter Beverly Stephen wrote, "nobody thought Reagan was going to put Gloria Steinem on the bench." O'Connor's middle-of-the road approach could be an advantage in a politically polarized environment. Stephen suggested, "She will be acceptable in ways that a harder-line feminist would not. She may be able to speak in a moderate voice that will be heard."[150] One Arizona Democrat said, "If you have to have a Republican on the court, well, she's about the best we could hope for."[151]

O'Connor and her supporters worked to win over skeptics, and the White House trumpeted her law-and-order conservatism as well as her commitment to states' rights and judicial restraint. O'Connor, they boasted, was a committed wife and mother who put her "career on hold" to raise three sons.[152] Responding to the Rev. Jerry Falwell's opposition to O'Connor's nomination, Arizona senator Barry Goldwater famously retorted, "every good Christian ought to kick Falwell right in the ass."[153] Fresh from a Rehnquist clerkship, John Roberts spent his first day as special assistant to the attorney general preparing draft answers for O'Connor's confirmation hearing. His goal was to "avoid giving specific responses to any direct questions on legal issues likely to come before the Court," while "demonstrating . . . a firm command" of relevant precedents and arguments.[154] O'Connor's careful and often cryptic replies won over key conservative legislators, and after a much-publicized phone conversation with Reagan, Falwell withdrew his opposition. Polls showed an overwhelming majority of Americans supported O'Connor, and editorial pages lent their endorsements. The first woman nominee to the Court was confirmed by a unanimous 99–0 vote.[155]

Nearly everyone agreed that President Reagan's choice was a masterstroke. He had kept a campaign promise and distanced himself from religious conservatives in a way that reassured secular allies. And he deflected feminists who assailed his dismal record on appointments.[156] Many observers predicted that O'Connor's elevation to the Court would not significantly change its ideological configuration. "Potter Stewart all over again" was how one observer characterized her likely voting patterns.[157] In cases involving sex discrimination, Stewart had been toward the right of center on a Court unsteadily retreating from its brief and partial embrace of sex equality.[158]

O'Connor's first sex discrimination case appeared just a few weeks into the term: Joe Hogan's challenge to the Mississippi University for Women (MUW)'s exclusion of men from its nursing school. Hogan did not represent all men seeking entrance into the nursing profession or women's colleges, nor was he opposing affirmative action as "reverse discrimination." The twenty-six-year-old Hogan was already a surgical nurse, and he simply wanted to get his degree without leaving Columbus.

Hogan's attorney personified the case's complicated relationship to the rights revolution. As a teenager in the early 1960s, Wilbur Colom and his parents had attended underground civil rights meetings in their hometown of Ripley, Mississippi. After Fannie Lou Hamer spoke at a local church, it "mysteriously" burned to the ground, and a team of Oberlin students arrived to rebuild. At their urging, Colom moved north for high school, spent a summer working for SNCC in Atlanta, and got "caught up in the excitement of 'black power' and militant advocacy." As a college student at Howard, he was active in the National Welfare Rights Organization. After earning his law degree at Antioch, a haven for activist lawyers, Colom returned to Mississippi in the mid-1970s and opened a law practice in an antebellum mansion adjacent to the Columbus courthouse.

But Colom had also been involved with the Republican Party since the early 1970s, and he had served on Reagan's transition team. His law firm had "deliberately taken on particularly controversial cases," developing a reputation as "mavericks not only among establishment lawyers, but among traditional black and female civil-rights lawyers as well."[159] His clients in the early 1980s included a white student attending a formerly all-black school and white police officers charged with brutality. Colom and his wife and law partner Dorothy Winston Colom believed the Hogan case would advance the feminist cause, and they joined forces with the ACLU of Mississippi to file a complaint on Hogan's behalf.

Feminists were at best ambivalent about Hogan's case. The national ACLU had declined to participate, and clashed with its Mississippi affiliate as the case made its way through the lower courts. As NOW LDEF attorney Anne Simon wrote in an internal memo, "The context of *Hogan* is not politically auspicious." Ideally, feminists could use the case to shore up robust judicial scrutiny for sex classifications while preserving "[t]he possibility that a sex-based classification [could] be used for affirmative action purposes." But many feminists worried that their participation would be seen as "attacking private women's colleges, institutions that [had] produced large numbers of feminists and that [were] supported by large numbers of feminists."[160]

The Fifth Circuit ruled for Hogan, but reinforced feminists' misgivings. The problem with MUW, wrote Judge Charles Clark, was not that the all-women's college was "based on role concepts for women that are no longer acceptable to many," including courses in "bookkeeping, photography, stenography, telegraphy, and typewriting," and "instruction in fancy, general and practical needlework." Rather, MUW's reasoning was circular: the nursing school could not justify excluding men because of the state's interest in providing educational opportunities to women. Clark wrote: "If a state were to urge that it has a compelling interest in educating white persons, its urging would be, at best, half true. But such a half-true premise could not support the maintenance of racially segregated schools. . . . Similarly, to justify gender-based discrimination in this case, Mississippi cannot advance a reason that is based on gender."[161] Clark's analogy to race—implicitly comparing the exclusion of *men* to the exclusion of blacks—suggested a symmetrical approach to equality unfriendly to affirmative action.[162]

On appeal to the Supreme Court, MUW defended its exclusion of men as affirmative action for women. "[W]omen still face pervasive, although at times more subtle, discrimination," they reminded the Court, quoting extensively from social science scholarship on the benefits of single-sex education for women.[163] MUW attorney Hunter Gholson, an Ole Miss alumnus, Republican county chairman, and unlikely champion of affirmative action, cited Justice Marshall's recent opinion affirming congressional funding set-asides for minority-owned businesses: "[I]f you change the words 'race' to 'gender' and 'white' to 'male' and 'black' to 'female,' it is a beautiful argument for the existence of MUW."[164] Once again, feminists had to explain how sex classifications that appeared to benefit women could instead reinforce women's subordination. Hogan's brief read like a primer on sex equality cases where the Justices had found men and women to be "similarly situated." Wilbur Colom argued that the policy's "actual purpose" reflected sex-stereotyped visions of women's proper role.

But feminists did not want to argue for sex-blindness. NOW LDEF attorneys assured NOW board members that the feminists' amicus brief "acknowledge[d] the validity of arguments that favor maintaining all-female schools in those instances where such segregation genuinely serves the goal of bringing women into full equality . . . to overcome the effects of past discrimination."[165] They hoped to preserve the constitutionality of some single-sex schools and of genuine affirmative action for women.

Law clerks once again tried, unsuccessfully, to persuade the swing Justices to vote in feminists' favor. Blackmun clerk Mary "Kit" Kinports echoed assurances from women's organizations that the Court's "opinion could be written narrowly" so as to avoid "any untoward policy effects."[166] But Blackmun's notes revealed his skepticism, which Powell shared. Like Blackmun, Powell was not persuaded by his clerk's memo arguing for a narrow affirmance that left open the possibility that another single-sex institution "with more consistent affirmative action interests" could be sustained.[167]

But for the first time in a sex equality case, a woman had a voice on the Court. O'Connor's vote in Hogan determined the outcome. At the Justices' conference after oral arguments, Burger recommended reversing the lower court on the ground that "no invidious purpose [existed] when this college was formed or now exists." Brennan voted to affirm on the "narrow" facts of the case, noting that the Court "need not reach [the] broader issue of uni-sex schools." Three more Justices lined up on each side, with Rehnquist, Blackmun, and Powell voting to reverse, and

White, Stevens, and Marshall agreeing with Brennan. That left O'Connor, who as the newest Justice spoke last. She did not believe Mississippi had carried its burden to "show [the] benefit of [single-sex] schools."[168] In the first constitutional sex equality case of her Supreme Court career, she parted ways with her conservative colleagues.

Assigned the majority opinion, O'Connor turned a narrow holding and close vote into a significant constitutional pronouncement.[169] O'Connor made clear that it was the government's burden to prove that a sex-based distinction was substantially related to an important interest. She also added a potent phrase: "[T]he State has fallen far short of establishing the *exceedingly persuasive justification* needed to sustain the gender-based classification." Leaving open the possibility that a genuine compensatory justification might pass muster, O'Connor dismissed the notion that affirmative action was the purpose or effect of MUW's policy. Instead, she wrote, "excluding males from admission to the School of Nursing tends to perpetuate the stereotyped view of nursing as an exclusively woman's job."[170] O'Connor placed *Hogan* squarely within the line of cases that rejected the imposition of traditional roles on women and men and scrutinized sex-based classifications even when they ostensibly benefited women.

In many ways, Powell and O'Connor shared a pragmatic instinct for seeking the middle ground. Later, commentators noted the striking similarities in their approaches to contentious issues like affirmative action.[171] In *Hogan*, however, they could not have been further apart. After reading O'Connor's draft opinion, Powell wrote in an internal memorandum: "There is no history of discrimination against men," he pointed out. "No ERA for men has been proposed."[172] The state provided other institutions of higher education for men to study nursing, and for a coeducational environment. Excluding Hogan did not, in Powell's view, offend the constitution.

Feminists knew better than to emphasize a race-sex analogy in *Hogan*, but the swing Justices reasoned from race reflexively. MUW, as one of many educational options, could not be compared to the "separate but equal" scheme condemned in *Brown*, they believed. "In a more fundamental sense, the racial classifications are examples of *invidious* discrimination," Powell wrote privately. Single-sex education remained a valuable educational choice, he insisted. "Perhaps I should add a footnote that I have experienced it personally with a wife and three daughters."[173] Blackmun, too, saw sex as fundamentally different from race. He wrote in his *Hogan* dissent: "I hope that we do not lose all values that some think are worthwhile (and are not based on differences of race or religion) and relegate ourselves to needless conformity."[174]

For the swing Justices as well as the Court's conservative wing, *Hogan* exemplified sex equality law's excesses. Blackmun said in dissent: "I have come to suspect that it is easy to go too far with rigid rules in this area of claimed sex discrimination." Powell's private notes revealed his mounting frustration with the Court's sex equality jurisprudence. "The Court, in this case, may have departed farther from the intent and purpose of the Equal Protection Clause than in any prior case."[175] In an early draft of his dissent, Powell called Hogan's claim "frivolous," and lamented that the "Court's decision comes close to trivializing the Equal Protection Clause of the Constitution."[176] Powell modulated his exasperation only somewhat in the final version, joined by Rehnquist: "Left without honor—indeed, held unconstitutional—is an element of diversity that has characterized much of American education and enriched much of American life," he began. His dissent concluded, "This simply is not a sex discrimination case. The Equal Protection Clause was never intended to be applied to this kind of case."[177]

The Court's opinions in *Hogan* were issued the day after the ERA's ratification deadline expired, on July 1, 1982. O'Connor "snatched partial victory from the jaws of total defeat," Colom later recalled, offering feminists "comfort in a bleak hour."[178] *New York Times* reporter Linda Greenhouse called *Hogan* "a ruling of limited practical impact but considerable constitutional importance."[179] "We felt that an enormous backlash was under way against women's rights," Wilbur Colom recalled. When he and his colleagues heard of the decision, "We brought out bottles of champagne. A man had won his sex discrimination case, yet we toasted the women of the feminist movement." For Colom, the *Hogan* case symbolized a new era in race and gender relations. Two decades earlier, "choosing sides was easy," he wrote. "The issues were simple and straightforward, black and white with little gray." Now, in contrast, "the issues [were] more complex," choosing sides more "complicated." The true legacy of the civil rights and feminist movements, Colom insisted, was to establish "principles that free everyone . . . whites as well as blacks, men as well as women."[180]

Hogan reflected the state of constitutional sex equality law in the early 1980s. *Hogan*'s author belonged to a politically ascendant demographic—

white, affluent, suburban women.[181] Race played a muted role in the case, despite its setting in the deep South.[182] And race-sex analogies were of little use to feminists. The exclusion of men from a nursing degree program bore little resemblance to the exclusion of African Americans from higher education or the separation of white and black children in school. Feminists wished to preserve the possibility of affirmative action for women and people of color in education and elsewhere. But men, unlike African Americans, were indisputably the dominant, privileged sex; Joe Hogan seemed exceptional in his desire to gain entrance to an all-female institution. The parallel between MUW and historically black colleges and universities might have been stronger, but that analogy, too, was politically fraught for both sides.[183]

Hogan preserved what advocates had gained in the 1970s and also suggested the limitations of those victories. Like many of the earlier women's rights cases, the facts of Hogan were less than compelling, its practical impact dwarfed by its significance for constitutional doctrine. Hogan affirmed that where men and women seemed "similarly situated," explicit sex-based classifications would be difficult to justify. The swing Justices were at pains to distinguish sex discrimination from race discrimination even as the Court's definition of race discrimination constricted.

Two weeks after the ERA's ratification deadline expired in the summer of 1982, more than two hundred senators and representatives reintroduced the amendment. House Speaker Thomas P. "Tip" O'Neill and Senator Ted Kennedy proclaimed their commitment to equality before a crowd of several hundred in front of the Capitol. Congressional hearings on "ERA II" and feminists' debates over how to approach the revived amendment reveal how both feminist legal advocacy and the resurgence of conservatism had transformed reasoning from race and the politics of amendment advocacy.[184]

The world had changed since the early 1970s. Partisan and ideological alignments shifted: formerly skeptical Democrats endorsed the amendment, and the GOP withdrew long-standing support. Feminists were ambivalent about the ERA's reintroduction, but Democrats hoped to exploit the emerging electoral "gender gap" to embarrass the Reagan administration. Litigation and legislative reform had removed many of the explicit sex-based classifications that the ERA originally was designed to vanquish. By the early 1980s, feminists had used the equal protection clause to eliminate most distinctions based on sex from the statute books, and Title VII had become a potent if imperfect weapon against employment discrimination.

What feminists wanted from the ERA had therefore evolved. The equal protection clause had proven more useful than predicted, but its limitations were increasingly apparent. Now feminists hoped to fill the gaps in the Court's equal protection jurisprudence by mandating disparate impact analysis, countenancing affirmative action, and making discrimination based on pregnancy unconstitutional. They demanded an ERA that went beyond "equality in theory" to achieve "equality in fact."

Feminists now reasoned beyond race; they demanded more from the Constitution than advocates for civil rights had achieved. For ERA II meaningfully to advance the feminist agenda, it needed to reach not only beyond what the equal protection clause had done for sex inequality, but also beyond what it had done to remedy racial injustice. But the conservative political milieu of the early 1980s made even a reliance on limited race equality precedents risky. Conservatives already wary of race equality law were unlikely to embrace a more expansive conception of sex equality.

Feminists found themselves besieged with specific and probing questions from opponents, and the comparison to race was relentlessly double-edged. A decade earlier, an analogy to race underscored the magnitude and gravity of discrimination against women and the government's relative apathy toward feminist goals. Then, skeptics generally assumed the legitimacy of race equality law but doubted its applicability to sex. Now, conservatives attacked the legal precedents established by the civil rights revolution as well as claims that sex should be treated like race. They recoiled from expansive federal power and judicial innovation in areas such as busing and abortion. Feminists hoped that "the ERA's stronger protection against laws that were sexist in impact would have a spillover effect extending stronger protection to blacks injured by laws that were racist in impact," as law professors Ann Freedman and Sylvia Law later wrote.[185] To ERA opponents, any such "spillover effect" justified passionate opposition.

The potential applications of disparate impact theory to sex equality law were threatening enough by themselves. Disparate impact could apply to everything from military regulations to veterans' employment preferences to decisions regarding child custody, as well as to abortion funding and government benefits programs like Social Security. In earlier cases challenging veterans' preferences, feminists had felt constrained by Court precedents that required proof of discriminatory intent. Now, feminist proponents of ERA II supported a bold approach that did not depend on such evidence of animus. NOW LDEF attorney Phyllis Segal hoped that exploring ERA II's implications for disparate impact cases would expand the amendment's "potential as a legal tool." But she worried that without further legislative history, the Court would import an intent requirement from equal protection case law. "While purpose or intent to discriminate would be definitive evidence" in a disparate impact case, Segal explained, "such evidence is not *required* (as it is in [equal protection] cases). This is the point that has not been articulated before." Segal also recognized that "[e]ven if proponents don't focus [on] the issue [of disparate impact], a smart 'undecided' legislator, or opponents, [would]."[186]

In the eyes of skeptics, such an expansive approach to sex equality threatened to wreak havoc on existing laws and regulations. If more women than men received public assistance, then cuts in benefits would have a disparate impact on women. Family law rules, from the financial consequences of divorce to child custody, would be susceptible to disparate impact analysis. Virtually every aspect of military service could be vulnerable. At congressional hearings in 1983 and 1984, ERA opponents and skeptics focused relentlessly on these questions. One anti-ERA witness worried that disparate impact analysis would "require that one-half the eligible married women be drafted, while their husbands stay home, and in many cases take care of the baby."[187] Another warned that the ERA debate was "no longer an argument about equal rights, but an argument about equal results."[188]

ERA supporters knew they needed a limiting principle for disparate impact theory. They could have quantified the degree of disparate impact necessary to trigger special judicial scrutiny. Instead, they proposed heightened scrutiny of disparate impact that was "traceable to and reinforce[d], or perpetuate[d], discriminatory patterns similar to those associated with facial discrimination."[189] Feminists were concerned about disparate negative effects on *women,* not with policies that harmed men. ERA II, they emphasized, would not affect the income tax just because progressive taxation fell more heavily on men than on women.

This reponse was hardly reassuring to conservatives. And the debate further revealed the conundrum feminists faced as they strove to clarify the relationship between the ERA and affirmative action.[190] Phyllis Segal defended the validity of affirmative action under the ERA. Any other approach, she wrote to colleagues, "would elevate 'equality in theory' over 'equality in fact.'" She asserted: "Where differential treatment is targeted to achieve equality it should survive scrutiny under the ERA." But Segal also hoped to "avoid the protracted reverse discrimination challenges that [were] being litigated in race cases."[191] For their part, opponents charged that the ERA would inevitably impose quotas on governments and public universities.[192] The congressional sponsors of Title VII never envisioned that the statute would permit affirmative action by employers, yet the Court had validated just such practices.[193] The same process would make the ERA a behemoth, they warned, further increasing federal intervention in work and home life.

In response to their opponents, ERA supporters found themselves embracing analogies to race as a limiting principle for affirmative action. When a witness claimed that the ERA would require 50 percent quotas for women in the military, including in combat roles, Columbia Law Professor Henry Monaghan responded, "That's plainly insupportable. . . . I mean, the race analogy is perfect. . . . There is just no basis for reading the Equal Rights Amendment as imposing quotas on the military."[194] In the Senate hearings, Hatch asked pro–ERA witness Antonia Chayes whether the ERA would permit or require affirmative action for women in the military. She carefully replied, "[W]here you are dealing with affirmative action issues, where the policies are designed to correct inequities of the past, just as in race cases, they will be very carefully scrutinized by the courts, if, indeed, they ever get to the courts."[195] When Utah Republican senator Orrin Hatch asked whether a 10 percent set-aside for women in government contracting would violate the ERA, Marsha Levick of the NOW Legal Defense and Education Fund responded that "such affirmative sex-conscious 'remedies' would be no more or less unconstitutional than the comparable race-conscious programs . . . if an 'institutionally competent actor' makes a finding of past discrimination vis-à-vis that institution, industry, etc. sex-conscious programs could be implemented."[196] The "etc." masked a key question that applied to race as well as sex: whether the existence of general, society-wide discrimination justified affirmative action.[197]

The debate over ERA II's effect on reproductive rights drove home the political hazards of reasoning from race. ERA opponents argued that the parallel to race foretold a vast expansion of abortion rights. Accepting a full-blown analogy between race and sex could imperil not only the separation between pregnancy discrimination and constitutional sex equality law, but limits on abortion funding. ERA opponents stressed the radical potential of the analogy to great effect. Rep. Henry Hyde, author of the Hyde amendment, testified at a Senate hearing on ERA II, "If sex discrimination were treated like race discrimination, Government refusal to fund abortions would be treated like a refusal to fund medical procedures that affect members of minority races."[198] Anti-ERA witness Grover Rees echoed many opponents when he testified, "[A] legislative program that funds other operations but not abortion would be constitutionally identical to a program that funded cures for every disease except sickle cell anemia, to which only blacks are susceptible."[199] Washington University professor Jules Gerard said that proponents of the amendment had pointed to "the potential of ERA to overturn statutes which have a disparate impact on women," so "for them to conclude that the classical statute which must have a disparate impact on women"—a restriction on abortion—"would be unaffected. . . . I don't understand their logic."[200]

Indeed, feminists' position was the product of an uneasy compromise between political expedience and their growing desire to reunite reproductive rights and constitutional sex equality.[201] Feminists had long disagreed over how to portray the relationship between the ERA and reproductive rights. Occasionally this tension bubbled to the surface, as it had in 1980 when Equal Rights Advocates attorney Mary Dunlap excoriated feminists who "trade[d]-off poor women's right to choose abortion" for "an illusory promise of constitutional equality applicable only to those women who [were] not poor, not pregnant, not in need of abortions."[202] Rhonda Copelon expressed the views of many feminists in a 1983 *Ms.* Magazine article: "[T]he separation of abortion from the campaign for the ERA has jeopardized abortion and produced a truncated version of liberation."[203] The connection between the ERA and abortion, Copelon suggested, should be embraced—if not with pride, then at least with grim determination. ERA opponents seized upon Copelon's article as evidence of feminists' true intentions for the ERA.

ERA proponents considered a range of approaches to abortion as they prepared for the ERA II hearings. Levick laid out three possible responses to one of the most pressing questions: "Is a woman's right to voluntarily choose to undergo an abortion enhanced, sustained or diminished by a federal equal rights amendment?" They first described abortion "as an aspect of the right *shared by men and women equally* to control their reproductive capacity, and to retain for themselves the right to decide when and under what circumstances they wish to become a parent."[204] This option linked abortion with both equality and privacy, and rejected outright the claim that pregnancy was a "unique physical characteristic" that justified differential treatment.[205] Levick's second alternative sacrificed this boldness at the altar of pragmatism: proponents could argue that abortion rights were "unaffected" by the ERA. But feminists did want to ensure that the ERA would encompass discrimination based on pregnancy. To that end, Levick suggested a third option: treat abortion regulations as involving "unique physical characteristics" subject to strict scrutiny under the ERA.[206]

Feminist attorneys briefed pro-ERA witnesses on how to respond to questions about abortion: abortion rights were protected by privacy jurisprudence under the Fourteenth Amendment. But feminists did not want pro-ERA witnesses to foreclose the ERA's applicability to reproductive rights. Striking this delicate balance proved very nearly impossible in the hearing room. When Rep. Mike DeWine asked women's rights advocate Bernice Sandler about the ERA's impact on the Hyde amendment, she deftly replied that "the Supreme Court [had] not viewed abortion under the Equal Protection Clause as a civil rights issue." Instead, she said, "[t]hey have always viewed it in terms of due process and privacy, and that is where the Court has been coming from all along."[207] DeWine pressed further: would "the passage of the ERA . . . in any way affect the right to an abortion or any legislation that might follow?" The next two witnesses declared outright that the ERA would have "no relationship" to abortion.[208]

Feminist lawyers were dismayed. The "no-relationship" language was memorialized by House counsel in a summary to be used by members of Congress in their testimony. "Obviously," ERA leader Sally Burns wrote, "legislative history to that effect is troubling to pro-choice concerns."[209] Meanwhile, congressional proponents of the amendment tried to dismiss the issue as a red herring.[210] Remarks like Rep. Chuck Schumer's compounded the problem. "Abortion has nothing to do with discrimination between men and women, period," he said, "until the time when a man can have an abortion or become pregnant, and then maybe it will have something to do with it. But until that point we ought to just abandon that argument and throw it out," Schumer declared to applause during one hearing.[211]

Proponents also disagreed about how to address the ERA's relationship to abortion funding. Ann Freedman, now a law professor at Rutgers, "believe[d] the ratification of the ERA [would] not affect Supreme Court decisions on Medicaid funding." Others, including Marcia Greenberger and Judy Lichtman, "think that it will (or hope that it will) if we don't have in the legislative history any statement that it won't have any effect or that ERA had 'no relation' to abortion." Greenberger and Lichtman counseled Freedman "to 'stonewall' if Congressman DeWine presse[d] her with questions and not to state her legal reasoning for thinking it [would] have no impact." Catherine East suggested instead that in order to ward off an antiabortion rider to the ERA, proponents offer "a clear unequivocal statement in the House Committee report that it is not the intent of the Congress that the ERA have any impact on abortion."[212] In the final House hearing, Freedman and Yale Law professor Tom Emerson testified that courts would decide abortion cases under the right to privacy, regardless of the ERA's fate. While feminist lawyers were careful not to disavow all connection between the new ERA and abortion, their strategy of circumvention shortchanged feminists' aspirations.

In the end, ERA II fell six votes short of the two-thirds majority needed for passage in the House and never came up for a vote in the Republican-controlled Senate. This final nail in the ERA's coffin liberated feminists even as it reinforced their political marginalization.[213] No longer encumbered by fears about the ERA's fate, leading feminists called for the reunification of abortion and sex equality arguments.[214] NYU Law professor Sylvia Law's 1984 article "Rethinking Sex and the Constitution" defended "a more integrated approach."[215] Ruth Bader Ginsburg, now a federal appeals court judge, promoted a "constitutionally based sex-equality perspective" on abortion, speculating that such a conception might have produced a different outcome in the abortion funding cases.[216] Feminist theorist Catharine MacKinnon lacerated the decision to rest the campaign for abortion rights on privacy grounds, rather than on equality or freedom, in an essay written around this time.[217] Once the amendment died, MacKinnon said, "There seemed little to lose, even from the truth."[218]

Feminists no longer had to fit every aspect of their legal agenda into a single, all-encompassing grand principle. They could, as young Stanford law professor Deborah Rhode recommended in 1983, "pause in the pursuit of an increasingly divisive constitutional symbol and focus on more concrete responses to structural inequities."[219] Judges and politicians had been wary of constitutional disparate impact theory's apparently limitless sweep. But a new generation of feminists joined their predecessors in exploring the concept's potential in specific contexts.[220] Feminist lawyer and professor Nancy Erickson had called for a disparate impact approach to pregnancy discrimination in 1978. Since then, judges' record had been mixed, but a few decisions gave reason to hope. In 1981, for instance, a D.C. Circuit panel including civil rights paragons Spottswood Robinson and J. Skelly Wright had allowed a labor union trainee to pursue her claim that a union policy limiting leave to ten days discriminated against women.[221]

Disparate impact analysis also had the potential to resolve the "equal treatment/special treatment" controversy, a sometimes divisive reprise of the earlier generation's debate over protective labor legislation. This time, feminists disagreed over laws and policies that gave pregnant women benefits not available to other employees temporarily unable to work. Wendy Webster Williams, a prominent proponent of the "equal treatment" position, wrote in 1982, "If we can't have it both ways, we need to think carefully about which way we want to have it." In her view, "for all of its problems, the equality approach"—treating pregnant workers the same as other temporarily disabled workers—was "the better one."[222] Linda Krieger of the Employment Law Project in San Francisco believed that the equal treatment approach was insufficient, but also recognized the pitfalls of advocating "special treatment" for women. Krieger and a student coauthor published an article in 1983 promoting an "adverse impact theory" as a way to "harmonize" the Pregnancy Discrimination Act (PDA) and "positive" legislation for pregnant workers.[223] They argued that employers should be forbidden to create special rules for pregnancy, but that judges should scrutinize employment policies that had a disparate impact on pregnant women.[224] In the coming years, Wendy Williams endorsed this third path, and Yale law student Reva Siegel offered a robust and detailed defense of disparate impact analysis under the PDA.[225] Disparate impact allowed feminists to have it both ways: they could attack policies that harmed pregnant women by changing the rules for all workers, male and female.

The ERA's defeat could also undermine the separation between race and sex equality that the amendment had sometimes symbolized. Reasoning beyond race had potentially dangerous implications for coalitions between feminists and civil rights advocates. As Ann Freedman and Sylvia Law recalled, "[ERA II] proponents had no desire to urge that women were entitled to a greater measure of constitutional protection than black people. Rather, most ERA proponents sought common cause between those who struggled against racism and sexism." They hoped that more expansive sex equality norms would "spill over" into race jurisprudence. But "it was difficult to use the actual words of the ERA to support this pragmatic belief."[226] U.S. Civil Rights Commissioner and legal historian Mary Frances Berry was among the very few people of color testifying on ERA II's behalf. Notably, while most ERA supporters claimed that the amendment would apply a higher standard of review to sex classifications than the strict scrutiny applicable to race under the equal protection clause, Berry testified that the standards would be identical.[227] To suggest otherwise seemed to threaten the already frayed bonds between civil rights and feminism.

Reasoning from race itself had become an easy target for condemnation. In her classic 1981 work *Ain't I a Woman*, the African American cultural critic bell hooks excoriated white feminists for their "constant comparison[s] of the plight of 'women' and 'blacks,'" charging that such analogies "support[ed] the exclusion of black women" and epitomized a "sexist-racist attitude endemic to the women's liberation movement." Hooks condemned parallels between racial and sexual oppression—especially by white women who "used black people as metaphors"—as parasitic and marginalizing.[228] A growing chorus of feminist scholars joined hooks in the early 1980s.[229]

These critiques reflected a renaissance in black and other "multicultural" women's studies. Anthologies of writing by and about women of color, classic works of black women's history and black feminist theory, and national conferences, such as "The Status of American Black Women: Their Influence on the American Economy" and "The Role of Black Women in the Civil Rights Struggle and Beyond," augured a broad new wave of interest and activism.[230] Some activists sought to unify racial and economic justice with feminism.[231] Others preferred independence from white-dominated women's groups.[232] In the 1970s, African American feminists placed women of color at the center of feminist analysis as they explored the interconnections between race, class, sex, and sexuality. Now they entered academia in larger and more influential numbers.[233]

This rebirth came later to the legal academy. Apart from pioneering scholars like Pauli Murray, Eleanor Holmes Norton (who taught at Georgetown and coauthored an important early sex discrimination casebook), and now Mary Frances Berry, relatively few feminist lawyers of color had obtained prestigious academic posts.[234] In the early 1980s, race and feminism remained largely separate in legal scholarship. There were exceptions: EEOC attorney Judy Trent Ellis theorized sexual harassment law through the lens of black women's experience; Illinois law professor Elaine Shoben explored the phenomenon of "compound" employment discrimination against women of color.[235]

By the late 1980s and early 1990s, women of color had revived "intersectionality" as a category of analysis in legal scholarship and activism.[236] They produced theoretically sophisticated scholarship, critiquing male-focused civil rights movements and white middle-class feminism that assumed the universality of white women's experience. These scholars sought to place women of color at the center, rather than the margins, of critical inquiry. Legal scholars of intersectionality rarely grappled with the legacies of women like Murray and Norton, however. The roots of reasoning from race in African American feminist legal advocacy had almost entirely disappeared from view.

For her part, Pauli Murray followed feminists' encounters with law from the pulpit. In a 1977 ceremony at Washington's National Cathedral, Murray became the first African American female priest in the Episcopal Church. After her inaugural sermon, delivered in the Chapel Hill sanctuary where her enslaved great-grandmother had been baptized more than a century earlier, Murray offered a prayer for the ERA's speedy passage.[237] She continued to speak and write about race, sex, and law, moving smoothly from statutory and constitutional text to Scripture and from legal to religious doctrine.[238] After ERA II failed in 1983, Murray wrote to feminist leaders to propose a new "Human Rights Amendment" that would encompass all "'downtrodden, weak and subordinate' groups" and allow "all minorities [to] come together in a coalition."[239] Once again, she hoped that bringing race and sex together in law would deliver on the promise of the rights revolution.

But the time for constitutional amendment had passed. Many advocates believed that feminists had wrung all the social change they could from the federal Constitution and looked primarily to other venues like legislation, lobbying, state constitutional litigation, and local activism. In the coming years, feminists would defend their gains in court and focus on new avenues of legal change in diverse arenas, from violence against women, to pay equity, to family leave, to reproductive freedom. They convinced the Supreme Court to recognize sexual harassment as a Title VII violation and to permit employers to engage in voluntary affirmative action for women. They struggled to form coalitions in the face of difference, to sustain a progressive vision in a conservative era.

Critics charged, then and since, that feminists sought a narrow version of formal equality in the 1970s, based on a simplistic and exploitive analogy between race and sex. The Supreme Court's early 1980s sex equality decisions, the ERA's demise, and the invisibility of race in sex equality jurisprudence all contributed to this perception. Given the Justices' narrow conception of race discrimination, the enduring legal and social meaning attributed to sex differences, and the erasure of women of color's experience, small wonder that reasoning from race seemed a discredited and bankrupt strategy.

But these shortcomings reflected the constraints feminists faced more than any poverty of ambition. The debate over ERA II reveals the disjuncture between feminists' aspirations and the dominant conservative political and legal environment. Ironically, by the early 1980s, the substantive equality feminists demanded resembled the racial justice movement's most expansive aspirations perhaps more than ever before. In seeking "equality in fact" through disparate impact, and in reuniting reproductive freedom with equality law, feminists' goals mirrored those of the civil rights struggle to an unprecedented degree. But the Reagan counterrevolution made the short-term success of both movements more tenuous than ever. Civil rights and feminism converged just as the civil rights era drew to a close.

CONCLUSION

In 2008, legal scholar Richard Thompson Ford questioned popular analogies between gay rights activism and the African American civil rights struggle. "Opposition to same-sex marriage isn't simply the 21st century's form of racism," he wrote. Rather, anxiety about changing sex roles was to blame. Many Americans, he suggested, "long for the kind of meaningful gender identities that traditional marriage seems to offer." The different treatment of race and sex discrimination in law, he wrote, "reflects this ambivalence about sex difference."[1]

Yet in the 1970s, dismantling government support for traditional sex roles within marriage was where feminists were most successful. Thanks to their legal advocacy, the Supreme Court invalidated laws that assumed or encouraged a male breadwinner/female homemaker family structure. At the same time, feminists won the enactment of antidiscrimination laws to support women's economic independence from men. Eventually, equal employment opportunity expanded to include affirmative action as well as freedom from pregnancy discrimination and sexual harassment. Feminists insisted that women's traditional responsibility for caregiving should not limit their jury service. By the early 1980s, feminists had vanquished the notion that law should reinforce women's place "at the center of home and family life."[2]

But feminists' success had limits. Sex equality law remained largely divorced from reproductive freedom, discriminatory intent requirements limited constitutional disparate impact claims, the scope of permissible affirmative action remained in doubt, and physical differences justified sex-specific laws such as women's exclusion from the military draft. Restrictions on abortion funding and access to reproductive health care threatened reproductive freedom for the young and poor. The public centerpiece of feminists' legal and political agenda, the ERA, went down to defeat.

Reasoning from race played a central role both in feminists' achievements and in their failures. Pauli Murray compared "women" and "Negroes" to persuade skeptics that sex discrimination should be included in the civil rights agenda. She also hoped to unite advocates for racial justice with the reemerging feminist movement. Murray and her allies convinced fellow feminists, civil rights advocates, and many legal decision makers to accept a parallel between race and sex. But analogies, when embraced by law, often became one-dimensional and abstract, reducing the meaning of race and sex discrimination to the lowest common denominator. Economic recession and conservative ascendancy made race equality law a less appealing template and intensified competition between "women" and "minorities." Analogies to race that once seemed full of promise became crabbed, co-optable, and constraining. By the time feminists created a legislative history for ERA II in the early 1980s, race parallels had become a means of limiting change. To many feminists then and since, race-sex analogies evoked white privilege and formal equality rather than interracial feminism and substantive justice.

This declension narrative tells only part of the story, though. Feminists responded creatively when their strategies foundered or backfired. Contrary to popular assumption, feminists did not seek only "formal equality" or "equal treatment" in the 1970s. Instead, they also drew on disparate impact theory, which probed much deeper than colorblindness. Advocates defended race equality precedents and used analogies to sex to expand remedies for racial inequality. African Americans brought pathbreaking sex equality cases featuring compelling intersections among race, sex, and sexuality. Feminists fought for women's right to combine motherhood and employment and to achieve economic independence without marriage. Despite setbacks, advocates continued to make sex equality arguments for reproductive freedom well into the 1970s. By the time the ERA was reintroduced in Congress in 1983, this onetime symbol of formal equality represented "equality in fact"—disparate impact and affirmative action.

When critiques of 1970s feminist advocacy began to appear in the early 1980s, reasoning from race seemed like a dead end. Feminists had lost control of the sex equality docket; Court cases largely featured challenges to laws whose demise seemed less than helpful to women. A narrow colorblindness theory of racial equality flourished under an administration committed to a civil rights counterrevolution. Feminists were demoralized by the ERA's demise and disgusted with the Court's refusal to apply sex equality principles in cases involving physical and reproductive differences between women and men. When the Justices did reason from race, they found that sex discrimination did not measure up. Abstract comparisons between "women" and "minorities" obscured the experiences of women of color. It is hardly surprising, then, that analogies between race and sex seemed inherently flawed.

At the same time, the goals of feminists and civil rights advocates had never been so closely aligned. Conservative mobilization actually strengthened the bonds between feminists and civil rights advocates. The antiabortion movement helped foster an alliance between abortion rights proponents and advocates for poor and minority women. Conservatives' "abortion-ERA connection" and unfavorable constitutional pregnancy discrimination rulings led feminists to focus their equal protection arguments on class and racial inequalities among women. Campaigns to undermine affirmative action inspired feminists and civil rights advocates to band together against a common adversary.

Even the triumph of conservatism in the 1980 elections could not reverse all of feminists' gains. In small but unprecedented numbers, women had joined the ranks of the judiciary and academe. Feminists spent the 1980s in political purgatory, but their exile proved intellectually and sometimes even legally productive.[3] Even the ERA's demise, the signal failure of feminism during this period, had a silver lining, freeing feminists from the straitjacket that had constrained creative constitutional arguments during the ratification debates. And in time, the strides feminists made through legislation, administrative interpretation, and litigation in the 1970s loomed larger than the failure of the ERA.[4]

In recent years, scholars have questioned the conventional picture of 1970s feminist legal advocacy. That picture had feminists preoccupied with a narrow, formal, assimilationist version of equality, ignoring or denying that there were differences between women and men and among women. It is indeed time to lay that mischaracterization to rest. Reasoning from race is often blamed, explicitly or implicitly, for the shortcomings of both feminist advocacy and the legal landscape it helped to produce. The story told here reveals, instead, a rich and complicated relationship between race and sex equality in feminist legal thought and advocacy. Despite their apparent separation in constitutional law, race and sex became more, not less, intertwined in the 1970s. Reasoning from race was neither inevitable nor inevitably doomed, but its incorporation into legal and political discourse had many unintended consequences.

Tracing the career of reasoning from race helps to explain why analogizing sex and race discrimination appealed to feminists generally, and to African American feminist legal advocates in particular. Linking sex equality to civil rights helped black feminists bridge a yawning gap between two movements that had little in common other than their marginalization of women of color. Race-sex analogies recast seemingly protective laws as discriminatory denials of basic rights, and placed black women at the center of both movements. These parallels proved useful in persuading the civil rights establishment, lawmakers, and judges who were already sympathetic to the cause of racial justice to see discrimination against women as a serious problem worthy of redress. African American feminists also counteracted policymakers' consensus that women's employment and economic independence undermined black progress and racial equality. Civil rights precedents helped feminists incorporate sex into antidiscrimination law, linking the fates of these two movements. White women's strength in numbers and resources made them attractive coalition partners for embattled civil rights advocates.

Race-sex analogies' purchase depended upon context as much as content. There was nothing inevitable or constant in how feminists reasoned from race or in how their arguments were received. In hindsight, it seems inevitable that the race-sex analogy would founder on women's reproductive capacity. But feminists persuaded many lower court judges that pregnancy discrimination resembled race discrimination enough to warrant similar constitutional remedies. It was not inherent differences between race and sex or between men and women that undermined the analogy, as much as the manipulation of perceived differences by opponents of feminism. Conservatives, too, reasoned from race, often with considerable creativity and savvy. And in the hands of judges, race-sex analogies were double-edged. Even sympathetic judges compared "women" and "blacks" but skipped over the complex historical relationship between civil rights and feminism. Those who were skeptical often argued that sex did not, in fact, resemble race, and that differences between race and sex—and between men and women—justified rejecting feminists' legal challenges.

Until now, we did not know or appreciate how feminists reconfigured their legal strategies in response to the crises they faced in the mid-1970s. In fact, feminists drew on expansive conceptions of substantive equality, including affirmative action and disparate impact. Often, they found themselves defending imperiled race precedents. By the end of the 1970s, far from insisting on formal equality based on an abstract parallel to race, feminists often emphasized differences between race and sex, and reasoned from sex discrimination law in the hope of achieving the more capacious versions of equality that had eluded civil rights advocates.

Paradoxically, sex equality law became a promising template in part because the perception that men and women were inherently different meant that many judges did not see formal equality as an option. Even judges who embraced a conservative version of colorblindness remained open to laws that treated men and women differently. In the early 1970s, that openness was a liability for feminists, because the laws they challenged "protected" women from first-class citizenship and reinforced their economic dependence. But once feminists persuaded the Court to distinguish between laws that perpetuated women's subordinate status and laws that promoted women's economic independence and advancement—between "invidious" classifications and "genuine affirmative action"—feminists used sex equality principles to combat the rise of colorblindness. They also fought to turn perceived differences between race and sex to their advantage, arguing that the relative subtlety of sex discrimination underscored the shortcomings of rules requiring proof of discriminatory intent. These efforts to reason from sex were seldom successful in the courts, but they belie the claim that feminists were divorced from the concerns that animated the civil rights movement.

Race and sex equality apparently diverged in the constitutional jurisprudence of the 1970s. In reality, though, race was never far from the minds of Justices and their clerks as they deliberated in cases involving everything from pregnancy discrimination to veterans' preferences. In Title VII cases, feminists could not convince the swing Justices to recognize pregnancy discrimination as sex discrimination per se. But they did manage to salvage a victory for the disparate impact theory. In constitutional cases, however, the specter of disparate impact writ large haunted the Justices. The swing Justices were instinctively sympathetic to feminists' challenge to veterans' preferences, and the preferences' discriminatory impact on women was unmistakable. But the pull of race precedents requiring a showing of discriminatory intent and the fear of the potentially sweeping ramifications of expanding disparate impact theory won the day.

Race and sex equality law were also politically connected in ways that threatened alliances between feminists and civil rights advocates. In the early 1970s, feminists attacked laws that purported to favor women at a time when race-based affirmative action had come under fire. Later, they walked a fine line in challenging veterans' preferences, which were linked to affirmative action in complicated ways. Conservatives certainly tried to drive a wedge between "women" and "minorities." On balance, however, the rise of conservatism in the 1970s united feminism and civil rights against a common foe more than it divided them.

The story of reasoning from race also reveals a rich intellectual and legal history of intersectionality. Court decisions in the 1970s rarely noted intersections between race and sex, reproductive freedom and sex equality, sexuality and economic independence. But many feminists saw the connections clearly, even those who were lawyers. This book has uncovered their stories and shown that African American women played pivotal roles in early sex equality litigation, long before "intersectionality" became a catchphrase. This was true not only in areas like sexual harassment law, where African American women's pioneering role has long been recognized, but in constitutional litigation, often considered the province of white middle-class interests. Even the classic cases brought by white plaintiffs had their roots in African American feminist challenges to the male breadwinner-female homemaker model that dominated American public policy but never captured the reality of black women's lives.

The history recounted here reconciles the conflicting pictures that emerge from historical and legal scholarship on 1970s feminism. Historians have discredited the notion that second-wave feminists were white middle-class and professional women, indifferent to and isolated from other social movements and causes. They have uncovered a rich array of feminists and feminisms, innovation and dynamism, coalition as well as fragmentation. And in recent years, historians have recognized that African American women often played pioneering roles in feminist theory and organizing.[5] This book adds to the growing body of literature arguing that feminist legal advocacy was no exception.[6] At the same time, it helps to explain why much of the creativity, diversity, and intersectionality of 1970s feminist advocacy did not appear in the sex equality law that emerged from the Supreme Court.

What produced the false impression that feminists got what they asked for, no more and no less?[7] For one thing, feminist attempts to expand legal equality often failed. Their efforts therefore rarely appeared in Supreme Court opinions, the primary texts that engage legal scholars and advocates. To some degree, then, the standard depiction of 1970s feminist legal advocacy simply confuses outcomes with inputs. The narrowness of the Court's vision has obscured the imaginative arguments advocates advanced.

The political context in which early impressions formed also played a role. Ironically, 1970s feminist advocates became "straw women" in part because of the same conservative ascendancy that radicalized feminist advocates and brought their goals into line with those of the civil rights movement. In the early 1980s, when the first wave of critiques appeared, prospects looked grim.[8] Feminists were demoralized by unfavorable Court rulings, the ERA's defeat, and women's abrupt ejection from positions of power they had only just begun to acquire. Most young feminists did not take a historical approach to their predecessors' legal strategies.[9] Frustrated with sex equality law's limitations in an increasingly conservative political climate, they soon found themselves embroiled in polarizing internecine disputes over sameness and difference, diversity and dominance.

1970s feminism became a "foil" in the debates that dominated feminist legal theory in the 1980s and 1990s: how to address differences between women and men; how to combat women's subordination to men; and how to make feminism responsive to differences of class, race, and sexuality among women.[10] If 1970s feminism had fallen short in each of these areas, reasoning from race seemed like a prime culprit. In part, this was because colorblindness had begun to eclipse more capacious notions of racial equality by the end of the decade. Colorblindness only made sense if there were no relevant differences between the races. Women apparently had to be just like men for the race analogy to work, so it seemed as if feminists must have denied sex differences entirely when they compared sex to race. Moreover, colorblindness precluded affirmative measures. It was therefore easy to blame analogies to race for rigid sexblindness and formal equality. And when incorporated into law as abstract parallels, race-sex analogies undeniably elided the experiences of women of color.

Feminist strategy also bears some responsibility for the invisibility of race in sex equality law. African American feminists challenged the male-breadwinner/female homemaker model early and often. But the impulse to universalize feminists' claims and make them applicable to all women was irresistible. Black plaintiffs and their lawyers brought cases that embodied intersections between race and sex: challenges to the exclusion of African American men and all women from jury service in the South, to the use of sex segregation in racial desegregation plans, to policies denying employment to unmarried mothers. Emphasizing the connection between race and sex sometimes won feminists a hearing with judges sympathetic to civil rights. But the very intersections between race, sex, sexuality, reproduction, and equality that so appealed to creative feminists and civil rights advocates made moderate and conservative judges profoundly uncomfortable. Feminist legal strategists thus faced a quandary. Some forged ahead; others tread more cautiously, avoiding or downplaying cases and arguments that forced courts to grapple with wideranging cultural, moral, and legal questions.

The story told here reinforces the need to look beyond published court opinions to the failed arguments of advocates, the internal deliberations of judges, and the social and legal context in which a case arose and made its way through the lower courts. Such research reveals a much richer picture of the legal strategy pursued by well-known feminist lawyers like Ruth Bader Ginsburg and organizations like NOW, Equal Rights Advocates, and the ACLU Women's Rights Project. It also suggests the importance of looking beyond the Supreme Court and organizations that focused solely on feminist causes. The NAACP Legal Defense Fund, the Southern Poverty Law Center, and the Center for Constitutional Rights all played important and underexplored roles in feminist legal advocacy in the 1970s and beyond. And examining the cases that never reached the Supreme Court can tell us as much about feminist legal strategy and its political constraints as the marquee cases featured in law school casebooks.

Reasoning from race has endured in the work of feminists and other proponents of civil and human rights. Lawyers for gay and lesbian Americans, the disabled, the aged, and others rely on race and sex equality cases, comparing their own causes to those of civil rights and feminist predecessors. Scholars in a variety of disciplines explore "intersectionality," probing what Pauli Murray once called the "conjunction" of multiple identities. Increasingly sophisticated critiques capture the peril as well as the promise of analogical reasoning. New activists who invoke parallels to race still face skepticism from legal decision makers and more established civil rights constituencies. Nevertheless, coalitions have borne fruit. And in the end, equality advocates have little choice but to seize the legacy of the civil rights struggle, its rhetorical power, and its ambivalent precedents; if they do not, their opponents will. However fraught, reasoning from race remains the currency of the American civil rights revolution.

In 1985, two years after she proposed a new Human Rights Amendment to her feminist colleagues, Pauli Murray died of cancer. As Eleanor Holmes Norton wrote of Murray, "history . . . placed her just ahead of her time."[1] Murray was always a relative outsider to the legal establishment, albeit a well-connected one. The next generation of feminist advocates joined the ranks of government and academe, acquiring power women had only dreamt of in the 1960s and 1970s. Many of those who argued, demonstrated, wrote, and cajoled decision makers during the early period later found themselves poised to make decisions themselves.

Like other social movements, feminism became professionalized and institutionalized.[2] By the 1980s, a small but increasing number of law professors found jobs and achieved tenure with scholarship on feminist topics. Feminist lawyers who came of age in the 1970s and early 1980s populated law school faculties, among them Catharine MacKinnon, Reva Siegel, Sylvia Law, Diane Zimmerman, Katharine Bartlett, Linda Hamilton Krieger, Judy Trent Ellis (now Scales-Trent), Deborah Rhode, Ann Freedman, Wendy Webster Williams, and Susan Deller Ross. Rhonda Copelon and Elizabeth Schneider were among those who combined activism with academics, playing central roles in litigation and policy advocacy while teaching law students and producing feminist scholarship.[3] President Carter's judicial appointments included several committed feminists. Most famously, Ruth Bader Ginsburg followed more than a dozen years on the D.C. Circuit with an appointment to the Supreme Court. Supreme Court clerks Diane Wood, Marsha Berzon, and Gerard "Jerry" Lynch now sit on the bench, as do Nancy Gertner and Inez Smith Reid.[4] Mary "Kit" Kinports and Sam Estreicher are law professors, and Richard Blumenthal became Connecticut's attorney general and U.S. senator.[5]

Several of the male protagonists in the story of 1970s legal feminism went on to prosper in private practice. Robert B. Barnett, whose law review student note tackled sex segregated schooling in 1970, became counselor to presidents as a partner at the prestigious Washington law firm Williams & Connolly. Former EEOC firebrand David Copus eventually built a practice defending employers against discrimination claims. Mississippi attorneys Wilbur Colom and Charles Victor McTeer enjoyed successful careers—Colom as a lawyer and Republican power-player-turned-Obama fundraiser and McTeer in a lucrative law practice whose clients included Jesse Jackson.[6]

Fannie Lou Hamer's health declined in the years after she testified in the Andrews case, and she died in 1977. Inspired by her father's stories of Hamer's heroism, McTeer's daughter became the first African American and first woman to serve as mayor of Greenville, Mississippi, in 2003. Mae Bertha Carter, the *Andrews* witness whose family desegregated the Drew schools, sent seven of her children to the University of Mississippi.[7] Mrs. Katie Mae Andrews Peacock served as a beloved teacher and librarian in the Mississippi public schools until her death in 2009.

Many of Pauli Murray's colleagues and protégés combined feminism with government service, teaching, and local activism. Norton fought for D.C. statehood as longtime nonvoting delegate to Congress from the District of Columbia. She also taught courses in employment law, alternative dispute resolution, and legislation at Georgetown University Law Center. After serving in the Carter administration, Barbara Babcock returned to Stanford Law School as its first tenured female professor. Aileen Hernandez combined equal employment opportunity consulting with community activism in California. Catherine East retired from government service in 1977, but not from feminism: after serving as women's issues coordinator for 1980 presidential candidate John Anderson, she became legislative director of the National Women's Political

Caucus and served on the board of the NOW Legal Defense and Education Fund. Mary Eastwood served in the special counsel's office of the Merit Systems Protection Board after twenty years in the Department of Justice's Office of Legal Counsel, ten of them as its equal opportunity adviser.

Feminists' antagonists, too, achieved influence and fame. Phyllis Schlafly has maintained a prolific stream of commentary that continues to this day.[8] William Rehnquist, ERA doubter and the lone dissenter in *Frontiero,* was a reliable vote and voice against feminist causes and for a rejuvenated brand of federalism throughout most of the late twentieth century, culminating in his opposition to the civil rights remedy of the Violence Against Women Act in the 1990s.[9] But as Chief Justice in 2003, he surprised everyone by writing a sweeping decision upholding the Family and Medical Leave Act's application to state governments as a valid exercise of congressional power to prevent and combat sex discrimination.[10] Having ascended to the federal bench at thirty-five, former Burger clerk Alex Kozinski built a reputation as a colorful libertarian who supplied overworked clerks to conservative Supreme Court Justices. But in 2006, he authored a spirited dissent to a Ninth Circuit decision that sustained a casino's requirement that its female employees wear makeup to work.[11]

Moderate Republican jurists such as Carolyn Dineen Randall (later Carolyn Dineen King) and Justice Sandra Day O'Connor balanced their predisposition toward pragmatic conservatism with their personal experiences as victims of discrimination and, arguably, as beneficiaries of affirmative action. By the time of her retirement in 2005, some feminists feted O'Connor for promoting sex equality and for her ambivalent but nevertheless crucial attempts to salvage affirmative action.[12]

For four years after O'Connor stepped down, Ginsburg served as the lone female Justice. In 2009, after confirmation hearings that highlighted lingering disagreements about the appropriate role of race and sex in judging, Sonia Sotomayor became the first woman of color to sit on the Court. Sotomayor grew up in a Bronx housing project and then spent the 1970s excelling in prestigious universities. Part of the third coeducational class to attend Princeton, she earned her degree summa cum laude in 1976 and graduated from Yale Law School in 1979.

Obama appointed Elena Kagan to replace Justice John Paul Stevens in 2010. A Jewish New Yorker like Ginsburg, Kagan's resume looked more like that of Harvard Law School dean and solicitor general Erwin Griswold. A contemporary of Obama, Kagan came of age during the 1970s. At twelve, determined to read from the Torah on Saturday morning as boys did for their bar mitzvahs, Kagan negotiated a compromise with her rabbi. Her synagogue's first bat mitzvah took place on a Friday evening in May 1973, four days after the Supreme Court handed down its decision in *Frontiero v. Richardson*. Instead of the Torah, Kagan read from the Book of Ruth.[13]

By the twenty-first century, gay advocates claimed Pauli Murray as one of their own. A GLBT History Month hagiography celebrated Murray as a "lifelong . . . activist against racial and sexual discrimination," noting that "[t]hough Murray never identified as a lesbian, her longest lasting relationships were with women." However Murray would have characterized her sexual identity, her words as quoted in the biography's epitaph spoke for themselves: "As an American, I inherit the magnificent tradition of an endless march toward freedom and toward the dignity of all mankind."[14]

NOTES

ACKNOWLEDGMENTS

INDEX

NOTES

Abbreviations

Individuals

BRW	Justice Byron R. White
HAB	Justice Harry A. Blackmun
JPS	Justice John Paul Stevens
LFP	Justice Lewis F. Powell, Jr.
PS	Justice Potter Stewart
RBG	Ruth Bader Ginsburg
TM	Justice Thurgood Marshall
WEB	Chief Justice Warren E. Burger
WHR	Justice William H. Rehnquist
WJB	Justice William J. Brennan, Jr.
WOD	Justice William O. Douglas

Organizations and Government Agencies

ABA	American Bar Association
DOL	Department of Labor
LCDC	Lawyers' Constitutional Defense Committee

Archival Sources

ACLU Records	Records of the American Civil Liberties Union, Mudd Library, Princeton University, Princeton, N.J.
BF Papers	Betty Friedan Papers, Schlesinger Library, Radcliffe Institute for Advanced Study, Harvard University, Cambridge, Mass.
CE Papers	Catherine East Papers, Schlesinger Library, Radcliffe In-

stitute for Advanced Study, Harvard University, Cambridge, Mass.

COASC	*The Complete Oral Arguments of the Supreme Court of the United States* (Frederick, MD: University Publications of America), Temple University Law Library, Philadelphia, PA.
DK Papers	Dorothy Kenyon Papers, Sophia Smith Collection, Smith College, Northampton, Mass.
EP Papers	Esther Peterson Papers, Schlesinger Library, Radcliffe Institute for Advanced Study, Harvard University, Cambridge, Mass.
ERAmerica Papers	Records of ERAmerica, Manuscripts Division, Library of Congress, Washington, D.C.
FMJ Papers	Frank M. Johnson, Jr., Papers, Manuscripts Division, Library of Congress, Washington, D.C.
HAB Papers	Justice Harry A. Blackmun Papers, Manuscripts Division, Library of Congress, Washington, D.C.
HRW Papers	Human Rights for Women Papers, Schlesinger Library, Radcliffe Institute for Advanced Study, Harvard University, Cambridge, Mass.
LCCR Papers	Leadership Conference on Civil Rights Records, Manuscripts Division, Library of Congress, Washington, D.C.
LFP Papers	Justice Lewis F. Powell, Jr. Archives, Washington and Lee University School of Law, Lexington, Va.
MacKinnon Papers	Judge George A. MacKinnon Papers, Minnesota Historical Society, Minneapolis, Minn.
ME Papers	Mary Eastwood Papers, Schlesinger Library, Radcliffe Institute for Advanced Study, Harvard University, Cambridge, Mass.
MR Papers	Marguerite Rawalt Papers, Schlesinger Library, Radcliffe Institute for Advanced Study, Harvard University, Cambridge, Mass.
NAACP Papers	Records of the NAACP, Manuscripts Division, Library of Congress, Washington, D.C.
NARA	National Archives and Records Administration
NCCRW	Newcomb Archives, Newcomb College Center for Research on Women, Tulane University, New Orleans, La.
NOW Papers	National Organization for Women Papers, Schlesinger

	Library, Radcliffe Institute for Advanced Study, Harvard University, Cambridge, Mass.
NOW LDEF Papers	NOW LDEF Papers, Schlesinger Library, Radcliffe Institute for Advanced Study, Harvard University, Cambridge, Mass.
NWP Papers	National Woman's Party Papers (microform), Sterling Memorial Library, Yale University, New Haven, Conn.
PCSW Papers	Presidential Commission on the Status of Women Papers, Schlesinger Library, Radcliffe Institute for Advanced Study, Harvard University, Cambridge, Mass.
PI Papers	Phineas Indritz Papers, Howard University School of Law, Washington, D.C.
PM Papers	Pauli Murray Papers, Schlesinger Library, Radcliffe Institute for Advanced Study, Harvard University, Cambridge, Mass.
RBG Papers	Ruth Bader Ginsburg Papers, Manuscripts Division, Library of Congress, Washington, D.C.
TE Papers	Thomas Emerson Papers, Manuscripts and Archives, Sterling Memorial Library, Yale University, New Haven, Conn.
TM Papers	Justice Thurgood Marshall Papers, Manuscripts Division, Library of Congress, Washington, D.C.
WCK Papers	William C. Keady Papers, Special Collections, Mississippi State University Library, Mississippi State, Miss.
WJB Papers	Justice William J. Brennan, Jr., Papers, Manuscripts Division, Library of Congress, Washington, D.C.
WSH Papers	Wilma Scott Heide Papers, Schlesinger Library, Radcliffe Institute for Advanced Study, Harvard University, Cambridge, Mass.

Periodicals

LAT	*Los Angeles Times*
NYT	*New York Times*
WP	*Washington Post*
WSJ	*Wall Street Journal*

Introduction

1. LaDoris Cordell, "Proposition 8 vs. Black Homophobia," *Salon.com,* October 30, 2008, accessed July 25, 2010, http://www.salon.com/news/opinion/feature/2008/10/30/proposition_8.

2. In fact, exit polls apparently overstated the African American vote for Prop 8 by at least ten points. See Patrick J. Egan and Kenneth Sherrill, "California's Proposition 8: What Happened, and What Does the Future Hold?," accessed November 3, 2010, http://www.thetaskforce.org/downloads/reports/reports/pi_prop8_1_6_09.pdf.

3. LaDoris H. Cordell, "The Court Will Overturn Prop 8," *San Francisco Chronicle,* November 11, 2008.

4. Cordell, "Court Will Overturn"; Cordell, "Proposition 8 vs. Black Homophobia."

5. *In re* Marriage Cases, 43 Cal. 4th 757, 782 (2008).

6. See, for example, Irene Monroe, "Gay Is *Not* the New Black," *Huffington Post,* December 16, 2008, accessed July 30, 2010, http://www.huffingtonpost.com/irene-monroe/gay-is-emnotem-the-new-bl_b_151573.html.

7. Richard Thompson Ford, "Analogy Lesson," *Slate,* November 14, 2008, accessed July 25, 2010, http://www.slate.com/id/2204661/.

8. For one example, see Michael J. Klarman, "Social Reform Litigation and Its Challenges: An Essay in Honor of Justice Ruth Bader Ginsburg," *Harvard Journal of Law & Gender* 32 (2009): 251–302. Klarman compares Ginsburg's legal advocacy with that of legendary civil rights lawyer Thurgood Marshall.

9. Catharine A. MacKinnon, "Reflections on Sex Equality under Law," *Yale Law Journal* 100 (1991): 1289.

10. Janet E. Halley, "Gay Rights and Identity Imitation: Issues in the Ethics of Representation," in *The Politics of Law: A Progressive Critique,* 3rd ed. (New York: Basic Books, 1998), 115.

11. Ellen Carol DuBois, *Feminism and Suffrage: The Emergence of an Independent Women's Movement in America, 1848–1869* (Ithaca, NY: Cornell University Press, 1999); Blanche Glassman Hersh, *The Slavery of Sex: Feminist-Abolitionists in America* (Urbana: University of Illinois Press, 1978).

12. For exceptions, see Dorothy Sue Cobble, *The Other Women's Movement: Workplace Justice and Social Rights in Modern America* (Princeton, NJ: Princeton University Press, 2004); Eileen Boris, "The Gender of Discrimination: Race, Sex, and Fair Employment," in *Women and the Constitution: History, Interpretation, and Practice,* ed. Sybil A. Schwarzenbach and Patricia Smith (New York: Columbia University Press, 2003), 273–291.

13. On the limitations of the "wave" metaphor, see Nancy Hewitt, ed., *No Permanent Waves: Recasting Histories of U.S. Feminism* (New Brunswick, NJ: Rutgers University Press, 2010); Linda K. Kerber, "'I Was Appalled': The Invisible Antecedents of Second-Wave Feminism," *Journal of Women's History* 14, no. 2 (2002): 90–101.

14. Gloria T. Hull, Patricia Bell Scott, and Barbara Smith, eds., *All the Women Are White, All the Blacks Are Men, But Some of Us Are Brave: Black Women's*

Studies (Old Westbury, NY: Feminist Press, 1982). See also bell hooks, *Ain't I a Woman: Black Women and Feminism* (Boston: South End Press, 1981); Margaret A. Simons, "Racism and Feminism: A Schism in the Sisterhood," *Feminist Studies* 5 (1979): 384–401; Elizabeth V. Spelman, "Theories of Race and Gender/The Erasure of Black Women," *Quest: A Feminist Quarterly* 5 (1982): 36–62.

15. The feminist campaign against sex-segregated job ads is well documented. See, for example, Hugh Davis Graham, *The Civil Rights Era: Origins and Development of National Policy, 1960–1972* (New York: Oxford University Press, 1990), Chapter 8.

16. Paulette M. Caldwell, "A Hair Piece: Perspectives on the Intersection of Race and Gender," *Duke Law Journal* (1991): 373.

17. The relatively few historical works to have examined interactions between these legal movements include Nancy MacLean, *Freedom Is Not Enough: The Opening of the American Workplace* (Cambridge, MA: Harvard University Press, 2006); Linda Kerber, *No Constitutional Right to Be Ladies: Women and the Obligations of Citizenship* (New York: Hill and Wang, 1998); and Susan M. Hartmann, *The Other Feminists: Activists in the Liberal Establishment* (New Haven, CT: Yale University Press, 1998). John David Skrentny's *Minority Rights Revolution* (Cambridge, MA: Harvard University Press, 2002) considers how subsequent movements, including feminism, built on the civil rights legacy; Graham's *Civil Rights Era* covers the early years of the feminist movement but ends in 1972.

18. See, for example, Craig J. Konnoth, "Created in Its Image: The Race Analogy, Gay Identity, and Gay Litigation in the 1950s–1970s," *Yale Law Journal* 119 (2009): 316–372.

19. MacLean, *Freedom Is Not Enough*, 225–264; Ian F. Haney-Lopez, "'A Nation of Minorities': Race, Ethnicity, and Reactionary Colorblindness," *Stanford Law Review* 59 (2007): 985–1064.

20. See, for example, Graham, *Civil Rights Era*; Skrentny, *Minority Rights Revolution*; Hartmann, *The Other Feminists*; Alice Kessler-Harris, *In Pursuit of Equity: Women, Men, and the Quest for Economic Citizenship in 20th-Century America* (Oxford: Oxford University Press, 2001); Kerber, *No Constitutional Right to Be Ladies*; Myra Marx Ferree and Beth B. Hess, *Controversy and Coalition: The New Feminist Movement Across Three Decades of Change*, rev. ed. (New York: Twayne, 1994); Donald G. Mathews and Jane S. DeHart, *Sex, Gender, and the Politics of the ERA: A State and the Nation* (New York: Oxford University Press, 1990); Benita Roth, *Separate Roads to Feminism: Black, Chicana, and White Feminist Movements in America's Second Wave* (New York: Cambridge University Press, 2004), 189.

Consideration and criticism of analogical reasoning and analogy-based advocacy abound in legal scholarship. See Serena Mayeri, "A Common Fate of

Discrimination: Race-Gender Analogies in Legal and Historical Perspective,"
Yale Law Journal 110 (2001): 1045–1088. For trenchant commentary on race-sex
analogies in legal doctrine, see Caldwell, "A Hair Piece"; Reva B. Siegel, "She
the People: The Nineteenth Amendment, Sex Equality, Federalism, and the
Family," *Harvard Law Review* 115 (2001): 961–963; and Mary Anne Case, "Reflections on Constitutionalizing Women's Equality," *California Law Review* 90
(2002): 765–769, 771–772. On the difficulty and necessity of incorporating
complex identities into equality law, see Kathryn Abrams, "The Constitution of
Women," *Alabama Law Review* 48 (1997): 861–884; Kathryn Abrams, "Title VII
and the Complex Female Subject," *Michigan Law Review* 92 (1994): 2479–2540.

21. John David Skrentny's study of affirmative action and Title IX implementation is an exception. See Skrentny, *Minority Rights Revolution,* chapters 4, 8.

22. See, for example, Stephanie Gilmore, ed., *Feminist Coalitions: Historical
Perspectives on Second-Wave Feminism in the United States* (Urbana: University of
Illinois Press, 2008); Cobble, *Other Women's Movement;* Hartmann, *The Other
Feminists;* Kimberly Springer, *Living for the Revolution: Black Feminist Organizations, 1968–1980* (Durham, NC: Duke University Press, 2005); Roth, *Separate
Roads to Feminism;* MacLean, *Freedom Is Not Enough;* Becky Thompson, "Multiracial Feminism: Recasting the Chronology of Second Wave Feminism," *Feminist Studies* 28 (2002): 336–360; Premilla Nadasen, "Expanding the Boundaries
of the Women's Movement: Black Feminism and the Struggle for Welfare
Rights," *Feminist Studies* 28 (2002): 270–301; Carrie N. Baker, "Race, Class,
and Sexual Harassment in the 1970s," *Feminist Studies* 30 (2004): 7–27.

23. See, for example, MacLean, *Freedom Is Not Enough;* Carrie N. Baker,
The Women's Movement against Sexual Harassment (Cambridge: Cambridge Uni-
versity Press, 2008); Jennifer Nelson, *Women of Color and the Reproductive Rights
Movement* (New York: New York University Press, 2003).

24. On Pauli Murray's increasing prominence in historical literature, see
Susan Ware, "Pauli Murray's Notable Connections," *Journal of Women's History*
14 (2002): 54-57; Nancy MacLean, "Response to Ken Mack—and New Questions for the History of African American Legal Liberalism in the Age of
Obama," *Law and History Review* 27 (2009): 671–680. On the underappreciated
role of African American women in the origins of second-wave feminism, see
Hartmann, *Other Feminists.*

25. I borrow this phrase from Risa Goluboff's pathbreaking study of civil
rights in the 1940s. See Risa Goluboff, *The Lost Promise of Civil Rights* (Cambridge: Harvard University Press, 2007).

26. Historians once treated the mid-1960s as the climax of civil rights, but
any definition of the civil rights era that omits the 1970s excludes the period
most essential to feminism. On the stakes of expanding our definition of the

civil rights movement and era, see Jacquelyn Dowd Hall, "The Long Civil Rights Movement and the Political Uses of the Past," *Journal of American History* 91 (2005): 1233–1263; MacLean, epilogue to *Freedom Is Not Enough.*

27. I do not mean to suggest that all civil rights or feminist activism during this period occurred among white and black Americans; my focus on these groups reflects how feminists framed their legal demands in relation to the African American civil rights movement.

28. Cordell, "Court Will Overturn."

1. The Rebirth of Race-Sex Analogies

1. Florynce Kennedy, "A Comparative Study: Accentuating the Similarities of the Societal Position of Women and Negroes," in *Words of Fire: An Anthology of African-American Feminist Thought,* ed. Beverly Guy-Sheftall (New York: W. W. Norton, 1995), 101–106.

2. Gunnar Myrdal, *An American Dilemma: The Negro Problem and Modern Democracy* (New York: Harper, 1944), appendix 5.

3. Ashley Montagu, *Man's Most Dangerous Myth: The Fallacy of Race* (New York: Columbia University Press, 1942); Ashley Montagu, *The Natural Superiority of Women* (New York: Macmillan, 1953).

4. Helen Mayer Hacker, "Women as a Minority Group," *Social Forces* 30 (1951): 60–69.

5. Simone de Beauvoir, *The Second Sex,* ed. and trans. H. M. Parshley (New York: Knopf, 1952).

6. Herbert Wechsler, "Toward Neutral Principles of Constitutional Law," *Harvard Law Review* 73 (1959): 33.

7. On the persistence of feminist activism between the "first" and "second" "waves," see Linda K. Kerber, "'I Was Appalled': The Invisible Antecedents of Second-Wave Feminism," *Journal of Women's History* 14 (2002): 90–101.

8. Kathleen M. Brown, *Good Wives, Nasty Wenches, and Anxious Patriarchs: Gender, Race, and Power in Colonial Virginia* (Chapel Hill: University of North Carolina Press, 1996).

9. Stephanie McCurry, *Masters of Small Worlds: Yeoman Households, Gender Relations, and the Political Culture of the Antebellum South Carolina Low Country* (New York: Oxford University Press, 1995).

10. Ellen Carol DuBois, *Feminism and Suffrage: The Emergence of an Independent Women's Movement in America, 1848–1869* (Ithaca, NY: Cornell University Press, 1999).

11. Nell Irvin Painter, *Sojourner Truth: A Life, a Symbol* (New York: W. W. Norton, 1996).

12. DuBois, *Feminism and Suffrage.* See also Jill Elaine Hasday, "Federalism and the Family Reconstructed," *UCLA Law Review* 45 (1998): 1297–1400.

13. DuBois, *Feminism and Suffrage,* 94–96; Paula Giddings, *When and Where I Enter: The Impact of Black Women on Race and Sex in America,* 1st ed. (New York: W. Morrow, 1984), 123–129.

14. "Votes for Women," *Crisis* 12 (November 1917), 178. See, for example, James Weldon Johnson, "About Aunties," *Crisis* 10 (August 1915), 180; Mary Church Terrell, "Woman Suffrage and the 15th Amendment," *Crisis* 10 (August 1915), 191. On African American advocates of woman suffrage, see Glenda Elizabeth Gilmore, *Gender and Jim Crow: Women and the Politics of White Supremacy in North Carolina, 1896–1920* (Chapel Hill: University of North Carolina Press, 1996); Ann D. Gordon and Bettye Collier-Thomas, eds., *African American Women and the Vote, 1837–1965* (Amherst: University of Massachusetts Press, 1997).

15. On the Nineteenth Amendment as being about more than suffrage, see Reva B. Siegel, "She, the People: The Nineteenth Amendment, Sex Equality, Federalism, and the Family," *Harvard Law Review* 115 (2002): 947-1046.

16. For more on the National Woman's Party, see Susan D. Becker, *The Origins of the Equal Rights Amendment: American Feminism between the Wars* (Westport, CT: Greenwood Press, 1981); Nancy F. Cott, *The Grounding of Modern Feminism* (New Haven, CT: Yale University Press, 1987); Leila J. Rupp and Verta A. Taylor, *Survival in the Doldrums: The American Women's Rights Movement, 1945 to the 1960s* (New York: Oxford University Press, 1987).

17. For more on the debates over protective labor legislation, see Vivien Hart, *Bound by Our Constitution: Women, Workers, and the Minimum Wage* (Princeton, NJ: Princeton University Press, 1994); Joan G. Zimmerman, "The Jurisprudence of Equality: The Women's Minimum Wage, the First Equal Rights Amendment, and Adkins v. Children's Hospital, 1905–1923," *Journal of American History* 78 (1991): 188–225. On women and feminism in the labor movement, see Dorothy Sue Cobble, *The Other Women's Movement: Workplace Justice and Social Rights in Modern America* (Princeton, NJ: Princeton University Press, 2004); Dennis A. Deslippe, *Rights Not Roses: Unions and the Rise of Working-Class Feminism, 1945–1980* (Urbana: University of Illinois Press, 2000); Nancy F. Gabin, *Feminism and the Labor Movement: Women and the United Auto Workers, 1935-1975* (Ithaca, NY: Cornell University Press, 1990).

18. Cynthia E. Harrison, *On Account of Sex: The Politics of Women's Issues, 1945–1968* (Berkeley: University of California Press, 1988), 30–38.

19. Blanche Crozier, "Constitutionality of Discrimination Based on Sex," *Boston University Law Review* 15 (1935): 723; Strauder v. West Virginia, 100 U.S. 303, 310 (1879).

20. See William E. Nelson, *The Fourteenth Amendment: From Political Principle to Judicial Doctrine* (Cambridge, MA: Harvard University Press, 1988).

21. See, for example, Alice Paul to Mabel Pollitzer, Acting Chairman, South Carolina Branch, NWP, February 7, 1955, NWP Papers, Film Misc 959, Reel 101; Helen Paul to Miss Brandon, July 20, 1956, NWP Papers, Film Misc 959, Reel 102.

22. For an insightful analysis of labor women's attitude toward gender differences, see Cobble, *Other Women's Movement*.

23. Catherine J. Tilson, "The Equal Rights Amendment to the Federal Constitution—Opposed," *Connecticut Bar Journal* 20 (1946): 66–74. See also Note, "Sex, Discrimination, and the Constitution," *Stanford Law Review* 2 (1950): 691–730.

24. There were other exceptions to the general dormancy of race-sex analogies during this period. See, for example, Cobble, *Other Women's Movement*, 87-92; Eileen Boris, "The Gender of Discrimination: Race, Sex, and Fair Employment," in *Women and the Constitution: History, Interpretation, and Practice*, ed. Sibyl A. Schwarzenbach and Patricia Smith (New York: Columbia University Press, 2003), 282–286.

25. Kate Weigand and Daniel Horowitz, "Dorothy Kenyon: Feminist Organizing, 1919–1963," *Journal of Women's History* 14 (2002): 126–131. See also Samantha Barbas, "Dorothy Kenyon and the Making of Modern Legal Feminism," *Stanford Journal of Civil Rights and Civil Liberties* 5 (2009): 423–446.

26. Rowland Watts to John M. Barron, June 25, 1959, ACLU Records, Box 1142, Folder 22.

27. Quoted in Heaton v. Bristol, 317 S.W.2d 86, 91 (Tex. Civ. App. 1958).

28. *Bristol,* 317 S.W.2d 86, *appeal dismissed, cert. denied,* 359 U.S. 230 (1959), *petition for rehearing denied,* 359 U.S. 999 (1959).

29. See Sweatt v. Painter, 339 U.S. 629 (1950); McLaurin v. Oklahoma State Regents, 339 U.S. 637 (1950).

30. For an excellent treatment of *Hoyt,* see Linda K. Kerber, *No Constitutional Right to Be Ladies: Women and the Obligations of Citizenship* (New York: Hill and Wang, 1998), 124-220.

31. Brief of the Florida Civil Liberties Union and the American Civil Liberties Union as Amici Curiae, 7, Hoyt v. Florida, 368 U.S. 57 (1961) (No. 31).

32. Hoyt v. Florida, 368 U.S. 57, 62 (1961).

33. See Alice Kessler-Harris, *In Pursuit of Equity: Women, Men, and the Quest for Economic Citizenship in 20th-Century America* (Oxford: Oxford University Press, 2001). See also Margot Canaday, *The Straight State: Sexuality and Citizenship in Twentieth-Century America* (Princeton, NJ: Princeton University Press, 2009).

34. Pauli Murray, *The Autobiography of a Black Activist, Feminist, Lawyer, Priest, and Poet* (Knoxville: University of Tennessee Press, 1989); Glenda

Elizabeth Gilmore, *Defying Dixie: The Radical Roots of Civil Rights, 1919–1950* (New York: W.W. Norton, 2008). Other histories that discuss Pauli Murray's contributions to theories about the parallels between race and sex discrimination include Harrison, *On Account of Sex;* Rosalind Rosenberg, *Divided Lives: American Women in the Twentieth Century,* rev. ed. (New York: Hill and Wang, 2008); Rosalind Rosenberg, "The Conjunction of Race and Gender," *Journal of Women's History* 14 (2002): 68–73; Kerber, *No Constitutional Right to Be Ladies;* Susan M. Hartmann, *The Other Feminists: Activists in the Liberal Establishment* (New Haven, CT: Yale University Press, 1998); Kessler-Harris, *In Pursuit of Equity;* Susan Ware, Symposium: "Pauli Murray's Notable Connections," *Journal of Women's History* 14(2002): 54-57; Nancy MacLean, *Freedom Is Not Enough: The Opening of the American Workplace* (Cambridge, MA: Harvard University Press, 2006). John David Skrentny calls Murray "[t]he most eloquent advocate of the analogy between blacks and women." Skrentny, *The Minority Rights Revolution* (Cambridge, MA: Harvard University Press), 244.

35. Murray, *Autobiography,* 221–222.

36. Ibid., 240.

37. Pauli Murray, "Pauli Murray's Appeal: For Admission to Harvard Law School," in *Rebels in Law: Voices in History of Black Women Lawyers,* ed. J. Clay Smith, Jr. (Ann Arbor: University of Michigan Press, 1998), 79–83. For more on Murray's exchanges with Harvard, see Mary Elizabeth Basile, "Pauli Murray's Campaign Against Harvard Law School's 'Jane Crow' Admissions Policy," *Journal of Legal Education* 57 (2007): 77-101.

38. Joanne J. Meyerowitz, *How Sex Changed: A History of Transsexuality in the United States* (Cambridge, MA: Harvard University Press, 2002), 36–37. For more on Murray's sexual identity, see Gilmore, *Defying Dixie;* Leila J. Rupp and Verta A. Taylor, "Pauli Murray: The Unasked Question," *Journal of Women's History* 14 (2002): 83-87; Rosenberg, "Conjunction of Race and Gender."

39. On Murray's time in Ghana, see Kevin K. Gaines, *American Africans in Ghana: Black Expatriates and the Civil Rights Era* (Chapel Hill: University of North Carolina Press, 2006).

40. Murray, *Autobiography,* 250, 255.

41. Pauli Murray, A Proposal to Reexamine the Applicability of the Fourteenth Amendment to State Laws and Practices Which Discriminate on the Basis of Sex Per Se, December 1962, 10, PCSW Papers, Doc. II-20, Box 8, Folder 62.

42. Gunnar Myrdal, *American Dilemma;* Hacker, "Women as a Minority Group"; Montagu, *Man's Most Dangerous Myth;* Montagu, *Natural Superiority of Women;* Eleanor Flexner, *Century of Struggle: The Woman's Rights Movement in the United States* (Cambridge, MA: Harvard University Press, 1959). On Montagu

and connections between theories of race and sexuality more generally, see Joanne J. Meyerowitz, "'How Common Culture Shapes the Separate Lives': Sexuality, Race, and Mid-Twentieth-Century Social Constructionist Thought," *Journal of American History* 96 (2010): 1057-1084.

43. Murray, *Autobiography*, 351–352.

44. See, for example, Goesaert v. Cleary, 335 U.S. 464 (1948).

45. Murray, Proposal to Reexamine, 8–9. As Ruth Feldstein writes, the "separation between womanhood and motherhood" in Murray's memo "countered long-standing assumptions within liberal discourse" and "allowed Murray to analyze sex and race discrimination in relation to each other." Ruth Feldstein, *Motherhood in Black and White: Race and Sex in American Liberalism, 1930–1965* (Ithaca, NY: Cornell University Press, 2000), 159.

46. Murray, Proposal to Reexamine, 17.

47. Statement of Mrs. Samuel Brown of the National Council of Jewish Women before the Civil and Political Rights Committee, March 8, 1963, 4, PM papers, MC 412, Box 49, Folder 883.

48. Erwin N. Griswold to Pauli Murray, January 31, 1963, PM papers, MC 412, Box 49, Folder 878.

49. Memorandum from Dorothy Kenyon, Chairman, ACLU Equality Committee, 4, March 28, 1963, PCSW Papers, B-26, Box 9, Folder 63; Paul A. Freund to Esther Peterson, March 11, 1963, ME Papers, 83-M257, Carton 1, Folder 58.

50. Murray, Proposal to Reexamine, 30; see also Statement of the AFL-CIO on Methods of Removing Legal Discrimination Against Women, Submitted to the CCPR of the PCSW, March 13, 1963, 4–5, PCSW Papers, B-26, Box 9, Folder 63.

51. See, for example, Pauli Murray to Edith Green, January 24, 1963, PM Papers, MC 412, Box 49, Folder 878.

52. Memorandum from Pauli Murray to Edith Green, Frank Sander, Harriet Pilpel, Marguerite Rawalt, Mary Eastwood, Katherine Ellickson, and Mrs. Hilton, Re: Fourteenth Amendment—Equal Rights Amendment Statement, March 12, 1963, ME Papers, 83-M257, Carton 1, Folder 59.

53. Murray, Proposal to Reexamine, 37; Pauli Murray, Draft Memorandum, August 24, 1962, 5, PCSW Papers, B-26, Box 8, Folder 61.

54. Report of Meeting Held August 24, 1962, PCSW Papers, B-26, Box 8, Folder 61.

55. See, for example, Miriam Y. Holden, "Argument in Favor of the Equal Rights Amendment, Made at the Request of the National Woman's Party," March 23, 1963, PM Papers, MC 412, Box 49, Folder 883.

56. Miriam Holden to Anita Pollitzer, February 16, 1963, NWP Papers, Film Misc 959, Reel 108. See also Nina Horton Avery, Report to the Member-

ship of the NWP on President Kennedy's Conference at the White House on July 9, 1963, with Group of Leaders of Women's Organizations, Concerning President's Proposed Civil Rights Act of 1963, July 15, 1963, NWP Papers, Misc 959, Reel 108.

57. See, for example, Pauli Murray to Richard Graham, EEOC Commissioner, March 28, 1966, PM Papers, MC 412, Box 55, Folder 959; Minutes, ACLU Equality Committee, November 30, 1967, 5, PM Papers, MC 412, Box 54, Folder 943.

58. Pauli Murray, Memorandum in Support of Retaining the Amendment to H. R. 7152, Title VII (Equal Employment Opportunity) to Prohibit Discrimination in Employment Because of Sex, April 14, 1964, 18–21, PM Papers, MC 412, Box 85, Folder 1485; Pauli Murray (address at the All-Women Conference Sponsored by the National Council of Women of the United States, New York, October 11, 1962), 4–5, NWP Papers, Misc 959, Reel 107.

59. Murray, "The Negro Woman in the Quest for Equality," *The Acorn* (June 1964), delivered as an address at the Leadership Council of the National Council of Negro Women, Nov. 14, 1963, Washington, DC.

60. 110 Cong. Rec. 2577–2583 (1964). For further discussion of the debate, see Kessler-Harris, *In Pursuit of Equity,* 241–246; Serena Mayeri, Note, "'A Common Fate of Discrimination': Race-Gender Analogies in Legal and Historical Perspective," *Yale Law Journal* 110 (2001): 1063–1067. On the addition of sex to Title VII and subsequent misrepresentations thereof, see Jo Freeman, "How 'Sex' Got Into Title VII: Persistent Opportunism as a Maker of Public Policy," *Law and Inequality* 9 (1991):163-184.

61. 110 Cong. Rec. 2581 (1964).

62. Nina Horton Avery, Chairman, Virginia Committee of the NWP, to Rep. J. Vaughan Gary (D-VA), January 8, 1964, NWP Papers, Misc 959, Reel 108. See also NWP, The Importance and Necessity of the Provisions in Title VII of the Civil Rights Bill Which Prevents Discrimination in Employment Against Women Workers, March 6, 1964, 8–9, NWP Papers, Misc 959, Reel 108; Emma Guffey Miller to Rep. Martha Griffiths (D-MI), January 20, 1964, NWP Papers, Reel 108; Message from NWP to Conference of Republican Women, April 1964, NWP Papers, Misc 959, Reel 109.

63. On the NWP's ideological diversity and relationship with the civil rights movement, see Rupp and Taylor, *Survival in the Doldrums,* 52, 153–165.

64. Meta Heller to Emma Guffey Miller, February 26, 1964, NWP Papers, Misc 959, Reel 108. See also Alma Lutz, Secretary, Massachusetts Committee for the Equal Rights Amendment, to Colleagues, January 21, 1964, NWP Papers, Misc 959, Reel 108.

65. Pauli Murray, Memorandum in Support of Retaining the Amendment to H. R. 7152, Title VII.

66. On the significance of Murray's Title VII memo, see, for example, Kessler-Harris, *In Pursuit of Equity*, 245-246; MacLean, *Freedom is Not Enough*, 120-123.

67. Compare, for example, Laura Roberts to Senators Sam Ervin and Everett Jordan, September 15, 1965, NWP Papers, Misc 959, Reel 109, with NWP Research Committee, Civil Rights for Women, August 1964, NWP Papers, Misc 959, Reel 109.

68. For more on the impact of Title VII on the feminist movement, see Kessler-Harris, *In Pursuit of Equity*, Chapter 6; Serena Mayeri, "Constitutional Choices: Legal Feminism and the Historical Dynamics of Change," *California Law Review* 92 (2004): 773–777; MacLean, *Freedom Is Not Enough*, Chapter 4.

69. For more on the EEOC's initial failure to enforce the sex discrimination provision of Title VII, see Jo Freeman, *The Politics of Women's Liberation: A Case Study of an Emerging Social Movement and Its Relation to the Policy Process* (New York: McKay, 1975), 76–79; Hugh Davis Graham, *The Civil Rights Era: Origins and Development of National Policy, 1960–1972* (New York: Oxford University Press, 1990), 205–232; Harrison, *On Account of Sex,* 192–206.

70. Pauli Murray and Mary O. Eastwood, "Jane Crow and the Law: Sex Discrimination and Title VII," *George Washington Law Review* 34 (1965): 232–233.

71. Pauli Murray to Marguerite Rawalt, July 21, 1965, ME Papers, 83-M257, Box 5, Folder 56.

72. Ibid., 2.

73. Edith Evans Asbury, "Protest Proposed on Women's Jobs," NYT, October 13, 1965; Remarks of Pauli Murray, Women and Title VII Conference, National Council of Women of the United States, October 12, 1965, ME Papers, 83-M257, Carton 1, Folder 34. See also Murray to Rawalt, July 21, 1965, 1.

74. Rawalt, too, had warmed up to Murray's approach. See Judith Paterson, *Be Somebody: A Biography of Marguerite Rawalt* (Austin, TX: Eakin Press, 1986), 155.

75. Miriam C. Holden to Alice Paul, October 16, 1965, 1–2, NWP Papers, Misc 959, Reel 109. Some NWP members were less enthusiastic, lamenting Murray's failure to embrace the ERA.

76. On women's role in the civil rights movement, see Belinda Robnett, *How Long, How Long?: African American Women in the Struggle for Civil Rights* (New York: Oxford University Press, 1997).

77. See Feldstein, *Motherhood in Black and White.*

78. Pauli Murray, Memorandum: The Role of the Negro Women in the Civil Rights Revolution, August 27, 1963, PM Papers, Box 129, Folder 2338; Cynthia Taylor, How Did the March on Washington Movement's Critique of American Democracy in the 1940s Awaken African American Women to the Problem of Jane Crow? (Binghamton, NY: State University of New York at Binghamton, 2007); see also Hartmann, *The Other Feminists*, 184.

79. Whitney M. Young, Jr., to Pauli Murray, November 29, 1963, 1–2, PM Papers, Box 127, Folder 2337.

80. James Forman to Pauli Murray, December 18, 1963, PM Papers, Box 129, Folder 2337.

81. James Farmer to Pauli Murray, January 22, 1964, PM Papers, Box 129, Folder 2337.

82. Murray, "The Negro Woman in the Quest for Equality.".

83. Office of Planning and Policy Research, *The Negro Family: The Case for National Action* (Washington, DC: U.S. Department of Labor, 1965), 5–14, 29–31, 35–36.

84. See, for example, Lee Rainwater, *The Moynihan Report and the Politics of Controversy* (Cambridge, MA: MIT Press, 1967).

85. See Marisa Chappell, *The War on Welfare: Family, Poverty, and Politics in Modern America* (Philadelphia: University of Pennsylvania Press, 2010), Chapter 2.

86. Lloyd Shearer, "Negro Problem: Women Rule the Roost," *Parade*, August 20, 1967, 4–5.

87. Catherine East to Editor, *Parade*, [1967], CE Papers, Box 10, Folder 48.

88. Catherine East to Rev. Rudolph Nemser, May 15, 1966, CE Papers, Box 9, Folder 9.

89. Martha Griffiths to Willard Wirtz, August 24, 1967, CE Papers, Box 1, Folder 33. It was not only liberal feminists who excoriated the indifference of civil rights sympathizers to feminist demands. As white Student Nonviolent Coordinating Committee (SNCC) members Casey Hayden and Mary King had written in their famous 1965 critique, "Many people who are very hip to the implications of the racial caste system, even people in the movement, don't seem to be able to see the sexual caste system." Casey Hayden and Mary King, "Sex and Caste: A Kind of Memo," in *"Takin' It To the Streets": A Sixties Reader*, ed. Alexander Bloom and Wini Breines (New York: Oxford University Press, 1995), 47–51. For more on the Hayden-King memo and the controversy over its provenance and meaning, see Wini Breines, *The Trouble between Us: An Uneasy History of White and Black Women in the Feminist Movement* (Oxford: Oxford University Press, 2006), 23–30.

90. On the fear of unrest as an impetus for EEO enforcement, see John David Skrentny, *The Ironies of Affirmative Action: Politics, Culture, and Justice in*

America (Chicago: University of Chicago Press, 1996). On masculinism and Black Power, see Deborah Gray White, *Too Heavy a Load: Black Women in Defense of Themselves, 1894–1994* (New York: W.W. Norton, 1999), Chapter 6.

91. White, *Too Heavy a Load,* 181.

92. See, for example, Alan Reitman to Catherine East, November 1, 1967, CE Papers, Box 10, Folder 48.

93. Quoted in Rainwater, *Moynihan Report,* 185.

94. Pauli Murray to William Yancey, January 25, 1966, CE Papers, Box 10, Folder 48.

95. "To Fulfill the Rights of Negro Women in Disadvantaged Families," A Statement for the White House Conference, "To Fulfill These Rights," June 1–2, 1966, Prepared by a Task Force on the Disadvantaged Family at the Request of the Citizens' Advisory Council on the Status of Women (by Dorothy Height and Caroline Ware). Height had expressed greater sympathy for Moynihan's position a few years earlier. See White, *Too Heavy a Load,* 202; Kessler-Harris, *In Pursuit of Equity,* 227–228.

96. African Americans were excluded, de facto, from jury service in many other Southern states as well. Many states differentiated between men and women with respect to jury service. Some automatically excluded women from jury rolls unless they specifically requested inclusion, with the practical effect that many juries throughout the United States were all-male. For a comprehensive discussion of women's jury service, see Kerber, *No Constitutional Right to Be Ladies,* 124–220.

97. Fred P. Graham, "Rights Case Yields Dividend for Women," NYT, February 13, 1966, 172.

98. Hoyt v. Florida, 368 U.S. 57, 62 (1961).

99. Margery Leonard to Dorothy Rogers, October 24, 1965, NWP Papers, Misc 959 Reel 109; Catherine East to Joseph Goldberg, November 3, 1965, EP papers, MC 450, Box 54, Folder 1062; Memorandum from Catherine East to Esther Peterson, December 7, 1965, Re: Discussions with Marguerite Rawalt and Others about Amicus Briefs in the Alabama Jury Exclusion Case, EP Papers, MC 450, Box 54, Folder 1062; East to Peterson, December 7, 1965 annotation; Esther Peterson to Richard Graham, EEOC Commissioner, January 10, 1966, EP papers, MC 450, Box 54, Folder 1062; Charles T. Duncan to Richard Graham, December 10, 1965, EP papers, MC 450, Box 54, Folder 1062; Esther Peterson to Nicholas deB. Katzenbach, February 4, 1966, ME Papers, 83-M257, Carton 1, Folder 16.

100. Deposition of Robert Coles, 33–39, White v. Crook, ACLU Records, Box 1832, Folder: White, G. v. Jury Commission. Coles discussed Helen Hacker's "Women as a Minority Group" at some length in his deposition, referring to her as "Mr. Hacker."

101. Plaintiff's Brief, White v. Crook, ACLU Records, Box 1840, Folder: Willis v. Carson.

102. Kerber, *No Constitutional Right to Be Ladies,* 198.

103. Jack Bass, "The Four from the Fifth," *Nation,* May 3, 2004, 799–800.

104. Judge Allgood lacked the pro-civil rights reputation of his colleagues. See James Barron, "Clarence Allgood, Federal Judge Since 1938," NYT, December 2, 1991, D10.

105. Judge Richard T. Rives to Judge Frank M. Johnson and Judge Clarence W. Allgood, September 7, 1965, Re: Gardenia White, et al. v. Bruce Cook [sic], et al., FMJ Papers, Container 42, Folder 2263-N: White v. Crook, 1966. Allgood replied that he "certainly hope[d] that [Rives's] first impression is correct," for "[i]f it is a case that we do not have to consider, I certainly do not wish to do so." Allgood to Rives and Johnson, September 8, 1965, Re: Gardenia White, et al., v. Bruce Crook, et al., FMJ Papers, Container 42, Folder 2263-N: White v. Crook, 1966. Three-judge district courts could only be convened in cases involving federal constitutional questions; otherwise a single district judge would hear the case.

106. Rives to Johnson and Allgood, September 7, 1965, Re: Gardenia White, et al. v. Bruce Cook [sic], et al., FMJ Papers, Container 42, Folder 2263-N: White v. Crook, 1966.

107. Dorothy Kenyon to Melvin Wulf, January 10, 196[6], Box 1832, Folder: White, G. v. Jury Commission, ACLU Records. See also Murray, *Autobiography,* 364.

108. White v. Crook, 251 F. Supp. 401, 408 (M.D. Ala. 1966).

109. Marguerite Rawalt to Mattie Belle, February 9, 1966, MR Papers, Box 30, Folder 38.

110. Mary Eastwood to Charles Morgan, Director, Southern Regional Office, ACLU, February 1966, ME Papers, 83-M257, Carton 1, Folder 28.

111. Dorothy Kenyon to Caroline Ware, March 23, 1966, DK Papers, Box 17, Folder 17, Sophia Smith Collection, Smith College; see also Press Release, ACLU Wins Case on Exclusion of Negroes and Women from Juries in Alabama, February 28, 1966, NWP Papers, Misc 959, Reel 110.

112. Pauli Murray to Alma Lutz, December 9, 1965, 1, PM Papers, MC 412, Box 97, Folder 1730. For more on the Murray-Lutz correspondence, see Mayeri, "Constitutional Choices," 781–783.

113. Pauli Murray to Marguerite Rawalt, February 16, 1966, MR Papers, Box 30, Folder 38.

114. Dan T. Carter, *The Politics of Rage: George Wallace, the Origins of the New Conservatism, and the Transformation of American Politics,* 2nd ed. (Baton Rouge: Louisiana State University Press, 2000), 276; Mary Eastwood to Jean Witter, September 2, 1968, ME papers, 83-M257, Box 4, Folder 50. Flowers had been

"shocked and amazed" at the grand jury's failure to indict the accused killers for first-degree murder, and condemned local officials' efforts to "whitewash" and "railroad" the case. Affidavit of Orzell Billingsley, Jr., to Support Motion [for Temporary Restraining Order or Preliminary Injunction], White v. Crook, ACLU Records, Box 1832, Folder: White, G. v. Jury Commission. The grand jury had returned an indictment for manslaughter.

115. Murray, *Autobiography,* 364.

116. Hartmann, *Other Feminists,* 65–66.

117. Pauli Murray to Marguerite Rawalt, February 2, 1966, PM Papers, MC 412, Box 59, Folder 999.

118. Ernest Angell, Chairman, Board of Directors, ACLU and John de J. Pemberton, Executive Director, ACLU, to the Editor of the NYT, February 15, 1966, ACLU Records, Box 1144, Folder 5; Text of Letter of the ACLU Urging Amendment of Civil Rights Protection Act of 1966 to Deal with Exclusion of Women from Service on State Juries, February 14, 1966, NWP papers, Misc 959, Reel 110.

119. Because some of the lawyers were employed full-time by the government, they often worked well into the night on briefs to which they could not sign their names.

120. Bowe v. Colgate Palmolive Co., 272 F. Supp. 332 (S.D. Ind. 1967).

121. On Lorena Weeks's case, see MacLean, *Freedom Is Not Enough,* 123–124.

122. Weeks v. Southern Bell, 277 F. Supp. 117 (D. Ga. 1967); Rosenfeld v. Southern Pacific Co., 293 F. Supp. 1219 (C.D. Calif. 1968).

123. Dorothy Kenyon expressed concern that such cases would confuse the protective labor law question with the larger Fourteenth Amendment issue. Dorothy Kenyon to Pauli Murray, October 13, 1966, PM Papers, Box 39, Folder 685.

124. Caroline F. Ware to Alice Rossi, February 18, 1967, NOW Papers, 72-25-79-M262; 81-M106, Box 14, Folder: Gov Board, NOW. For the fascinating correspondence between Ware and Murray, see Anne Firor Scott, ed., *Pauli Murray and Caroline Ware: Forty Years of Letters in Black and White* (Chapel Hill: University of North Carolina Press, 2006).

125. In a letter to her colleagues at the ACLU of Southern California, Murray called *Mengelkoch* a "possible test case" under Title VII in which "the constitutional issue of the Fourteenth Amendment with respect to women may be reached." Pauli Murray to A. L. Wirin and Fred Okrand, ACLU of Southern California, September 25, 1966, PM Papers, Box 39, Folder 685. Believing she was about to be appointed to an official position at the EEOC, Murray could not take the case herself, but she urged dubious ACLU officials to do so. See Alan Reitman to Dorothy Kenyon, September 29, 1966, ACLU Records, MC #001, Box 1144, Folder 3.

126. [Catherine East], Memorandum for the Secretary, Subject: Should Labor Department Recommend that the U.S. Government Intervene in the Mengelkoch Case, 3, CE Papers, Box 10, Folder 9.

127. NOW, Late Bulletin, The Mengelkoch case, NOW, January 13, 1967, BF papers, 71-62-81-M23, Carton 44, Folder 1551.

128. Rawalt's biographer Judith Paterson wrote later that "[a]lthough [Rawalt] saw parallels between racial and sexual discrimination and immediately recognized the brilliance of civil rights strategy, her identification with that movement would remain slim." Paterson, *Be Somebody*, 126.

129. Murray recognized Rawalt as a fellow pragmatist. See, for example, Pauli Murray to Marguerite Rawalt, February 16, 1966, MR Papers, Box 30, Folder 38.

130. Bill Farr, "Autonetics Women Land 'Equality' Blow," *Orange County Register* (Santa Ana, CA), April 2, 1966, CE Papers, Box 10, Folder 9.

131. Ted James, "Silver Joins Autonetics Women in Fighting for Right to Overtime," *Orange County Register* (Santa Ana, CA), October 9, 1966, 1, CE Papers, Box 10, Folder 9.

132. Brief of the National Organization for Women as Amicus Curiae, in opposition to defendant's motion to dismiss, 6, 11, 14, 16, 18–21, Mengelkoch v. Industrial Welfare Commission, No. 66-16-18-S, U.S. District Court for the Central District of California, [1967?], PM Papers, Box 39, Folder 687.

133. Among other cases, the court cited Muller v. Oregon (1908), in which the Supreme Court upheld a minimum wage law for women on the ground that women's physical weakness and responsibilities for family care justified protective laws that would be unconstitutional if applied to men.

134. Jurisdictional Statement, Mengelkoch v. Industrial Welfare Commission, PM Papers, Box 39, Folder 687; see also Ronald J. Ostrow, "Crusade Against Women's Work Law Kept Alive," LAT, October 29, 1968, 3.

135. Jurisdictional Statement, 7–10.

136. Bowe v. Colgate Palmolive, 272 F. Supp. 332, 362 (S.D. Ind. 1967); Wolfgang Saxon, "W. E. Steckler, 81, U.S. District Judge Serving 45th Year," NYT, March 11, 1995, 10.

137. Weeks v. Southern Bell, 277 F. Supp. 117 (S.D. Ga. 1967). A dearth of funds and increasing personal friction among Mengelkoch's attorneys compounded the disappointment of these initial legal setbacks. See, for example, Mary Eastwood oral history, Tully-Crenshaw Oral History Project, Schlesinger Library, Radcliffe Institute, Harvard University.

138. Brief for Plaintiffs-Appellants, 20, Bowe v. Colgate Palmolive, 416 F.2d 711 (7th Cir. 1969) (Nos. 16624-16626, 16632), PI Papers, Box B11, Folder: Bowe v. Colgate Palmolive.

139. Mengelkoch v. Industrial Welfare Commission, 393 U.S. 83 (1968). The Ninth Circuit later ruled that Mengelkoch had presented a substantial federal question. Mengelkoch v. Industrial Welfare Commission, 442 F. 2d 1119 (9th Cir. 1971).

140. Skrentny observes that in congressional hearings on sex discrimination during this period, "[b]y far the most prevalent way of establishing the injustice of women's inequality was not by reference to specific instances of crushed aspirations, but rather the analogy of women with blacks." Skrentny, *Minority Rights Revolution,* 243.

141. Pauli Murray to Mary Eastwood, January 19, 1966, ME Papers, 83-M257, Box 5, Folder 56.

142. See, for example, Minutes, NOW Executive Board, November 20, 1966, 2–4, BF Papers, Carton 44, Folder 1563.

143. Minutes, NOW Board of Directors Meeting, February 22–23, 1967, 6, BF Papers, Carton 44, Folder 1550.

144. Freeman, *Politics of Women's Liberation,* 80. See also Minutes of the First Board Meeting, NOW, October 30, 1966, 4, BF Papers, Carton 44, Folder 1551.

145. Human Rights Amendment, in Proposal for NOW, January 1, 1967, Mary Eastwood Papers, 83-M257, Carton 3, Folder 12, on file with the Schlesinger Library, Radcliffe Institute, Harvard University.

146. See For Discussion Purposes Only: Proposal: That NOW Support a Constitutional Amendment, but with New Language, April 21, 1967, ME Papers, 83-M257, Carton 3, Folder 12. For an account of Paul's rejection of the proposal, see Amelia Fry to Mary Eastwood, October 12, 1979, and attached oral history, ME Papers, 83-M257, Carton 3, Folder 12. Other slight alterations in wording were also rejected out of hand. See, for example, Harriet Bradford, Proposed Rewording of the Equal Rights Amendment, Spring 1967, BF Papers, Box 42, Folder 1486; Alma Lutz to Betty Friedan, March 13, 1967, BF Papers, Box 42, Folder 1486; Alma Lutz to Betty Friedan, April 24, 1967, BF Papers, Box 42, Folder 1486.

147. For instance, in 1967, Miriam Holden would turn 74, Alma Lutz 77, Emma Guffey Miller 93, and Alice Paul 82.

148. Miriam Holden to Miss Newell, February 11, 1967, NWP Papers, Misc 959, Reel 110.

149. A year earlier, Eastwood had been hesitant to suggest that NOW tackle the ERA issue right away. See Mary Eastwood to Inka O'Hanrahan, July 25, 1966, 2, BF Papers, Box 42, Folder 1481; Mary Eastwood to Betty Friedan, August 1966, BF Papers, Box 42, Folder 1481.

150. National Capital Area NOW, Resolution, November 19, 1967, NWP Papers, Misc 959, Reel 110.

151. 1967 National Conference of N.O.W. Schedule, November 1, 1967, BF Papers, Carton 44, Folder 1550. The leadership of NOW anticipated a variety of diversionary tactics on the part of ERA opponents. Confidential Notes for Betty Friedan, President of NOW, November 11, 1967, BF Papers, Box 42, Folder 1491.

152. Paterson, *Be Somebody,* 180. See also Minutes of the NOW Conference, November 18, 1967, BF Papers, Box 44, Folder 1553. As Dorothy Sue Cobble shows, Caroline Davis had been one of the few union women to argue for similar treatment of race and sex discrimination. Cobble, *Other Women's Movement,* 90.

153. Murray spoke of her concern that a strong stance on the ERA would "alienate organizations who have given us support until now." Minutes of the NOW Conference, November 18, 1967, BF Papers, Box 44, Folder 1553.

154. Minutes of National Conference of NOW, November 18–19, 1967, BF Papers, Carton 44, Folder 1550.

155. Dorothy Haener to Betty Friedan, December 26, 1967, 4, PI Papers, Box 6, Folder: NOW conference, 1967.

156. Hartmann, *Other Feminists,* 189. Aileen Hernandez and others also spoke out on behalf of building connections with racial minority groups. See, for example, Aileen Hernandez to Muriel Fox, October 21, 1967, BF Papers, Box 42, Folder 1484.

157. Pauli Murray to Kathryn Clarenbach, November 21, 1967, PM Papers, Box 51, Folder 899, quoted in Hartmann, *Other Feminists,* 189–190.

158. NOW also considered a freestanding reproductive freedom amendment. See NOW, The Right of a Woman to Determine Her Own Reproductive Process, Document II, BF Papers, Carton 44, Folder 1553.

159. Minutes of National Conference of NOW.

160. More radical groups of mostly younger women also appeared during this period. For more, see Alice Echols, *Daring to Be Bad: Radical Feminism in America, 1967–75* (Minneapolis: University of Minnesota Press, 1989), 167–169; Freeman, *Politics of Women's Liberation,* 81–83; Susan M. Hartmann, *From Margin to Mainstream: American Women and Politics Since 1960* (Philadelphia: Temple University Press, 1989), 62–66; Ruth Rosen, *The World Split Open: How the Modern Women's Movement Changed America* (New York: Viking, 2000), 81–89.

161. Mary Eastwood to Pauli Murray, October 26, 1967, 2, ME Papers, 83-M257, Carton 3, Folder 12 ("[T]he more support [there] is for a new amendment, the better the chances for winning under the 14th. . . . [T]he converse is also true: winning under the 14th improves chances for ERA passage.").

162. Mary Eastwood, Proposal for NOW, January 1, 1967, ME Papers, 83-

M257, Carton 3, Folder 12; see also Mary O. Eastwood, Constitutional Protection Against Sex Discrimination: An Informational Memorandum Prepared for the National Organization for Women (NOW) Regarding the Equal Rights Amendment and Similar Proposals, November 1967, NWP Papers, Misc 959, Reel 110.

163. NOW, NOW Bill of Rights for 1968, NWP Papers, Misc 959, Reel 111 (describing the ERA as the top priority); Jean Witter, Suggested Future Directions for N.O.W., July 20, 1968, ME Papers, 83-M257, Box 4, Folder 50 (indicating continued support for litigation).

164. Caruthers G. Berger, Comments on Questions and Answers on the Equal Rights Amendment, September 22, 1967, NWP Papers, Misc 959, Reel 110 (emphasis in original). I discuss how feminists coalesced around the dual strategy in much greater detail in Mayeri, "Constitutional Choices."

165. See, for example, Minutes, ACLU Equality Committee, November 30, 1967, 4, PM Papers, MC 412, Box 54, Folder 943; Minutes, ACLU Equality Committee, December 28, 1967, PM Papers, MC 412, Box 54, Folder 943.

166. Pauli Murray to Catherine East, November 24, 1967, CE Papers, Box 2, Folder 11; Pauli Murray to Mary Eastwood, January 25, 1968, ME Papers, 83-M257, Carton 1, Folder 4.

167. See, for example, Minutes, ACLU Equality Committee, June 6, 1968, PM Papers, MC 412, Box 54, Folder 943; Minutes, ACLU Equality Committee, December 28, 1967, 4; Kerber, No Constitutional Right to Be Ladies, 195–196.

168. Hartmann, Other Feminists, 72–73.

169. Dorothy Kenyon to Rolland O'Hare, April 20, 1970, 1–2, DK Papers, Box 29, Folder 1.

170. Dorothy Kenyon to Betsy Nolan, ACLU, June 29, 1970, DK Papers, Box 29, Folder 1.

171. See, for example, Pauli Murray to Mary Eastwood, January 3, 1969, ME Papers, 83-M257, Carton 1, Folder 4.

172. Hartmann, Other Feminists, 74; Memorandum from Susan Deller Ross, ACLU Position on Sex Discrimination and Protective Legislation, March 17, 1970, PM Papers, MC 412, Box 55, Folder 958.

173. Memorandum from Pauli Murray to ACLU Equality Committee, Re: ACLU Position on Sex Discrimination, March 30, 1970, 1–3, PM Papers, MC 412, Box 55, Folder 959 (emphasis added). Hartmann, Other Feminists, 80; Dorothy Kenyon to Larry Speiser, June 3, 1971, DK Papers, Box 29, Folder 2.

174. Memorandum from Murray, March 30, 1970, 3.

175. Memorandum from Pauli Murray & Dorothy Kenyon to the Board of the ACLU, Re: Women's Rights. The Equal Rights Amendment: Should We

Favor It, and If So, Why? September 24, 1970, PM Papers, MC 412, Box 55, Folder 956. See also Memorandum from Dorothy Kenyon to the ACLU Board of Directors, Re: Why the Equal Rights Amendment for Women? December 1, 1970, 2, PM Papers, MC 412, Box 55, Folder 956.

176. Press Release, ACLU, October 2, 1970, ME Papers, 83-M257, Carton 3, Folder 12. Hartmann shows that the change in ACLU policy was due not only to external events and to the internal pressures from Murray and Kenyon, but also to grassroots organization on behalf of the ERA by women in the ACLU's local affiliates. Hartmann, *Other Feminists,* 75.

177. Esther Peterson to Martha Griffiths, October 12, 1971, 1–2, EP Papers, MC 450, Box 54, Folder 1061.

178. For more on feminists' strong commitment to the dual strategy, see Mayeri, "Constitutional Choices," 808–813.

179. See Kessler-Harris, *In Pursuit of Equity,* 278–279; Skrentny, *Minority Rights Revolution,* 136–141, 242–245.

180. *The "Equal Rights" Amendment: Hearings Before the Subcommittee on Constitutional Amendments, Senate Judiciary Committee,* 91st Cong., 1st Sess., May 5–7, 1970, 35.

181. *Equal Rights 1970: Hearings Before the Senate Committee on the Judiciary on S.J. Res. 61 and S.J. Res. 231,* 91st Cong., 2d Sess., September 9, 10, 11 and 15, 1970.

182. *Equal Rights for Men and Women,* S. Rep. No. 92-689, 92d Cong., 2d Sess., 12–13. On the evolution of the ERA's "unique physical characteristics" exemption, see Siegel, "Constitutional Culture."

183. See Barbara A. Brown, Thomas I. Emerson, Gail Falk, and Ann E. Freedman, "The Equal Rights Amendment: A Constitutional Basis for Equal Rights for Women," *Yale Law Journal* 80 (1971): 871–985.

184. Paul A. Freund, "The Equal Rights Amendment Is Not the Way," *Harvard Civil Rights-Civil Liberties Law Review* 6 (1971): 234, 240.

185. For in-depth analysis of Ervin's opposition to the ERA, see Jane Sherron DeHart and Donald G. Mathews, *Sex, Gender, and the Politics of ERA: A State and the Nation* (New York: Oxford University Press, 1990), Chapter 2.

186. See *Equal Rights 1970,* 77–91.

2. "Women and Minorities"

1. Aileen Hernandez to Merrillee A. Dolan, December 15, 1970, NOW Papers, Box 48, Folder 30.

2. Aileen Hernandez to Merrillee A. Dolan, January 21, 1971, NOW Papers, Box 7, Folder 60.

3. Merrillee A. Dolan, "Moynihan, Poverty Programs, and Women: A Female Perspective," [NOW Task Force on Women and Poverty, 1971], NOW

Papers, Box 48, Folder 35. For more on Dolan and her antipoverty efforts within NOW, see Marissa Chappell, *The War on Welfare: Family, Poverty, and Politics in Modern America* (Philadelphia: University of Pennsylvania Press, 2010), 102–103, 136, 169–171.

4. Ann Scott and Lucy Komisar, And Justice For All: Federal Equal Opportunity Enforcement Effort against Sex Discrimination, [1971], 14, NOW, NOW Papers, 72-8-82-M211, Carton 18, Folder: NOW Compliance for Affirmative Action.

5. See Hugh Davis Graham, *The Civil Rights Era: Origins and Development of National Policy, 1960–1972* (New York: Oxford University Press, 1990); John David Skrentny, *The Minority Rights Revolution* (Cambridge, MA: Harvard University Press, 2002).

6. [Ann Scott], National Organization for Women, Federal Compliance Committee, Federal Compliance Programs, NOW Papers, 72-25-79-M262, 81-M106, Carton 1, Folder: Denver Board Meeting.

7. Press Release, U.S. Commission on Civil Rights, July 1, 1970, Leadership Conference on Civil Rights Papers, 1:151, Folder: Women's Equal Rights Amendment. On the history of the Commission, see Mary Frances Berry, *And Justice for All: The United States Commission on Civil Rights and the Continuing Struggle for Freedom in America* (New York: Random House, 2009).

8. See, for example, Lacey Fosburgh, "Dealing with Feminism in Black and White," LAT, March 20, 1974, E1. Benita Roth writes that "[i]n mainstream accounts, black women's resistance to feminism became a kind of trope" in the 1970s. Benita Roth, *Separate Roads to Feminism: Black, Chicana, and White Feminist Movements in America's Second Wave* (Cambridge: Cambridge University Press, 2004), 97–98.

9. Almena Lomax, "Speaking Out: Women's Lib Reductio Ad Absurdum," *Ebony*, July 1973, 122. See also Roth, *Separate Roads*, 43–44.

10. Quoted in Mary Ellen Perry, "Minority Women Differ on 'Movement,'" *Oakland Post*, October 5, 1972, 8.

11. "A Black Woman Responds to Women's Liberation," *Off Our Backs*, April 17, 1971, 18.

12. Toni Morrison, "What the Black Woman Thinks about Women's Lib," *NYT Magazine*, August 22, 1971, SM14. As Mae C. King put it two years later, "There is reason to believe that white women in the 1970's, like those of an earlier period, will disassociate themselves from the issue of racial justice whenever it appears advantageous for them to do so." Mae C. King, "The Politics of Sexual Stereotypes," *Black Scholar*, vol. 4, no. 6-7, March–April 1973, 12, 22.

13. "Mrs. King Faults Lib for 'Elitism,'" *Atlanta Journal*, May 29, 1972, WSH Papers, 72-120-74-233, Carton 3, Folder: 1972 Corr. (May–Aug).

14. Bayard Rustin, "Feminism and Equality," August 27, 1970, PM Papers, Box 99, Folder 1784 (news release from A. Philip Randolph Institute).

15. After all, Murray wrote, "The women's movement has sprung up with renewed vitality primarily because it was impossible to convince our brethren, including *you*, dear Bayard, that women's rights were and *are* an integral part of the civil rights-human rights revolution, and that human rights are indivisible!" Pauli Murray to Bayard Rustin, September 9, 1970, PM Papers, Box 99, Folder 1770.

16. Ibid.

17. Pauli Murray, *The Autobiography of a Black Activist, Feminist, Lawyer, Priest, and Poet* (Knoxville: University of Tennessee Press, 1989), 393, 389–390, 414.

18. Ibid., 416.

19. Nancy MacLean notes that "the women who most appreciated the potential of Title VII were those who had benefited least from the family wage bargain"—particularly black women. Nancy MacLean, *Freedom Is Not Enough: The Opening of the American Workplace* (Cambridge, MA: Harvard University Press, 2006), 118–119; see also Dorothy Sue Cobble, *The Other Women's Movement: Workplace Justice and Social Rights in Modern America* (Princeton: Princeton University Press, 2004), 91–92.

20. Aileen C. Hernandez, "The Women's Movement: 1965–1975, for the Symposium on the Tenth Anniversary of the EEOC," sponsored by Rutgers University Law School, November 28–29, 1975, 6–7, 23–24, PM Papers, Box 96, Folder 1704.

21. Quoted in Vera Glaser, "U.S. Job Bias Agency Is Hit by Resignation," *Detroit News*, November 13, 1966, CE Papers, Box 16, Folder 9.

22. Toni Carabillo interview, conducted by Muriel Fox, Tully-Crenshaw Oral History Project, Schlesinger Library, Radcliffe Institute, Harvard University. See also Winifred Wandersee, *On the Move: American Women in the 1970s* (Boston: Twayne, 1988), 44.

23. See, for example, Gene Reid, "Feminist Leader Says: Women and Minorities Face Similar Problems," *New Pittsburgh Courier*, December 7, 1974, 1.

24. Aileen Hernandez and Ann Scott to FCC Commissioner Dean Burch, October 6, 1970, CE Papers, Box 16, Folder 27.

25. Aileen Hernandez to Members of the Legal Defense and Education Fund Board, December 10, 1971, PI Papers, Box 319, Folder: Weeks v. Southern Bell. On Hernandez's support for making lesbian rights a feminist issue, see also Carabillo interview; Wilma Scott Heide interview, conducted by Muriel Fox, Tully-Crenshaw Oral History Project, Schlesinger Library, Radcliffe Institute, Harvard University. On NOW and lesbian feminists, see Stephanie Gilmore and Elizabeth Kaminski, "A Part and Apart: Lesbian and Straight Feminists Negotiate Identity in a Second-Wave Organization," *Journal of the History of Sexuality* 16 (2007): 95–113.

26. For more on Norton's early career, see Susan Hartmann, *The Other Feminists: Activists in the Liberal Establishment* (New Haven, CT: Yale University Press, 1998); Joan Steinau Lester, *Fire in My Soul: The Life of Eleanor Holmes Norton* (New York: Atria Books, 2003), 107, 176. Hartmann notes the generational contrast between Norton's and Murray's professional opportunities. Hartmann, *Other Feminists,* 182.

27. See *Women's Role in Contemporary Society: The Report of the New York City Commission on Human Rights* New York: Avon Books, 1972).

28. "Black Lawyer in Women's Lib Fight," *Chicago Daily Defender,* September 25, 1971, 17.

29. Eleanor Holmes Norton, "A Strategy for Change," in *Women's Role in Contemporary Society,* 55. See also Eleanor Holmes Norton, "Black Women as Women," *Social Policy,* Vol. 3, No. 2, July/August 1972, 2.

30. Like Murray, Chisholm grouped "racism and anti-feminism" in the broader, unifying category of "Anti-Humanism." Shirley Chisholm, "Racism and Anti-Feminism," *Black Scholar,* Vol. 1, Nos. 3-4, January–February 1970, 40, 45. See also Shirley Chisholm, "Race, Revolution and Women," *Black Scholar,* Vol. 3, No. 4, December 1971, 17–21.

31. See, for example, Aileen Hernandez to Wilma Scott Heide, June 29, 1972, NOW Papers, Box 7, Folder 60 (suggesting steps NOW could take to attract and ally itself with Chicana, Asian, and Native American as well as black women); Report of the Task Force, Minority Women and Women's Rights, May 1974, NOW Papers, Box 48, Folder 18. As Hernandez said, "I am a woman and a member of a minority race. I can't be schizoid. I have to deal with both questions, both problems, and integrate both of them in my life. I think the women's movement has to do the same thing. It has to encompass racism as well as sexism." Quoted in Lacey Fosburgh, "Dealing with Feminism in Black and White," LAT, March 20, 1974, E1. On black women's "quandary" during this period, see Deborah Gray White, *Too Heavy a Load: Black Women in Defense of Themselves, 1894–1994* (New York: W.W. Norton, 1999), 249.

32. Quoted in Enid Nemy, "Toting Up Dollars and Cents Cost of Sex Discrimination," NYT, May 14, 1971.

33. "The Negro/Black Woman: Myth and Reality," Remarks of Dr. Pauli Murray, Stulberg Professor of Law and Politics, Brandeis University, Symposium II, Women Today and Tomorrow, May 12, 1973, 5, George Washington University, PM Papers, Box 89, Folder 1558.

34. As Benita Roth notes, "all of the women [who founded BFOA] had connections to NOW." Roth, *Separate Roads,* 125. See also Kimberly Springer, *Living for the Revolution: Black Feminist Organizations, 1968–1980* (Durham, NC: Duke University Press, 2005), 62.

35. Barbara Campbell, "Black Feminists Hold Parley Here," NYT, December 2, 1973. For more on the NBFO, see White, *Too Heavy a Load*, Chapter 7; Springer, *Living for the Revolution*; Roth, *Separate Roads*; Wini Breines, *The Trouble Between Us: An Uneasy History of White and Black Women in the Feminist Movement* (Oxford: Oxford University Press, 2006), 50–51.

36. Quoted in Lester, *Fire in My Soul*, 148.

37. "On the road to equality," Norton wrote, "there is no better place for blacks to detour around American values than in foregoing its example in the treatment of its women and the organization of its family life." Eleanor Holmes Norton, "For Sadie and Maude," *Rutgers Law Review* 25 (1970): 23. See also MacLean, *Freedom Is Not Enough*, 144.

38. Charlayne Hunter, "Many Blacks Wary of 'Women's Liberation' Movement in U.S.," NYT, November 17, 1970.

39. Eleanor Holmes Norton, "For Black Women, Opportunities Open," NYT, January 10, 1971.

40. On black women's feminist leadership during this period, see Hartmann, *Other Feminists*; MacLean, *Freedom Is Not Enough*, 151.

41. Quoted in Scott and Komisar, *And Justice for All*.

42. Quoted in Caroline Bird, "Black Womanpower," *New York* (1973), PM Papers, Box 118, Folder 2104. Murray and Harris had led sit-ins together while at Howard in the 1940s. See Pauli Murray, letter to the editor, NYT, October 25, 1971; Harry McAlpin, "Howard Students Picket Jim Crow Restaurant," *Chicago Defender*, April 24, 1943, 5.

43. Bird, "Black Womanpower," 38. See also Cynthia Fuchs Epstein, "Black and Female: The Double Whammy," *Psychology Today*, August 1973, 57. Hernandez often made similar points. See, for example, Gail Berkley, "'Black Women Should Join Movement'—Aileen Hernandez," *Oakland Post*, September 12, 1972, 7.

44. On Harris and her husband, William Beasley Harris, see Linda Charlton, "Patricia Roberts Harris," NYT, December 22, 1976, 16.

45. Quoted in Lester, *Fire in My Soul*, 176.

46. Lester, *Fire in My Soul*, 154, 160.

47. Pauli Murray, "Why Negro Girls Stay Single," *Negro Digest*, July 1947, 4–8.

48. For example, see Aileen Hernandez, "Small Change for Black Women," *Ms.*, August 1974, 16–18.

49. Eleanor Holmes Norton, "Commencement Address," *Vassar Quarterly*, Summer 1971, CE Papers, Box 2, Folder 14.

50. The early 1970s saw an unprecedented outpouring of writing by and about African American women. See, for example, Toni Cade Bambara, *The Black Woman* (New York: New American Library, 1970); Joyce A. Ladner, *To-*

morrow's Tomorrow: The Black Woman (Garden City, NY: Anchor Books, 1972); Cellestine Ware, *Woman Power: The Movement for Women's Liberation* (New York: Tower Publications, 1970).

51. Frances Beale, "Double Jeopardy: To Be Black and Female," in *Black Woman,* 98.

52. Linda LaRue, "The Black Movement and Women's Liberation," *Black Scholar,* Vol. 1, No. 7, May 1970, 36.

53. Catharine R. Stimpson, "'Thy Neighbor's Wife, Thy Neighbor's Servants': Women's Liberation and Black Civil Rights," in *Woman in Sexist Society,* ed. Vivian Gornick and Barbara K. Moran (New York: Basic Books, 1971), 452, 473–474. See also Catharine R. Stimpson, "Conflict: Probable; Coalition, Possible: Feminism and the Black Movement," in *Women in Higher Education,* ed. W. Todd Furniss and Patricia Albjerg Graham (Washington, DC: American Council on Education, 1974). For other contemporaneous critiques of the parallel by white feminists, see, for example, Alice Rossi, "Sex Equality: The Beginnings of Ideology," in *Voices of the New Feminism,* ed. Mary Lou Thompson (Boston: Beacon Press, 1971), 59; Alice Rossi, "Women—Terms of Liberation," *Dissent,* November/December 1970, 540–541.

54. For example, see LaRue, "Black Movement," 42. See also Barbara Sizemore, "Sexism and the Black Male," *Black Scholar,* Vol. 4, Nos. 6–7, March–April 1973, 2; King, "The Politics of Sexual Stereotypes." For more, see Roth, *Separate Roads to Feminism,* 85–87; Breines, *Trouble Between Us,* 144–145.

55. See Roth, *Separate Roads to Feminism,* 99–101.

56. MacLean notes that "[w]hite women as individuals usually had more social power than black men or women, but now feminists as a group needed to affiliate and cooperate with black civil rights forces to make political headway." MacLean, *Freedom Is Not Enough,* 148.

57. Board of Directors and Other Involved Members, Re: Report of the President Since November 22, 1971, February 19, 1972, WSH Papers, 72-120-74-233, Carton 1, Folder: Board agendas, forms.

58. Wilma Scott Heide, Revolution: Tomorrow Is NOW! Keynote Address at the Sixth National Conference of NOW, at Statler Hilton Hotel, Washington, DC, February 17, 1973, WSH Papers, 72-120-74-233, Box 4, Folder: WSH Testimony.

59. RBG to Jameson Doig, Chairman, Committee on Educational Programs, Princeton University, Woodrow Wilson School of Public and International Affairs, December 6, 1971, RBG Papers, Container 9, Folder: Upward Bound Program, Princeton University, 1969–1971.

60. Quoted in Barbara Campbell, "Black Feminists Form Group Here," *NYT,* August 16, 1973, 36. U.S. Civil Rights Commissioner Frankie Muse Freeman's declaration the same year that "the achievement of women's rights is

essential to the achievement of racial justice" meant all the more given her ear-lier reluctance to prioritize feminist claims. Frankie Freeman, "Women's Rights in the 1970s," reprinted from Jacksonville, Florida, NOW newsletter, from re-marks delivered August 16, 1973, NOW Papers, Box 48, Folder 18.

61. Kermit J. Scott, "Women's Lib and the Black Community," *Oakland Post*, September 2, 1971.

62. On the "natural alliance" between feminists and civil rights advocates as a "novel idea" made possible by mobilization around Title VII, see MacLean, *Freedom Is Not Enough*, 117–119. MacLean notes, "Today's organizers take for granted the pressure for identical reform and for inter-group collaboration against discrimination, but that outcome was anything but inevitable given the prior history." MacLean, *Freedom Is Not Enough*, 147. See also Serena Mayeri, "Constitutional Choices: Legal Feminism and the Historical Dynamics of Change," California Law Review 92 (2004): 755–839.

63. Judith Michaelson, "The Justices Saw It Her Way," *New York Post*, Jan-uary 30, 1971, quoted in *Women's Rights Law Reporter*, Vol. 1, No. 1 (1971): 21.

64. Brief for the EEOC as Amicus Curiae, Phillips v. Martin-Marietta Corp., 8–9, Fifth Circuit, No. 26825, PM Papers, Box 39, Folder 696.

65. Phillips v. Martin-Marietta, 411 F.2d 1, 3–4 (5th Cir. 1969).

66. Phillips v. Martin-Marietta, 416 F.2d 1257, 1259–1261 (5th Cir. 1969) (Brown, C.J., dissenting from denial of rehearing en banc).

67. Brief for the United States as Amicus Curiae, 13, Phillips v. Martin-Marietta, 400 U.S. 542 (1971) (No. 69-1058).

68. Motion for Leave to File a Brief Amicus Curiae and Brief Amicus Cu-riae of the National Organization for Women, Phillips v. Martin-Marietta (No. 69-1058); Brief for Human Rights for Women, Inc., as Amicus Curiae, Phillips v. Martin-Marietta (No. 69-1058). See also Oral Argument, Phillips v. Martin-Marietta, COASC, 10.

69. Motion for Leave to File Brief Amicus Curiae and Brief of the Amer-ican Civil Liberties Union as Amicus Curiae, 22, *Phillips* (No. 69-1058).

70. Brief for Petitioner, 13–14, *Phillips* (No. 69-1058). While the brief mentioned "the economic weakness of Negro males" and cited the Moynihan Report in a footnote, the text emphasized the plight of black women "suffer-ing under the double discrimination of race and sex," characterizing these women as "the most oppressed group of workers in the society."

71. Brief for the United States as Amicus Curiae, 4-5, *Phillips* (No. 69-1058), 1970 WL 122567. See also Brief for the ACLU as Amicus Curiae, 14-16, *Phillips* (No. 69-1058). Martin-Marietta's attorneys denied that their policy had anything to do with racism. The company protested the charge that its pol-icy had a disproportionate impact on blacks, emphasizing that no evidence of

racial discrimination appeared in the record: "Indeed, petitioner carefully re-frains from suggesting that she is black herself and the record shows she is not." Brief for Respondent, 22, *Phillips* (No. 69-1058).

72. Burger would threaten immediate resignation when Nixon's administra-tion floated women's names as possible Supreme Court nominees the following year. John W. Dean, *The Rehnquist Choice: The Untold Story of the Nixon Appointment That Redefined the Supreme Court* (New York: Free Press, 2001), 181–184. Around this time, Nixon himself stated, "I don't think a woman should be in any govern-ment job whatever," but he recognized the political advantages of appointing a woman to the Court. See Dean, *Rehnquist Choice,* 113, 155.

73. Ann Marie Boylan, "Ida Phillips v. Martin-Marietta Corporation," *Women's Rights Law Reporter,* Vol. 1, No. 1 (1971): 11, 19–20.

74. Sandler wrote: "I went down to the Supreme Court to hear arguments on Martin Marietta and was most disappointed. The lawyers didn't know all the ins and outs of the law and did not field the questions nearly as well as could have been done." Bernice Sandler to Pauli Murray, March 7, 1971, PM Papers, MC 412, Box 140, Folder 2551.

75. Phillips v. Martin-Marietta, 400 U.S. 542 (1971). A per curiam decision is an unsigned opinion "for the court."

76. Harry A. Blackmun, No. 73—Phillips v. Martin-Marietta Corp., De-cember 7, 1970, HAB Papers, Box 122, Folder 8, LOC.

77. Harry A. Blackmun to Warren E. Burger, January 7, 1971, HAB Papers, Box 122, Folder 8, LOC.

78. Warren E. Burger to Conference, January 7, 1971, HAB Papers, Box 122, Folder 8, LOC.

79. Phillips v. Martin-Marietta Corp., 400 U.S. 542, 545 (1970) (Marshall, J., concurring in the judgment).

80. See *Hearings on Nomination of George Harrold Carswell of Florida, to Be As-sociate Justice of the Supreme Court of the United States, January 27–29, February 2–3, 1970, Before the Committee on the Judiciary, U.S. Senate,* 91st Cong., 2d Sess. (1970).

81. Quoted in Ethel L. Payne, "Women Gird for Political Action," *New Pittsburgh Courier,* July 24, 1971, 21. Historian Sara Evans writes that the NWPC, like NOW, was a venue for interracial feminist coalitions in a way that radical women's groups were not. Sara M. Evans, *Tidal Wave: How Women Changed America at Century's End* (New York: Free Press, 2003), 116. For more on the NWPC, see Susan M. Hartmann, *From Margin to Mainstream: American Women and Politics Since 1960* (New York: Alfred A. Knopf, 1989), 74–79.

82. Quoted in Marylin Bender, "Black Woman in Civil Rights," NYT, September 2, 1969.

83. Roy Wilkins, "Women Join Racial Minorities to Make a Formidable Alliance," LAT, July 26, 1971, B7.

84. Wilma Scott Heide, President, NOW, to Roy Wilkins, Chairman, Leadership Conference on Civil Rights (LCCR), December 16, 1972, LCCR Papers, 2:38, Folder 5; Arnold Aronson to various women leaders, March 28, 1973, LCCR Papers, 2:38, Folder 5. The LCCR women's rights committee was chaired by NOW's Ann London Scott. Arnold Aronson to Ann Scott, NOW, March 28, 1973, LCCR Papers, 2:38, Folder 5.

85. As MacLean observes, "Women's numbers and their distribution through all groups helped their challenge penetrate the culture's very core, including, ultimately, the white upper-class elite." MacLean, *Freedom Is Not Enough*, 153.

86. Donald Allen Robinson, "Two Movements in Pursuit of Equal Employment Opportunity," *Signs* 4 (1979): 413–433.

87. *Hearings on H. R. 1746, March 18, 1971, Before the General Subcommittee on Labor of the Committee on Education and Labor, House of Representatives*, 92d Cong., 1st Sess. 290 (statement of Hon. Bella Abzug). See also *Hearings on H. R. 1746, March 18, 1971, Before the House General Subcommittee on Labor of the Committee on Education and Labor*, 92d Cong., 1st Sess. 303 (statement of Hon. Shirley Chisholm). On Abzug's early civil rights and feminist activism, see Leandra Zarnow, "Braving Jim Crow to Save Willie McGee: Bella Abzug, the Legal Left, and Civil Rights Innovation, 1948–1951," *Law and Social Inquiry* 33 (2008): 1003–1041.

88. *Equal Employment Opportunities Enforcement Act of 1971*, H.R. Rep. 92-928 (1971) (to accompany H.R. 1746), 5.

89. *Equal Employment Opportunities Enforcement Act of 1971, Hearing, October 4, 1971, Before the Senate Subcommittee on Labor of the Committee on Labor and Public Welfare*, 92d Cong. (prepared statement of William H. Brown III, Chairman, EEOC), 51.

90. Heide characterized her new relationship with Brown as "very warm and friendly." Wilma Scott Heide interview, by Frances Kolb, 1980, Tully-Crenshaw Oral History Project, Schlesinger Library, Radcliffe Institute, Harvard University

91. See Lois Kathryn Herr, *Women, Power, and AT&T: Winning Rights in the Workplace* (Boston: Northeastern University Press, 2003), 19. Pressman also took a public position on the topic of black women and employment. See, for example, Sonia Pressman, "Job Discrimination and the Black Woman," *Crisis*, March 1970, 103–104. On Pressman's role as a "double agent," see MacLean, *Freedom Is Not Enough*, 127–128.

92. For a contemporaneous view on the impact of feminist pressure, see, for example, Statement of Ms. Aileen C. Hernandez, to the Joint Economic Com-

mittee, U.S. Congress, Hearings on Federal Efforts to Achieve Equal Employment Opportunities for Women, July 11, 1973, NOW Papers, Box 46, Folder 18. See also MacLean, *Freedom Is Not Enough*, 129–130.

93. Skrentny, *Minority Rights Revolution*, 127. See also Robinson, "Two Movements in Pursuit of Equal Employment Opportunity." Scholars of Nixon's civil rights policy suggest that members of the administration were acutely aware of white women's electoral power, and felt the need to appease feminists. See, for example, Skrentny, *Minority Rights Revolution*, 234–239.

94. Sylvia Danovitch, "Humanizing Institutional History: Oral History at the EEOC," *Prologue* 27(1995): 335–346. Marjorie Stockford notes that many of the male EEOC lawyers left government to pursue lucrative careers in private law firms. Marjorie A. Stockford, *The Bellwomen: The Story of the Landmark AT&T Sex Discrimination Case* (New Brunswick, NJ: Rutgers University Press, 2004), 219.

95. NOW, Suggested Press Release for General Mills Action, NOW Papers, Box 42, Folder 45 (emphasis added).

96. Memorandum from Joan Hull, Coordinator, National Task Force on Compliance and Enforcement, to Chapter TF Coordinators Re: Action: Demonstration against General Mills for Sex and Race Discrimination in Employment, NOW Papers, 72-25—79-M262, Carton 8, Folder: TF: Compliance—mimeos.

97. Do It NOW, October/November [1972], WSH Papers, 72-120—74-233, Carton 1, Folder: Board-related.

98. See "Big Three Car Makers Biased, UAW Charges, On Pregnancy Benefits," WSJ, October 11, 1972, 15; "Du Pont, Hughes Tool, Are Accused by EEOC of Job Discrimination," WSJ, November 14, 1972, 4; "EEOC Files 9 More Suits Charging Discrimination," *New Pittsburgh Courier*, May 5, 1973, 21.

99. MacLean, *Freedom Is Not Enough*, 131–132.

100. Harvey D. Shapiro, "Women on the Line, Men at the Switchboard," *NYT Magazine*, May 20, 1973, 208.

101. Women's organizations also pushed for hiring goals for men in traditionally female clerical positions to elevate those jobs' status and compensation, a position often opposed by black organizations "on the ground that as many as possible of the low-paid jobs should be left open for members of groups that are discriminated against." Eileen Shanahan, "AT&T to Grant 15,000 Back Pay in Job Inequities; Women and Minority Men Will Get $15 Million Along with $23 Million Raises," NYT, January 13, 1973. For a negative assessment of the consent decrees' effects, particularly for African American women, see Venus Green, *Race on the Line: Gender, Labor, and Technology in the Bell System, 1880–1980* (Durham, NC: Duke University Press, 2001).

102. Whereas a search of several major American newspapers for the phrase "women and minorities" or "minorities and women" yields less than a dozen

results for the year 1970, by 1973 these phrases appeared in almost two hundred articles.

103. NOW Press Release, "N.O.W. President Charges Government Improperly Excludes Equal Opportunity for Women from Federal Compliance Programs; Files Complaint Asking for Labor Secretary to Investigate Federal Contractors Among 1300 Corporations," June 25, 1970, 3–5, NOW Papers, 72-8-82-M211, Box 20, Folder: Nat. NOW. Aileen Hernandez noted that in federal contracting, "minority group women are counted as statistics in setting goal standards, but they can be totally excluded from employment, upgrading, or training programs without this showing up in the compliance reports." Such an oversight was an "outrageous interpretation" and a "deliberate distortion" of government edicts "which have made it clear that discrimination against women is to be considered on a par with discrimination against racial and ethnic minorities." Aileen Hernandez to Hon. James D. Hodgson, Sec. of Labor, June 25, 1970, NOW Papers, Box 42, Folder 42.

104. NOW, Federal Compliance Committee, Ann Scott—Coordinator, NOW Papers, 72-25—79-M262, Carton 8, Folder: TF Compliance—Internal; Wilma Scott Heide to John Wilke, Deputy Assistant Secretary for Employment Standards, DOL, September 27, 1971, CE Papers, Box 1, Folder 39. See also NOW, National Compliance and Enforcement Committee, Affirmative Action: The Key to Ending Job Discrimination, 1971, NOW papers, 72-8—82-M211, Carton 18, Folder: NOW Compliance. NOW frequently criticized the reporting of employment statistics that compared black women's earnings to those of white women's, rather than to those of white men's. See, for example, Testimony of Dr. Sally Hacker, NOW, Hearings before the US EEOC on Utilization of Minority and Women Workers in Certain Major Industries, Houston, Texas, June 2–4, 1970, Papers of Luther Holcomb, Vice Chairman, EEOC, 1965–1974, LBJ Library, Box 9; NOW Press Release, "N.O.W. President Charges Government Improperly Excludes."

105. Testimony of Ann London Scott, Legislative Vice President, NOW, [1973], NOW Papers, Box 46, Folder 18.

106. See NOW Says Women Lose in Federal WIN Program, NOW Papers, Box 48, Folder 35. In 1971, Shelley Thorn, a young unmarried mother, successfully challenged the HEW policy instructing states to give first priority to unemployed fathers in referring job and training applicants to federally funded programs. See Thorn v. Richardson, 1971 WL 201 (W.D. Wash.); Memorandum from Stephen Randels, Re: Thorn v. Richardson, December 2, 1971, PI Papers, Box B10, Folder: Struck, LaFleur.

107. NOW, "H.R. 1 and the Poverty of Women," testimony submitted to the Senate Committee on Finance, February 11, 1972, reprinted in *Welfare: A*

Documentary History of U.S. Policy and Politics, ed. Gwendolyn Mink and Rickie Solinger (New York: New York University Press, 2003), 380–384.

108. Hernandez to Dolan, January 21, 1971(emphasis in original).

109. Statement of Ms. Aileen C. Hernandez, Urban Consultant, to the Joint Committee on Legal Equality, California State Legislature, Sacramento, California, August 12, 1974, CE Papers, Box 1, Folder 42. Benita Roth argues that the tendency of white feminists to take a "gender universalist stance" was linked to "the analogy of gender oppression to racial oppression." She notes that this move "had an unintended negative effect: By blurring racial/ethnic and class differences among women," gender universalism "made it difficult for feminists of color to defend feminism to the men in their communities." Roth, *Separate Roads,* 194–195. See also Breines, *Trouble Between Us,* 115. On antipoverty advocates' shift from championing the rights of minorities in particular to making universalist arguments for more general social spending, see Chappell, *The War on Welfare,* 116–117.

110. For a compelling argument that constitutional sex discrimination law drew on ideas and legal theories developed in Title VII cases, see Mary Anne Case, " 'The Very Stereotype the Law Condemns': Constitutional Sex Discrimination Law as a Quest for Perfect Proxies," *Cornell Law Review* 85 (2000): 1463–1464; Mary Anne Case, "Reflections on Constitutionalizing Women's Equality," *California Law Review* 90 (2002): 766–770.

111. Vera Glaser, "The Female Revolt: Laws Discriminate Against Women (Part III)," *Baltimore Evening Sun,* March 19, 1969, CE Papers, Box 16, Folder 27; Associated Press, "Girl, 13, Wins Entry to All-Male School," *Evening Star* (Washington, DC), May 3, 1969, A2, CE Papers, MC 477, Box 9, Folder 44; United Press International, "Sex Makes Difference in Legal Disputes," *Fayetteville (NC) Observer,* April 10, 1969, CE Papers, MC 477, Box 9, Folder 44.

112. "Girl, 13," A2.

113. Memorandum of Law in Support of Petition, 4–9, DeRivera v. Fliedner, No. 00938-69 (N.Y. Sup. Ct. June 5, 1969), CE Papers, MC 477, Box 9, Folder 44.

114. Catherine East to Mayor John Lindsay, January 24, 1969, CE Papers, MC 477, Box 9, Folder 44.

115. East also noted that Judge Sandifer "made life difficult for the corporation counsel." Memorandum from Catherine East to Elizabeth Duncan Koontz, May 2, 1969, Re: New Developments in the De Rivera Case, CE Papers, MC 477, Box 9, Folder 44.

116. See William E. Nelson, *Fighting for the City: A History of the New York City Corporation Counsel* (New York: New York Law Journal, 2008).

117. "Girl, 13," A2.

118. For more on Hirschkop, see Jason McLure, "A Liberal Lion in Winter," *Legal Times*, January 17, 2006. Hirschkop also made a name for himself defending anti-Vietnam War protesters.

119. Memorandum, Kirstein v. Univ. of Virginia, No. 220-69-R, September 8, 1969, 2, CE Papers, MC 477, Box 10, Folder 7.

120. Kirstein v. Univ. of Virginia, 309 F. Supp. 184, 187 (E.D. Va. February 9, 1970).

121. Philip J. Hirschkop to Mel Wulf, Re: Kirstein v. Rector and Visitors of the University of Virginia, February 12, 1970, HRW Papers, 83-M229, Box 1, Folder: Kirstein. Rutgers law professor and ACLU lawyer Ruth Bader Ginsburg was more upbeat, calling the decision a "landmark" and a "path-breaker." Ruth Bader Ginsburg to Bernice Sandler, September 8, 1970, RBG Papers, Container 7, Folder: Rutgers College, New Brunswick, NJ, Coeducation, 1970.

122. In 1969, Peters had issued a landmark decision declaring that women had a fundamental right to choose whether or not to bear children. See People v. Belous, 71 Cal. 2d 954 (1969).

123. Sail'er Inn v. Kirby, 5 Cal. 3d 1, 19–20 (1971).

124. For more on Williams's role in *Kirby*, see Fred Strebeigh, *Equal: Women Reshape American Law* (New York: W.W. Norton, 2009), 86–89. On the changing gender composition of the United States Supreme Court clerk pool, see Mark R. Brown, "Gender Discrimination in the Supreme Court's Clerkship Selection Process," *Oregon Law Review* 75 (1996): 359–388.

125. On the Supreme Court clerkship as an institution, see Todd C. Peppers, *Courtiers of the Marble Palace: The Rise and Influence of the Supreme Court Law Clerk* (Stanford, CA: Stanford Law and Politics, 2006); Artemus Ward, *Sorcerers' Apprentices: 100 Years of Law Clerks at the United States Supreme Court* (New York: New York University Press, 2006); William E. Nelson, Harvey Rishikof, I. Scott Messinger, and Michael Jo, "The Liberal Tradition of the Supreme Court Clerkship: Its Rise, Fall, and Reincarnation?" *Vanderbilt Law Review* 62 (2009): 1747–1814. Bernard Schwartz argues that the role of clerks expanded significantly during the Burger Court era. See Bernard Schwartz, *The Ascent of Pragmatism: The Burger Court in Action* (Reading, MA: Addison-Wesley, 1990), 35–39.

126. Reed v. Reed, 404 U.S. 71 (1971).

127. See Ruth Bader Ginsburg to Melvin Wulf, March 2, 1971, ACLU Records, Box 1645, Folder: Reed v. Reed (requesting information about the case); Melvin Wulf to Ruth Bader Ginsburg, March 9, 1971, ACLU Records, Box 1645, Folder: Reed v. Reed (requesting Ginsburg's assistance). See also Linda K. Kerber, *No Constitutional Right to Be Ladies: Women and the Obligations of Citizenship* (New York: Hill and Wang, 1998), 199–204; Strebeigh, *Equal,*

24–27. Ginsburg had already developed equal protection arguments for sex equality in a Tenth Circuit case involving the Internal Revenue Service's denial of a tax exemption to unmarried male but not unmarried female caregivers. For more, see Cary Franklin, "The Anti-Stereotyping Principle in Constitutional Sex Discrimination Law," *New York University Law Review* 85 (2010): 140–143.

128. Ginsburg's focus on Swedish law and the time she spent in Sweden also influenced her feminism. See Franklin, "The Anti-Stereotyping Principle," 115–123.

129. Diana Klebanow and Franklin L. Jonas, *People's Lawyers: Crusaders for Justice in American History* (Armonk, NY: M.E. Sharpe, 2003), 359, 361.

130. Strebeigh, *Equal,* 12–13.

131. Ibid., 19. Historian Jane S. DeHart is completing a fascinating biography of Ginsburg, tentatively titled, *Becoming Justice Ruth Bader Ginsburg.*

132. Murray and Kenyon were both credited as the brief's coauthors.

133. Brief for Appellant, 5, 12–13, 31, Reed v. Reed, 404 U.S. 71 (1971) (No. 70–4). On the brief-writing process, see Strebeigh, *Equal,* 34–41.

134. Joint Brief of Amici Curiae American Veterans Committee and NOW Legal Defense and Education Fund, 10–12, *Reed* (No. 70-4); Brief of Amicus Curiae the City of New York, 16, *Reed* (No. 70-4); Brief of Amicus Curiae the National Federation of Business and Professional Women's Clubs, 8, *Reed* (No. 70-4).

135. Wulf wrote one amicus: "Our brief argued firstly and predominantly that sex should be denominated as 'suspect.' Our second point is that the classification is irrational. Your brief reverses those positions. Thus, to the extent that your brief will have any influence at all with the Court, it will injure our position. Such favors I don't need." Melvin Wulf to Norman Redlich, Office of Corporation Counsel, July 1, 1971, 1, ACLU Records, Box 1645, Folder: Reed v. Reed.

136. Wulf lobbied Sally Reed directly: "The woman we have in mind to argue the case is Eleanor Holmes Norton. . . . She is a national figure—both on behalf of civil rights and women's rights—and is one of the most persuasive lawyers I know. I don't know anyone who could argue the case better." Melvin Wulf to Sally Reed, September 29, 1971, ACLU Records, MC #001, Box 1645. See also RBG to Mel Wulf, April 6, 1971, RBG Papers, Container 5, Folder: Moritz v. Commissioner, Jan.-Apr. 1971; Wilma Scott Heide, NOW, to Mel Wulf, September 14, 1971, ACLU Records, MC #001, Box 1645; Mel Wulf to Martha Griffiths, September 16, 1971, ACLU Records, MC #001, Box 1645; Melvin L. Wulf to Allen R. Derr, June 4, 1971; Melvin L. Wulf to Allen R. Derr, October 8, 1971; Melvin L. Wulf to Allen R. Derr, December 20, 1971; Telegram from Allen R. Derr to Melvin L. Wulf, December 26, 1971, ACLU Records, Box 1645, Folder: Reed v. Reed.

137. For more on *Reed*, see Linda K. Kerber, "November 22, 1971: Sally Reed Demands Equal Treatment," in *Days of Destiny: Crossroads in American History*, ed. David Rubel (New York: DK, 2001): 441–451; Mayeri, "Constitutional Choices;" Strebeigh, *Equal*, 42–44.

138. Reed v. Reed, 404 U.S. 71, 76–77 (1971).

139. Melvin L. Wulf to Allen R. Derr, December 20, 1971. See also "Court Rules Out Bias by Legislators," Associated Press, November 23, 1971, ACLU Records, Box 1646, Folder: Reed v. Reed.

140. Pauli Murray to Mary Dublin Keyserling, December 7, 1971, 1, Pauli Murray Papers, MC 412, Box 95, Folder 1657.

141. Strebeigh, *Equal*, 40.

142. Ibid., 45.

143. Quoted in Linda Greenhouse, "Westchester Women Testify on Employment Bias," NYT, April 1, 1973, 72.

144. LaFleur v. Cleveland Board of Education, 326 F. Supp. 1208, 1213 (D. Ohio February 1971). The disruptions that concerned Connell included "children pointing, giggling, laughing and making snide remarks causing interruption and interference with the classroom program of study." Ibid., 1210. For more, see Peter Irons, *The Courage of their Convictions: Sixteen Americans Who Fought Their Way to the Supreme Court* (New York: Penguin Books, 1988), Chapter 13.

145. Schattman v. Texas Employment Commission, 459 F.2d 32 (5th Cir. 1972).

146. Ronald J. Bacigal, *May It Please the Court: A Biography of Judge Robert R. Merhige, Jr.* (Lanham, MD: University Press of America, 1992).

147. Plaintiff's Brief, Cohen v. Chesterfield County School Board, U.S. Court of Appeals for the Fourth Circuit, PI Papers (uncatalogued materials).

148. Cohen v. Chesterfield County School Board, 326 F. Supp. 1159, 1161 (E. D. Va. May 17, 1971). On feminists' reaction to Merhige's decision, see Strebeigh, *Equal*, 119.

149. Struck v. Secretary of Defense, 460 F.2d 1372, 1375 (9th Cir. 1972). Judge Madden was a senior judge on the Federal Court of Claims, sitting by designation. The Ninth Circuit found "no merit" in Struck's claims that her rights to privacy and religious free exercise had been infringed.

150. Three other judges also voted to grant a rehearing.

151. Duniway had joined the original panel's decision, issued before *Reed*.

152. 460 F.2d at 1380 (Duniway, J., dissenting from denial of rehearing en banc).

153. The Fourth Circuit panel declared: "That the regulation is a discrim-

ination based on sex is, we think, self-evident." Cohen v. Chesterfield County Board of Education, 1972 WL 2594 (4th Cir. 1972), reversed en banc, 474 F. 2d 395 (4th Cir. 1973). Cohen's brief to the Fourth Circuit echoed the plaintiff's argument in *Reed* that classifications based on sex should be subject to strict scrutiny.

154. Griswold v. Connecticut, 381 U.S. 479 (1965); Eisenstadt v. Baird, 405 U.S. 438 (1972). On the litigation campaign that produced these decisions, see David J. Garrow, *Liberty and Sexuality: The Right to Privacy and the Making of Roe v. Wade* (Berkeley: University of California Press, 1998).

155. Brief for the Petitioner, 9, 34, 26, 52, 55, Struck v. Secretary of Defense, 1972 WL 135840 (No. 72–178).

156. For more on the lost promise of *Struck*, see Neil S. Siegel and Reva B. Siegel, "Struck by Stereotype: Ruth Bader Ginsburg on Pregnancy Discrimination as Sex Discrimination," *Duke Law Journal* 59 (2010): 771–798. On Ginsburg's lasting disappointment that *Struck* did not produce a Supreme Court decision, see Ruth Bader Ginsburg, "A Postscript to Struck By Stereotype," *Duke Law Journal* 59 (2010): 799–800; Amy Leigh Campbell, "Raising the Bar: Ruth Bader Ginsburg and the ACLU Women's Rights Project," *Texas Journal of Women and the Law* 11 (2001): 195.

157. Linda Mathews, "Surprise Move: Unwed AF Nurse Wins Right to Stay," LAT, December 2, 1972, 23.

158. Gutierrez v. Laird, 346 F. Supp. 289 (D.D.C. 1972); Robinson v. Rand, 340 F. Supp. 37 (D. Colo. 1972).

159. Crawford v. Cushman, 531 F.2d 1114 (2d Cir. 1976). Kathleen Peratis argued the case, with Ginsburg and Wulf on the brief.

160. LaFleur v. Cleveland Board of Education, 465 F.2d 1184, 1187–1188 (6th Cir. 1972).

161. Monell v. Dept. of Social Services, 357 F. Supp. 1051, 1053 (S.D.N.Y. 1972). The case was brought by the Center for Constitutional Rights (CCR) and argued by Nancy Stearns. Motley noted the passage of the ERA and other federal legislation against sex discrimination, declaring that "[s]ex legislation is thus automatically suspect." On Motley's relationship to feminism, see Nancy MacLean, "Using the Law for Social Change: Judge Constance Baker Motley," *Journal of Women's History* 14 (2002): 136–139.

162. Heath v. Westerville Board of Educ., 345 F. Supp. 501, 505 and n. 1 (D. Ohio 1972). A 1973 Harvard Law Review note on military discharges for pregnancy compared these policies to racial classifications and charged that they "appear to be . . . premised on a belief that a woman's primary function is child rearing and that career interests should not be allowed to compete with that function," a rationale out of step with then-current equal protection analysis.

Note, "Pregnancy Discharges in the Military: The Air Force Experience," *Harvard Law Review* 86 (1973): 587–588. The Second Circuit relied heavily on the analysis of this note in striking down a similar Marines policy in 1976. See Crawford v. Cushman, 531 F.2d 1114 (2d Cir. 1976).

163. Cohen v. Chesterfield County School Board, 474 F.2d 395, 397–398 (4th Cir. 1973) (en banc).

164. See Reva B. Siegel, "*Roe's* Roots: The Women's Rights Claims that Engendered *Roe*," *Boston University Law Review* 90 (2010): 1875–1907; Linda Greenhouse and Reva B. Siegel, *Before Roe v. Wade: Voices that Shaped the Abortion Debate before the Supreme Court's Ruling* (New York: Kaplan, 2010).

165. For more on the unresolved nature of this relationship, see Deborah Dinner, "Recovering the *LaFleur* Doctrine," *Yale Journal of Law and Feminism* 22 (2010).

166. See Reva B. Siegel, "Sex Equality Arguments for Reproductive Rights: Their Critical Basis and Evolving Constitutional Expression," *Emory Law Journal* 56 (2007): 815–842; Siegel, "*Roe's* Roots"; Greenhouse and Siegel, *Before Roe v. Wade.*

167. Ruth Bader Ginsburg, "Some Thoughts on Autonomy and Equality in Relation to *Roe v. Wade*," *North Carolina Law Review* 63 (1984): 386.

168. See, for example, Lawrence Van Gelder, "Cardinals Shocked—Reaction Mixed," NYT, January 23, 1973, 81; Linda Mathews, "Supreme Court Gives Women Right to Have Abortions," LAT, January 23, 1973, A1; Editorial, "Abortions and the Right of Privacy," LAT, January 23, 1973, C6.

169. Janice Goodman, Rhonda Copelon Schoenbrod, and Nancy Stearns, "*Doe* and *Roe*: Where Do We Go from Here," *Women's Rights Law Reporter,* Vol. 1, No. 4 (1973): 20.

170. Goodman, Schoenbrod, and Stearns, "*Doe* and *Roe*," 26. Nancy Stearns concluded: "Given . . . that the Supreme Court has . . . not had a whole lot of education about women's rights, I think we came out surprisingly well."

171. The brief, which was signed by conservative Solicitor General Robert Bork as well as attorneys from the EEOC and Department of Justice, continued: "On the contrary, precisely because pregnancy is a condition unique to women, treating the pregnant less favorably is, at least presumptively, a discrimination based on sex." Memorandum for the United States as Amicus Curiae, 9, Cleveland Board of Education v. LaFleur, 414 U.S. 632 (1974) (No. 72-777).

172. Eleanor Holmes Norton was Babcock's close friend and law school roommate. See Lester, *Fire in My Soul.*

173. Summary Minutes, Legal Philosophy of Feminism, 1–4, Ford Foundation Equal Rights Advocates Conference, PM Papers, Box 125, Folder 2250.

Murray did not mention that her challenge to the university's racial exclusion was not the only time the NAACP LDF shied away from using her for a test case; on another occasion, her gender non-conformity likely was the obstacle. See Glenda E. Gilmore, *Defying Dixie: The Radical Roots of Civil Rights, 1919–1950* (New York: W. W. Norton, 2008), 316–329.

174. Summary Minutes, Legal Philosophy of Feminism, 5.

175. Marguerite Rawalt, [submission to Equal Rights Advocates conference, 1973], PM Papers, Box 123, Folder 2200; Marguerite Rawalt to Ruth Bader Ginsburg, May 20, 1973, RBG Papers, Container 20, Folder: Equal Rights Amend. Conference of Equal Rights Advocates, New York, NY, 1973. Despite vast differences in background, Murray and Rawalt had in common both the institutional memory of movement veterans and a commitment to pragmatism in pursuit of feminist goals. Murray promised to visit Rawalt in the hospital and keep her informed.

176. Pauli Murray, Notes from Ford Foundation Equal Rights Advocates Conference, April 26–27, 1973, PM Papers, Box 125, Folder 2250.

177. Murray, *Autobiography*, 422, 426.

178. Pauli Murray to Family and Friends, December 20, 1973, CE Papers, Box 2, Folder 12.

179. Murray, *Autobiography*, 417–419.

180. The Negro/Black Woman: Myth and Reality, Remarks of Dr. Pauli Murray, Stulberg Professor of Law and Politics, Brandeis University, Symposium II, Women Today and Tomorrow, May 12, 1973, George Washington University, 4, PM papers, Box 89, Folder 1558.

181. For a more detailed account of the *Frontiero* case, see Serena Mayeri, " 'When the Trouble Started': The Story of *Frontiero v. Richardson*," in *Women and the Law Stories*, ed. Elizabeth M. Schneider and Stephanie M. Wildman (New York: Foundation Press, 2011). See also Strebeigh, *Equal*, 48–64; Campbell, "Raising the Bar," 180–195.

182. Quoted in Chris Carmody, "Judge Ginsburg's Ex-Clients Reflect Upon Their Cases," *National Law Journal*, June 28, 1993, 34; and Kay Lazar, "Fight for Equality Recalled," *Boston Herald*, March 16, 2003, 7.

183. Weeks v. Southern Bell, 408 F.2d 228 (5th Cir. 1969). Johnson, a district judge, was sitting on the appeals court by designation.

184. Billings enumerated the political and economic discrimination suffered by women, "albeit generally less blatant than that visited upon minorities," and urged Johnson to declare sex suspect. Both "prior cases" and the "growing recognition of women's subjugation," supported such an outcome, Billings argued. Memorandum from Jack Billings to Judge Frank M. Johnson, Jr., July 8, 1971, Re: Frontiero v. Laird, FMJ Papers, Container 64, Folder: 3232-N, Frontiero v. Laird, 1971 (1).

185. Frontiero v. Laird, 341 F. Supp. 201 (M.D. Ala. 1972).

186. Charles F. Abernathy to Brenda Fasteau, October 19, 1972, RBG Papers, Container 3, Folder: Frontiero v. Richardson, 1972. By "preoccupation," Abernathy apparently meant that the political climate on the Court had recently become hostile toward the judicial innovations that many perceived as the legacy of the Warren Court.

187. Joseph Levin to Melvin Wulf, October 17, 1972, RBG Papers, Container 3, Folder: Frontiero v. Richardson, 1972.

188. With its emphasis on the sex-as-suspect argument, the WRP brief's "approach and substantive content . . . differ[ed] substantially" from the SPLC's brief for the appellants, as Ginsburg put it. RBG to Joseph Levin, December 5, 1972, RBG Papers, Container 3, Folder: Frontiero v. Richardson, 1972.

189. At the Justices' weekly conference, discussion centered on whether the Court should view *Frontiero* as "kin to *Reed*," in Ginsburg's words, a proposition with which seven Justices agreed. Strebeigh, *Equal*, 55.

190. Ruth B. Cowan, "Women's Rights through Litigation: An Examination of the American Civil Liberties Union Women's Rights Project, 1971–1976," *Columbia Human Rights Law Review* 8 (1976): 381; Peppers, *Courtiers of the Marble Palace*, 157.

191. Ruth Bader Ginsburg and Wendy Webster Williams, "Court Architect of Gender Equality: Setting a Firm Foundation for the Equal Stature of Men and Women," in *Reason and Passion: Justice Brennan's Enduring Influence*, ed. E. Joshua Rosenkranz and Bernard Schwartz (New York: Norton, 1997), 186. A long-awaited biography of Justice Brennan appeared just as this book was going to press. See Seth Stern and Stephen Wermiel, *Justice Brennan: Liberal Champion* (Boston: Houghton Mifflin Harcourt, 2010).

192. Memorandum from BRW to WJB, February 15, 1973, WJB Papers, Part 1: 299, Folder 11.

193. Memorandum from WOD to WJB, Mar. 3, 1973, PS Papers, Group 1367, Series 1, Box 269, Folder 3208.

194. Memorandum from LFP to WJB, February 15, 1973, WJB Papers, Part 1: 299, Folder 11.

195. Memorandum from PS to WJB, February 16, 1973, WJB Papers, Part 1: 299, Folder 11.

196. Memorandum from WJB to LFP, March 6, 1973, WJB Papers, Part 1: 299, Folder 11.

197. Frontiero v. Richardson, 411 U.S. 677, 685 (1973).

198. Ibid., 686–687. Some of the language in Brennan's opinion was strikingly similar to the wording of the California Supreme Court's decision in *Sail'er Inn v. Kirby*.

199. Memorandum from J[ames] W[.] Z[iglar] to HAB, Re: Frontiero v. Laird, March 3, 1973, HAB Papers, Box 163, Folder 9, Supreme Court Case File.

200. For more, see Linda Greenhouse, *Becoming Justice Blackmun: Harry Blackmun's Supreme Court Journey* (New York: Henry Holt, 2005), 207–227.

201. *Frontiero*, 411 U.S. at 691.

202. See also Memorandum from LFP to WJB, March 2, 1973, WJB Papers, Part 1: 299, Folder 11.

203. For more on the legacies of *Frontiero,* see Mayeri, " 'When the Trouble Started, ' " 79–92.

204. Ruth Bader Ginsburg to Jane Lifset, May 15, 1973, RBG Papers, Container 10, Folder: Weinberger v. Wiesenfeld, Correspondence, 1972–1973.

205. Rehnquist based his dissent on the lower court opinion authored by Judge Rives. *Frontiero,* 411 U.S at 691.

206. Feminist lawyers did not let their euphoria over *Roe* blind them to the real challenges of implementation. Foremost among them was what the CCR's Janice Goodman and her colleague Nancy Stearns called "the development of affirmative ways to assure access to abortion," especially for poor women. Goodman, Schoenbrod, and Stearns, "*Doe* and *Roe,*" 29.

207. I discuss in much greater depth the dilemmas of feminists' "dual strategy" elsewhere. See Mayeri, "Constitutional Choices"; Serena Mayeri, "A New ERA or a New Era: Amendment Advocacy and the Reconstitution of Feminism," *Northwestern University Law Review* 103 (2009): 1280–1287.

208. See Jane Mansbridge, *Why We Lost the ERA* (Chicago: University of Chicago Press, 1986); Mayeri, "Constitutional Choices." Ironically, Rehnquist, who as a DOJ official had equivocated about the ERA's desirability and had predicted judicial reinterpretation of the Fourteenth Amendment, was the lone dissenter in *Frontiero.* See *Frontiero,* 411 U.S. at 691 (Rehnquist, J., dissenting).

209. Press coverage on the likelihood of ratification began to shift in early 1973. See, for example, Jenkin Lloyd Jones, "Women Are Having Second Thoughts About Equal Rights Amendment," *Human Events,* February 10, 1973, 13 (citing *Newsweek's* assessment that "amendment-pushers can't even count on 10 additional 'sure' states. They need 16.").

210. LFP to WJB, March 1, 1973, 71–1694, Frontiero v. Laird, LFP Papers.

211. Memorandum from LFP to WJB, March 2, 1973, WJB Papers, Part 1: 299, Folder 11.

212. See Kenji Yoshino, "Assimilationist Bias in Equal Protection: The Visibility Presumption and the Case of 'Don't Ask, Don't Tell,' " *Yale Law Journal* 108 (1998): 560–563; Reva B. Siegel, "Collective Memory and the Nineteenth

Amendment: Reasoning About 'The Woman Question' in the Discourse of Sex Discrimination," in *History, Memory, and the Law,* ed. Austin Sarat and Thomas R. Kearns (Ann Arbor: University of Michigan Press, 1999), 131. The Court's refusal to make wealth a suspect classification two months earlier in a case involving funding for public schools did not bode well. See San Antonio v. Rodriguez, 411 U.S. 1 (1973).

213. On the failure of the *Frontiero* plurality opinion to grapple with the history of subordination based on race and sex, see Reva B. Siegel, "She, the People: The Nineteenth Amendment, Sex Equality, Federalism, and the Family," *Harvard Law Review* 115 (2002): 961–965.

3. Recession, Reaction, Retrenchment

1. A labor official predicted "race war" if equal employment goals eclipsed the prerogatives of seniority. Quoted in Nina Totenberg, "Recession's Special Victims: Newly Hired Blacks, Women," NYT, March 9, 1975, E1.

2. Quoted in Charlayne Hunter, "Job Rights Gains Called Imperiled," NYT, December 1, 1975, 17. See also Francis X. Clines, "City Layoffs Hurt Minorities Most," NYT, February 20, 1976, 69.

3. Aileen C. Hernandez to Lynn Darcy, NOW Task Force on Compliance, January 22, 1975, NOW Papers, Carton 18, Folder: Unfiled: '73–'76.

4. Nancy MacLean, *Freedom Is Not Enough: The Opening of the American Workplace* (Cambridge, MA: Harvard University Press, 2006); Laura Kalman, *Right Star Rising: A New Politics, 1974–1980* (New York: W.W. Norton, 2010).

5. Thomas J. Sugrue, *Sweet Land of Liberty: The Struggle for Civil Rights in the North* (New York: Random House, 2008), Chapter 13.

6. Historian Laura Kalman writes, "During the Ford years . . . liberals lost control of the Court." Kalman, *Right Star Rising,* 136.

7. Alan David Freeman, "Legitimizing Racial Discrimination through Antidiscrimination Law: A Critical Review of Supreme Court Doctrine," *Minnesota Law Review* 62 (1978): 1102. Among the cases that prompted this observation were the school funding and integration cases San Antonio v. Rodriguez (1973) and Milliken v. Bradley (1974). Kalman identifies 1974 as the beginning of a new era in American politics. See Kalman, *Right Star Rising.*

8. On the potency of affirmative action as an issue around which conservatives of various stripes could unite, see MacLean, *Freedom Is Not Enough,* 231.

9. Ruth Bader Ginsburg, "Gender and the Constitution," *University of Cincinnati Law Review* 44 (1975): 29. For a thoughtful contemporaneous exploration of race-sex analogies by a leading historian of American women, see William H. Chafe, *Women and Equality: Changing Patterns in American Culture* (Oxford: Oxford University Press, 1977).

10. Women were "a harder category" for Owen M. Fiss, a leading propo-
nent of race-based remedies for inequality. See *Affirmative Action: The Answer to
Discrimination? American Enterprise Institute Roundtable, May 29, 1975* (Washing-
ton, DC: American Enterprise Institute, 1976), 21–22. See also, for example,
John Hart Ely, "The Wages of Crying Wolf: A Comment on *Roe v. Wade,*" *Yale
Law Journal* 82 (1973): 920–949.

11. Thomas Nagel, introduction to *Equality and Preferential Treatment,* ed.
Marshall Cohen et al. (Princeton, NJ: Princeton University Press, 1977).

12. Richard Wasserstrom, "Racism, Sexism, and Preferential Treatment:
An Approach to the Topics," *UCLA Law Review* 24 (1976): 589.

13. Quotes are from Wasserstrom, "Racism, Sexism," 590.

14. *A Conversation with Commissioner Eleanor Holmes Norton* (Washington,
DC: American Enterprise Institute, 1979). See also, for example, F. K. Barasch,
"HEW, the University, and Women," in *Reverse Discrimination,* ed. Barry R.
Gross (Buffalo, NY: Prometheus Books, 1977), 54–65.

15. For more on Schlafly's life and political career, see Donald T. Critchlow,
Phyllis Schlafly and Grassroots Conservatism: A Woman's Crusade (Princeton, NJ:
Princeton University Press, 2005); Carol Felsenthal, *The Sweetheart of the Silent
Majority: The Biography of Phyllis Schlafly* (Garden City, NY: Doubleday, 1981).
Biographical details on Schlafly are taken from these accounts. I describe
Schlafly's early life in similar terms in Serena Mayeri, "Two Women, Two His-
tories," *Harvard Magazine,* November/December 2007, 29–31. On Schlafly's ac-
tivism in the GOP, see also Catherine E. Rymph, *Republican Women: Feminism
and Conservatism from Suffrage through the Rise of the New Right* (Chapel Hill: University of North Carolina Press, 2006).

16. Phyllis Schlafly, *The Power of the Positive Woman* (New Rochelle, NY:
Arlington House, 1977), 113–114, 142, 24. Virtually the same language had appeared earlier in "Sexist Mischief in Schools and Colleges," *PS Report,* September 1975, vol. 9, no. 2, sec. 2, p. 1.

17. "The Right to Be A Woman," *PS Report,* November 1972, vol. 6, no.
4, p. 2.

18. "Will ERA Force All Private Schools Coed?" *PS Report,* December
1976, vol. 10, no. 5, sec. 2, p. 1.

19. In certain contexts, such as university hiring, affirmative action for
women played a somewhat more prominent role in the debate. But even when
white women were among the primary beneficiaries of affirmative action initiatives, sex-based affirmative action often was subsumed under race-based
remedies. Many discussions of affirmative action either omitted references to
women altogether, or mentioned women only in passing. On the debate over
affirmative action in university hiring, see MacLean, *Freedom Is Not Enough,*
189–192.

20. Butler D. Shaffer and J. Brad Chapman, "Hiring Quotas—Will They Work?" *Labor Law Journal* 26 (March 1975): 152, 153, 157, 158.

21. Thomas Sowell, "A Black 'Conservative' Dissents," NYT, August 8, 1976, 152.

22. Thomas Sowell, "Affirmative Action Reconsidered," in *Reverse Discrimination,* 121–122.

23. "What's Wrong with 'Equal Rights' for Women?" *PS Report,* February 1972, vol. 5, no. 7, p. 4.

24. On Schlafly's acceptance of a limited set of sex equality principles, see Reva B. Siegel, "Constitutional Culture, Social Movement Conflict and the Constitutional Change: The Case of the de Facto ERA," *California Law Review* 94 (2006): 1405–1406.

25. See, for example, Phyllis Schlafly, "The Vital Political Role of Conservative Women," *Human Events,* April 12, 1969, 6.

26. "How the ERA Will Hurt Men," *PS Report,* May 1975, vol. 8, no. 10, p. 3; Schlafly, *Power of the Positive Woman,* 18.

27. "Sexist Mischief in Schools and Colleges," 1.

28. "Unemployment—Causes and Solutions," *PS Report,* November 1975, vol. 9, no. 4, sec. 1, p. 1.

29. "How the ERA Will Hurt Men," 3; Schlafly, *Power of the Positive Woman,* 118.

30. Schlafly, *Power of the Positive Woman,* 60–61.

31. Ibid., 141.

32. Schlafly made these connections even more explicit in later congressional testimony.

33. Both of her biographers note that Schlafly had never invoked explicitly racist arguments in her political writings and speeches, even when more blatantly racially charged language was common in American political discourse. On the conflation of racial and sexual integration among ERA opponents, see Donald G. Mathews and Jane Sherron De Hart, *Sex, Gender, and the Politics of ERA: A State and the Nation* (New York: Oxford University Press, 1990), 165–174.

34. Conservative male commentators also utilized this technique. See, for example, Morrie Ryskind, "Some Random Thoughts About Women's Lib," *Human Events,* September 29, 1973, 18 ("It seems to me that the employer has the right to want a female receptionist or a male lumberjack without some government agency charging him with being 'discriminatory.' Those who rant about 'civil rights' in such matters are destroying the civil rights of the employer."). See also Rep. Trent Lott to Mrs. Moxon [mass mailing], November 28, 1973, NOW Papers, Box 46, Folder 24 (urging conservatives to

oppose NOW's campaign to introduce affirmative action into broadcasting context).

35. Schlafly, *Power of the Positive Woman,* 133–135, 211. See also "The Hypocrisy of ERA Proponents," *PS Report,* July 1975, vol. 8, no. 12, sec. 2, p. 2 (criticizing AT&T settlement).

36. "Sexist Mischief in Schools and Colleges," 2.

37. Occasionally, Schlafly linked race- and sex-based affirmative action more explicitly. In a 1975 policy statement on unemployment, she condemned "federal bureaucrats" for interpreting antidiscrimination laws "to require job preference for certain minorities, including employed women, in order to achieve arbitrary race and sex quotas." "Unemployment—Causes and Solutions," 1. In the months that followed, she frequently contended that the "biggest discrimination at the present time is the employment discrimination against the husband and father who is trying to provide for his family [but] . . . has been shunted aside while reverse discrimination has been given to second wage-earner families." "What Are Your Community Problems?" *PS Report,* April 1976, vol. 9, no. 9, sec. 2, p. 1.

38. "Unemployment—Causes and Solutions," 1; "What Are Your Community Problems?" 1.

39. Schlafly, *Power of the Positive Woman,* 119.

40. For a perceptive account of the evolution of liberal and conservative versions of the "male breadwinner" ideal in the context of debates over welfare, see Marisa Chappell, *The War on Welfare: Family, Poverty, and Politics in Modern America* (Philadelphia: University of Pennsylvania Press, 2010).

41. "Right to Be A Woman," 2.

42. "Will ERA Force All Private Schools Coed?" 1.

43. For a few of many examples, see "The Problem of the Supreme Court," *PS Report,* December 1975, vol. 9, no. 5, sec. 1; Evelyn Pitschke, "The Effect of Section 2," *PS Report,* November 1976, vol. 10, no. 4, sec. 2, p. 4. Though they often portrayed judges as the primary villains in their tales of civil rights provisions run amok, all branches of the federal government came under attack. On the ERA as the target of conservative attacks on the federal government, see Mathews and De Hart, 172–173, 205–206; Mary Frances Berry, *Why ERA Failed: Politics, Women's Rights, and the Amending Process of the Constitution* (Bloomington: Indiana University Press, 1986), 85.

44. James J. Kilpatrick, "Women's Rights: Uncertainties Surround the New Amendment," LAT, December 2, 1974, C7. As Evelyn Pitschke wrote in 1976, "We have seen the courts determine what public policy should be when they interpreted civil rights under the Fourteenth Amendment." Pitschke, "Effect of Section 2," 4.

45. See Ruth Bader Ginsburg to Catherine East, January 24, 1974, RBG Papers, Container 20, Folder: Equal Rights Amend. Correspondence, 1974; Testimony of Thomas I. Emerson, Lines Professor of Law Emeritus, Yale Law School, on ratification of the Equal Rights Amendment, Baton Rouge, Louisiana, June 7, 1977, TE Papers, SML, 1622, 92-M-56, Box 24, Folder: ERA—Current Basic Materials; Marjorie Longwell to Thomas Emerson, February 10, 1971, TE Papers, SML, 1622, 92-M-56, Box 26, Folder: ERA—Congress 1971 and 1972; Thomas Emerson to Marjorie Longwell, February 17, 1971, TE Papers, SML, 1622, 92-M-56, Box 26, Folder: ERA—Congress 1971 and 1972.

46. "Don't Stoop to Equality," *PS Report,* February 1978, vol. 11, no. 7, sec. 2.

47. "Will ERA Force All Private Schools Coed?" 1. For one of the most comprehensive analyses Schlafly offered of Section 2's effects, see "Section 2 of ERA: The Federal Power Grab," *PS Report,* July 1979, vol. 12, no. 12, sec. 2. Most of the cases Schlafly cited had been decided in the 1960s. She often pointed to *Katzenbach v. Morgan,* 384 U.S. 641 (1966) and *Jones v. Alfred Mayer,* 392 U.S. 409 (1968), which affirmed congressional power to enact civil rights legislation under the Reconstruction Amendments, as models for ERA enforcement.

48. See, for example, PS Report, April 1976, vol. 9, no. 9, sec. 2.

49. "The Hypocrisy of ERA Proponents."

50. Schlafly, *Power of the Positive Woman,* 142.

51. *PS Report,* June 1976, vol. 9, no. 11, sec. 2, p. 1.

52. See Sarah Barringer Gordon, *The Spirit of the Law: Religious Voices and the Constitution* (Cambridge, MA: Harvard University Press, 2010), 182–183; Peggy Pascoe, "Sex, Gender, and Same-Sex Marriage," in *Is Academic Feminism Dead? Theory and Practice* (New York: New York University Press, 2000), 86, 91–103.

53. See Siegel, "Constitutional Culture."

54. See, for example, Natasha Zaretsky, *No Direction Home: The American Family and the Fear of National Decline, 1968-1980* (Chapel Hill: University of North Carolina Press, 2007).

55. As Reva Siegel writes, "In retrospect, the [ERA] debate has an Alice-in-Wonderland quality about it, as Schlafly offers a more robust reading of the feminist movement's claims than the movement itself felt able publicly to own." Siegel, "Constitutional Culture," 1395.

56. See, for example, "What's Wrong with 'Equal Rights' for Women?" 1.

57. For examples of antiprotectionist and pro-affirmative action sentiments coexisting peacefully and without comment in the early 1970s, see Mary East-

wood, "The Double Standard of Justice: Women's Rights under the Constitution," *Valparaiso University Law Review* 5 (1971): 281–317; Robert Allen Sedler, "The Legal Dimensions of Women's Liberation: An Overview," *Indiana Law Journal* 47 (1972): 419–456.

58. While *DeFunis* received extensive media coverage as a bellwether in the heated debate over affirmative action, *Kahn* attracted little notice outside the legal community.

59. Ruth Bader Ginsburg to Marc [Fasteau], Brenda [Feigen Fasteau], and Christine [Cassaday Curtis], November 13, 1973, RBG Papers, Container 4, Folder: Kahn v. Shevin Correspondence, 1973–1975. Though often characterized as a $500 property tax exemption, the $500 referred to the value of property exempt from the tax. The actual tax saving was approximately $15. Ruth Bader Ginsburg to James M. Klein, Harry W. Zanville, and Stephen E. Klein, Civil Law Clinic, University of Toledo College of Law, May 28, 1974, RBG Papers, Container 1, Folder: Califano v. Coffin.

60. Brief for Appellees, 3, 9–10, Kahn v. Shevin, 416 U.S. 351 (1974) (No. 73–78).

61. Ruth Bader Ginsburg to Mary McGowan Davis, January 30, 1974, 1, RBG Papers, Container 4, Folder: Kahn v. Shevin Correspondence, 1973–1975. Ginsburg had hoped to bring *Weinberger v. Wiesenfeld* (discussed in Chapter 4) as the next WRP case after *Frontiero*. Ruth Bader Ginsburg to John H. Fleming et al., Harvard Law Review, December 16, 1974, RBG Papers, Container 4, Folder: Kahn v. Shevin, 1973–74.

62. The parallels between the two cases were self-evident, at least to Justices Brennan and Blackmun's clerks. See Memo from T[homas] M[.] J[orde] (clerk) to WJB, Re: Kahn v. Shevin [no date], WJB Papers, Box 1: 325, Folder 12; Bench Memorandum from [Robert I.] Richter to Justice Harry A. Blackmun, February 16, 1974, Re: No. 73–78, Kahn v. Shevin, HAB Papers, Box 185, Folder 6.

63. At oral argument, too, Ginsburg contrasted the property tax exemption with Title VII remedies "that are realistically designed to promote equal opportunity, free from gender-based discrimination." Oral Argument, Kahn v. Shevin, COASC, 12.

64. "Generalized provisions based on gender stereotypes of the variety here at issue must be distinguished from affirmative action measures tailored narrowly and specifically to rectify the effects of past discrimination against women in a particular setting. Such measures deal directly with economic and social conditions that underlie and support a subordinate status for women." Brief for Appellants, 4, *Kahn v. Shevin,* 416 U.S. 351 (1974) (No. 73-78). See also ibid., 11, 24, note 19.

65. Oral Argument, Kahn v. Shevin, COASC, 7. Ginsburg was optimistic after oral argument. Ruth Bader Ginsburg to Bill Hoppe, Law Office of Colson & Hicks, March 8, 1974, RBG Papers, Container 4, Folder: *Kahn v. Shevin, 1973–75.*

66. Ibid.

67. Kahn v. Shevin, 416 U.S 351, 356 n. 10 (1974).

68. *Kahn,* 416 U.S. at 359–361 (Brennan, J., dissenting).

69. *Kahn,* 416 U.S. at 361–362 (White, J., dissenting).

70. Ruth Bader Ginsburg to Sara-Ann Determan, Hogan & Hartson, April 26, 1974, RBG Papers, Container 4, Folder: Kahn v. Shevin, 1973–75. Cary Franklin suggests that Ginsburg was skeptical that a pure "anti-subordination" approach would suffice to vanquish government support for traditional sex roles. Instead, Franklin contends, Ginsburg promoted an anti-stereotyping theory of equal protection. See Cary Franklin, "The Anti-Stereotyping Principle in Constitutional Sex Discrimination Law," *New York University Law Review* 85 (2010): 138.

71. In Ginsburg's estimation, Douglas had betrayed his vote in *Frontiero* for strict scrutiny by joining the "deplorable" *Kahn* majority position, and had compounded his error by reaching the opposite conclusion in his *DeFunis* dissent. Ruth Bader Ginsburg to Sara-Ann Determan, April 26, 1974.

72. Ruth Bader Ginsburg to Sara-Ann Determan, April 30, 1974, RBG Papers, Container 4, Folder: Kahn v. Shevin, 1973–75. For a similar critique, see John D. Johnston. Jr., "Sex Discrimination and the Supreme Court, 1971–74," *New York University Law Review* 49 (1974): 664. The inconsistency was obvious even to those who disagreed with Ginsburg and Johnston on the merits. See, for example, Jack B. Owen's handwritten notes on First draft of Douglas Opinion in *Kahn,* Circulated March 12, 1974, 73–78 Kahn v. Shevin, LFP Papers; Robert I. Richter, Memorandum to Justice Blackmun, Re: No. 73–78 Kahn v. Shevin, Circulation by Justice Douglas, March 12, 1974, HAB Papers, Box 185, Folder 6, Library of Congress.

73. Ruth Bader Ginsburg, "Gender in the Supreme Court: The 1973 and 1974 Terms," *Supreme Court Review* (1975): 21.

74. Ruth Bader Ginsburg to Stephanie W. Kanwit, Regional Director, Federal Trade Commission, April 30, 1974, RBG Papers, Container 12, Folder: Speech File, April–May 1974. See also Ruth B. Cowan, "Women's Rights through Litigation: An Examination of the American Civil Liberties Union Women's Rights Project, 1971–1976," *Columbia Human Rights Law Review* 8 (1976): 393.

75. W[illiam] C. K[elly], Supplemental Memo Re: Relisting No. 72-777 Cleveland Board of Educ. v. LaFleur, February 11, 1973, LFP Papers.

76. LFP, Summer Memorandum, No. 72-777 Cleveland Board of Education v. LaFleur, August 24, 1973, LFP Papers.

77. Jack B. Owens, Bench Memorandum, to LFP, September 24, 1973, LFP Papers, 72-777 Cleveland Board of Educ. v. LaFleur.

78. Ibid. Owens did not mention these advantages per se, but he sounded a cautionary note: "[I]t will be important to avoid Victorian viewpoints in these cases. . . . Whatever one's view about the wonders of motherhood," the clerk wrote, "it must be recognized that continued employment . . . may be terribly important financially to some women teachers, particularly in the inner cities. In too many families, such women act as breadwinners." Owens encouraged Powell to frame the issue as "a clinical analysis of two essentially unemotional and competing interests—a teacher's desire or perhaps need to retain her employment and a school board's obligation to protect the educational requirements of its students." Powell indicated his agreement with Owens in the margins; indeed, he had made similar observations in his earlier assessment of the cases.

79. HAB, Memo, Cleveland Board of Education v. LaFleur; Cohen v. Chesterfield County School Board, October 15, 1973, 5, HAB Papers, Box 175, Folder 1.

80. Ibid.

81. Jack B. Owens, Bench Memorandum, to LFP, September 24, 1973. Powell's oral argument notes described the teachers' stance as requiring that "any rule, to be valid, must apply to *all* disability 'across the board,' " which Powell labeled an "extreme position." At conference, only Justice Marshall appeared to agree with this analysis, causing Powell to write beside his notes, "Wow." Of the other Justices, Brennan came the closest to embracing the teachers' position, stating his view that requiring teachers to take leave at four or five months was "irrational and arbitrary," and that any requirement that teachers provide notice of their pregnancy should apply across the board to all foreseeable temporary disabilities. Burger and Rehnquist voted to uphold the regulations as reasonable. LFP Conference Notes, No. 72-777 Cleveland Board of Education v. LaFleur, Conference—October 19, 1973, LFP Papers.

82. Ibid. Stewart's "irrebuttable presumption" analysis was widely criticized. Legal historian Deborah Dinner makes the intriguing argument that the doctrinal weaknesses of the majority's decision in *LaFleur* have obscured more expansive conceptions of sex equality embodied in the case. See Deborah Dinner, "Recovering the *LaFleur* Doctrine," *Yale Journal of Law and Feminism* 22 (2010).

83. Robert Richter to HAB, December 3, 1973, Re: Maternity Leave Cases, HAB Papers, Box 175, Folder 1. Richter also critiqued Powell's concur-

rence, concluding, "I thought Justice Powell's opinion typified the application sub-silentio of middle-level equal protection. I don't necessarily think it is wrong, but I think it is weakened by the failure to indicate precisely that a standard is being applied that is more stringent than the traditional 'rational basis' test which the opinion purports to be applying." RR to HAB, Re: Maternity Leave Cases, Justice Powell's Concurrence, January 16, 1974, HAB Papers, Box 175, Folder 1, LOC.

84. Cleveland Board of Education v. LaFleur, 414 U.S. 632, 653 n. 2 (Powell, J., concurring). Powell wrote to Stewart: "I am concerned . . . as to where the due process analysis will lead us and whether the concept of 'irrebuttable presumption' may frustrate reasonable classifications of employees for various purposes." LFP to PS, December 11, 1973, Re: Pregnant Teachers' Cases, HAB Papers, Box 175, Folder 1.

85. Memorandum of the United States as Amicus Curiae, Cohen and LaFleur (No. 72-777, 72-1129) The government's brief also offered another alternative argument for striking down the policies—their interference with the fundamental right to bear children.

86. California Unemployment Insurance Code § 2626 ("In no case shall the term 'disability' or 'disabled' include any injury or illness caused by or arising in connection with pregnancy.").

87. For more on the stories behind the pregnancy discrimination cases, see Fred Strebeigh, *Equal: Women Reshape American Law,* 1st ed. (New York: W.W. Norton, 2009), Chapters 5–8.

88. See Dinner, "Recovering the LaFleur Doctrine."

89. Editorial, "Examining Sex Discrimination," WSJ, April 12, 1974, 6.

90. Quoted in James C. Hyatt, "Sex and the Federal Contractor: Firms, Colleges Denounce as Too Costly Proposed Rules to Bar Employment Bias," WSJ, April 5, 1974, 28.

91. Anastasia T. Dunau, letter to the editor, "Sex Discrimination," WSJ, April 29, 1974, 15.

92. Strebeigh, *Equal,* 84–89. *Kirby* had declared sex a suspect classification under the state constitution and provided key language both for Ginsburg's *Reed* brief and for Justice Brennan's plurality opinion in *Frontiero.* See Chapter 2.

93. Linda Mathews, "State Fights Disability Pay for Pregnancies," LAT, March 28, 1974, A3. For further discussion, see Strebeigh, *Equal,* 91.

94. Aiello v. Hansen, 359 F. Supp. 792, 794–799 (N.D. Cal. 1973).

95. *Aiello,* 359 F. Supp at 806 (Williams, J., dissenting).

96. Brief for Appellees, Geduldig v. Aiello, 49-50, 417 U.S. 484 (1974) (No. 73-640). The plaintiffs' brief argued that strict scrutiny was applicable for two reasons: the similarities between sex and existing suspect classifications like

race, and the policies' interference with women's fundamental right to bear children. An amicus brief filed by the ACLU WRP, NOW, and the Center for Constitutional Rights took a different tack, arguing that the state's policy violated even the less stringent rational basis test articulated in *Reed*. Brief Amici Curiae of the ACLU, the Center for Constitutional Rights and the National Organization for Women, 31, *Geduldig* (No. 73-640).

97. HAB, Geduldig v. Aiello, March 25, 1974, HAB Papers, Box 188, Folder 12.

98. Draft concurrence, Geduldig v. Aiello (never filed), HAB Papers, Box 188, Folder 12.

99. R[obert] R[ichter] to HAB, May 20, 1974, HAB Papers, Box 188, Folder 12.

100. Brief for Appellant, 27, *Geduldig* (No. 73-640). The plaintiffs countered that pregnancy was not substantially different from other temporary disabilities. Linda Mathews, "State Fights Disability Pay for Pregnancies," LAT, March 28, 1974, A3.

101. Mathews, "State Fights," A3.

102. "There is no risk from which men are protected and women are not. Likewise, there is no risk from which women are protected and men are not." Geduldig v. Aiello, 417 U.S. 484, 496 n.20, 496–497 (1974).

103. *Geduldig*, 417 U.S. at 501 (Brennan, J., dissenting).

104. Sylvia A. Law, "Rethinking Sex and the Constitution," *University of Pennsylvania Law Review* 132 (1984): 955, 983.

105. Quoted in Linda Mathews, "California Upheld on Denial of Disability Pay for Pregnancy," LAT, June 18, 1974, A3.

106. For more on the "abortion-ERA connection," see Chapter 6; Jane Mansbridge, *Why We Lost the ERA* (University of Chicago Press, 1986), 122–128; De Hart and Mathews, *Sex, Gender, and the Politics of ERA*, 158-160; Siegel, "Constitutional Culture."

107. *PS Report*, July 1975, vol. 8, no. 12, sec. 2.

108. Ann Scott to Del Martin, August 10, 1973, NOW Papers, Box 99, Folder 16.

109. Jan Liebman, Abortion Amendment Strategy [1973], NOW Papers, Box 99, Folder 17.

110. For further discussion, see Siegel, "Constitutional Culture," 1393.

111. Katharine T. Bartlett, Comment, "Pregnancy and the Constitution: The Uniqueness Trap," *California Law Review* 62 (1974): 1548–49.

112. For more on the Vorchheimer case, see Martha Minow, "Single-Sex Public Schools: The Story of *Vorchheimer v. School District of Philadelphia*," in *Women and the Law Stories*, ed. Elizabeth M. Schneider and Stephanie M. Wildman (New York: Foundation Press, 2011), 101–110; Philippa Strum, *Women in*

the Barracks: The VMI Case and Equal Rights (Lawrence: University Press of Kansas, 2002), Chapter 5.

113. Appendix, 9a, Vorchheimer v. Sch. Dist., 430 U.S. 703 (1977) (No. 76-37).

114. Appendix, 9a–10a, *Vorchheimer* (No. 76-37); Vorchheimer v. Sch. Dist., 400 F. Supp. 326, 328 (E.D. Pa. 1975).

115. Appendix, 9a, *Vorchheimer* (No. 76-37).

116. This statement is somewhat odd because the decision in *Brown* did not depend upon a showing that school facilities provided to black and white children were materially unequal. Brown v. Bd. of Educ., 347 U.S. 483, 495 (1954).

117. *Vorchheimer,* 400 F. Supp. 326, 342 (E.D. Pa. 1975). When the court ordered Central High to admit female students, the district initially moved to comply with the ruling, but irate alumni convinced the school board to appeal. See Ewart Rouse and Steve Twomey, "Judge Tells Central High to Go Co-ed," *Philadelphia Inquirer,* August 8, 1975, 1A; Editorial, "Central High Will Survive," *Philadelphia Inquirer,* August 15, 1975; Robert Fowler, "Central Alumni Taken by Surprise," *Philadelphia Inquirer,* August 8, 1975, 2C.

118. Vorchheimer v. Sch. Dist., 532 F.2d 880, 887–888 (3d Cir. 1976).

119. Gibbons wrote: "I was under the distinct impression . . . that 'separate but equal' analysis, especially in the field of public education, passed from the fourteenth amendment jurisprudential scene over twenty years ago. The majority opinion in establishing a twentieth-century sexual equivalent to the *Plessy* decision, reminds us that the doctrine can and will be invoked to support sexual discrimination in the same manner that it supported discrimination prior to *Brown.*"

120. 532 F. 2d at 889 (Gibbons, J., dissenting).

121. See, for example, Michael Heise, "Are Single-Sex Schools Inherently Unequal?" *Michigan Law Review* 102 (2004): 1228–1229. Before examining archival sources, I too assumed that the WRP was in control of the *Vorchheimer* litigation. See Serena Mayeri, "'A Common Fate of Discrimination': Race/ Gender Analogies in Legal and Historical Perspective," *Yale Law Journal* 110 (2001): 1078 n. 162.

122. Ruth Bader Ginsburg to Jill Goodman, May 11, 1976, RBG Papers, Container 9, Folder: Vorchheimer v. School Dist, Correspondence, 1976.

123. Ruth Bader Ginsburg to Jill Goodman, June 11, 1976, 1–2, RBG Papers, Container 9, Folder: Vorchheimer v. School Dist., Correspondence, 1976.

124. Ruth Bader Ginsburg to Sharon K. Wallis, Jill Laurie Goodman, and Lynn Hecht Schafran, January 11, 1977, 1, RBG Papers, Container 9, Folder: Vorchheimer v. School Dist., Correspondence, 1977.

125. See Spencer Coxe to Kathleen Peratis, Ruth Bader Ginsburg, and Lou Pollak, February 23, 1977, RBG Papers, Container 9, Folder: Vorchheimer v. School Dist., Correspondence, 1977. Justice Powell, for one, found Wallis's oral argument "entirely confusing . . . no help." LFP, Oral Argument Notes, 76–37 Vorchheimer v. Sch. Dist., February 22, 1977, LFP Papers.

126. Ruth Bader Ginsburg, Reply Brief for the Petitioners, 7–11, Vorchheimer v. Sch. Dist., No. 76-37, RBG Papers, Container 10, Folder: Vorchheimer v. School Dist. Pleadings, 1976–1977 (draft: never filed).

127. See letters contained in RBG Papers, Container 9, Folder: Vorchheimer v. School Dist., Correspondence, 1977.

128. Memorandum from J. L. [Jerry Lynch] to WJB, Jr., 1, Re: The Lineup in Vorchheimer, 76-37, WJB Papers, 1:421, Folder: Vorchheimer v. School Dist. This was also the position of the United States. *See* Memorandum for the United States as Amicus Curiae, Vorchheimer v. School Dist., 430 U.S. 703 (1977) (No. 76-37).

129. When neither remand nor reargument commanded a majority of Justices, White voted to affirm. See LFP Conference Notes, 76-37 Vorchheimer v. Sch. Dist., March 25, 1977, LFP Papers.

130. Memorandum from WEB to the Conference, April 11, 1977, WJB Papers, 1:421, Folder: Vorchheimer v. School Dist.

131. Memorandum from WEB to the Conference, Re: Vorchheimer v. Sch. Dist. of Philadelphia, March 9, 1977, WJB Papers, 1:421, Folder: Vorchheimer v. School Dist.

132. Justice Powell noted that four Justices disagreed with Chief Justice Burger's judgment that the "separate is inherently unequal" question was properly presented. See Memorandum WEB to the Conference, Re: 76-37 Vorchheimer v. Sch. Dist. of Philadelphia, March 9, 1977, LFP Papers. The Justices who might vote to reverse the Third Circuit's decision were not doing so on the grounds that all sex separation was unconstitutional per se. Rather, they were confining themselves to the specific facts of the Philadelphia case, where girls were excluded from a school with superior tangible and intangible qualities.

133. Blackmun agreed that "the Court [would] look bad, or at least awkward" if an equally divided vote were the result, and thus voted to reargue. White, too, favored reargument. Stevens did not, however, and apparently only one other Justice did. Memorandum from HAB to WEB, Re: Vorchheimer v. Sch. Dist. of Philadelphia, April 18, 1977, WJB Papers, 1:421, Folder: Vorchheimer v. School Dist.; BRW to WEB, April 18, 1977, WJB Papers, 1:421, Folder: Vorchheimer v. School Dist.; JPS to WEB, April 18, 1977, WJB Papers, 1:421, Folder: Vorchheimer v. School Dist. See also LFP to WEB, Re: No. 76-37 Vorchheimer v. Sch. Dist., April 18, 1977, LFP Papers ("As I view

the case as involving unique facts, I am content to 'let the chips lie where they fell' ").

134. WEB to HAB, April 18, 1977, WJB Papers, 1:421, Folder: Vorchheimer v. School Dist.

135. Quoted in Lesley Oelsner, "Recent Supreme Court Rulings Have Set Back Women's Rights," NYT, July 7, 1977, A8. Reflecting on the 1976–1977 term as a whole, Oelsner declared that the Supreme Court's year "went against women—heavily."

136. "*Brown v. Board of Education* had been preceded by a generation of litigation in which decisions turned on the markedly inferior opportunities afforded blacks, on inequalities solidly demonstrated at trial. . . . *Vorchheimer* may have been a case brought to the Court too soon, and with too spare a record." Ruth Bader Ginsburg, George Abel Dreyfous Lecture on Civil Liberties, Tulane University School of Law, February 13, 1978, 39, RBG Papers, Container 13, Folder: Speech File, February 13, 1978.

137. Inez Smith Reid, "Equal Protection or Equal Denial? Is It Time for Racial Minorities, the Poor, Women, and Other Oppressed People to Regroup?" *Hofstra Law Review* 3 (1975): 2.

138. MacLean, *Freedom Is Not Enough,* 77–89.

139. See, for example, Kimberle Crenshaw, "Demarginalizing the Intersection of Race and Sex: A Black Feminist Critique of Antidiscrimination Doctrine, Feminist Theory, and Antiracist Politics, *University of Chicago Legal Forum* (1989): 139–168; Eileen Boris, "The Gender of Discrimination: Race, Sex, and Fair Employment," in *Women and the Constitution: History, Interpretation, and Practice,* ed. Sibyl A. Schwarzenbach and Patricia Smith (New York: Columbia University Press, 2003), 273–291.

140. DeGraffenreid v. General Motors Assembly Division, 558 F. 2d 480, 483 (8th Cir. 1977)

141. Ibid., 482–83.

142. DeGraffenreid v. General Motors Assembly Division, 413 F. Supp. 142–144 (E.D.Mo. May 4, 1976).

143. Ibid., 145.

144. Brief for the Equal Employment Opportunity Commission as Amicus Curiae, 20, DeGraffenreid v. General Motors Corp., 558 F.2d 480 (8th Cir. 1977) (No. 76-1599), NARA Central Plains Regional Div., Kansas City, MO.

145. International Brotherhood of Teamsters v. United States, 431 U.S. 324 (1977). As one commentator put it, *Teamsters* "involved racial discrimination, but [its] logic applied to sex discrimination as well." Lesley Oelsner, "Recent Supreme Court Rulings Have Set Back Women's Rights," NYT, July 8, 1977, 32.

146. DeGraffenreid v. General Motors, 558 F. 2d 480 (8th Cir. 1977).

147. Washington v. Davis, 426 U.S. 229 (1976).

148. Carol H. Falk, "The Supreme Court and Civil Rights," WSJ, December 30, 1976, 4.

4. Reasoning from Sex

1. Smith v. City of East Cleveland, 363 F. Supp. 1131 (N.D. Ohio 1973). The court relied on 42 U.S.C. section 1983 as well as the equal protection clause of the Fourteenth Amendment.

2. Griggs v. Duke Power Co., 401 U.S. 424 (1971). For a range of perspectives on the emergence of disparate impact, see Hugh Davis Graham, *The Civil Rights Era: Origins of National Policy* (New York: Oxford University Press, 1990); Neal Devins, "The Civil Rights Hydra," *Michigan Law Review* 89 (1991): 1723–1765; Susan Carle, "A Social Movement History of Disparate Impact Analysis," Social Science Research Network, accessed August 10, 2010, http://ssrn.com/abstract=1538525.

3. NettaBell Girard Larson, "Concept of Equal Rights," *Women Lawyers Journal* 58 (1972): 101.

4. Disparate impact analysis did make an appearance in LaFleur's case. See Memorandum for the United States as Amicus Curiae, 10, Cleveland Board of Education v. LaFleur, 414 U.S. 632 (1974) (No. 72-777).

5. For more on the story behind the *Gilbert* litigation, see Fred Strebeigh, *Equal: Women Reshape American Law,* 1st ed. (New York: W.W. Norton, 2009), Chapter 7.

6. See Chapter 2.

7. Gilbert v. General Electric, 375 F. Supp. 367, 381–382 (E.D. Va. April 13, 1974).

8. Commentators had predicted that the outcome of the constitutional pregnancy cases would influence the interpretation of Title VII. See, for example, Linda Mathews, "Court to Decide Whether Pregnant Teachers Can Be Forced to Quit," LAT, April 24, 1973, 7. At first, it seemed as if lower courts were following *Geduldig* even in Title VII cases, but feminists kept the issue alive by arguing that the Court's interpretation of the equal protection clause should not constrain Title VII litigation. Paradoxically, feminists found themselves highlighting the weakness of a race-sex parallel under the equal protection clause in order to stress that Title VII's race-sex equivalence was comparatively robust. See, for example, Brief of the American Civil Liberties Union and Equal Rights Advocates, Inc., as Amici Curiae, 33–34, 42–43, General Electric Co. v. Gilbert, 519 F.2d 661 (4th Cir. 1975) (No. 74-1557), RBG Papers, Container 3, Folder: General Elec. Co. v. Gilbert, 1974.

9. See Nancy Erickson, "Pregnancy Discrimination: An Analytical Approach," *Women's Rights Law Reporter* 5 (1979): 83, 87.

10. Diane L. Zimmerman, "*Geduldig v. Aiello:* Pregnancy Classifications

and the Definition of Sex Discrimination," *Columbia Law Review* 75 (1975): 457, 459.

11. Kathleen Peratis and Elisabeth Rindskopf, "Pregnancy Discrimination as a Sex Discrimination Issue," *Women's Rights Law Reporter* 2 (1975): 26–34.

12. Gilbert v. General Electric, 519 F.2d 661, 664 n.9 (4th Cir. 1975).

13. Peratis and Rindskopf, "Pregnancy Discrimination as a Sex Discrimination Issue," 30. In September, Peratis told a reporter, "We're really making headway now. . . . I just hope the Supreme Court doesn't mess us up." Quoted in Virginia Lee Warren, "The Fight for Disability Benefits in Pregnancy," NYT, September 16, 1975, 36.

14. Brief for Respondents Gilbert and IUE, 88, GE v. Gilbert, 429 U.S. 125 (1976) (Nos. 74-1589 and 74-1590); Brief for the AFL-CIO and International Union UAW as Amici Curiae, *Gilbert;* Brief for the United States and the EEOC as Amici Curiae, *Gilbert.* (Nos. 74-1589 and 74-1590).

15. Amicus Brief of the ACLU and NEA, Wetzel v. Liberty Mutual (No. 74-1245), 1975 WL 173653. *Wetzel* raised substantially the same question as *Gilbert,* and Ginsburg called it the "most important case since *Roe."* Ginsburg later wrote: "We filed a slim (and not very good) *Gilbert* brief limited to the ERA issue GE raised." Ruth Bader Ginsburg to Jeffrey S. Saltz, Executive Editor, *Harvard Law Review,* August 15, 1977, RBG Papers, Container 2, Folder: Califano v. Goldfarb: Correspondence, 1977–1979.

16. Supplemental Brief of Respondents, 10–12, *Gilbert* (Nos. 74-1589 and 74-1590).

17. Washington v. Davis, 426 U.S. 229 (1976).

18. Supplemental Brief of General Electric at Reargument, 10, 15–16, *Gilbert* (Nos. 74-1589 and 74-1590).

19. Brief for Petitioner, 21, *Gilbert* (Nos. 74-1589 and 74-1590).

20. Brief of AT&T as Amicus Curie, 16, *Wetzel* (No. 74-1245), 1975 WL 173663.

21. Blackmun did not hear the first set of arguments in *Gilbert,* based upon an apparent disqualification, though in the end he did participate in the Court's deliberations.

22. Conference Notes, Gilbert v. GE, January 26, 1976, LFP Papers.

23. Donna Murasky, Bench Memorandum, Gilbert v. GE, August 14, 1976, 15, 18, 25–26, HAB Papers, Box 238, Folder 8.

24. Harry A. Blackmun, Notes, General Electric v. Gilbert, August 31, 1976, HAB Papers, Box 238, Folder 8.

25. Block analogized to *Griggs,* "where it seems to be insufficient for Blacks to show that they get a certain number of questions on the test wrong in a higher proportion than Whites—they must show rather that they failed the test

as a whole in a disproportionate number." William H. Block to HAB, Re: Supplemental Briefs in Gilbert v. General Electric, October 5, 1976, HAB Papers, Box 238, Folder 8.

26. Gene Comey to LFP, October 12, 1976, LFP Papers. See also Gene Comey to LFP, Bobtail Bench Memorandum, Gilbert v. General Electric, October 11, 1976, LFP Papers.

27. Powell, Conference Notes, GE v. Gilbert, Conf. October 15, 1976, LFP Papers.

28. Then-Nixon aide John Dean and some scholars have cast doubt on Rehnquist's alternative explanation for the memo. See John W. Dean, *The Rehnquist Choice: The Untold Story of the Nixon Appointment That Redefined the Supreme Court* (New York: Free Press, 2001), 274–284 and n. 60.

29. "William H. Rehnquist," Supreme Court Historical Society, accessed October 12, 2010, http://www.supremecourthistory.org.

30. Memorandum from William H. Rehnquist, Assistant Attorney General, Office of Legal Counsel, DOJ, to Leonard Garment, Special Counsel to the President (1970), reprinted in *Legal Times,* September 15, 1986, 4–5. Rehnquist's memo, a response to a brief for the ERA by Mary Eastwood, his DOJ subordinate, was exhumed by opponents of his nomination to become Chief Justice of the Supreme Court in 1986.

31. See Chapter 2.

32. Diane Wood to HAB, Re: General Electric v. Gilbert, Comments on opinion circulated by WHR, October 29, 1976, 2–6, HAB Papers, Box 238, Folder 8. Wood argued that Rehnquist's assertions that *Geduldig* controlled the outcome in *Gilbert* would fatally undermine *Griggs*. All that can be drawn from *Geduldig,*" Wood asserted, "is that an intentional adoption of a plan that excludes pregnancy benefits cannot be equated to intentional discrimination on the basis of gender. Thus, it is the *Griggs* 'effect' test that must control." She also told Blackmun that she "would be delighted" to discuss her objections to the majority's holding if he so desired. Ibid.

33. Powell, handwritten note on copy of changes, November 6, 1976, LFP Papers. Wood "heard through the grapevine that Justice Powell [might] be preparing a memorandum setting out objections" to Justice Rehnquist's draft opinion "insofar as it overrule[d] *Griggs* sub rosa." Diane Wood to HAB, Addendum, November 1, 1976, HAB Papers, Box 238, Folder 8.

34. William H. Block to HAB, Re: General Electric v. Gilbert, November 8, 1976, HAB Papers, Box 238, Folder 8.

35. William H. Block to HAB, Re: General Electric v. Gilbert, November 22, 1976, HAB Papers, Box 238, Folder 8. Block added: "I think that getting the opinion changed might be more beneficial in the long run than the separate concurrence." Stewart, too, supported the changes Blackmun suggested. Ibid.

36. Three of the five changes "designed as they apparently are to restrict the test of violation to 'effect' alone, run more of a risk than I want to do of deciding *sub silentio* that effect alone is sufficient under all of the various provisions of Title VII," Rehnquist wrote, adding, "[I]f I am correct in my ascription of reasons, I would prefer not to make the changes you suggest." WHR to HAB, Re: General Electric v. Gilbert, November 22, 1976, HAB Papers, Box 238, Folder 7, LOC.

37. Gilbert v. General Electric, 429 U.S. 125, 146 (Blackmun, J., concurring in part); *Gilbert*, 429 U.S. at 146 (Stewart, J., concurring).

38. *Gilbert*, 429 U.S. at 136, 153–155 (Brennan, J., dissenting).

39. RBG to Herma Hill Kay, Harvard Law School, December 7, 1976, RBG Papers, Container 9, Folder: Vorchheimer v. School Dist, Correspondence, 1976.

40. Quoted in Gail Bronson, "Group to Map Plan to Sidestep Decision of Justices on Pregnancy Disability Pay," WSJ, December 13, 1976, 12.

41. Quoted in Philip Hager, "Court Upholds Bar to Benefits for Pregnancy," LAT, December 8, 1976, B1.

42. Marian F. Sabetny-Dzvonik to HAB, December 9, 1976, and Alexander Buchman to HAB, December 9, 1976, HAB Papers, Box 238, Folder 8.

43. Editorial, "Equality Sometimes," NYT, December 11, 1976, 17; Editorial, "Women and the Court," WSJ, December 16, 1976, 18.

44. Quoted in Carol H. Falk, "Disability Plans That Exclude Pregnancy Don't Violate Sex Bias Law, Justices Rule," WSJ, December 8, 1976, 3.

45. The *New York Times* ran one of the few press accounts that mentioned this aspect of the case. See "High Court Says Pregnancy Pay Is No Legal Right," NYT, December 12, 1976, E1; see also William B. Gould, "The High Court Discriminates between Sex and Race," NYT, June 12, 1977, 153.

46. Clare Cushman, ed., *Supreme Court Decisions and Women's Rights: Milestones to Equality* (Washington, DC: CQ Press, 2001), 124–126.

47. Brief for Appellants, Dothard v. Mieth, 433 U.S 321 (1977) (No. 76-422), 1977 WL 189472.

48. [Alex] Kozinski, Preliminary Memo, Dothard v. Mieth, No. 76-422, November 12, 1976 Conference, List 1, Sheet 1, LFP Papers.

49. WEB to PS, June 9, 1977, Re: Dothard v. Mieth, HAB Papers, Box 253, Folder 1.

50. LFP, Conference Notes, Dothard v. Mieth, No. 76-422, LFP Papers.

51. Dothard v. Rawlinson, 433 U.S. 321, 329–335 (1977).

52. *Dothard*, 433 U.S. at 343 (quoting Marshall's opinion in *Phillips v. Martin-Marietta*) (Marshall, J., dissenting in part). The Court's rationale, in Marshall's view, "regrettably perpetuate[d] one of the most insidious old myths about women that women, wittingly or not, are seductive sexual objects." Ibid., 345.

53. Ibid., 343–347.

54. Ibid., 336 n. 23. Justice Powell had objected to this footnote, afraid it would "encourage some other pioneer women like Ms. Rawlinson to institute similar suits," but joined the opinion anyway. LFP to PS, June 9, 1977, Re: Dothard v. Mieth, No. 76-422, HAB Papers, Box 253, Folder 1.

55. *Dothard*, 433 U.S. at 339–340 (Rehnquist, J., concurring in the result and concurring in part). Blackmun's clerk, William Block, had encouraged him to join the dissent. See WHB to HAB, June 9, 1977, Re: Dothard v. Mieth: Justice Stewart's proposed draft, No. 76-422, HAB Papers, Box 253, Folder 1, LOC; WHB to HAB, Re: Dothard v. Mieth, Justice Rehnquist's concurrence, June 17, 1977, HAB Papers, Box 253, Folder 1.

56. Quoted in Lesley Oelsner, "Recent Supreme Court Rulings Have Set Back Women's Rights," NYT, July 8, 1977, 32.

57. Bench Memo, Dothard, HAB Papers, Box 253, Folder 1. The clerk's "penchant [sic] for narrowness" was "fueled, of course, by [his] belief that certain members of the Court . . . would like to use the case to cut back significantly on the reach and effectiveness of Title VII." Ibid.

58. Some commentators did worry that the decision left the door open for tests of strength that would disproportionately exclude women applicants. See, for example, James B. Jacobs, "The Sexual Integration of the Prison's Guard Force: A Few Comments on *Dothard v. Rawlinson*," *University of Toledo Law Review* 10 (1978): 389–418.

59. Nashville Gas Co. v. Satty, 434 U.S. 136 (1977).

60. Brief for the Respondent, Nashville Gas Co. v. Satty; Brief Amici Curiae of American Civil Liberties Union and Women's Legal Defense Fund, 22–23, Nashville Gas Co. v. Satty, 434 U.S. 136 (1977) (No. 75-536), 1977 WL 189752.

61. Motion for Leave to File a Brief Amici Curiae and Brief for the American Federation of Labor and Congress of Industrial Organizations and International Union, UAW as Amici Curiae, 4, *Satty* (No. 75-536), 1977 WL 189753.

62. Steven A. Reiss to WJB, Re: No. 75-436, Nashville Gas Co. v. Satty, 1, WJB Papers, I:410, Folder 5.

63. *Satty*, 434 U.S. at 141–142.

64. *Satty*, 434 U.S. at 154–155 (Stevens, J., concurring); see also Respondent's Brief, 9, *Satty* (No. 75-536).

65. Miles N. Ruthberg to TM, Re: No. 75-576, TM Papers, Box 200, Folder 7.

66. LFP to Sam [Estreicher], [Re: No. 85-536 Nashville Gas Co. v. Satty], November 3, 1977, LFP Papers. Powell's concurrence argued that the Court's remand for reconsideration of the sick leave policy should allow the employees to present not only evidence of pretext, but also evidence that the policy had a

disparate impact on women. Powell essentially said that it was unfair to preclude the women from making a disparate impact argument since, prior to *Gilbert,* they were not required to do so. *Satty,* 434 U.S. at 151 (Powell, J., concurring in the result and concurring in part).

67. Powell wrote that he would "prefer not to make [the intent vs. effect] issue the centerpiece of my opinion." See draft attached to LFP to Sam [Estreicher], November 3, 1977.

68. Quoted in Carol H. Falk, "Justices Rule Gas Firm's Seniority Policy on Pregnancy Leave Amounts to Sex Bias," WSJ, December 7, 1977, 5.

69. Quoted in Warren Weaver, Jr., "Seniority is Upheld on Maternity Leave," NYT, December 7, 1977, 1. On the promise of disparate impact theory after *Satty,* see Erickson, "Pregnancy Discrimination: An Analytical Approach."

70. Carol H. Falk, "Backtracking on Job Bias?" WSJ, February 9, 1978, 18.

71. Damon Stetson, "Women Vow Fight for Pregnancy Pay," NYT, December 9, 1976, 19.

72. "Feminist Leaders Plan Coalition for Law Aiding Pregnant Women," NYT, December 15, 1976, 40; Synopsis of Meeting for Campaign to End Discrimination Against Pregnant Workers, January 14, 1977, NOW Papers, Box 55, Folder 12.

73. Quoted in Bronson, "Group to Map Plan," 12.

74. Quoted in "Pregnancy Benefit Bill Is Disputed at Hearing," NYT, April 7, 1977, 22.

75. Letty Cottin Pogrebin, "Anatomy Isn't Destiny," NYT, May 6, 1977, 21.

76. Erica Black Grubb and Andrea Hricko, "Pregnancy Ruling: Who's Responsible for Propagation?," LAT, January 30, 1977, D2. See also Wendy Susco, "Pregnant with Sexism," NYT, February 6, 1977, O24.

77. CEDAPW, Fact Sheet, December 1976, NOW Papers, Box 55, Folder 12.

78. *Legislative History of the Pregnancy Discrimination Act of 1978, Public Law 95–555, Prepared for the Committee on Labor and Human Resources, U.S. Senate* (Washington, DC: U.S. Government Printing Office, 1979), 3, 166 (hereinafter *PDA Legislative History*).

79. On the equal treatment/special treatment debate, see Jane S. DeHart, "Equality Challenged: Equal Rights and Sexual Difference," in *Civil Rights in the United States,* ed. Hugh Davis Graham (University Park: Pennsylvania State University Press, 1994), 40–72.

80. *PDA Legislative History,* 40–41. See also *Hearing on Legislation to Prohibit Sex Discrimination on the Basis of Pregnancy, House of Representatives, Subcommittee on*

Employment Opportunities of the Committee on Education and Labor, 80 (April 6, 1977) (testimony of Laurence Gold, General Counsel, AFL-CIO).

81. "By making clear that distinctions based on pregnancy are per se violations of Title VII, the bill would eliminate the need in most instances to rely on the impact approach, and thus would obviate the difficulties in applying the distinctions created in *Satty." PDA Legislative History,* 149.

82. *PDA Legislative History,* 201. PDA supporters frequently cited the dissenters' opinions in *Gilbert,* emphasizing their "commonsense" definitions of "sex" as including pregnancy. The dissenters had also argued for a broad interpretation of *Griggs* and its application to the pregnancy context. But none of the lawmakers' citations referred to this element of their opinions, as they were focused on bolstering the argument that pregnancy discrimination was sex discrimination per se.

83. *PDA Legislative History,* 148 (quoting House Report 95-948). See also *Hearing on Legislation to Prohibit Sex Discrimination on the Basis of Pregnancy, House of Representatives, Subcommittee on Employment Opportunities of the Committee on Education and Labor,* 34 (Wednesday, April 6, 1977) (testimony of Susan Deller Ross) ("In adopting the standard of equal treatment for those who are similar in their ability or inability to work, HR 5055 incorporates the theory of the EEOC pregnancy guidelines which the Supreme Court declined to follow.") The EEOC guidelines also approved disparate impact analysis in the context of pregnancy discrimination.

84. An early Senate report was typical in describing the employer obligations created by the PDA: "[The bill] would require employers who provide a general income support program for disabled workers to provide the same benefits to women disabled by pregnancy, childbirth, or related medical occurrences. . . . An employer who does not provide disability benefits or paid sick leave to other employees will not, because of [the PDA], have to provide these benefits. And, an employer will not have to allow pregnant women to use paid sick leave or receive disability benefits simply because they are pregnant; benefits need to be paid only on the same terms applicable to other employees." *PDA Legislative History,* 41 (Senate Report 95-331). For similar descriptions, see *PDA Legislative History,* 151. See also *Hearing on Legislation to Prohibit Sex Discrimination on the Basis of Pregnancy, House of Representatives, Subcommittee on Employment Opportunities of the Committee on Education and Labor* 121 (April 6, 1977) (testimony of Drew Days, Assistant Attorney General for Civil Rights); *PDA Legislative History,* 63, 83.

85. Indeed, the Supreme Court eventually so found in *California Savings and Loan v. Guerra,* 479 U.S. 272 (1987).

86. Erickson, "Pregnancy Discrimination: An Analytical Approach," 105.

87. For an early critique of these cases, see Reva B. Siegel, "Employment Equality under the Pregnancy Discrimination Act of 1978," *Yale Law Journal* 94 (1985): 929–956.

88. Ruth Bader Ginsburg, "Gender and the Constitution," *University of Cincinnati Law Review* 44 (1975): 27–40.

89. On the history of feminist campaigns for child care and the conservative response, see Mary Frances Berry, *The Politics of Parenthood: Child Care, Women's Rights, and the Myth of the Good Mother* (New York: Viking, 1993); Kimberly J. Morgan, "A Child of the Sixties: The Great Society, the New Right, and the Politics of Federal Child Care," *Journal of Policy History* 13 (2001): 215–250; Deborah Dinner, "The Universal Childcare Debate: Rights Mobilization, Social Policy, and the Dynamics of Feminist Activism, 1966–1974," *Law and History Review* 28 (2010): 577–628.

90. NOW Compliance Committee, Guidelines on Questions to Be Used in Evaluating Affirmative Action Plans, September 20, 1972, NOW Papers, Box 209, Folders 58, 65.

91. The N.O.W. Model Affirmative Action Program, NOW Papers, Box 209, Folder 69. See also, for example, The N.O.W. Phone Company Anti-Discrimination Affirmative Action Kit, NOW Papers, Box 209, Folder 69; NOW Federal Compliance Committee, Newsletter #3, NOW Papers, Box 209, Folder 85 (listing as a "good feature" that "[c]hildcare is suggested as an element of affirmative action"). Feminists' stated objections to the AT&T consent decree included the company's failure to implement effective leave and child-care policies.

92. The quote is from Strebeigh, *Equal,* 10.

93. Weinberger v. Wiesenfeld, 420 U.S. 636, 641 n. 7 (1975) (plurality opinion). For more on the Wiesenfelds' story, see Strebeigh, *Equal,* Chapters 1, 4.

94. Oral Argument, Weinberger v. Wiesenfeld, in *Landmark Briefs and Oral Arguments of the Supreme Court of the United States,* ed. Philip B. Kurland and Gerhard Casper (Arlington, VA: University Publications of America, 1975), 430.

95. "An Open Discussion with Justice Ruth Bader Ginsburg," *Connecticut Law Review* 36 (2004): 1037–1038.

96. The "cert. pool memo," in which a clerk summarizes the case in order to help the Justices decide whether to hear it, recommended summarily reversing the lower court's invalidation of the distinction in light of *Kahn v. Shevin.* O'Neill, Preliminary Memorandum on 73-1892 Weinberger v. Wiesenfeld, July 19, 1974, 3, LFP Papers ("The case should be reversed in light of *Kahn,* probably summarily.").

97. Bench Memorandum from Richard Blumenthal to HAB, Decem-

ber 23, 1974, Re: Weinberger v. Wiesenfeld, No. 73-1892, HAB Papers, Box 203, Folder 6. Moynihan supervised Blumenthal's Harvard senior thesis on the failure of government anti-poverty programs, and Blumenthal later worked for Moynihan in the Nixon White House. See David Plotz, "Just Call Him Senator," *Slate,* January 6, 2010, http://www.slate.com/id/2240729/.

98. See LFP, Conference Notes, January 22, 1975, Weinberger v. Wiesenfeld, LFP Papers.

99. Memorandum from Julia "Penny" Clark, law clerk, to Justice Lewis F. Powell, Jr., January 17, 1975, 3, LFP Papers. Powell accepted Penny Clark's recommendation that the challenged statute be invalidated, but stopped short of agreeing with her statement that "unless it is rational for society to insist that men work rather than care for children, there is no rational basis for the gender classification in the existing statutory scheme." Powell's marginalia revealed his ambivalence: "This [classification] may have some rationality."

Before choosing Clark over a similarly qualified male, the Justice consulted the appellate judge for whom Clark had worked to make sure she was not "the kind of girl who's going to break down in tears when the going gets tough." Still, Powell was a gentleman in both manner and deed: his female clerks, including the feminist scholars Mary Becker and Christina Brooks Whitman, remember him as unfailingly courteous and respectful of their intellectual abilities. See John C. Jeffries, Jr., *Justice Lewis F. Powell, Jr.* (New York: Scribner's, 1994), 502–508.

100. LFP, Conference Notes, January 22, 1975.

101. Powell agreed that the "statutory scheme . . . impermissibly discriminates against a female wage earner because it provides her family less protection than it provides that of a male wage earner, even though the family needs may be identical." Powell "attach[ed] less significance" than the plurality, though, to fathers' right to care for their children: "In light of the long experience to the contrary, one may doubt that fathers generally will forgo work and remain at home to care for children to the same extent that mothers may make this choice." *Wiesenfeld,* 420 U.S. at 654–655, n.★ (Powell, J., concurring). Justice Rehnquist concurred in the result without reaching the sex discrimination question. Memorandum from Julia "Penny" Clark to LFP, January 17, 1975, LFP Papers.

102. On Blackmun's evolving attitude toward *Wiesenfeld,* see Linda Greenhouse, *Becoming Justice Blackmun: Harry Blackmun's Supreme Court Journey* (New York: Times Books, 2005), 216–217.

103. *Wiesenfeld,* 420 U.S. at 645, 652.

104. Strebeigh, *Equal,* 75. Strebeigh surmises that Berzon, following clues in Ginsburg's brief, wrote a historical analysis of the origins of the challenged provision that "apparently lifted *Wiesenfeld* to unanimity." Ibid.

105. For more on the importance of *Wiesenfeld* and Ginsburg's often misunderstood reliance on male plaintiffs, see Cary Franklin, "The Anti-Stereotyping Principle in Constitutional Sex Discrimination Law," *New York University Law Review* 85 (2010): 150–159.

106. Bill Barnhart and Gene Schlickman, *John Paul Stevens: An Independent Life* (DeKalb: Northern Illinois University Press, 2010), 206.

107. Ginsburg observed, "The tendency has been to deal with each case in its own frame, and to write an opinion for that case and that day alone." Ruth Bader Ginsburg, "Gender and the Supreme Court: The 1973 and 1974 Terms," *Supreme Court Review* (1975): 22.

108. Craig v. Boren, 429 U.S. 190, 197 (1976).

109. Burger wrote to Brennan, "You read into Reed v. Reed what is not there." WEB to WJB, November 15, 1976, LFP Papers, Folder: Craig v. Boren. Powell's concurrence expressed his reservations about intermediate scrutiny. *Craig,* 429 U.S. at 210–211 (Powell, J., concurring).

110. Memorandum from Tyler Baker to LFP, November 2, 1976, Re: 75-628 Craig v. Boren, LFP Papers; WEB to WJB, November 15, 1976, Re: 75-628 Craig v. Boren, LFP Papers; HAB, Notes, No. 73–78—Kahn v. Shevin, February 18, 1974, 2, HAB Papers, Box 185, Folder 6.

111. Brief for Appellee, 10, 35, Califano v. Goldfarb, 430 U.S 199 (1977) (No. 75-699), 1976 WL 181387.

112. Powell initially thought *Frontiero* and *Wiesenfeld* controlled the outcome, but then had second thoughts. He requested further analysis from his clerk, who found himself in a "quandary." "Aid to Memory" Memorandum of LFP, August 2, 1976, 4–5, Re: 75-699 Mathews v. Goldfarb, LFP Papers; Memorandum from Tyler Baker to LFP, August 12, 1976, 14, Re: 75-699 Matthews v. Goldfarb, LFP Papers.

113. LFP, Conference Notes, October 8, 1976, Re: 75-699 Mathews v. Goldfarb, LFP Papers; Docket Sheet, No. 75-699 Mathews v. Goldfarb, WJB Papers, Box 1:401, Folder 7; HAB Notes, No. 75-699 Mathews v. Goldfarb, September 27, 1976, HAB Papers, Box 241, Folder 5. See also Greenhouse, *Becoming Justice Blackmun,* 219–220.

114. "She's Not Sure about Anti-Male Prejudice," October 6, 1976, RBG Papers, Container 2, Folder: Califano v. Goldfarb: Correspondence, 1976. Justice Powell noted that Ginsburg "simply ducked this" question. LFP, Oral Argument Notes, October 5, 1976, Re: 75-699 Mathews v. Goldfarb, LFP Papers.

115. Ruth Bader Ginsburg to E. Richard Larson, October 14, 1976, RBG Papers, Container 2, Folder: Califano v. Goldfarb: Correspondence, 1976.

116. Ruth Bader Ginsburg to Jane Stevens, Legal Services for the Elderly Poor, October 15, 1976, RBG Papers, Container 2, Folder: Califano v. Goldfarb: Correspondence, 1976.

117. The center Justices wavered during the Court's deliberations in *Goldfarb*. For more, see Serena Mayeri, "Reconstructing the Race-Sex Analogy," *William and Mary Law Review* 49 (2008): 1820–1822. Ginsburg was drawn to Stevens's approach in his concurring opinion. Ruth Bader Ginsburg to John H. Fleming, Sutherland, Asbill & Brennan, August 15, 1977, RBG Papers, Container 2, Folder: Califano v. Goldfarb: Correspondence, 1977–1979; Carol H. Falk, "Social Security Law on Widower Benefits Is Ruled Discriminatory by High Court," WSJ, March 3, 1977, 2.

118. The extension of benefits to widowers cost the government an estimated $200 million annually. Lesley Oelsner, "Social Security Rules Upset over Sex Bias," NYT, March 3, 1977, 69.

119. Under the provision, a female wage earner could exclude from the computation of her average monthly wage three more lower-earning years than a male wage earner for the purposes of calculating benefits.

120. Webster v. Sec'y of Health, Education and Welfare, 413 F. Supp. 127 (E.D.N.Y. May 3, 1976).

121. Jerry Lynch to RBG, March 23, 1977, RBG Papers, Container 2, Folder: Califano v. Goldfarb: Correspondence, 1977–1979. See also Jerry Lynch, Draft 4, No. 76-457 Califano v. Webster [undated], WJB Papers, I: 425, Folder 6.

122. Lynch wrote to Ginsburg, "Dave Barrett tells me you said you felt like kissing Justice Brennan when you heard about *Goldfarb*. If so, you should save at least a handshake for the draftsman." Lynch to RBG, March 23, 1977, 1.

123. Califano v. Webster, 430 U.S. 313, 317, 320-321 (1977) (citation omitted).

124. Ruth Bader Ginsburg to Jerry Lynch, March 28, 1977, RBG Papers, Container 2, Folder: Califano v. Goldfarb: Correspondence, 1977–1979. As Ginsburg later noted, the *Webster* synthesis bore a strong resemblance to the ACLU's brief in *Goldfarb*. Ruth Bader Ginsburg, Chapel Hill Address, September 22, 1978, RBG Papers, Container 14, Folder: Speech File. Justice Powell called the ACLU's *Goldfarb* brief "elaborate and sophisticated." "Aid to Memory" Memorandum of LFP, August 2, 1976, 4.

125. *Webster*, Ginsburg wrote, "attempt[ed] to preserve and bolster a general rule of equal treatment while leaving a corridor open for genuinely compensatory classifications," and clarified "[t]he line between impermissible adverse discrimination and permissible rectification." Ruth Bader Ginsburg, letter to the

editor, *New Republic,* April 30, 1977, 9. See also Ruth Bader Ginsburg, "Women, Equality, and the *Bakke* Case," *Civil Liberties Review,* November–December 1977, 8, 14; Ruth Bader Ginsburg, "Sex Equality and the Constitution: The State of the Art," *Women's Rights Law Reporter,* vol. 4 (1978): 146; Ruth Bader Ginsburg, "Some Thoughts on Benign Classification in the Context of Sex," *Connecticut Law Review* 10 (1978): 824.

126. On the Burger Court's solicitude for suburban women, see Mark V. Tushnet, "The Warren Court as History: An Interpretation," in *The Warren Court in Historical and Political Perspective,* Constitutionalism and Democracy (Charlottesville: University Press of Virginia, 1993), 32.

127. Brief for the Bar Ass'n of San Francisco and the Los Angeles County Bar Ass'n as Amici Curiae Supporting Petitioner, 549–550, *Bakke,* 438 U.S. 265 (No. 76-811); Brief for Petitioner, 177, *Bakke* (No. 76-811); Brief for the State of Washington and the University of Washington as Amicus Curiae, 23, *Bakke* (No. 76-811).

128. Brief for the Bar Ass'n of San Francisco, 45–46, *Bakke* (No. 76-811).

129. On controversy within the administration over its *Bakke* brief, see Laura Kalman, *Right Star Rising: A New Politics, 1974–1980* (New York: W. W. Norton, 2010), 184–201.

130. Brief for the United States as Amicus Curiae, 39–40, 64–65, *Bakke* (No. 76-811).

131. See, for example, United Jewish Organizations v. Carey, 430 U.S. 144, 173–174 (1977) (Brennan, J.); Owen M. Fiss, "Groups and the Equal Protection Clause," *Philosophy and Public Affairs,* Vol. 5, No. 2 (Winter 1976): 107–177; Owen M. Fiss, "A Theory of Fair Employment Laws," *University of Chicago Law Review* 38 (1971): 235.

132. For a rare mention, see John Kaplan, "Equal Justice in an Unequal World: Equality for the Negro—The Problem of Special Treatment," *Northwestern University Law Review* 61 (1966): 365.

133. For additional sources and quotations supporting this section, see Mayeri, "Reconstructing the Race-Sex Analogy."

134. Bob Comfort to LFP, Bench Memo in *Bakke,* August 29, 1977, 16, 35–37, LFP Papers.

135. See WJB, First Working Draft of Bakke, June 9, 1978, 16–23, LFP Papers.

136. WJB to the Conference, 6, 13–14, November 23, 1977, LFP Papers (citation omitted).

137. Though he joined Brennan's opinion, Justice White wrote privately, "I am frank to say that I don't see much help in the gender classification cases, but if they don't rub someone else the wrong way, I don't object." BRW to WJB, Re: 76-811 Regents of the University of California v. Bakke, June 13,

1978, WJB Papers, I:442, Folder 3. Blackmun, on the other hand, expressed to his colleagues his "doubt[s] that the sex classification cases [were] so easily brushed aside [by Powell] just because they [were] 'relatively manageable' and less complex." HAB to the Conference, Re: No. 76-811. Regents of the University of California v. Bakke, May 1, 1978, HAB Papers, Box 260, Folder 8.

138. Regents of the Univ. of Cal. v. Bakke, 438 U.S. 265, 269-272 (1978).

139. Ibid., 300–303.

140. In contrast, Brennan's opinion on behalf of himself, White, Marshall, and Blackmun accepted many elements of the petitioner's analogy to the Court's sex equality jurisprudence. *Bakke,* 438 U.S. at 324, 360, 365 (Brennan, J., concurring in part). Justice Marshall's separate opinion also cited *Webster* as "recogniz[ing] the permissibility of remedying past societal discrimination through the use of otherwise disfavored classifications." *Bakke,* 438 U.S. at 399 (Marshall, J., concurring in part and dissenting in part).

141. See, for example, Anthony Lewis, "A Solomonic Decision," NYT, June 29, 1978, A25.

142. Nancy Gertner, "*Bakke* on Affirmative Action for Women: Pedestal or Cage?" *Harvard Civil Rights–Civil Liberties Law Review* 14 (1979): 173.

143. Ruth Bader Ginsburg, Panel Discussion at the ABA Annual Meeting: Affirmative Action: The Impact of the *Bakke* Decision, August 7, 1978, 6, RBG Papers, Container 13, Folder: Speech File, August 7–30, 1978. See also Ginsburg, "Women, Equality, and the Bakke Case."

144. Ginsburg, Panel Discussion, August 7, 1978, 6–7. See also Gertner, "*Bakke* on Affirmative Action for Women," 189.

145. Gertner, "*Bakke* on Affirmative Action for Women," 191, 194–196.

146. Mieth deposition, cited in Plaintiff's Brief on the Merits, 6, Mieth v. Dothard, 418 F. Supp. 1169, 1174 (M.D. Ala. 1976) (No. 75-433-N), FMJ Papers, Box 111, Folder 10.

147. The quote is from the district court's opinion. Mieth v. Dothard, 418 F. Supp. 1169, 1174 (M.D. Ala. 1976).

148. Plaintiff's Brief on the Merits, 7, 9, 12, 21, *Dothard* (No. 75-433-N), FMJ Papers, Box 111, Folder 10.

149. The third judge on the case was Robert E. Varner.

150. For a description of the Department of Public Safety's compliance efforts, see Compliance Report, Mieth v. Dothard, Civ. Action No. 75-433-N, December 28, 1976, FMJ Papers, Box 111, Folder 11, LOC; State of Alabama Board of Corrections, Administrative Regulation 206, Equal Employment Opportunity Program Affirmative Action Plan, August 11, 1976, FMJ Papers, Box 111, Folder 11.

151. Colonel E. C. Dothard, Director, Alabama State Troopers, news release, June 12, 1976; Phyllis Wesley, "Moral, Morale Troubles Viewed," *Daily Ledger,* July 30, 1976; "Stewart Speaks to Rotary Club," *Selma Shopper,* July 22, 1976; "The Un-Welcome Mat," *Troy Messenger,* July 18, 1976.

152. "Your Career in the Alabama State Troopers," 3; "Outfitting Woman Trooper Not What It Seamed to Be," *Alabama Journal,* July 27, 1976; *Observer* (Pell City, AL), August 12, 1976, 12; Radio Spots—Recruitment, July 1976; Greg MacArthur, "Hiring Limits Erased," *Montgomery Advertiser,* July 1, 1976. All of the sources cited in this and the previous note were found in FMJ Papers, Box 111, Folder 11.

153. One woman was scheduled to begin training the following year, out of fifty trainees.

154. Ala. Code, Tit. 36-26-15 (1975). In order to be considered for a job opening, an applicant for the state trooper position had to be in one of the top three positions on the eligibility lists, which were compiled separately by race under the state's affirmative action plan. Ranking on the eligibility lists was determined by adding applicable veterans' preference points to an applicant's score on an exam.

155. Motion for Reconsideration, 6, Mieth v. Dothard, Civ. Action No. 75-433-N, June 27, 1978, FMJ Papers, Box 111, Folder 10.

156. Order, Mieth v. Hilyer, Civ. Action No. 75-433-N, June 29, 1978, FMJ Papers Box 111, Folder 10; Judge Frank M. Johnson, Jr. to Honorable Richard T. Rives and Honorable Robert E. Varner, June 6, 1978, FMJ Papers, Box 111, Folder 10.

157. For a contemporaneous summary of various forms of veterans' preference, see John H. Fleming and Charles A. Shanor, "Veterans' Preferences in Public Employment: Unconstitutional Gender Discrimination?" *Emory Law Journal* 26 (1977): 13–64.

158. Linda Kerber, *No Constitutional Right to Be Ladies: Women and the Obligations of Citizenship,* 1st ed. (New York: Hill and Wang, 1998), 227–229.

159. Resolution quoted in Report of the Compliance Task Force, September 1971–September 1972, October 7, 1972, WSH Papers, 72-120–74-233, Carton 1, Folder: Board related.

160. The Civil Rights Commission proposed that veterans should only be allowed to exercise their preferences for a maximum of five years after leaving the service. Ernest Holsendolph, "Action to Assure Job Rights Urged," NYT, July 20, 1975, 23.

161. In southern California, for example, NOW, the League of Women Voters, and other groups lobbied local authorities to reconsider such preferences in light of their disproportionate impact on women's employment opportunities. See "County Votes Job Preference for Veterans," LAT, May 2, 1973, E3;

Celeste Durant, "Veterans' Point Bonus on City Job Exams May Face Vote Test," LAT, September 3, 1974, B1; Mike Ward, "Veteran Preference: A Lifetime Benefit?" LAT, January 12, 1975, SG1; Don Snyder, "Hearing Set on Veterans' Preference," LAT, July 25, 1976, GB1. On New Jersey, see "Job Status Accorded to Veterans May Change," NYT, February 16, 1975, NJ86.

162. Editorial, "The Preference Is Unfair," LAT, February 7, 1978, C6.

163. Judith Lonnquist, National Legal Vice President, NOW, to Sylvia Roberts and Marilyn Patel, September 22, 1973, NOW LDEF papers, 86-M94, Carton 4, Folder: Veteran's Preference; Ruth B. Cowan, "Women's Rights through Litigation: An Examination of the American Civil Liberties Union Women's Rights Project, 1971–1976," *Columbia Human Rights Law Review* 8 (1976): 392.

164. Kerber, *No Constitutional Right to Be Ladies,* 236.

165. See Linda Charlton, "Support in Congress Rated Good for Carter Civil Service Changes," NYT, March 4, 1978, 8; Associated Press, "Veterans' Preference Limits Won't Be OKd, Cranston Says," LAT, March 10, 1978, B10.

166. Celeste Durant, "Veterans' Point Bonus on City Job Exams May Face Vote Test," LAT, September 3, 1974, B1.

167. See, for example, Warren Weaver, Jr., "Veterans' Preference: How Much Is Enough?" NYT, January 15, 1978, E7.

168. See, for example, Franklin D. Epstein, letter to the editor, LAT, February 24, 1978, C6.

169. John Wasylik, Commander-in-Chief, Veterans of Foreign Wars of the United States, letter to the editor, WSJ, August 25, 1978, 8.

170. "Veterans Win Fight to Keep Job Preference," in *Congress and the Nation,* vol. 5 (Washington, DC: CQ Press, 1981), 836. The administration figures revealed that women were much better represented at the lowest levels of federal government employment, holding 77.3 percent of job at levels GS-1 to GS-4.

171. Erwin Baker, "Women Win Key City Hall Battle," LAT, February 8, 1978, D2.

172. See, for example, Jerry Flint, "Change in Veteran Preference Tied to Civil Service Reform, NYT, May 13,1978, 9.

173. Charles G. Gant, letter to the editor, LAT, February 24, 1978, C6.

174. Wilma Scott Heide, "Revolution: Tomorrow Is NOW!" Keynote Address at the Sixth National Conference of NOW, at Statler Hilton Hotel, Washington, DC, February 17, 1973, WSH Papers, 72-120–74-233, Box 4, Folder: WSH Testimony.

175. Leroy Knox, letter to the editor, "Who Benefits Most from 'Affirmative Action'?" *Philadelphia Tribune,* October 31, 1978, 6.

176. Regents v. Bakke, 438 U.S. 265, 406 (Blackmun, J.).

177. *Civil Service Reform Act of 1978: Hearings on S. 2640, S. 2707, and S. 2830, April 13, 1978, Before the Committee on Governmental Affairs,* U.S. Senate, 95th Cong., 2d. Sess. 710 (testimony of Mae M. Walterhouse, National President, Federally Employed Women).

178. Ellen Goodman, "Against Affirmative Action—Veterans' Preference," LAT, January 15, 1979, C7.

179. See, for example, Grace Ganz Blumberg, "De Facto and de Jure Sex Discrimination under the Equal Protection Clause: A Reconsideration of the Veterans' Preference in Public Employment," *Buffalo Law Review* 26 (1976), 1, 21.

180. Castro v. Beecher, 459 F.2d 725, 732 (1st Cir. 1972). As law professor Grace Ganz Blumberg observed in 1977, the years 1971–1976 witnessed a "short-lived constitutionalization of *Griggs.*" This constitutionalization of *Griggs* in the public employment context became less consequential overall after the 1972 amendments applied Title VII to public employers, but not in the realm of veterans' preferences, for which Title VII provided an explicit statutory exemption.

181. Feinerman v. Jones, 356 F. Supp. 252, 261–262 (M.D. Pa. 1973).

182. Ginsburg noted that the "ACLU has not done well in the past in veterans' preferences cases." RBG to John H. Fleming, January 22, 1975, RBG Papers, Container 4, Folder: Kahn v. Shevin, 1973–1975.

183. In another footnote, Judge Tauro distinguished *Geduldig.* See Anthony v. Massachusetts, 415 F. Supp. 487, 498, 504 notes 7–8 (D. Mass. 1976).

184. *Anthony,* 415 F. Supp at 501 (Campbell, J., concurring).

185. *Anthony,* 415 F. Supp. at 504 (Murray, J., dissenting).

186. Plaintiffs' Supplementary Memorandum of Law, Feeney v. Commonwealth of Mass., Civil Action No. 75-1991-T, (D. Mass), NOW LDEF Papers, 95-M99, Carton 5, Folder: Feeney—Legal File.

187. Tauro found that the extent of the veterans' preference's disparate impact on women was sufficient evidence of intent, while Campbell relied, in his more measured concurrence, on the "inevitability" of the disproportionate effects. Feeney v. Mass., 451 F. Supp. 143 (D. Mass. 1978). Again in dissent, Judge Murray found the "attempted distinction between the test in *Davis* and the statute here . . . totally unconvincing." *Feeney,* 451 F. Supp. at 153 (Murray, J., dissenting).

188. Then-DOJ Civil Rights Division attorney Bob Reinstein recalls that he attempted to draft a brief on Feeney's behalf and felt stymied by the federal government's investment in various preferences for veterans. Author conversation with Bob Reinstein, February 15, 2010.

189. Biographical details on McCree are from The United States Department of Justice website, accessed October 24, 2009, http://www.usdoj.gov/osg/aboutosg/wadebio.html.

190. See correspondence contained in [Bell, Griffin B.] SG[Solicitor General]/Veterans Preference, Subject Files of the Attorney General, Container 100, Record Group 60, NARA—College Park, MD [hereinafter Bell File]. The SG's *Feeney* brief took a somewhat less equivocal position than the U.S. presentation in *Bakke:* while emphasizing the importance of looking beneath the facial neutrality of a law to discern discriminatory purpose, the brief rejected the district court's capacious conception of intent. See Brief for the United States, Personnel Administrator v. Feeney, 442 U.S. 256 (1979) (No. 78-233).

191. See, for example, Mailgram from Phyllis Segal, NOW LDEF Legal Director, to President Carter et al., December 3, 1978, NOW LDEF Papers, 95-M99, Carton 5, Folder: Feeney correspondence; Ira Glasser, Executive Director, ACLU, to Anne Wexler, Special Assistant to the President, December 20, 1978, RBG Papers, Container 31, Folder: Massachusetts v. Feeney, 1978–1979.

192. Rep. Robert F. Drinan et al., to Griffin Bell, December 6, 1978, Bell File; Telegram from Gov. Michael Dukakis to Griffin Bell, December 8, 1978, Bell File.

193. Ruth Bader Ginsburg and Phyllis Segal, Memorandum to the Attorney General, December 7, 1978, Re: Massachusetts v. Feeney, Bell File.

194. See, for example, Memorandum from Wade McCree, Jr. to Patricia M. Wald, Assistant AG, Office of Legislative Affairs, December 13, 1978, Bell File; Memorandum from J. Philip Jordan to Griffin Bell, December 19, 1978, Re: Veterans' Preference Case, Bell File; Frank H. Easterbrook, Memorandum for the SG, December 8, 1978, Re: The Ginsburg-Segal Memorandum on *Feeney,* Bell File.

195. Memorandum from Patricia M. Wald to Griffin Bell, December 11, 1978, Re: Supplemental Filing in *Feeney* Case; Memorandum from Eleanor Holmes Norton to Alan K. Campbell, Carin A. Clauss, and Patricia M. Wald, December 22, 1978, and attached letter from Norton to Wade McCree, Jr., December 21, 1978, Bell File.

196. Frank H. Easterbrook, Memorandum for the Solicitor General, February 1, 1979, Re: Personnel Administrator of Massachusetts v. Feeney; Memorandum from William C. Bryson to the Solicitor General, January 30, 1979, Bell File.

197. Frank H. Easterbrook, Memorandum for the Solicitor General, February 3, 1979, Re: Personnel Administrator of Massachusetts v. Feeney, Bell File.

198. Brief for the Appellee, 24, *Feeney* (No. 78-233) (quoting Craig v. Boren, 429 U.S. 190, 198–199 (1976)) (citations omitted).

199. Brief of NOW et al., 16, *Feeney,* (No. 78-233).

200. Brief of Appellees, 27, 31, *Feeney* (No. 78-233).

201. Brief of NOW et al., 3, *Feeney* (No. 78-233).

202. Blumberg, "De Facto and de Jure," 40; Ginsburg-Segal memo, (December) 7, 1978.

203. Brief of NOW et al., 6 n.2, *Feeney* (No. 78-233). The brief also cited the grandfather clause cases. Ibid., 13.

204. Quoted in Kerber, *No Constitutional Right to Be Ladies,* 236.

205. Brief of the Washington Legal Foundation as Amicus Curiae, 16, *Feeney* (No. 78-233).

206. Kenneth Labich et al, "Women vs. Veterans," *Newsweek,* March 5, 1979, 59. See also Brief for the United States as Amicus Curiae, *Feeney* (No. 78-233), 1978 WL 207300, *7–8. The women's organizations' brief was joined and partially written by the American Jewish Committee, which had taken an ambivalent position in *Bakke*—opposing the U.C. Davis program as a "quota" but endorsing other forms of affirmative action.

207. See Phyllis Segal to Ruth Bader Ginsburg, Re: Feeney Amicus Brief, December 17, 1978, NOW LDEF Papers, 95-M99, Carton 5, Folder: Feeney Correspondence. ("You will note that citations to *Bakke* are sprinkled throughout. Do you think we should tie the analogy together more directly?")

208. Brief of NOW et al., 7, 23, *Feeney* (No. 78-233); Brief of the Appellee, 28, 60, *Feeney* (No. 78-233).

209. LFP Draft concurrence in Feeney, May 8, 1979, 78-233 Personnel Administrator of Massachusetts v. Feeney, LFP Papers.

210. HAB, Notes, Admin. v. Feeney, 78-233, February 24, 1979, HAB Papers, Box 293, Folder 1.

211. Powell did not want "to place equal protection analysis on an 'effects' basis comparable to Title VII." LFP to David [Westin], 3, February 20, 1979, 78-233 Personnel Administrator v. Feeney, LFP Papers.

212. Powell wrote in the margin, "Yes." "Bobtail Bench Memorandum," from David W[estin] to LFP, February 26, 1979, 6, 78-233 Personnel Administrator v. Feeney, LFP Papers.

213. LFP, Oral Argument Notes, 78-233 Personnel Administrator v. Feeney, LFP Papers.

214. Clerk William McDaniel wrote to Blackmun, "The opinion was written by Ginny Kerr, with whom we had breakfast today. She was (and is, I assume) opposed personally to the Court's judgment in this case. I believe that accounts for the opinion's sharp criticisms of vets' preference statutes and its

emphasis of the history, such as it is, of women in the military." Memorandum from William McDaniel, Jr., to HAB, May 8, 1979, Re: No. 78-233, Personnel Administrator v. Feeney, HAB Papers, Box 293, Folder 1. McDaniel, too, was uncomfortable with the outcome in Feeney. He had written to Blackmun, "I find this a hard case to make a recommendation on: not so much because it is difficult analytically, but because I am out of sympathy with the result I believe *Washington v. Davis* and *Arlington Heights* require." Bench Memorandum from William McDaniel, Jr. to HAB, February 23, 1979, Re: Personnel Administrator v. Feeney, HAB Papers, Box 293, Folder 1.

215. Personnel Administrator v. Feeney, 442 U.S. 256, 272–279 (1979).

216. Linda Greenhouse, "High Court Upholds a Civil Service Edge for Wars' Veterans," NYT, June 6, 1979, A1.

217. Quoted in Sheila Rule, "Veterans and Feminists Clash on Hiring Decision," NYT, June 6, 1979, A17.

218. FEW, Press Release, June 6, 1979, NOW LDEF Papers, 95-M99, Carton 5, Folder: Feeney press.

219. Linda Greenhouse, "Women's Rights v. Court: Scorecard Less Than Even," NYT, June 10, 1979, E20.

220. See, for example, Reva Siegel, "Why Equal Protection No Longer Protects: The Evolving Forms of Status-Enforcing State Action," *Stanford Law Review* 49 (1997): 1111.

221. Brief for the Appellant, 8, Califano v. Westcott, 443 U.S. 76 (1979) (Nos. 78-437, 78-689), 1979 WL 199804.

222. On feminism and welfare reform during the Carter administration, see Marissa Chappell, *The War on Welfare: Family, Poverty, and Politics in Modern America* (Philadelphia: University of Pennsylvania Press, 2010), Chapter 4.

223. Thomas Merrill to HAB, Bench Memorandum, Califano v. Westcott, No. 78-437, April 9, 1979, 23, HAB Papers, Box 294, Folder 5.

224. LFP Conference Notes, Califano v. Westcott, No. 78-437, March 18, 1979. In the end, four Justices dissented from the majority's secondary ruling that extended benefits to families with unemployed mothers, rather than invalidating the law and leaving extension up to Congress.

225. For a compelling argument that *Personnel Administrator v. Feeney*, too, fundamentally challenged the male breadwinner/female homemaker model, see Melissa Murray, "Made with Men in Mind: The GI Bill and Its Reinforcement of Gendered Work after World War II," in *Feminist Legal History: Essays on Women and Law*, ed. Tracy Thomas and Tracey Jean Boisseau (New York: New York University Press, 2011).

226. Califano v. Westcott, 443 U.S. 76, 77 (1979).

227. RBG to Stephen Wiesenfeld, May 31, 1979, RBG Papers, Container 10, Folder: Weinberger v. Wiesenfeld Correspondence 1976–1980.

228. RBG to Gerald Gunther, June 29, 1979, RBG Papers, Container 2, Folder: Califano v. Westcott, 1978–1979.

5. Lost Intersections

1. Carrie N. Baker, *The Women's Movement against Sexual Harassment* (Cambridge: Cambridge University Press, 2008), 16–17, 56; Miller v. Bank of America, 418 F. Supp. 233 (N.D. Cal. 1976); Munford v. James T. Barnes and Company, 441 F. Supp. 459 (E.D. Mich. 1977); Continental Can Company v. Minnesota, 297 Nw. 2d. 241 (Minn. 1980).

2. Paulette Barnes, the plaintiff in the first successful sexual harassment case at the appellate level, is one example. See Baker, *Women's Movement,* 16–17, 180–184; Carrie N. Baker, "Race, Class, and Sexual Harassment in the 1970s," *Feminist Studies* 30 (2004): 14–15; Barnes v. Costle, 561 F.2d 983 (D.C. Cir. 1977).

3. For more on Norton's role in the development of sexual harassment law, see Baker, *Women's Movement;* Baker, "Race, Class, and Sexual Harassment in the 1970s," 14–15.

4. Catharine MacKinnon, *Sexual Harassment of Working Women* (New Haven, CT: Yale University Press, 1979). See also Fred Strebeigh, *Equal: Women Reshape American Law* (New York: W.W. Norton, 2009), Chapter 16.

5. See, for example, Plaintiff-Appellants' Brief, Tomkins v. Public Service Electric and Gas Company, 568 F.2d 1044 (3d Cir. 1977) reprinted in Carrie N. Baker, *How Did Diverse Activists in the Second Wave of the Women's Movement Shape Emerging Public Policy on Sexual Harassment?* (Binghamton, NY: State University of New York at Binghamton, 2005), Document 23; Comment, "Employment Discrimination—Sexual Harassment and Title VII," *New York University Law Review* 51 (1976): 148–167. The leading racial harassment case was Rogers v. EEOC, 454 F.2d 234 (5th Cir. 1971).

6. Judges in early cases were skeptical of sexual harassment claims, seeing them as "personal," "sexual" rather than discriminatory, and prone to turn every harmless office flirtation into a federal case. On the early decisions, see MacKinnon, *Sexual Harassment,* 57–99; Baker, *Women's Movement,* 15–26. Reva Siegel (a former clerk to Judge Spottswood Robinson) has read Robinson's landmark ruling in *Barnes v. Costle* as reasoning from race in order to understand sexual harassment as sex discrimination that "perpetuat[ed] group status inequalities." Reva B. Siegel, "A Short History of Sexual Harassment," in *Directions in Sexual Harassment Law,* ed. Reva B. Siegel and Catharine MacKinnon (New Haven, CT: Yale University Press, 2003), 11–18. Correspondence in the files of Judge George MacKinnon suggests that Robinson's reasoning from race also helped to convince his initially dubious colleagues of the merit of Paulette Barnes's claim.

See George MacKinnon Papers, File 74–2026, 142-B-16-13-B, Minnesota Historical Society. For an intriguing account of the deliberations in *Barnes v. Costle,* see Strebeigh, *Equal,* Chapters 16–17.

7. See Baker, "Race, Class, and Sexual Harassment in the 1970s," 12–13.

8. The Alliance Against Sexual Coercion (AASC)'s comments on the EEOC's proposed sexual harassment guidelines contended that black women had been "discouraged from filing race discrimination complaints because of prevailing attitudes, media presentations of the issue, and the history of complaints of sexual harassment being filed as Title VII *sex* discrimination suits." AASC warned: "Although sexual harassment may be directed at *any* woman, it may at times be used as a tool to discriminate against a woman not *because* of her sex but *because* of her race, age, etc. In particular, we have assisted Black women harassed by their white male supervisors, a number of whom have articulated and documented their belief that the harassment (comments about their sexuality, sexual jokes, demands for sexual favors, etc.) was a form of race discrimination. It was designed either to (1) keep them as *black* women in unequal positions to whites in the workplace, or (2) encourage them to quit their jobs because as *black* women they were not wanted in the workplace. Or, the harassment was directed at them rather than at white women because of myths and other discriminatory practices which made them seem to be more vulnerable targets." Denise Wells, Alliance Against Sexual Coercion, to EEOC, June 6, 1980, reprinted in Baker, *How Did Diverse Activists,* Document 33C. See also Baker, "Race, Class, and Sexual Harassment in the 1970s," 21–22.

9. Historians have noted the pioneering role of African American women in the passage and early implementation of Title VII and in organizations like the ACLU. See, for example, Susan Hartmann, *The Other Feminists: Activists in the Liberal Establishment* (New Haven, CT: Yale University Press, 1998); Alice Kessler-Harris, *In Pursuit of Equity: Women, Men, and the Quest for Economic Citizenship in Twentieth-Century America* (Oxford: Oxford University Press, 2001); Nancy MacLean, *Freedom Is Not Enough: The Opening of the American Workplace* (Cambridge, MA: Harvard University Press, 2006). Black women's predominance as plaintiffs in early sexual harassment cases is widely recognized in legal scholarship and among historians. See, for example, Baker, *Women's Movement;* Kimberle Crenshaw, "Race, Gender, and Sexual Harassment," *Southern California Law Review* 65 (1992): 1467–1476; Siegel, "A Short History of Sexual Harassment." However, the role of African Americans and what scholars later would call "intersectionality" in constitutional sex equality cases has remained largely hidden from view. One notable exception is Linda Kerber's excellent treatment of the jury service cases, though this is not the primary focus of her

account. See Linda K. Kerber, *No Constitutional Right to Be Ladies: Women and the Obligations of American Citizenship* (New York: Hill and Wang, 1998).

10. See United States v. Tunica County School District, 323 F. Supp. 1019 (N.D. Miss. July 16, 1970).

11. On the struggle to desegregate the Drew school system, see Constance Curry, *Silver Rights* (San Diego, CA: Harcourt, Brace, 1995).

12. Jane Dailey, "Sex, Segregation, and the Sacred after *Brown*," *Journal of American History* 91 (2004): 119–144.

13. For more on moral regulation as resistance to desegregation, see Anders Walker, *The Ghost of Jim Crow: How Southern Moderates Used Brown v. Board of Education to Stall Civil Rights* (Oxford: Oxford University Press, 2009).

14. On the civil rights struggle in the Mississippi Delta, see Charles M. Payne, *I've Got the Light of Freedom: The Organizing Tradition and the Mississippi Freedom Struggle* (Berkeley: University of California Press, 2007); John Dittmer, *Local People: The Struggle for Civil Rights in Mississippi* (Urbana: University of Illinois Press, 1994).

15. Quoted in Kay Mills, *This Little Light of Mine: The Life of Fannie Lou Hamer* (New York: Dutton, 1993), 287.

16. See Rickie Solinger, *Wake up Little Susie: Single Pregnancy and Race after Roe v. Wade*, 2nd ed. (New York: Routledge, 2000).

17. As a college graduate, Andrews could make $5,400 in nine months as a teacher's aide in the recently desegregated public schools, compared with a similar amount in a year at her factory job. A high school graduate like Rogers would earn $3,000 per year. By comparison, the Aid to Families with Dependent Children (AFDC) benefits available to a single unemployed mother with one child in Mississippi totaled $360 annually, supplemented by food stamps worth $760 per year.

18. William C. Keady, *All Rise: Memoirs of a Mississippi Federal Judge*, limited ed. (Boston: Recollections Bound, 1988), 97.

19. Green v. New Kent County School Board, 391 U.S. 430 (1968).

20. Keady, *All Rise*, 104–106.

21. See Gates v. Collier, 349 F. Supp. 881 (N.D. Miss. 1972); H. Eric Semler, "William C. Keady, 76, U.S. Judge in Overhaul of Mississippi Prisons," NYT, June 18, 1989, 30; David M. Oshinsky, *Worse Than Slavery: Parchman Farm and the Ordeal of Jim Crow Justice* (New York: Simon and Schuster, 1996).

22. See Keady, *All Rise*.

23. Oral History: Charles Victor McTeer, Delta Project, Community Studies Archives, Dickinson College, Carlisle, PA.

24. Mills, *This Little Light of Mine*, 241–246.

25. Appendix, 101, Drew Municipal Separate School District v. Andrews 423 U.S. 820 (1975) (No. 74-1318).

26. Ibid., 126.

27. Ibid., 142.

28. Ibid., 102–103, 106–107, 109.

29. Carter v. Drew Municipal Separate School District, 451 F. 2d 599 (5th Cir. 1971). The Carters were represented by NAACP LDF lawyers, including Marian Wright and Jack Greenberg. On the Carter family's struggle, see Curry, *Silver Rights*.

30. Appendix, 113-114, *Andrews* (No. 74-1318). For more on school desegregation in Mississippi, see Charles C. Bolton, *The Hardest Deal of All: The Battle Over School Integration in Mississippi, 1870–1980* (Jackson: University Press of Mississippi, 2005).

31. Appendix, 188, 192, 196–197, 199, *Andrews,* (No. 74-1318).

32. McTeer also relied on Title VI of the Civil Rights Act, which prohibited racial discrimination by entities receiving federal funds.

33. Parham v. Southwestern Bell, 1969 WL 109, *9.

34. EEOC Decision No. 71-332, 1970 WL 3569, 1 (EEOC).

35. 321 N.Y.S. 2d 493, 450, 451 (N.Y. Sup. Ct. Apr. 30, 1971). On New York's progressive case law, see William E. Nelson, *The Legalist Reformation: Law, Politics, and Ideology in New York, 1920–1980* (Chapel Hill: University of North Carolina Press, 2001).

36. See San Antonio v. Rodriguez, 411 U.S. 1 (1973); Geduldig v. Aiello, 417 U.S. 484 (1974).

37. Brief for the Center for Constitutional Rights (CCR) as Amicus Curiae, 13-14, Andrews v. Drew Municipal Separate School District, 371 F. Supp. 27 (N.D. Miss. 1973) (No. GC 73-20-K), WCK Papers.

38. Ibid. The brief cited Reed v. Reed and Sail'er Inn v. Kirby (see Chapter 2).

39. As the EEOC's brief put it, "Courts have increasingly applied Title VII guidelines to determine the constitutionality of a state practice under the equal protection clause." Brief of the EEOC as Amicus Curiae, *Andrews* (District Court), WCK Papers.

40. Brief for CCR, 16, *Andrews* (District Court), WCK Papers.

41. McTeer's original filings did not emphasize reproductive freedom. CCR's briefs made procreative choice central to the constitutional questions presented by *Andrews*.

42. Author interview with Rhonda Copelon, March 2, 2009.

43. Motion for Leave to Participate as Amicus Curiae (and affidavit of Rhonda Copelon), March 16, 1973, *Andrews* (District Court), WCK Papers.

44. See Chapter 2.

45. Appendix, 94, *Andrews* (No. 74-1318). Even if Andrews had wished to terminate her pregnancy, to do so would likely have been a criminal act prior to

Roe v. Wade. On abortion in the pre-*Roe* years, see Leslie J. Reagan, *When Abortion Was a Crime: Women, Medicine, and Law in the United States, 1867–1973* (Berkeley: University of California Press, 1997).

46. See Chana Kai Lee, *For Freedom's Sake: The Life of Fannie Lou Hamer* (Urbana: University of Illinois Press, 1999), 80–81.

47. See Jennifer Nelson, *Women of Color and the Reproductive Rights Movement* (New York: New York University Press, 2003), Chapter 5. On race and fertility control, see Dorothy Roberts, *Killing the Black Body: Race, Reproduction, and the Meaning of Liberty* (New York: Random House, 1997). For more on the history of eugenic sterilization, see Alexandra Minna Stern, *Eugenic Nation: Faults and Frontiers of Better Breeding in Modern America* (Berkeley: University of California Press, 2005).

48. Complaint, Relf v. Weinberger, Civ. A. No. 73-1557 (U.S. District Court for the District of Columbia) (filed July 17, 1973).

49. For more on *Relf*, see Lisa Ikemoto, "Infertile by Force and Federal Complicity: The Story of *Relf v. Weinberger*," in *Women and the Law Stories*, ed. Elizabeth M. Schneider and Stephanie M. Wildman (New York: Foundation Press, 2010), 179–206.

50. Andrews v. Drew Municipal Separate School District, 371 F. Supp. 27, 33–36 (N.D. Miss. 1973).

51. Author interview with Rhonda Copelon, March 2, 2009.

52. Letter to the editor, *Jackson Clarion-Ledger*, n.d., WCK Papers.

53. [Unsigned handwritten note, n.d.], WCK Papers.

54. Frank Wallace and H.V. Mahan to Judge William C. Keady, July 27, 1973, WCK Papers.

55. Andrews v. Drew Municipal Separate School District, 507 F.2d 611, 617 n.10 (5th Cir. 1975).

56. The panel included Judges Griffin Bell, John Simpson, and Joe Ingraham.

57. Petition for a Writ of Certiorari, Drew Municipal Separate School District v. Katie Mae Andrews et al., 7-8, 423 U.S. 820 (1975) (No. 74-1318).

58. Brief for the Petitioners, 30, *Andrews* (No. 74-1318).

59. Plaintiffs' Supplemental Memorandum of Law in Support of the Motion for a Preliminary Injunction, *Andrews* (District Court), March 27, 1973, WCK Papers.

60. Records of the Center for Constitutional Rights, Schomburg Center for Research in Black Culture, Box 127 (unprocessed).

61. Brief for Respondents, 69-71, *Andrews* (No. 74-1318).

62. The Court granted certiorari in Washington v. Davis in October 1975.

63. The plaintiffs were careful to distinguish *Andrews,* an employment case, from cases involving social welfare benefits, in which the Court had found

disparate impact insufficient to trigger an equal protection violation. See Jefferson v. Hackney, 406 U.S. 535 (1972); Dandridge v. Williams, 397 U.S. 471 (1970).

64. Brief for Respondents, 69, n. 42, *Andrews* (No. 74-1318). For more on the evolution of van den Haag's racial views, see John P. Jackson, Jr., *Science for Segregation: Race, Law, and the Case Against Brown v. Board of Education* (New York: New York University Press, 2005).

65. Copelon recalled receiving this information from the "Inc. Fund, the NAACP LDF" Author interview with Rhonda Copelon, March 2, 2009.

66. Respondents' Supplemental Brief Pursuant to Rule 42(5), 3-4, *Andrews* (No. 74-1318).

67. Stanley v. Illinois, 400 U.S. 1020 (1971).

68. See Chapter 3.

69. Motion for Leave to File Brief Amici Curiae and Brief Amici Curiae of Equal Rights Advocates, Inc. and the ACLU, 46-47, *Andrews* (No. 74-1318).

70. ACLU/ERA Brief, 46, *Andrews* (No. 74-1318).

71. The Supreme Court's "illegitimacy" jurisprudence was criticized, then and since, as incoherent. See, for example, Earl M. Maltz, "Illegitimacy and Equal Protection," *Arizona State Law Journal* (1980): 831–851.

72. Levy v. Louisiana, 391 U.S. 68 (1968); Weber v. Aetna Casualty and Surety Company, 406 U.S. 164 (1972); Gomez v. Perez, 409 U.S. 535 (1973) (per curiam); New Jersey Welfare Rights Organization v. Cahill, 411 U.S. 619 (1973) (per curiam).

73. See Martha F. Davis, "Male Coverture: Law and the Illegitimate Family," *Rutgers Law Review* 56 (2003): 73–118.

74. Brief for the Child Welfare League of America, 65, *Andrews* (No. 74-1318).

75. Author interview with Rhonda Copelon, March 2, 2009; Nelson, *Women of Color and the Reproductive Rights Movement.*

76. For a fascinating discussion, see Deborah Dinner, "Recovering the *LaFleur* Doctrine," *Yale Journal of Law and Feminism* 22 (2010).

77. Brief for the Petitioners, 73, *Andrews* (No. 74-1318) (citing Cleveland Board of Education v. LaFleur).

78. Author interview with Rhonda Copelon, March 2, 2009.

79. See LFP, Handwritten notes on cert pool memo, *Andrews,* LFP Papers.

80. Brief for the National Educational Association as Amicus Curiae, 7, *Andrews* (No. 74-1318).

81. Mason, Preliminary Memorandum, Re: Drew Municipal Separate School District v. Andrews, July 11, 1975, LFP Papers. Powell was determined to avoid a reprise of *LaFleur,* in which Stewart's majority opinion had resolved

what Powell believed was an equal protection question on a dubious due process theory. Powell clerk Penny Clark did not think the case was close: the school district had summarily disqualified teachers from employment without granting them so much as a hearing. Powell initially responded, "Altho[ugh] reasons of CA5 may be questioned (I'm not sure of this), I think result was right." Accordingly, he saw "no purpose in taking" the case.

82. Carl R. Schencker to LFP, Bobtail Memorandum, January 23, 1976, Re: Drew Municipal Separate School Dist. v. Andrews, LFP Papers.

83. Ibid.

84. HAB Notes, No. 74-1318, Drew Municipal Separate School District v. Andrews, 5–8, February 17, 1976, HAB Papers, Box 223, Folder 1. Like Powell, Blackmun hoped to avoid the irrebuttable presumption theory. "I hope we have rounded the turn and will never follow that road again." Ibid.

85. HAB, Oral Argument Notes, No. 74-1318, Drew Municipal Separate School District v. Andrews, March 3, 1976, HAB Papers, Box 223, Folder 1.

86. 40 Fed. Reg. 24140, 24144, Sections 86.60(a), 86.57(a)(1) and (b).

87. 40 Fed. Reg. 24143.

88. Brief for the NEA, 10-11, *Andrews* (No. 74-1318).

89. Memorandum for the United States as Amicus Curiae, 1, *Andrews* (No. 74-1318), 1976 WL 181172.

90. HAB, Conference Notes, Drew Municipal Separate School District v. Andrews, No. 74-1318, March 5, 1976, HAB Papers, Box 223, Folder 1.

91. Nelson, *Women of Color and the Reproductive Rights Movement;* Author interview with Rhonda Copelon, March 2, 2009.

92. See Martha F. Davis, *Brutal Need: Lawyers and the Welfare Rights Movement* (New Haven, CT: Yale University Press, 1993); Davis, "Male Coverture."

93. Later cases involving unwed mothers as teachers included Reinhardt v. Alton Community Unit Sch. Dist., 1973 WL 15004 (Ill. Cir. Ct.); Wardlaw v. Austin Indep. Sch. Dist., 1975 WL 182 (W.D.Tex.); Leechburg Area Sch. Dist. v. Penn. Hum. Rel. Comm'n, 339 A.2d 850 (Pa. Cmwlth. Ct. 1975).

94. Some material from this section is drawn from Serena Mayeri, "The Strange Career of Jane Crow: Sex Segregation and the Transformation of Anti-Discrimination Discourse," *Yale Journal of Law and the Humanities* 18 (2006): 187–272. More extensive discussion and citations can be found therein.

95. Arthur Krock, "In the Nation: 'Gradual,' in the Frame of History," NYT, March 27, 1956, 34.

96. Mitchell Rawson, letter to the editor, "Segregation by Sexes," NYT, December 2, 1954, 30.

97. United States v. Carroll County, No. 6541K (N.D.Miss 1969), quoted in Order, United States v. Lincoln County, Nos. 1400 and 1420 (S.D. Ga. Apr. 27, 1970).

98. Brief of Appellants, at 9, Smith v. Concordia Parish Sch. Bd., No. 28342 (5th Cir. October 1, 1969) NARA, Southwest Regional Division, RG 276, Fifth Circuit Case Files, Box 4235, 28342–28349.

99. See Mayeri, "Strange Career of Jane Crow," 209–217.

100. Ibid., 217–224.

101. The suit was filed on behalf of Kenlee Helwig by her parents, Carl and Jeanne Helwig, and William Helis by his parents, Kathleen and James Helis. "Sex Separation in Schools Hit," *New Orleans Times-Picayune,* August 2, 1974, sec.1, 6. Later, Peebles filed another suit on behalf of two other female students, challenging the constitutionality of the Louisiana statute authorizing sex-segregated school assignments. "Suit Attacks Jeff Non-Coed School Setup," *New Orleans Times-Picayune,* July 20, 1976, sec. 1, 1.

102. Joyce Trotter, interview with Superintendent Bertucci, October 13, 1969, Mindy Milam Papers, NCCRW, Box 1—NAC 284.

103. Mauna P. Brooke, quoted in Fred Barry, "Jefferson Board Tables Coed Vote," *New Orleans Times-Picayune,* February 8, 1973, sec. 1, 3. See also Mayeri, "Strange Career of Jane Crow," 230–237.

104. Note, "The Constitutionality of Sex Separation in School Desegregation Plans," *University of Chicago Law Review* 37 (1970): 296–327.

105. American Friends Service Committee, *Almost as Fairly: The First Year of Title IX Implementation in Six Southern States* (Atlanta: Southeastern Public Education Program, 1977), 93.

106. Tom Herman, Evasive Action: Schools in Deep South Slow Integration Tide with Subtler Tactics, WSJ, Oct. 15, 1970, 1. Two years later, the *Christian Science Monitor* called sex segregation "a palliative for white parents worried about interracial dating and marriage that they saw coming from integration." John Dillin, To Integrate, Set Boys, Girls Apart?, *Christian Science Monitor,* Apr. 8, 1972, 1.

107. Quoted in Stanford Maxwell Brown, "Equalization, Freedom of Choice, and Sex Segregation: School Desegregation in Taylor and Baker Counties" (master's thesis, University of Georgia, 1994), iii.

108. Jeanne Helwig, Letter to the Editor, "Artificial Segregation," *New Orleans Times-Picayune,* March 19, 1977, sec.1, 16.

109. Quoted in Complainants' Trial Memorandum, *Helwig v. Jefferson Parish Sch. Bd.,* on file with author. My thanks to Naveen Kabir of the ACLU Women's Rights Project for sharing this and other documents from the *Helwig* case.

110. Emmett C. Burns to Judges Griffin Bell, Homer Thornberry, and Lewis Morgan, United States Court of Appeals for the Fifth Circuit, August 4, 1976, Library of Congress, Records of the NAACP, 5:2570, Folder: Branches—States—Mississippi: A–J Misc., 1956–81.

111. Quoted in Dillin, "To Integrate, Set Boys, Girls Apart?" 1.

112. United States v. Hinds County School Board, 560 F.2d 619 (5th Cir. 1977).

113. Legislative history on this provision has proven difficult to find. On the role of the busing controversy in "running interference" for sex discrimination legislation, see John David Skrentny, *The Minority Rights Revolution* (Cambridge, MA: Harvard University Press, 2002), 248.

114. For a comprehensive discussion of the jury service cases, see Kerber, *No Constitutional Right to Be Ladies,* 124–220.

115. Hoyt v. Florida, 368 U.S. 57, 62, 68-69 (1961) (citations omitted).

116. Taylor v. Louisiana, 419 U.S. 522, 531 (1975).

117. No women sat on the venire of 175 persons from which his jury was drawn.

118. Only Justice Rehnquist dissented in *Taylor.*

119. Peters v. Kiff, 407 U.S. 493 (1972).

120. Duren v. Missouri, 439 U.S. 357 (1979). While Taylor challenged an "opt-in" system, Duren questioned an "opt-out" exemption for women.

121. Complaint, Willis v. Carson, Civil Action No. 1145(w)(R), in the U.S. District Court for the Southern District of Mississippi, Western Division, PM Papers, Box 40, Folder 706.

122. See drafts and correspondence in ACLU Records, Box 1840, Folder: Willis v. Carson.

123. "FBI Searches for Auto in Mississippi Shooting," WP, December 4, 1966, A17. Murray and Kenyon offered their assistance in *Willis,* but the LCDC politely declined. See Henry Schwartzschild to Dorothy Kenyon and Pauli Murray, March 8, 1966, PM Papers, MC 412, Box 40, Folder 706.

124. Alvin J. Bronstein, Lawyers Constitutional Defense Committee of the ACLU, to Catherine East, Executive Secretary, Interdepartmental Committee on the Status of Women, Department of Labor, November 16, 1966, PM Papers, MC 412, Box 40, Folder 706; see also Willis v. Carson, 324 F. Supp. 1144, 1149 (S.D. Miss. 1971).

125. Willis v. Carson, 324 F. Supp. 1144 (S.D. Miss. 1971).

126. Alexander v. Louisiana, 405 U.S. 625 (1972).

127. Kerber, *No Constitutional Right to Be Ladies,* 204–205.

128. Initially, Marshall drafted a per curiam opinion summarily reversing Alexander's conviction on race discrimination grounds.

129. G[eorge]T[.]F[rampton] to HAB, March 8, 1972, Re: Alexander v. Louisiana, HAB Papers, Box 143, Folder 5.

130. WOD, First draft of concurrence in Alexander v. Louisiana, March 13, 1972, WJB Papers, I:274, Folder 4.

131. Ibid., 6 (quoting Bradwell v. Illinois).

132. Ibid., 9 (citing White v. Crook). Douglas also cited *Reed v. Reed*, decided a few months earlier.

133. HAB notes on Alexander v. Louisiana, December 6, 1971, HAB Papers, Box 143, Folder 5.

134. Oral Argument, *Alexander v. Louisiana*, COASC, 13.

135. According to the district attorney, the clerk had asked an assistant district attorney. "who happen[ed] to be a lady . . . to talk to the women's clubs and get them interested" in jury service. Oral Argument, *Alexander*, COASC, 25.

136. Oral Argument, *Alexander*, COASC, 39.

137. As Blackmun put it, "A man has a stronger case under D[ue] P[rocess]." Alexander's equal protection claim raised a "standing question," Blackmun noted. HAB notes on Alexander v. Louisiana, December 6, 1971, HAB Papers, Box 143, Folder 5.

138. Kerber, *No Constitutional Right to Be Ladies*, 207.

139. Since *Alexander*, the Court had decided both *Frontiero* and *Peters v. Kiff*, giving Healy's supporters favorable sex discrimination/equal protection and race discrimination/due process precedents to rely upon.

140. Healy v. Edwards, 363 F. Supp. 1110, 1117 (D.C. La. 1973).

141. Penn v. Eubanks, 360 F. Supp. 699 (M.D. Ala. 1971).

142. Kerber, *No Constitutional Right to Be Ladies*, 206.

143. Stubblefield was originally convicted of first-degree murder; on appeal the court reduced the charge to second-degree murder.

144. William R. Neese, Law Offices of Marvin P. Morton, Jr., to RBG, February 21, 1974 [Re: Stubblefield], RBG Papers, ACLU File, Folder: Stubblefield v. Tennessee, January–March 1974.

145. Stubblefield v. Tennessee, Court of Criminal Appeals of Tennessee, Jackson, September Session 1973, No. 1, Henry County, Hon. Dick Jerman, Judge (First Degree Murder), October 30, 1973, Modified and Affirmed, Robert K. Dwyer, Judge.

146. William R. Neese to ACLU WRP, January 24, 1974, RBG Papers, ACLU File, Folder: Stubblefield v. Tennessee, January–March 1974.

147. RBG to William R. Neese, January 31, 1974, RBG Papers, RBG Papers, ACLU File, Folder: Stubblefield v. Tennessee, January–March 1974.

148. It is also possible that Ginsburg raised this issue in a telephone conversation. Alternatively, her concern may have been based primarily on her belief that the record below was just not very strong, an opinion confirmed in a research memo by one of her students. See RBG to Morton and Neese, October 3, 1974, RBG Papers, ACLU File, Folder: Stubblefield v. Tennessee, January–March 1974.

149. RBG to Neese and Morton, April 1, 1974 [Re: Stubblefield], RBG Papers, ACLU File, Folder: Stubblefield v. Tennessee, April–October 1974; RBG 0409 1438 William R. Neese to RBG, April 9, 1974, [Re: Stubblefield], RBG Papers, ACLU File, Folder: Stubblefield v. Tennessee, April–October 1974.

150. RBG to Kathleen Peratis, April 12, 1974, RBG Papers, ACLU File, Folder: Stubblefield v. Tennessee, April–October 1974.

151. Jurisdictional Statement, Stubblefield v. Tennessee, at 6, RBG Papers, RBG Papers, ACLU File, Folder: Stubblefield v. Tennessee, April–October 1974.

152. HAB, Notes, [Healy and Taylor], September 23, 1974, HAB Papers, Box 205, Folder 4.

153. Julia Penny Clark to LFP, October 1, 1974, Re: Edwards v. Healy; Schlesinger v. Ballard; Taylor v. Louisiana, LFP Papers, Folder: Edwards v. Healy.

154. As Blackmun put it, "The *Taylor* case is more akin to *Peters v. Kiff* because the male defendant was convicted by an all-male jury. Nevertheless, race does not enter into [*Taylor*]. Thus, of the two, *Peters v. Kiff* is closer to the *Taylor* case than it is to the *Healy* case and yet, because of the race aspect is not precisely the same." HAB Notes, No. 73-759-Edwards v. Healy; No. 73-5744-Taylor v. Louisiana, September 23, 1974, HAB Papers, Box 205, Folder 4.

155. Taylor v. Louisiana, 419 U.S. 522, 537 (1975).

156. Editorial, "The Court Views Women as People," LAT, January 24, 1975, C6.

157. Rhonda Copelon, Elizabeth M. Schneider, and Nancy Stearns, "Constitutional Perspectives on Sex Discrimination in Jury Selection," *Women's Rights Law Reporter* 2 (1975): 12. See also Kerber, *No Constitutional Right to Be Ladies,* 206–213.

158. Carter v. Jury Commission of Greene County, 396 U.S. 320, 329–330 (1970).

159. Copelon, Schneider, and Stearns, "Constitutional Perspectives on Sex Discrimination in Jury Selection," 11.

160. William R. Neese to RBG, October 9, 1974; RBG to William R. Neese, Law Offices of Marvin P. Morton, Jr., October 17, 1974, RBG Papers, Container 9, Folder: Stubblefield v. Tennessee, April–October 1974.

161. Memorandum from BRW to the Conference, Re: Cases Held for Taylor v. Louisiana, No. 73-5744, December 18, 1974, HAB Papers, Box 205, Folder 4.

162. Kerber writes that Ginsburg still speaks "wistful[ly]" of the case. Kerber, *No Constitutional Right to Be Ladies,* 206.

163. Angela Davis, "Joanne Little: The Dialectics of Rape," *Ms.,* June 1975, 74, 108.

164. See also, for example, Buckley v. Coyle Public School System, 476 F.2d 92 (10th Cir. 1973).

165. See Jack Bass, "The Fifth Circuit Four," *Nation,* May 3, 2004, 30.

166. See, for example, Danielson v. Board of Higher Education, 358 F. Supp. 22 (S.D.N.Y. 1972); Strebeigh, *Equal,* 173–192; Cynthia Grant Bowman, "The Entry of Women into Wall Street Law Firms: The Story of *Blank v. Sullivan & Cromwell,*" in *Women and the Law Stories,* ed. Elizabeth M. Schneider and Stephanie M. Wildman (New York: Foundation Press, 2011): 415–452; Nancy MacLean, "Using the Law for Social Change: Judge Constance Baker Motley," *Journal of Women's History* 14 (2002): 136–139.

167. Patricia Sullivan, "Federal Judge Robert R. Merhige Dies," WP, February 20, 2005, C8.

168. See Davis, *Brutal Need;* Davis, "Male Coverture."

169. Author interview with Rhonda Copelon, March 2, 2009.

170. Memorandum from WRP to Members of WRP Advisory Committee Re: Minutes of Advisory Committee Meeting of June 20, 1977, TE Papers, Group No. 1622, Box 11, Folder 162. ("In the wake of [the] defeat [in *Vorchheimer*], the Project began investigating and soliciting information from ACLU affiliates on other sex-segregated schools. We are eager to locate plaintiffs for such a case since most of the sex-segregated schools were sexually segregated in response to court orders to integrate racially.") See also Report of Litigation Committee Meeting, February 18, 1977, TE Papers, Box 11, Folder 163. ("In education, Ruth suggested that we concentrate our efforts on sex-segregated public schools which have sometimes been a by-product of court-ordered integration plans.")

6. The Late Civil Rights Era

1. For more on IWY, see Marjorie J. Spruill, "Gender and America's Right Turn," in *Rightward Bound: Making America Conservative in the 1970s,* ed. Bruce J. Schulman and Julian E. Zelizer (Cambridge, MA: Harvard University Press, 2008). Historian Sara Evans argues that in the mid-1970s, "as the crescendo of activism continued to swell, creativity outpaced disintegration." Sara M. Evans, *Tidal Wave: How Women Changed America at Century's End* (New York: Free Press, 2003), 128. On the late 1970s as a time of interracial feminist coalition-building, see Wini Breines, *The Trouble Between Us: An Uneasy History of White and Black Women in the Feminist Movement* (Oxford: Oxford University Press, 2006), 17; Benita Roth, *Separate Roads to Feminism: Black, Chicana, and White Feminist Movements in America's Second Wave* (Cambridge: Cambridge University Press, 2004), 220; Becky W. Thompson, *A Promise and a Way of Life: White Antiracist Activism* (Minneapolis: University of Minnesota Press, 2001), 117. See also Stephanie Gilmore, ed., *Feminist Coalitions: New Perspectives on*

Second-Wave Feminism in the United States (Urbana: University of Illinois Press, 2008).

2. "The Combahee River Collective: A Black Feminist Statement," in *All the Women Are White, All the Blacks Are Men, But Some of Us Are Brave,* ed. Gloria T. Hull, Patricia Bell Scott, and Barbara Smith (Old Westbury, NY: Feminist Press, 1982), 13–22.

3. See, for example, Celeste Durant, "Carter Vows Support for ERA Passage," LAT, October 8, 1976, A36; Blythe Babyak, "All the President's Women," NYT, January 22, 1978, SM3. On the fate of feminist agendas in the Carter administration, see Susan M. Hartmann, "Feminism, Public Policy, and the Carter Administration," in *The Carter Presidency: Policy Choices in the Post–New Deal Era,* ed. Gary M. Fink and Hugh Davis Graham (Lawrence: University Press of Kansas, 1998), 224–243.

4. "Does the Women's Movement Compromise the Struggle of Minorities?" *Women's Rights Law Reporter* 4 (1977): 30–31.

5. Nancy Hicks, "Eleanor Norton Called in Line for Jobs Post," NYT, March 24, 1977, A17.

6. Richard V. Clarke, "The World of Work: Ms. Norton Will Revitalize EEOC," *Tri-State Defender* (Memphis), April 16, 1977, 5.

7. Ernest Holsendolph, "Norton Optimistic on E.E.O.C.'s Goals," NYT, June 6, 1977, 56.

8. A. H. Raskin, "Jim Crow, Union Member," NYT, June 12, 1977, 230.

9. "EEOC Head Wishes to Improve Effectiveness of U.S. Agency," *Philadelphia Tribune,* May 31, 1977, 4.

10. United States v. International Brotherhood of Teamsters, 431 U.S. 324 (1977).

11. Quoted in Lesley Oelsner, "Supreme Court's Year Is Marked by Changes in Patterns of Voting," NYT, July 4, 1977, 1. See also A. H. Raskin, "Labor–Civil Rights Friction," NYT, June 4, 1977, 33; Nancy MacLean, *Freedom Is Not Enough: The Opening of the American Workplace* (Cambridge, MA: Harvard University Press, 2006), 288–289.

12. "83% in Poll Oppose Reverse Bias Plans," NYT, May 1, 1977, 33. The question posed was: "Some people say that to make up for past discrimination, women and members of minority groups should be given preferential treatment in getting jobs and places in college. Others say that ability, as determined by test scores, should be the main consideration. Which point of view comes closest to how you feel on this matter?" See also, "An Eager New Team Tackles Job Discrimination," *Business Week,* July 25, 1977, 116.

13. Quoted in Laura Kalman, *Right Star Rising: A New Politics, 1974–1980* (New York: W.W. Norton, 2010), 259–260.

14. Steven V. Roberts, "The *Bakke* Case Moves to the Factory," *NYT Magazine,* February 25, 1979, SM10.

15. As historian Nancy MacLean has demonstrated, although an interracial, cross-class coalition of women and men sought to open doors to women seeking nontraditional employment in the mid-to-late 1970s, this effort went almost entirely unnoticed in media accounts. See Nancy MacLean, "The Hidden History of Affirmative Action: Working Women's Struggles in the 1970s and the Gender of Class," *Feminist Studies* 25 (1999): 42–78; MacLean, *Freedom Is Not Enough.*

16. Memorandum from Sue to Phyllis and Stephanie, Re: Report on Affirmative Action Coordinating Center meeting of today re Weber case, December 27, 1978, NOW LDEF Papers, 95-M79, Carton 8, Folder: Weber v. Kaiser Aluminum.

17. Frances M. Beal, Kathleen A. Gmeiner, and Gerald C. Horne to Friends, March 9, 1979, NOW LDEF Papers, 95-M79, Carton 8, Folder: Kaiser v. Weber.

18. See, for example, Kathe Karlson, Coordinator, NY Affirmative Action Task Force, Dear Friend [of the National Anti-Weber Mobilization Committee, [June 1979], NOW LDEF Papers, 95-M79, Carton 8, Folder: Weber v. Kaiser Aluminum.

19. Brief of Amici Curiae American GI Forum et al., Appendix A: Statement of Principles, United Steelworkers v. Weber, 443 U.S. 193 (1979) (Nos. 78-432, 78-435 and 78-436).

20. Wendy Webster Williams, by now a law professor, provided assistance. Brief Amici Curiae of the Hon. Patricia Schroeder, et al., 17, *Weber* (Nos. 78-432, 78-435 and 78-436). In January 1979, Phyllis Segal of NOW LDEF recommended that her organization sign on to the brief and offer comments on the WLDF draft. Memorandum from Phyllis N. Segal to NOW LDEF Defense Committee, cc: NOW LDEF Board, January 12, 1979, Re: Litigation Support Request, Kaiser Aluminum v. Weber, NOW LDEF Papers, 95-M79, Carton 8, Folder: Weber v. Kaiser.

21. Motion of Rudy Gorden, et al., individually and on behalf of Black and Women Workers at Gramercy, for Special Leave to Intervene and for an Order Vacating the Judgment Below and Remanding for a New Trial with Intervenors as Party Defendants and to File a Brief in Support, *Weber* (Nos. 78-432, 78-435 and 78-436).

22. United Steelworkers of America v. Weber, 443 U.S. 193 (1979). Justices Powell and Stevens did not take part. *Weber* was decided three weeks after the feminists' defeat in Personnel Administrator v. Feeney.

23. Urban C. Lehner and Carol H. Falk, "Beyond *Bakke:* High Court Approves Affirmative Action in Hiring, Promotion," WSJ, June 28, 1979,

1; Morton Mintz, "Racial Quotas in Job Training Backed," WP, June 28, 1979, A1; Editorial, "The *Weber* Solution," NYT, June 28, 1979, A18; Philip Taubman, "Rights Leaders Hail Weber Case Decision," NYT, June 28, 1979, B13.

24. Linda LaRue, "The Black Movement and Women's Liberation," *Black Scholar,* Vol. 1, No. 7(May 1970): 36, 37.

25. On the evolution of the racial politics of abortion rights, see Jennifer Nelson, *Women of Color and the Reproductive Rights Movement* (New York: New York University Press, 2003); Mary Ziegler, "The Framing of a Right to Choose: *Roe v. Wade* and the Changing Debate on Abortion Law," *Law and History Review* 27 (2009): 326–329.

26. Author interviews with Rhonda Copelon, March 2 and May 7, 2009; Nelson, *Women of Color and the Reproductive Rights Movement.*

27. Jennifer Nelson makes a similar point in reference to a particular feminist organization, the Committee for Abortion Rights and Against Sterilization Abuse. See Nelson, *Women of Color and the Reproductive Rights Movement,* 150.

28. "Plank 11: Equal Rights Amendment," in National Commission on the Observance of International Women's Year, *The Spirit of Houston: The First National Women's Conference* (Washington, DC: U.S. Government Printing Office, 1978), 51.

29. Author interview with Rhonda Copelon, May 7, 2009.

30. Jane J. Mansbridge, *Why We Lost the ERA* (Chicago: University of Chicago Press, 1986); Reva B. Siegel, "Constitutional Culture, Social Movement Conflict, and Constitutional Change: The Case of the de facto ERA," *California Law Review* 94 (2006): 1395–1397. Rhonda Copelon suggests that litigators may have been more focused on doctrinal barriers like *Geduldig v. Aiello,* while legislative lobbyists were more concerned with the ERA's fate. Author interview with Rhonda Copelon, May 7, 2009. See also Sylvia A. Law, "Rethinking Sex and the Constitution," *University of Pennsylvania Law Review* 132 (1984): 955–1040.

31. Neither these arguments nor sex equality arguments for abortion rights were new; both originated in pre-Roe v. Wade litigation. For more, see Leslie J. Reagan, *When Abortion Was a Crime: Women, Medicine, and Law in the United States, 1867-1973* (Berkeley: University of California Press, 1997), 234–237; Linda Greenhouse and Reva B. Siegel, *Beyond Roe v. Wade: Voices that Shaped the Abortion Debate Before the Supreme Court's Ruling* (New York: Kaplan, 2010); Reva B. Siegel, "*Roe's* Roots: The Women's Rights Claims that Engendered *Roe,*" *Boston University Law Review* 90 (2010): 1875–1907.

32. Brief for the American Public Health Association, NOW, et al, as Am-

icus Curiae, 8, Maher v. Roe, 432 U.S. 454 (1977) (Nos. 75-1440 and 75-442), 1976 WL 181644.

33. Brief for Respondents, Poelker v. Doe, 11 (No. 75-442), 1976 WL 181351.

34. McRae v. Califano, 491 F. Supp. 630, 768 (E.D.N.Y. 1980).

35. Rep. Robert Dornan of California said he was aware that "some of the conservative members of the Congress supported pro-abortion legislation as a means of controlling the growth in the population of blacks, Puerto Ricans or other Latins or whomever they thought should not bear more than a polite one or two 'burdens on society.'" *McRae,* 491 F. Supp. at 775.

36. Maher v. Roe, 432 U.S 454, 483 (1977) (Brennan, J., dissenting).

37. 432 U.S. at 462 (Blackmun, J., dissenting).

38. Beal v. Doe, 432 U.S. 454, 456 (Marshall, J., dissenting).

39. 432 U.S. at 456, 460 (Marshall, J., dissenting).

40. 432 U.S. at 456–457 (Marshall, J., dissenting).

41. For more on *Harris v. McRae,* see Rhonda Copelon and Sylvia A. Law, "'Nearly Allied with Her Right to Be'—Medicaid Funding for Abortion: The Story of *Harris v. McRae,*" in *Women and the Law Stories,* ed. Elizabeth M. Schneider and Stephanie M. Wildman (New York: Foundation Press, 2011).

42. Stevens said, according to Powell's notes, "Under *Roe v. Wade* a state couldn't impose a fine on a woman who aborts. Nor can a state impose the risk of poor health or death as a penalty for getting pregnant." LFP conference notes, *Harris v. McRae,* LFP Papers.

43. Marginal notations in Richey Bench Memo and in LFP conference notes, *Harris v. McRae,* 2.

44. Powell joined Stewart's opinion for the Court unconditionally, but did suggest, at clerk Ellen Richey's urging, that he "emphasiz[e] the elasticity of the 'medically necessary' standard" and note the testimony of a physician in the related Zbaraz case that the mortality rate for pregnant women was very low. He also suggested that Stewart include statistics on the high rate of abortions in the U.S. populations, particularly in cities such as Washington, D.C. Powell asserted that this information helped to support the rationality of Congress's weighing of interests. LFP to PS, June 12, 1980, Re: Harris v. McRae, LFP Papers.

45. Harris v. McRae, 448 U.S. 297, 316 (1980).

46. Ibid., 356–357 (Stevens, J., dissenting).

47. All quoted in Robin Herman, "After Decision, Focus Turns to Lower Courts and Abortion Politics," NYT, July 1, 1980, A1.

48. Jennifer Nelson explains that "[m]any middle-class women, who had stayed neutral in the political battle to end sterilization abuse . . . felt compelled

to join a movement protecting abortion rights when these seemed threatened." Nelson, *Women of Color and the Reproductive Rights Movement,* 154.

49. On the "new energy" of the ERA ratification campaign during its final years, see Evans, *Tidal Wave,* 174.

50. On the ERA and public opinion, see Mansbridge, *Why We Lost the ERA;* Serena Mayeri et al., "Gender Equality," in *Public Opinion and Constitutional Controversy,* ed. Nathaniel Persily et al. (New York: Oxford University Press, 2008), 139–161.

51. "Black Women's Plan of Action," in *The Spirit of Houston: The First National Women's Conference,* 272–277.

52. Jesse Jackson, for instance, declared that he was for the ERA, but warned that competition from white women workers would "reduce the black labor market; not the black *women's* labor market, but for all blacks." He asserted: [W]hite women can be expected to be as racist and reactionary as white men when it comes to a fight to keep their economic advantages and stability. . . . For blacks and browns in the women's movement, the challenge is not only to see what they have in common with white women but also to see what divides them." Jesse Jackson on ERA, ERAmerica Coalition Update, March 1978, Records of ERAmerica, Container 22, Folder: Black Piece.

53. Joye Brown, "Group Braves Sour Weather to Back ERA," *Raleigh News & Observer,* October 26, 1980, 21.

54. Working Draft, ERAmerica Multi-Cultural Task Force on ERA, Report on Strategies to Involve Multi-Cultural Communities, Records of ERAmerica, Container 73, Folder: Field: General.

55. Cathy Sedwick and Reba Williams, "Black Women and the Equal Rights Amendment," *Black Scholar,* Vol. 7, No. 10 (July–August 1976): 24, 28; Sylvia Crudup Cole, "ERA: Why Should We Care," *Essence,* October 1978, 143.

56. See, for example, Internal Memorandum from Jane C. to S/M/L, December 1, 1980, at 4, Re: Field operation review and planning, Records of ERAmerica, Container 74, Folder: Multi-Cultural Outreach-Job Description.

57. Proposal, ERAmerica Papers, Box 22, Folder: Blacks, LOC.

58. Minority Task Force on ERA, Report on Meeting, March 24, 1980, convened by Willi Delaney, Women's Bureau, U.S. DOL, ERAmerica Papers, Box 73, Folder: ERA Readings.

59. NOW Minority Women's Committee, Minority Women and the Equal Rights Amendment (1977), NOW Papers, Box 209, Folder 18.

60. ERA Georgia and South Carolina ERA Coalition, *The E.R.A. and the Black Community,* Records of ERAmerica, Container 73, Folder: Georgia Literature. See also, [Announcement of People of Color Conference, ERAmerica

[1981], Records of ERAmerica, Container 73, Folder: Women of Color; NOW, *The Equal Rights Amendment: What Does it Mean to You?* NOW Papers, Box 209, Folder 18 (quoting Aileen Hernandez).

61. See, for example, ACLU Women's Rights Project Report, Fall 1979, ERAmerica, Box 22, Folder: Blacks.

62. NOW Minority Women's Committee, Minority Women and Feminism (1977), NOW Papers, Box 209, Folder 29.

63. Sedwick and Williams, "Black Women and the Equal Rights Amendment," 27.

64. ERA Georgia and South Carolina ERA Coalition, "The E.R.A. and the Black Community."

65. NOW Minority Women's Committee, Minority Women and the Equal Rights Amendment (1977), NOW Papers, Box 209, Folder 18. See also, for example, Jane Glover, Speech to the Partners in Ecumenism Platform Committee, [Black Church Conference?], September 16, 1980, Records of ERAmerica, Container 73, Folder: Black Church Strategy. For a report on "multi-cultural outreach" generally, see Multi-Cultural Outreach, 1980–1981, Records of ERAmerica, Container 75, Folder: MCTC originals.

66. Memorandum from Mike McClister to ERAmerica, September 30, 1977, Re: The ERA in South Carolina, Records of ERAmerica, Container 69, Folder: South Carolina 79; Barbara W. Moxon, Chair, ERA South Carolina, to Sheila Greenwald and David Abrams, ERAmerica, September 12, 1978, Records of ERAmerica, Container 69, Folder: South Carolina (indicating that ERA South Carolina was in contact and cooperation with NAACP and some other, smaller black organizations).

67. See, for example, Kristin Kalsem and Verna L. Williams, "Social Justice Feminism," University of Cincinnati College of Law Public Law and Legal Theory Research Paper Series, No. 08-14, March 21, 2008, accessed September 12, 2010, http://ssrn.com/abstract=1112105.

68. Other plaintiffs had brought "combined" race and sex discrimination claims, but none had yielded as definitive a discussion of the phenomenon.

69. Jefferies v. Harris County Community Action Association, 425 F. Supp. 1208 (S.D. Tex. 1977).

70. Staff Counsel, Screening Memo, Jefferies v. Harris County Community Action Association, et al., No. 77-1848, February 27, 1978, NARA Southwest Regional Division, Accession No. 276-81-0001, Location: 9-A2-800-3-7, Box 175. As attorney Jesse Funchess put it in his brief, the trial judge "fail[ed] to recognize the minority with whom it [was] dealing, to-wit: Black women." Brief for the Appellant, 12, Jefferies, No. 77-1848, (5th Cir.), NARA Southwest Regional Division, Ft. Worth, Texas, Accession No. 276-81-0001, Location: 9-A2-800-3-7, Box 175.

71. ABA Commission on Women in the Profession, "Carolyn Dineen King," accessed August 14, 2008, http://www.abanet.org/women/bios/king.html.

72. Jefferies v. Harris County Community Action Association, 615 F.2d 1025, 1032–1034 (5th Cir. 1980).

73. Given that the district court had not considered the issue directly, and that the only court to have done so explicitly—in *DeGraffenreid*—had "held that black women [were] not a special Title VII class," Randall would have preferred to reserve judgment until the trial court addressed the question.

74. *Jefferies*, 615 F.2d at 1034 n. 7.

75. Jefferies v. Harris County Community Action Association, 693 F.2d 589 (5th Cir. 1982).

76. See, for example, Kimberle Crenshaw, "Demarginalizing the Intersection of Race and Sex: A Black Feminist Critique of Antidiscrimination Doctrine, Feminist Theory, and Antiracist Politics," *University of Chicago Legal Forum* (1989): 139–168; Minna J. Kotkin, "Diversity and Discrimination: A Look at Complex Bias," *William and Mary Law Review* 50 (2009): 1439–1500.

77. Sissy Farenthold, "Is Carter Just Whistling Dixie about Women in His Government?" LAT, January 28, 1979, E3.

78. Hartmann, "Feminism, Public Policy and the Carter Administration," 226.

79. Quoted in "Weighing the Worth of Jimmy Carter's Presidency," LAT, March 4, 1979, G3.

80. Quoted in Marlene Cimons and Don Irwin, "Carter Promises 25 Women's Groups He'll Keep Pressing for ERA Enactment," LAT, December 14, 1979, B14.

81. Anderson's chief aide for women's issues was Catherine East. On Republican feminist support for Anderson, see Marlene Cimons, "GOP Feminists Distraught: A Task Force without a Task," LAT, July 18, 1980, F1. On Anderson's positions and polls showing the social liberalism of his supporters as compared to Carter's and Reagan's, see E. J. Dionne, Jr., "Social Issues Prompt Sharp Divisions," NYT, October 4, 1980, 8.

82. Leslie Bennetts, "Democratic Parley in Contrast with GOP's on Feminist Delegates and Issues," NYT, August 8, 1980, A14.

83. Leslie Bennetts, "Republicans and Women's Issues: For Some, a Painful Conflict," NYT, September 2, 1980, B12. See also Catherine Rymph, *Republican Women: Feminism and Conservatism from Suffrage through the Rise of the New Right* (Chapel Hill: University of North Carolina Press, 2006), 227–232.

84. Leslie Bennetts, "NOW Leans to No Endorsement," NYT, October 4, 1980, 9.

85. Quoted in Marlene Cimons, "Women's Movement in Wake of Reagan Win," LAT, Nov. 6, 1980, G1.

86. D'Amato had defeated liberal Republican senator Jacob Javits in the primary; many attributed Holtzman's defeat to her splitting the vote with Javits, who was the Liberal Party's candidate in the general election.

87. On the Reagan Revolution and civil rights enforcement, see, for example, MacLean, *Freedom Is Not Enough;* Carrie N. Baker, *The Women's Movement Against Sexual Harassment* (Cambridge: Cambridge University Press, 2008), 135–140; Mary Frances Berry, *And Justice For All: The United States Commission on Civil Rights and the Continuing Struggle for Freedom in America* (New York: Alfred A. Knopf, 2009).

88. Brief of Women's Legal Defense Fund as Amicus Curiae in Support of Petitioner, 4, Michael M. v. Superior Court of Sonoma County, 450 U.S. 464 (1981) (No. 79-1344). See also Michael M. v. Superior Court, 25 Cal. 3d. 608 (1979) (Mosk, J., dissenting).

89. LFP Conference Notes, Michael M., November 7, 1980, LFP Papers, Folder: Michael M.

90. Lahne added, "I worry generally about the extent to which your joining this opinion (in its present form) would conflict with your current position on abortion and privacy rights." Susan G. Lahne to HAB, 3–4, December 15, 1980, Re: No. 79-1344 Michael M., HAB Papers, Box 326, Folder 12.

91. HAB to WHR, December 17, 1980, Re: Michael M., HAB Papers, Box 326, Folder 11.

92. Susan G. Lahne to HAB, December 31, 1980, Re: Michael M., HAB Papers, Box 326, Folder 12. At one point, she tried to offer him an alternative that would limit the Court's holding, suggesting that he might vote to invalidate this particular application of the statute but suggest circumstances in which a sex-based classification might be valid. Susan G. Lahne to HAB, January 5, 1981, Re: Michael M., HAB Papers, Box 326, Folder 12. See also Susan G. Lahne to HAB, December 18, 1980, Re: Michael M., HAB Papers, Box 326, Folder 12.

93. Blackmun's concurrence argued that the statutory rape law was sustainable under *Craig,* emphasizing that he in no way condoned any implied incursion into the privacy/abortion line of cases, and quoting at length from the hearing transcript to demonstrate what he considered to be the unfairness of Michael M.'s conviction in light of the victim's own culpability.

94. Morgan replied, "I might be persuaded . . . if this case were the first gender-discrimination case to reach this Court, for commonsense about the way of the teenage world suggests that respondent's generalization is accurate. But the Court's precedents," he emphasized, "have held this type of generalization is insufficient." Greg Morgan to LFP, Bench Memorandum, October 29, 1980, 10–12, Re: Michael M., LFP Papers (and annotations by LFP).

95. Greg Morgan to LFP, Bench Memorandum, October 29, 1980, Re: Michael M, LFP Papers (annotation by LFP, handwritten).

96. Second draft of Rehnquist opinion in *Michael M.*, December 10, 1980, LFP papers (annotation by LFP).

97. Michael M. v. Superior Court of Sonoma County, 450 U.S. 464, 470 (1981).

98. *Michael M.*, 450 U.S. at 478 (Stewart, J., concurring).

99. Lahne to HAB, December 18, 1980, 4 (annotation by HAB).

100. *Michael M.* 450 U.S. at 478 (Stewart, J., concurring).

101. Kerber, *No Constitutional Right to be Ladies,* 274.

102. Ibid., 284–285.

103. ACLU, Draft Press Release, [n.d., 1980], ACLU Records, Box 1662, Folder: Rostker v. Goldberg.

104. For more, see Jane Mansbridge, "Who's in Charge Here? Decision by Accretion and Gatekeeping in the Struggle for the ERA," *Politics and Society* 13 (1984): 343–382.

105. As *New York Times* reporter Linda Greenhouse put it, anti-ERA propaganda had "injected political risk to any focus of attention on the issue." Linda Greenhouse, "Women Join Battle on All-Male Draft," NYT, March 22, 1981, 19.

106. Muriel Fox to Stephanie [Clohesy] and Phyllis [Segal], [n.d.], NOW LDEF Papers, 95-M99, Carton 5, Folder: Rostker v. Goldberg corresp. & memoranda.

107. Virginia Watkins to Muriel Fox, September 15, 1980, NOW LDEF Papers, 95-M99, Carton 5, Folder: Rostker v. Goldberg corresp. & memoranda.

108. See, for example, Julie B. Doron to Barbara Brown, February 6, 1981, NOW LDEF Papers, 95-M99, Carton 5, Folder: Rostker v. Goldberg corresp. & memoranda.

109. See Kim E. Greene to Barbara Brown, February 10, 1981, NOW LDEF Papers, Carton 5, Folder: Rostker v. Goldberg corresp. & memoranda (describing conversation with Epstein re: amicus brief).

110. Brief for Amicus Curiae National Organization for Women, Rostker v. Goldberg, 453 U.S. 57 (No. 80-251), 1981 WL 390369, 24. See also Brief for Amici Curiae Women's Equity Action League et al., 17, *Rostker,* (No. 80-251), 1980 WL 390514.

111. Brief for the Appellees, 17, *Rostker* (No. 80-251), 1980 WL 339849 (emphasis added).

112. Jim Mann, "All-Male Draft Issue Reaches Supreme Court," LAT, March 23, 1981, B1.

113. See, for example, Metzloff, Preliminary Memo, Rostker v. Goldberg, No. 80-251, November 16, 1980 Conference, LFP Papers. ("[G]iven the funda-

mental importance of the question raised, and the potentially serious impact of the district court's judgment on the conduct of the Nation's military operations, the Court should note probable jurisdiction.") Selective Service registration had gone ahead despite the lower court ruling, due to a stay issued by Justice Brennan the day after the district court's decision.

114. Burger believed, according to Powell's notes, that "[if *Craig's* intermediate scrutiny] test were applied, the exclusion of women flunks the test." LFP Conference Notes, Rostker v. Goldberg, March 27, 1981, LFP Papers.

115. It is unclear from Powell's notes how Blackmun voted at this point. White was "very tentative," according to Powell's notes. Ibid.

116. In Rehnquist's view, the classification easily survived the *Craig* test. Ibid.

117. Paul Smith to LFP, May 2, 1981, Re: Justice Rehnquist's Opinion in Rostker v. Goldberg, 1–2, LFP Papers.

118. Handwritten note on page 1 of Paul Smith to LFP, March 17, 1981, Re: Rostker v. Goldberg, LFP Papers.

119. "It is not easy," he wrote in his notes on the lower court's opinion, "to think of many greater intrusions on military affairs, as well as on the authority of Congress than for the judiciary to decide the sex of the armed services."

120. LFP, Comments on Opinion of Three-Judge Court, [Rostker v.] Goldberg, March 20, 1981, 4, 11–12, LFP Papers.

121. Paul Smith, Bench Memo, March 10, 1981, Re: No. 80-251 Rostker v. Goldberg, 16, LFP Papers.

122. The district court opinion, he pointed out, left "open (i) whether women must serve in combat, and (ii) must be 'conscripted in equal numbers to men.'" LFP, Comments on Opinion of Three-Judge Court, 3.

123. LFP Notes, for conference, undated, LFP Papers, Folder: Rostker v. Goldberg (emphasis in original). See also marginal notations on Paul Smith to LFP, March 17, 1981, Re: Rostker v. Goldberg, 5, LFP Papers.

124. LFP, handwritten notes on first draft of Rehnquist's opinion for the Court, Rostker v. Goldberg, May 1, 1981, 1, LFP Papers (emphasis in original). Powell thought that the discussion of the proper standard of review improved between Rehnquist's first and second drafts.

125. Handwritten notes on second draft of Rehnquist's opinion for the Court, Rostker v. Goldberg, May 6, 1981, 1, LFP Papers. Powell was characteristically polite in a note to Rehnquist, declaring, "Your opinion is quite persuasive, although I have rarely seen Justice Rehnquist so 'deferential' to anything or anybody!" LFP to WHR, May 7, 1981, Re: Rostker v. Goldberg, No. 80-251, LFP Papers. The language to which Powell referred largely survived in Rehnquist's final opinion for the Court: "The case arises in the context of Congress' authority over national defense and military affairs, and perhaps in no other area

has the Court accorded Congress greater deference." Rostker v. Goldberg, 453 U.S. 57, 64–65 (1981).

126. LFP to WHR, May 7, 1981. On the role of such arguments in the congressional debate over women and draft registration, see Jill Elaine Hasday, "Fighting Women: The Military, Sex, and Extrajudicial Constitutional Change," *Minnesota Law Review* 93 (2008): 110–121.

127. Rehnquist reminded Powell of "broad language in previous opinions about 'sexual stereotyping,' most if not all of which [Rehnquist] dissented from." Ultimately, Rehnquist "did not think it worthwhile to confuse the case by a possibly divisive discussion of societal considerations." WHR to LFP, Re: Rostker, May 11, 1981, 1, LFP Papers.

128. Rostker v. Goldberg, 453 U.S. 57, 79 (1981).

129. *Rostker,* 453 U.S. at 78.

130. Linda Greenhouse, "Justices, 6–3, Rule Draft Registration May Exclude Women," NYT, June 26, 1981, A1.

131. *Rostker,* 453 U.S. at 86 (Marshall, J., dissenting).

132. Ibid., 94 n.10 (Marshall, J., dissenting).

133. This was the thrust of Catharine MacKinnon's critique of antidiscrimination law in *Sexual Harassment of Working Women* (1979).

134. Feminists noted the irony that the Court considered pregnancy a sex-based distinction when sustaining a discriminatory law in *Michael M.,* just a few years after denying that discrimination against pregnant women was sex-based in *Geduldig.* See, for example, Catherine A. MacKinnon, "Introduction," *Capital University Law Review* 10 (1980): xiii.

135. Quoted in Colin Campbell, "Conservatives Are Generally Pleased, Feminists Dismayed by Court's Ruling," NYT, June 26, 1981, A12.

136. Quoted in Campbell, "Conservatives Are Generally Pleased."

137. Greenhouse, "Justices, 6–3."

138. Editorial, "Three States, One Year," LAT, June 30, 1981, 6.

139. Leslie Bennetts, "Women Stage Fifth Ave. Rally for Equal Rights Amendment," NYT, July 1, 1981, A1.

140. Quoted in Harry Bernstein, "Anti-Reagan Feeling Unites Divided Groups," LAT, September 26, 1981, SD1. See also Bernard Weinraub, "Liberal Groups Report Surge Since Reagan Election," NYT, December 9, 1980, B23.

141. Anita Hill, *Speaking Truth to Power* (New York: Anchor Books, 1997), 76–77.

142. Johnson v. Transportation Agency of Santa Clara, 480 U.S. 616 (1987).

143. On O'Connor's abortion record, see Joan Biskupic, *Sandra Day O'Connor: How the First Woman on the Supreme Court Became Its Most Influential Justice,* 1st ed. (New York: Ecco, 2005), 58–59.

144. Stephen Wermiel et al., "First Woman Chosen: Sandra O'Connor, Arizona Judge, Nominated for Supreme Court," WSJ, July 8, 1981, 2.

145. Quoted in Francis X. Clines, "Baker Vows Support for Nominee," NYT, July 8, 1981, A1.

146. Biskupic, *Sandra Day O'Connor*, 52; Wermiel et al., "First Woman Chosen," 2.

147. Biskupic, *Sandra Day O'Connor*, 60–61, 64.

148. Richard A. Viguerie, "Court Choice Could Be Devastating," LAT, July 14, 1981, C5.

149. Quoted in Clines, "Baker Vows Support," A12.

150. Beverly Stephen, "The Supreme Court's Newest Member," LAT, August 4, 1981, F8.

151. Quoted in B. Drummond Ayres, Jr., "'A Reputation for Excelling': Sandra Day O'Connor," NYT, July 8, 1981, A1.

152. In fact, O'Connor had remained active in politics and civic life throughout her sons' childhood. See Biskupic, *Sandra Day O'Connor*.

153. Quoted in George Skelton, "Reagan Tries to Assuage Critics of Court Nominee," LAT, July 9, 1981, OC1. See also, for example, Alan Baron, "Reagan Basks in the Warmth of a Popular Choice," LAT, July 12, 1981, F2.

154. Memorandum from John Roberts to Kenneth Starr, Re: Internal History of Supreme Court Appointment, September 17, 1981, Subject files of the Assistant to the Attorney General, John G. Roberts Jr. (Special Assistant), 1981–9/1982, Folder: [Roberts, John G.] JR/Sandra Day O'Connor, Box 123, ARC ID 1402143, Entry P42 (location RG 60, Stack 230, Row 60, Compartment 21, Shelf 4).

155. Linda Greenhouse, "Panel Approves Judge O'Connor," NYT, September 16, 1981, A1; Editorial, "It's About Time," LAT, September 13, 1981, D4; Editorial, "A Judge Well Chosen," NYT, September 13, 1981, E20; Associated Press, "Poll Samples Diverse Groups: O'Connor Support Is 'Overwhelming,'" LAT, July 17, 1981, B5.

156. See Hedrick Smith, "Reagan's Court Choice: A Deft Maneuver," NYT, July 9, 1981, A17.

157. The observer was "Phoenix attorney and longtime Supreme Court watcher John Frank." "Sandra O'Connor, Arizona Judge, Nominated for the Supreme Court," WSJ, July 8, 1981, 2. But see Linda Greenhouse, "New Right Loses on Judge but Gains New Zeal," NYT, September 17, 1981, A20.

158. Stewart was the author of *Geduldig v. Aiello, Personnel Administrator v. Feeney* and *Harris v. McRae,* and he was part of the majority in *Gilbert v. General Electric, Maher v. Roe, Michael M. v. Superior Court,* and *Rostker v. Goldberg.* He had concurred in the result in *Frontiero v. Richarson* but had not embraced heightened

scrutiny for sex classifications, and his ambivalence persisted throughout the 1970s.

159. Wilbur Colom, "The Trials of a Mississippi Lawyer," NYT, May 15, 1983, 295.

160. See Memorandum from Anne E. Simon to NOW LDEF Defense Committee, December 16, 1981, Re: Litigation Support Request for Amicus Participation, NOW LDEF Papers, 95-M79, Carton 5, Folder: Miss. Univ. Corr.

161. Hogan v. Mississippi University for Women, 646 F.2d 1116, 1118–1119 (5th Cir. 1981).

162. The logic of Clark's opinion also suggested that single-sex education might always be unconstitutional.

163. Brief for the Petitioners, 11, *Mississippi University for Women v. Hogan*, 458 U.S 718 (1982) (No. 81-406); see also Brief of Mississippi University for Women Alumnae Association Amicus Curiae, *Hogan*, (No. 81-406). MUW had not made the affirmative action argument in the lower courts.

164. "Hunter M. Gholson," *Clarion Ledger* (Jackson, MS), August 14, 2008; Oral Argument, MUW v. Hogan, 1982 U.S. Trans. LEXIS 101, *14–*15. Gholson was referring to *Fullilove v. Klutznick,* 448 U.S. 448 (1980).

165. Memorandum from Stephanie J. Clohesy and Phyllis N. Segal to NOW National Board Members, Re: Single-Sex Schools, February 9, 1982, NOW LDEF Papers, 95-M79, Carton 5, Folder: Miss. Univ. Corr.

166. Mary K. "Kit" Kinports to HAB, Re: MUW v. Hogan, [n.d.], HAB Papers, Box 359, Folder 10.

167. John Wiley, Bobtail Bench Memorandum, Mississippi v. Hogan, March 21, 1982, LFP Papers.

168. LFP Conference Notes, March 24, 1982, *Hogan,* No. 81-406, LFP Papers.

169. One observer called her opinion "a clear departure from her campaign for judicial restraint." Kathleen Sylvester, "Justice O'Connor Makes Her Mark on High Court," *National Law Journal,* July 19, 1982, 8, 24.

170. Mississippi University for Women v. Hogan, 458 U.S. 718, 731, 729 (1982).

171. See, for example, Keith J. Bybee, "The Political Significance of Legal Ambiguity: The Case of Affirmative Action," *Law and Society Review* 34 (2000): 269–290; Linda Greenhouse, "Context and the Court," NYT, June 25, 2003, A1.

172. LFP, Memorandum for File, 1, June 7, 1982, Re: No. 81-406 Mississippi University for Women v. Hogan, LFP Papers. Powell also objected to the use of language about "stereotypes" in a case involving what he believed to be nothing more than "inconvenience" to a man, rather than "discrimination against women." Ibid.

173. Powell did not wish to carry the distinction between race and sex segregation too far, he told clerk Richard Fallon. Beside a footnote distinguishing single-sex schooling from "hostile" racial segregation, Powell wrote, "Dick—it was *not* hostile in my State. It was unreasoning acceptance of a system that had prevailed for centuries and been approved by *Plessy*."

174. *Hogan,* 458 U.S. at 734–735 (Blackmun, J., dissenting).

175. LFP, Memorandum for File, June 7, 1982, Mississippi University for Women v. Hogan, LFP Papers.

176. LFP draft, Rider A, Part IV, *Hogan,* June 16, 1982, LFP Papers.

177. *Hogan,* 458 U.S. at 745 (Powell, J., dissenting). On Blackmun's evolving views on O'Connor's *Hogan* opinion, see Linda Greenhouse, *Becoming Justice Blackmun: Harry Blackmun's Supreme Court Journey* (New York: Times Books, 2005), 220–224.

178. Colom, "Trials of a Mississippi Lawyer," 69.

179. As she noted, "[F]eminist lawyers were worried that a majority might use the case as a vehicle to put an end to the heightened scrutiny approach." Linda Greenhouse, "Court Says School Cannot Bar Men," NYT, July 2, 1982, A1.

180. Colom, "Trials of a Mississippi Lawyer," 69–71.

181. Legal scholar Mark Tushnet later described the Burger Court's "constituency" as the "middle class." Mark Tushnet, "The Warren Court as History: An Interpretation," in *The Warren Court in Historical and Political Perspective* (Charlottesville: University Press of Virginia, 1993), 32. See also Mark Tushnet, "The Burger Court in Historical Perspective: The Triumph of Country-Club Republicanism," in *The Burger Court: Counter-Revolution or Confirmation?* (New York: Oxford University Press, 1998), 203–215.

182. O'Connor's opinion mentioned that MUW had been founded to educate white women in the 1880s, but did not acknowledge that racial integration in Mississippi's universities was incomplete and of recent vintage.

183. Only a handful of black women attended MUW between 1954 and 1962; by 1974, the student body had the highest percentage of black students among the historically white Mississippi universities, at about thirteen percent. See also United States v. Fordice, 505 U.S. 717 (1992).

184. For more comprehensive discussions of the ERA II debate, see Mary Frances Berry, *Why ERA Failed: Politics, Women's Rights, and the Amending Process of the Constitution* (Bloomington: Indiana University Press, 1986), Chapter 9; Serena Mayeri, "A New ERA or a New Era? Amendment Advocacy and the Reconstitution of Feminism," *Northwestern University Law Review* 103 (2009): 1223–1302. On the ERA ratification struggle, see Berry, *Why ERA Failed;* Mansbridge, *Why We Lost the ERA;* Donald Mathews and Jane Sherron DeHart, *Sex, Gender, and the Politics of the ERA: A State and the Nation* (New York: Oxford University Press, 1990).

185. Ann E. Freedman and Sylvia A. Law, "Thomas I. Emerson: A Pioneer for Women's Equality," *Case Western Reserve Law Review* 38 (1988): 554.

186. Memorandum from Phyllis Segal to ERA Legislative History Project, March 21, 1983, CE Papers, Box 23, Folder 29.

187. See *Equal Rights Amendment: Hearings on House Joint Resolution 1, before the Subcommittee on Civil and Constitutional Rights of the House Committee on the Judiciary*, 98th Congress [hereafter *House Hearings*] 653 (1983) (testimony of William A. Stanmeyer).

188. *The Impact of the Equal Rights Amendment: Hearings on Senate Joint Resolution 10, Before the Subcommittee on the Constitution of the Senate Committee on the Judiciary*, 98th Congress [hereafter *Senate Hearings*] Part I, 895 (1983–1984) (testimony of Edward Erler).

189. *House Hearings* 787 (November 3, 1983) (statement of Professor Ann Freedman).

190. Memorandum from Sally Burns, ERA Legislative History Project, to The Attorneys for the ERA and Working Groups for the ERA, July 19, 1983, Re: Answers to Hatch Questions and Meeting with Hill Staff, CE Papers, Box 23, Folder 31.

191. Memorandum from Segal to ERA Legislative History Project, March 21, 1983, 1–3.

192. *United Steelworkers v. Weber* was opponents' favorite example of unintended consequences.

193. *Senate Hearing* Part II, 187 (September 19, 1984).

194. *House Hearings,* 685 (October 26, 1983).

195. *Senate Hearings* Part I, 341–342, 352 (November 1, 1983).

196. Memorandum from Marsha Levick to NOW-NOW LDEF ERA Legislative History Committee (internal use only), 7, Re: Questions posed by Senator Hatch during ERA hearing 5/26/83, along with suggested framework for answers, as worked out at Fem. Litig. Strat. Mtg. 5/26–5/27, CE Papers, Box 23, Folder 32.

197. ERA Q's and A's (Kennedy), CE Papers, Box 23, Folder 30. When making the case to pro-ERA legislators, ERA proponents described congressional power expansively: "By equating a sexual classification with a racial classification, the ERA would permit [remedial] legislation in favor of women." For more on the relationship between constitutional standards for sex- and race-based affirmative action, see Chapter 4.

198. *Senate Hearings* Part I, 84 (May 26, 1983).

199. *House Hearings* (July 13, 1983) (statement of Grover Rees III, Assistant Professor of Law, University of Texas). Rep. DeWine asked nearly every witness about the validity of the sickle-cell anemia analogy, which proved difficult to refute.

200. *House Hearings,* 803 (November 3, 1983).

201. For more, see Siegel, "Constitutional Culture," 1400.

202. Mary C. Dunlap, "Harris v. McRae," *Women's Rights Law Reporter* 6 (1979): 166.

203. Quoted in *Senate Hearings* Part I, 263 (January 24, 1984).

204. Memorandum from Marsha Levick to [NOW/NOW LDEF] ERA Legislative History Committee, April 11, 1983, 1–3, CE Papers, Box 23, Folder 29.

205. Ibid.

206. "If pregnancy-based discrimination is sex discrimination," Levick wrote, "it is difficult to substantiate the position that disparate or discriminatory treatment of women wishing to undergo abortion is *not* sex discrimination since abortion, like pregnancy, can only be experienced by women, and is clearly 'pregnancy-related.' " Distinguishing abortion from pregnancy would compromise an important feminist principle, Levick argued. "To accept that abortion is *unlike* pregnancy would seem to suggest an acceptance of the right to life position. . . . This seems to be an untenable position for the women's movement to endorse, and a major step backwards." The challenge for feminists, she said, was "[t]o ensure that pregnancy is subsumed in the definition of sex discrimination at the same time that we strive to maintain a low profile on abortion." Ibid., 2.

207. *House Hearings,* 164 (September 14, 1983).

208. Ibid., 165 (September 4, 1983).

209. Memorandum from Sarah E. Burns, ERA Legislative History Project, to ERA Attorneys, October 4, 1983, 2, TE Papers, Box 23, Folder 344.

210. *Senate Hearings,* 264 (November 1, 1983).

211. *House Hearings,* 237 (September 14, 1983).

212. Catherine East, ERA—Major Issues, October 11, 1983, 1, CE Papers, Box 23, Folder 47.

213. Feminists did reintroduce the ERA in subsequent Congresses. For more, see Jane Mansbridge, "What Ever Happened to the ERA," in *Women and the United States Constitution: History, Interpretation, and Practice,* ed. Sibyl A. Schwarzenbach and Patricia Smith (New York: Columbia University Press, 2003), 365–378.

214. See Siegel, "Constitutional Culture," 1399–1403.

215. Law, "Rethinking Sex and the Constitution."

216. Ruth Bader Ginsburg, "Some Thoughts on Autonomy and Equality in Relation to *Roe v. Wade,*" *North Carolina Law Review* 63 (1984): 386.

217. Catharine A. MacKinnon, "Privacy versus Equality: Beyond *Roe v. Wade* (1983)," in *Feminism Unmodified: Discourses on Life and Law* (Cambridge, MA: Harvard University Press, 1987), 93–102.

218. Catharine A. MacKinnon, "Excerpts from MacKinnon/Schlafly Debate," *Law and Inequality: A Journal of Theory and Practice* 1 (1983): 341.

219. Deborah L. Rhode, "Equal Rights in Retrospect," *Law and Inequality: A Journal of Theory and Practice* 1 (1983): 72.

220. See, for example, Mary Joe Frug, "Securing Job Equality for Women: Labor Market Hostility Toward Working Mothers, *Boston University Law Review* 59 (1979): 55–104.

221. Abraham v. Graphic Arts International Union, 660 F.2d 811 (D.C. Cir. 1981).

222. Wendy W. Williams, "The Equality Crisis: Some Reflections on Culture, Courts, and Feminism," *Women's Rights Law Reporter* 7 (1982): 196.

223. Linda J. Krieger and Patricia N. Cooney, "The Miller-Wohl Controversy: Equal Treatment, Positive Action, and the Meaning of Women's Equality," *Golden Gate University Law Review* 13 (1983): 525.

224. Nadine Taub and Wendy W. Williams, "Will Equality Require More Than Assimilation, Accommodation, or Separation from the Existing Social Structure?" *Rutgers Law Review* 37 (1985): 825–844.

225. Reva B. Siegel, "Employment Equality under the Pregnancy Discrimination Act of 1978," *Yale Law Journal* 94 (1985): 929–956.

226. Freedman and Law, "Thomas I. Emerson," 554.

227. *House Hearings,* 52.

228. bell hooks, *Ain't I a Woman: Black Women and Feminism* (Boston: South End Press, 1981), 8, 140–141.

229. See, for example, Margaret Simons, "Racism and Feminism: A Schism in the Sisterhood," *Feminist Studies* 5 (1979): 384–401; Elizabeth V. Spelman, "Theories of Race and Gender/The Erasure of Black Women," *Quest: A Feminist Quarterly* 5 (1982): 36–62.

230. See, for example, *This Bridge Called My Back* (1981), *All the Women Are White, All the Blacks Are Men, But Some of Us Are Brave* (1982), *Home Girls: A Black Feminist Anthology* (1983), and *Sister-Outsider* (1984). As Sara Evans observes, the issue of race also loomed large on the agenda of predominantly white women's organizations in the late 1970s and early 1980s. See Evans, *Tidal Wave,* 175. On the impact of including black women's writing and activism in the periodization of second wave feminism, see Becky Thompson, "Multiracial Feminism: Recasting the Chronology of Second Wave Feminism," *Feminist Studies* 28 (2002): 337–360. The conference titles are examples of gatherings attended by Pauli Murray in the early 1980s, as documented in her papers.

231. MacLean, *Freedom Is Not Enough,* 331–332.

232. On black feminist organizing, see Kimberly Springer, *Living for the Revolution: Black Feminist Organizations, 1968–1980* (Durham, NC: Duke Uni-

versity Press, 2005); *Still Lifting, Still Climbing: Contemporary African American Women's Activism* (New York: New York University Press, 1999); Roth, *Separate Roads to Feminism;* Breines, *Trouble Between Us;* Deborah Gray White, *Too Heavy a Load: Black Women in Defense of Themselves, 1894–1994* (New York: W.W. Norton, 1999). On the emergence of black women's studies, see Beverly Guy-Sheftall, "Black Women's Studies: The Interface of Women's Studies and Black Studies," *Phylon* 49 (1992): 33–41.

233. By the early 1980s, as Sara Evans notes, academia was home to most feminist theorists, and race had become an important focus of their work. Evans, *Tidal Wave,* 206–220. On the "porous" boundary between feminist activism and academia in these years, see Breines, *Trouble Between Us,* 184. See also Thompson, *Promise and a Way of Life,* 207.

234. On Murray's time at Brandeis, see Joyce Antler, "Pauli Murray: The Brandeis Years," *Journal of Women's History* 14 (2002): 78–82. Phyllis Wallace, the EEOC researcher, was not a lawyer but an economist who taught at MIT. See Julianne Malveaux, "Tilting Against the Wind: Reflections on the Life of Phyllis Ann Wallace," *American Economic Review* 84 (1994): 93–97.

235. Elaine W. Shoben, "Compound Discrimination: The Interaction of Race and Sex in Employment Discrimination," *New York University Law Review* 55 (1980): 793–837; Judy Trent Ellis, "Sexual Harassment and Race: A Legal Analysis of Discrimination," *Journal of Legislation* 8 (1981): 30–45.

236. For classic legal scholarship on intersectionality from this period, see, for example, Regina Austin, "Sapphire Bound," *Wisconsin Law Review* 1989: 539–578; Kimberle Crenshaw, "Demarginalizing the Intersection of Race and Sex;" Kimberle Crenshaw, "Mapping the Margins: Intersectionality, Identity Politics, and Violence Against Women of Color," *Stanford Law Review* 43 (1990): 1241–1300; Angela P. Harris, "Race and Essentialism in Feminist Legal Theory," *Stanford Law Review* 42 (1990): 581–616; Mari J. Matsuda, "Beside My Sister, Facing the Enemy: Legal Theory out of Coalition," *Stanford Law Review* 43 (1990): 1183–1192; Paulette M. Caldwell, "A Hair Piece: Perspectives on the Intersection of Race and Gender," *Duke Law Journal* (1991): 365–396.

237. "1st Negro Woman Priest Holds Service in N.C.," WP, Feb. 25, 1977, D14.

238. See Pauli Murray, *Pauli Murray: Selected Sermons and Writings* (Maryknoll, NY: Orbis Books, 2006).

239. Pauli Murray to Judy Goldsmith, 1, November 30, 1983, PM Papers, MC 412, Box 125, Folder 2248; Memorandum from Pauli Murray to Judith Goldsmith, Gloria Steinem, Marjorie Fine Knowles, Eleanor Holmes Norton, Marguerie Rawalt, Sonia Pressman Fuentes, Catherine East, Caroline F. Ware, Ann Fagan Ginger, Isabelle Katz Pinzler, Betty Friedan, Mary O. Eastwood, Kay

Clarenbach, Re: A Proposed Human Rights Amendment to Replace the Campaign for ERA, November 30, 1983, PM Papers, MC 412, Box 125, Folder 2248.

Conclusion

1. Richard Thompson Ford, "Analogy Lesson," *Slate,* November 14, 2008, accessed July 25, 2010, http://www.slate.com/id/2204661/.

2. Hoyt v. Florida, 368 U.S. 57, 62 (1961).

3. Feminist legal scholar Martha Chamallas writes: "although the 1980s was a bad time for the nation, it was a very productive period for feminist legal theory." Martha Chamallas, Past as Prologue: Old and New Feminisms," *Michigan Journal of Gender and the Law* 17 (2010): 161.

4. On feminists' achievement of many of the ERA's goals through other means, see Cynthia Harrison, " 'Heightened Scrutiny': An Alternative Route to Equality for U.S. Women," in *Women and the United States Constitution: History, Interpretation, and Practice,* ed. Sybil A. Schwarzenbach and Patricia Smith (New York: Columbia University Press, 2003), 347–364; Reva B. Siegel, "Constitutional Culture, Social Movement Conflict, and Constitutional Change: The Case of the de Facto ERA," *California Law Review* 94 (2006): 1324.

5. For examples, see sources cited in the Introduction.

6. See, for example, Joan Williams, *Unbending Gender: Why Family and Work Conflict and What to Do About It* (New York: Oxford University Press, 2000), Chapter 7; Nancy MacLean, *Freedom Is Not Enough: The Opening of the American Workplace* (Cambridge: Harvard University Press, 2006); Carrie N. Baker, *The Women's Movement Against Sexual Harassment* (New York: Cambridge University Press, 2008); Cary Franklin, "The Anti-Stereotyping Principle in Constitutional Sex Discrimination Law," *New York University Law Review* 85 (2010): 83–173; Neil Siegel and Reva B. Siegel, "Struck by Stereotype: Ruth Bader Ginsburg on Pregnancy Discrimination as Sex Discrimination," *Duke Law Journal* 59 (2010): 771–798; Deborah Dinner, "Recovering the *LaFleur* Doctrine," *Yale Journal of Law and Feminism* 22 (forthcoming 2010).

7. As Cary Franklin notes in relation to the ACLU WRP, "Many scholars in the 1980s concluded that the WRP won from the Court precisely what it sought: a commitment to treat men and women the same when the law deemed them similarly situated." Franklin, "The Anti-Stereotyping Principle," 149.

8. Franklin observes, "Much of this criticism [of Ginsburg's 1970s strategy] was generated at a low point in the struggle for women's rights." Ibid., 147.

9. For a similar observation about feminism more generally, see Sara M. Evans, foreword to *Feminist Coalitions: Historical Perspectives on Second-Wave Feminisms in the United States,* ed. Stephanie Gilmore (Urbana: University of Illinois Press, 2008), viii.

10. I borrow the term "foil" from Sara Evans. Ibid., ix–x.

Postscript

1. Eleanor Holmes Norton, introduction to Pauli Murray, *Pauli Murray: The Autobiography of a Black Activist, Feminist, Lawyer, Priest, and Poet* (Knoxville: University of Tennessee Press, 1989), ix.

2. On the professionalization and institutionalization of feminism, see Sara M. Evans, *Tidal Wave: How Women Changed America at Century's End* (New York: Free Press, 2003), 190–212; Nancy MacLean, *Freedom Is Not Enough: The Opening of the American Workplace* (Cambridge, MA: Harvard University Press, 2006), 298.

3. MacKinnon held posts at the University of Michigan and the University of Chicago; Siegel at Berkeley and Yale; Zimmerman and Law at New York University; Barlett at Duke, where she served as dean; Scales-Trent at the State University of New York–Buffalo; Freedman at Rutgers; Williams and Ross (as well as Norton) at Georgetown; Copelon and Schneider at New York–area law schools.

4. Wood, a Seventh Circuit judge, made President Obama's short list for the seats eventually filled by Sotomayor and Kagan. Berzon sits on the Ninth Circuit, Lynch on the Second Circuit, and Gertner is a federal district court judge in Massachusetts. Reid is a judge on the District of Columbia Court of Appeals.

5. Kinports has taught at the University of Illinois College of Law and at Penn State University Law School, Estreicher at New York University School of Law.

6. Colom cofounded the Innocence Project at the University of Mississippi with John Grisham, served as one of Mississippi's delegates to the 2004 Republican National Convention, and represented Ike Brown, a black politician accused by the Justice Department of intimidating white voters in Mississippi. In 2008, he co-wrote a book about why Republicans should vote for Obama. See Wilbur O. Colom and James W. Parkinson, *Turning Red States Blue: Obama's Mission to Win the Republican Vote* (Genesis Press, 2008).

7. Mrs. Carter's daughter Beverly became the first African American member of the Drew school board in 1986. The Carter children later remembered Ruby Nell Stancill, the math teacher who testified for the school district in *Andrews,* as an important positive influence in their lives. Constance Curry, *Silver Rights* (San Diego, CA: Harcourt, Brace, 1997), 118, 126–127, 129–131, 187, 229, 232.

8. See, for example, Phyllis Schlafly, "How the Feminists Want to Change Our Laws," *Stanford Law & Policy Review* 5 (1993): 65; republished on Eagle Forum website, accessed September 2, 2010, http://www.eagleforum.org.

9. Rehnquist's concurrence in the result in *United States v. Virginia* (1996), which held the Virginia Military Institute's exclusion of women unconstitutional, is a partial exception.

10. See Reva B. Siegel, "You've Come a Long Way, Baby: Rehnquist's New Approach to Pregnancy Discrimination in *Hibbs*," *Stanford Law Review* 58 (2005): 1871; Nevada Department of Human Resources v. Hibbs, 538 U.S. 721 (2003).

11. Jespersen v. Harrah's Operating Co., 444 F.3d 1104 (9th Cir. 2006) (en banc) (Kozinski, J., dissenting).

12. See, for example, Ann Bartow, "Farewell, Justice O'Connor," accessed August 10, 2010, http://feministlawprofs.law.sc.edu/. But see Hanna Rosin, "Feminists on O'Connor: A Mixed Verdict," WP, July 3, 2005.

13. The rabbi was modern Orthodox pioneer Shlomo Riskin. Stewart Ain, "A Pioneer at Age 12," *New York Jewish Week,* May 12, 2010; Lisa W. Foderaro, "Growing Up, Kagan Tested Boundaries of Her Faith," NYT, May 12, 2010. Kagan later clerked for Justice Thurgood Marshall, known mainly for his civil rights advocacy but also an important feminist ally on the Court. On Marshall's "pragmatic feminism," see Taunya Lovell Banks, "Thurgood Marshall, the Race Man, and Gender Equality in the Courts," *Virginia Journal of Social Policy and the Law* 18 (2010): 15–43.

14. "Pauli Murray" [Day 19], GLBT History Month, accessed November 6, 2009. http://www.glbthistorymonth.com/glbthistorymonth/2009/multimedia/Murray19.pdf.

ACKNOWLEDGMENTS

To properly thank everyone who contributed to this book would require an-other chapter, perhaps another volume entirely. The support and example pro-vided by colleagues, friends, and mentors have been truly extraordinary. My dissertation advisor, Nancy Cott, has been unfailingly generous with her time and invaluable advice throughout. Together with committee members Glenda Gilmore and Robert W. Gordon, she provided a shining example of erudition as well as crucial intellectual and moral support as the project developed. For more than a decade, Reva Siegel has provided wise counsel on substance and strategy at every turn, not to mention infinite patience in enduring early drafts so numerous we both lost count. I am thankful to have crossed paths with Laura Kalman during my final year of law school; since then, her friendship and guidance have been both unstinting and indispensable. She also read the entire manuscript multiple times and offered insightful feedback and much-needed encouragement in equal measure. Sarah Barringer Gordon provided transformative input on many drafts along the way and then improved literally every sentence as a huge and unwieldy manuscript became a book of reasonable length. She is the consummate mentor and colleague in every way.

My interest in this topic had its origins in my undergraduate years, when Ellen Herman, Linda Greenhouse, James Goodman, Claudia Goldin, Florence Graves, Keith Bybee, and Lee Daniels all provided inspiration. I learned from other wonderful teachers and scholars in law and graduate school, including Bruce Ackerman, David Brion Davis, Drew Days, William Eskridge, and Judith Resnik. I had the privilege of serving as a law clerk to Judge Guido Calabresi in 2003–2004, and benefit still from his rare confluence of brilliance and human-ity and from the lasting friendship of my co-clerks, Amy Kapczynski, Roberto Gonzalez, and Jacob Sullivan. I was fortunate to take part in the Samuel I. Golieb Fellowship program at the New York University School of Law, where

William Nelson, Daniel Hulsebosch, and Deborah Malamud gave generously of their time and prodigious knowledge, and members of the Legal History Colloquium provided excellent feedback.

Draft chapters benefited immeasurably from the keen eyes of my dissertation support group: Rebecca Louise Davis, Michael Jo, Bethany Moreton, Julia Ott, Philipp Ziesche, and especially Rebecca Ann Rix. Deborah Dinner provided knowledgeable and perceptive comments at several pivotal moments, including a thoughtful read of the whole manuscript. As the book came together, several chapters benefited immensely from close readings by Regina Austin, Cary Coglianese, and Seth Kreimer, each of whom offered expert advice on both form and substance. Rebecca Davis's careful and discerning editing in the final stages was both heroic and invaluable.

The circle of patient, generous readers and interlocutors is even wider. To mention just a few: Kerry Abrams, Anita Allen, Aditi Bagchi, Felice Batlan, Richard Bernstein, Mary Frances Berry, Susanna Blumenthal, Cynthia Grant Bowman, Tomiko Brown-Nagin, Stephen Burbank, Dorothy Sue Cobble, Kristin Collins, Ann Coughlin, Bridget Crawford, Adrienne Davis, Jane DeHart, Davison Douglas, Ariela Dubler, Thomas Dublin, Mary Dudziak, Elizabeth Emens, Daniel Ernst, Katie Eyer, Jill Fisch, Cary Franklin, Barry Friedman, Risa Goluboff, Frank Goodman, Craig Green, Jamal Greene, Ariela Gross, Daniel Hamilton, Cheryl Harris, Jill Hasday, Taja-Nia Henderson, Nancy Hirschmann, Olati Johnson, Martha Jones, Linda Kerber, Alice Kessler-Harris, Anne Kringel, Alison LaCroix, Sylvia Law, Sophia Lee, Howard Lesnick, Nancy MacLean, Daniel Markovits, Joanne Meyerowitz, Bernadette Meyler, Gwendolyn Mink, Maribel Morey, Melissa Murray, William Novak, Sarah Paoletti, Nicholas Parrillo, Robert Post, Richard Primus, Wendell Pritchett, Gretchen Ritter, Cristina M. Rodriguez, Kermit Roosevelt, Rosalind Rosenberg, Darren Rosenblum, Jed Rubenfeld, David Rudovsky, Theodore Ruger, Elizabeth Schneider, Patricia Seith, Robert Self, Jed Shugerman, Kathryn Kish Sklar, Rogers Smith, Ilya Somin, Carla Spivack, Catherine Struve, Susan Sturm, Thomas Sugrue, Karen Tani, Joshua Tate, Steven Teles, Martha Umphrey, Rose Cuison Villazor, Michael Wachter, Anders Walker, Amy Wax, Barbara Welke, Stephanie Wildman, David Wilkins, John F. Witt, Tobias Wolff, Kenji Yoshino, and Mary Ziegler. During the course of this project, I had the honor of learning from Rhonda Copelon, Ruth Emerson, Alan Lerner, and Peggy Pascoe, whose memories and legacies I will cherish always.

Generous support from Dean Michael Fitts and the University of Pennsylvania Law School, Yale Law School, the Yale Department of History, New York University School of Law, the Golieb family, Richard and Barbara Franke, and the Mellon Foundation made this book possible. I could not have completed my research without the patient assistance of archivists at institutions including the Library of Congress; the Schlesinger Library, Radcliffe Institute, Harvard

University; the Justice Lewis F. Powell, Jr., Archives, Washington and Lee School of Law; the Schomburg Center for Research in Black Culture; the Jimmy Carter Presidential Library; the Sophia Smith Collection at Smith College; the Seeley Mudd Library at Princeton University; the Newcomb Archives, Newcomb College Center for Research on Women, Tulane University; the Southwest Regional Division of the National Archives and Records Administration; the Lillian Goldman Library at Yale Law School; and Yale's Manuscripts and Archives collection at the Sterling Memorial Library. The librarians and staff of the University of Pennsylvania's Biddle Law Library have been immensely helpful and intrepid in tracking down sources. Special thanks are due to Paul George, Joe Parsio, Merle Slyhoff, and especially Alvin Dong, who has gone above and beyond the call of duty on countless occasions. I owe Ben Meltzer a debt of gratitude for crucial help in preparing the final manuscript. Breanna Forni, John Jacob, Patrick Kerwin, Stephanie Nestor, and Ann Trevor helped me to gather sources from afar. Zain Lakhani and Ke Wan provided shrewd research assistance. Lynne Hecht Schafran and Naveen Kabir are among those who graciously shared information and documents with me. I am grateful to Michael Aronson and his colleagues at Harvard University Press for discerning potential in this project and for patiently seeing it through.

Early versions of some material in this book appeared in "'A Common Fate of Discrimination': Race-Gender Analogies in Legal and Historical Perspective," *Yale Law Journal* 110 (2001): 1045–1088; "Constitutional Choices: Legal Feminism and the Historical Dynamics of Change," *California Law Review* 92 (2004): 755–840; "The Strange Career of Jane Crow: Sex Segregation and the Transformation of Anti-Discrimination Discourse," *Yale Journal of Law and the Humanities* 18 (2006): 187–272; "Reconstructing the Race-Sex Analogy," *William and Mary Law Review* 49 (2008): 1789–1858; and "A New ERA or a New Era? Amendment Advocacy and the Reconstitution of Feminism," *Northwestern University Law Review* 103 (2009): 1223–1302. I thank the staffs of each of those publications, and especially Deborah Dinner, Katherine Florey, Jean Galbraith, Wendie Schneider, and R. Owen Williams, for superb editorial assistance.

Drafts also benefited greatly from feedback provided by participants in workshops, colloquia, and conferences, including those held at Penn's Alice Paul Center for Research on Women, Gender, and Sexuality, the American Bar Foundation, Boston University, Brooklyn Law School, Columbia, Cornell, New York University, Pace, Princeton, St. John's University, Southern Methodist University, and Yale; the Universities of Akron, Delaware, Maryland, Minnesota, Michigan, Oregon, Santa Clara, and Virginia; as well as the New York Law and Humanities Consortium, the Colloquium on Current Scholarship in Labor and Employment Law, the Law and Humanities Interdisciplinary Junior Scholar Workshop, annual meetings of the American Society for Legal History and the

Association for the Study of Law, Culture and the Humanities, and especially, the University of Pennsylvania Law School's faculty workshop and the Penn-Chicago Legal History Consortium.

Many others have given me support, shelter, and friendship over the course of this project. In addition to those already mentioned, they include roommates Rachel Thompson, Maame Ewusi-Mensah Frimpong, and Jamie Z. Goodson, as well as dear friends Robin Meezan, Lorraine Paterson, Kristie Starr, and Aditi Shrikhande. Amelia and Bronwyn Glaser and their parents, Carol and John Glaser, have been like family for more than three decades. I am now incredibly fortunate to count the Klenoffs and Brumbergs among my family as well. If she were here, I know that my grandmother, Touba Ezri Mayeri, would say, *Mashallah*.

I can never sufficiently thank my mother, Harriet Mayeri, who has read innumerable drafts and provided support of literally every kind imaginable for as long as I can remember. The patience, encouragement, and love of my parents, my husband, Jason Klenoff, and our son, Sam, truly make everything worthwhile.

Harvard University Press is a member of Green Press Initiative
(greenpressinitiative.org), a nonprofit organization working to
help publishers and printers increase their use of recycled paper
and decrease their use of fiber derived from endangered forests.
This book was printed on recycled paper containing 30%
post-consumer waste and processed chlorine free.